THE STRUCTURE OF WOOD

THE STRUCTURE OF WOOD

F. W. JANE, Ph.D., D.Sc.

FORMERLY PROFESSOR OF BOTANY IN THE UNIVERSITY
OF LONDON, AT ROYAL HOLLOWAY COLLEGE

SECOND EDITION

Completely revised by

K. WILSON, Ph.D., F.I.Biol.

PROFESSOR OF BOTANY IN THE UNIVERSITY
OF LONDON, AT ROYAL HOLLOWAY COLLEGE

AND

D. J. B. WHITE, Ph.D., F.I.W.Sc.

UNIVERSITY COLLEGE, LONDON

WITH OVER 500 PHOTOGRAPHS
AND DRAWINGS

LONDON
ADAM & CHARLES BLACK

FIRST PUBLISHED 1956

REPRINTED WITH MINOR CORRECTIONS AND ADDITIONS 1962
SECOND EDITION, REVISED AND RESET 1970
A. AND C. BLACK LTD.
4, 5 AND 6 SOHO SQUARE LONDON W.1

ISBN 0 7136 0912 5

To the Memory
of
my Father

PRINTED IN GREAT BRITAIN BY
NEILL AND COMPANY LTD., EDINBURGH

PREFACE TO THE SECOND EDITION

When Frank Jane died in 1963 he had revised or re-written most of the text in readiness for a second edition. Both of us had, at his invitation, read and commented on parts of this revision, but it was not possible, immediately after his death, to proceed with it. Now, with the exhaustion of the reprint of the first edition, we have undertaken to complete the preparation of the second edition along the lines clearly laid down by the author.

We have attempted to bring the book up to date, while preserving its character as a work of proved interest and value, on the one hand to students of timber technology, and on the other to those whose interests lie in the more purely botanical aspects of wood structure. The principal changes are in the appendix to Chapter 1 and in Chapters 8 and 9; in addition the bibliography has been somewhat expanded.

The appendix to Chapter 1 is substantially as the author left it, revised in the light of British Standard 881 and 589 (1955). He has placed on record his grateful acknowledgement to the British Standards Institution for permission to make full use of their standard. The name proposed as the standard name for each timber is printed in heavy type, and the scientific names used in the standard have also been adhered to, even though nomenclatural changes since 1955 have rendered some of them out of date: synonyms have been indicated where it seems to us appropriate.

We have rewritten Chapters 8 and 9, because the study of the ultra-structure of wood, and of the formation, structure and properties of reaction wood, are fields which have attracted a good deal of attention in recent years. Here we have aimed at presenting modern views without losing sight of the essential simplicity of treatment of these matters which Jane intended.

Otherwise the text has been generally further revised throughout, and most, at least, of the minor errors and ambiguities in it have, we hope, been eliminated.

Generally the terminology of the "International Glossary of Terms used in Wood Anatomy" (1957) has been followed, though the somewhat involved terminology proposed for rays is referred to only briefly and some old terms have been retained: we share with Jane a feeling that it is unnecessarily pedantic to replace "callitroid" by "callitrisoid".

We are grateful to Dr. A. W. Robards for providing us with Figures 99, 100 A and B, 114 and 118, and it is our particular pleasure to record our indebtedness to Mrs. Inge Judd and Mrs. Mary Collins, of the Botany Department of Royal Holloway College, for their assistance

v

with the secretarial and clerical work involved. Both of them had assisted Jane in the earlier stages of the revision, and have supplied an essential link of continuity in our taking up this work from the stage at which it lay at the time of his death.

K. W.
D. J. B. W.

PREFACE TO THE FIRST EDITION

Apart from the intrinsic interest of the structure of so complex and variable a plant tissue, wood structure is most likely at the present time to interest students who are working, mainly from the technical colleges, for a qualification in wood technology. In writing the present book, the needs of such students have been kept in mind and I have tried to present a simple but comprehensive account of wood structure in its several aspects, assuming no knowledge of botany. The book is, therefore, not exhaustive, nor is it as fully documented as it might have been had the treatment been more advanced.

For the University student, reading for the first degree in botany, the field which I have covered will reasonably be regarded as too specialized an aspect of plant anatomy to merit much attention. Nevertheless, the author is of the opinion that a sound grounding in the elements of vegetable histology should be regarded as a necessary introduction to the study of plant anatomy, and this grounding might, with advantage, be obtained by a detailed study of one tissue in a range of plants. Because of the variety of its elements and its complexity as a tissue, the xylem, and especially the secondary xylem, has much to commend it for this purpose, besides which it is one of the easiest plant tissues to examine in detail. Moreover, since it is readily available in large pieces, it can also be studied in the solid, with the unaided eye or with a hand-lens, thereby emphasising that plant anatomy need not, and should not, be restricted to the examination of sections and macerations under the microscope. The relevant chapters of the present book should serve as a guide to work along these lines.

The book has its origin in several series of articles on wood structure which have appeared in *Timber News, Timber Technology* and *Wood* during the last nine years. It was intended that some of these articles, dealing with the structure of specific woods, should be reprinted as leaflets, but preference was given to an expanded treatment in the form of the present book. Many of the illustrations derive from blocks used for my original articles, while most of the remainder are new and were prepared by myself or, under my direction, by Mr R. Brinsden, whose help with the photographic work has been invaluable. The Forest Products Research Laboratory, Princes Risborough, and the Timber Development Association have generously helped me with the loan of specimens for many of the illustrations, and Mr. G. Hart, of the latter organization, has been at great pains to see that my needs, which were sometimes exacting, have been satisfied.

I am grateful to Dr. C. D. Adams, Professor A. S. Boughey, Mr. B. A.

Jay, Professor R. D. Preston, Dr. D. J. B. White and Dr. K. Wilson for lending me photographs from which a few of the blocks have been made, and also to the authors, the Australian Commonwealth Scientific and Industrial Research Organisation and the Forest Products Research Laboratories of Canada, for permission to use certain published figures. The origin of each of these illustrations is indicated in the text.

Mr. B. A. Jay and Dr. D. J. B. White read through the manuscript and their helpful criticism enabled me to remove at least some of its original imperfections. For the chapter on the "Ultimate Structure of Wood" I had the advantage of Dr. K. Wilson's specialized knowledge and he did so much to help me present a difficult subject as simply as possible that he must take a large share of the credit for such merits as this chapter may possess. During the preparation of the book I had lengthy discussions with Mr. T. J. Price and was able to profit by his wide knowledge of wood and more particularly of wood as a commercial product. I also have to thank Miss B. J. Saunders for the help she has given in many ways, and in particular for her assistance with much tedious clerical work while the book was passing through the press.

FRANK W. JANE

Royal Holloway College
(*University of London*)
Englefield Green, Surrey
April, 1955

CONTENTS

CHAPTER I

THE NAMES AND CLASSIFICATION
OF TIMBERS

The name of anything is no more than a convenient shorthand notation, which makes it possible to refer to an object tersely and with more or less precision. The same end would be attained, but more laboriously and generally less precisely, by a description of the object in question.

For many purposes the name "tree" is sufficiently exact in that it serves to describe a particular type of plant habit. For map-making, however, it is customary to go a little farther and to distinguish certain types of trees; groups of trees may be differentiated into deciduous (broad-leaved) or coniferous woods, and orchards. To the majority of people coniferous trees are pines or firs, while of the broad-leaved trees certain poplars, oak, ash, beech and a few others are about all that are known. Similarly with timbers—oak, walnut, mahogany and deal represent about the sum total of the knowledge of the average man on this subject. The botanist, however, recognises thousands of sorts of trees and potentially, at least, there is a correspondingly large number of timbers. Hence precision in their naming becomes important.

Timbers have often received their names from common names of the trees from which they are derived, a practice which has led to much confusion. When a new country has been opened up, the native trees have often become known by familiar names, from a real or fancied resemblance to those of the settlers' homeland. Australian tulip oak, which is not an oak, is also known as brown oak, silky elm, black ash and hickory. The particular maple which is known in England as sycamore, is termed plane in Scotland, while the sycamore of North America is, in fact, a plane tree and the sycamore of the Bible appears to have been one of the fig trees. To the botanist, maples, planes and figs are very different sorts of plants.

Timbers sometimes receive their names from a supposed resemblance to some better-known wood. A large number of woods pass under the name of oak, with some distinguishing prefix; some, because of a superficial similarity in appearance, like the Australian silky oaks, others because of a supposed resemblance in properties, like the African oaks. Others again, no doubt, are so called for want of a better name, or perhaps because, in the early days of their appearance on the market, they were considered to be more likely to meet with a satisfactory reception if they bore a familiar name. The use of the word "pine" extends to coniferous woods from most parts of the world, although the true pines are almost confined to north temperate regions.

Purely commercial names, quite unrelated to botanical names or relationships, have sometimes been invented for newly available timbers, a practice which is to be deprecated, and is indefensible when attempts are made to restrict such names to the exclusive use of one trading organisation.

Because of the confusion which has arisen in this way, attempts have been made to standardize names for commercial woods. The British Standards Institution (1955) has published a list of proposed standard names to cover the woods in use in Britain, while similar attempts have been made in Australia by the Standards Association of Australia (1940), and also by the South African Bureau of Standards (1947). These are steps in the right direction, but they do not entirely solve the problem. One serious difficulty is that such lists are drawn up on a national basis and the parochial method can never be entirely successful. The only sound basis for standardization of names is a world-wide one, and even then it will only achieve its end if it is accepted and adhered to internationally.

An international basis does exist for the scientific names of plants, and until such time as there is a similar method for the standardization of common or commercial names of timbers, the botanical system, in which woods are known by the same names as the trees from which they are derived, will remain the only reliable system of nomenclature.

Botanical nomenclature passed through many vicissitudes before it became standardized. The old herbalists and botanists found the common names of plants, as used by the layman, insufficient for their needs. Oak, for example, was an accurate enough designation for use by the man in the streeet, but it was apparent to anyone looking closely at oaks that there was more than one kind of oak; thus it became necessary to sort out the different kinds or species of oak, which comprised the group or genus of oaks in general. Nor would the sorting be sufficient unless it enabled the various species to be recognised by anyone, of whatever nationality, in any part of the world, who cared to take enough trouble to study the genus. All educated men were then conversant with Latin and it was natural that this language should have become accepted as the international language of the botanist. Precision in nomenclature was obtained by the use of a common or generic name for all the species of a genus, followed by a longer or shorter description of the features peculiar to the species. Thus, in one of the works of John Ray (1724), several species of blackberry are described as follows:

Rubus major fructu nigro   The common Bramble or Black-
[The large blackberry with black   berry bush
   fruits]

Rubus minor fructu coeruleo   Dew-berry bush or small Bramble
[The small blackberry with blue
   fruits]

Rubus Idaeus spinosus fructu rubro	The Rasp-berry-bush, Framboise
[The spiny blackberry of Mount Ida, with red fruits]	or Hind-berry

Some of the specific descriptions are much longer, others are confined to one word. Thus Ray divided the apples into:

Malus sativa	The Apple-tree
Malus sylvestris	The Crab-Tree or Wilding

This division of the apples is a poor one for international usage, since a botanist in another country, unfamiliar with crab apples, would have no means of knowing, from a specimen, whether he was handling a wild or a cultivated plant. The specific descriptions of the blackberries are more satisfactory.

It is to the Swedish botanist, Carl Linnaeus or Linné (1707–1778), that botanists owe the standardization of this method of naming plants. Linnaeus adopted the binomial system, by which every plant received two names, a generic name, indicative of the group to which is belonged, and a specific, or trivial name, applying to it and to no other kind of plant, a system analogous to our use of surnames and christian names. The binomial system was not invented by Linnaeus; binomials had been used previously, as in the example from Ray which has just been quoted. Linnaeus's genius lay in the standardization of this binomial system, which made possible a rational, international system of nomenclature by which any new kind of plant could be accurately and precisely named, and recognised by a competent botanist. Under this system the several blackberries, described by Ray, became:

Rubus fruticosus	(= shrubby)	Bramble
Rubus caesius	(= blue-grey)	Dewberry
Rubus idaeus	(= of Mount Ida)	Raspberry

It will immediately be objected that these Linnaean names are less precise than those of Ray: after all, there are several sorts of shrubby blackberry and no one could know, from an inspection of the plant, that the raspberry originated on Mount Ida, in Crete, even if it did so. Linnaeus, however, described each plant tersely and accurately, so that it is possible to look up his descriptions under their appropriate names and to attempt to match any plants which he described. Clearly, it is not enough merely to know the shorthand notation; we must be able to interpret it, and this the descriptions enable us to do.

It might be thought that so simple a device for naming plants and animals would have solved the difficulty for all time, but the system, now in world-wide use, has many complications, although it is accepted as the basis for nomenclature by botanists and zoologists alike. To mention a few of the more obvious difficulties: what happens when two botanists, working independently, give the same plant different names? or when two workers happen to select the same name for different plants? and further, how does a name for a new plant become established, and accepted universally? Linnaeus established certain rules of nomenclature (see Green, 1931) which were amplified and amended as occasion arose, until in 1905 at the International Botanical Congress at Vienna they were codified as the rules of botanical nomenclature. Since 1905 sundry modifications have been made to these rules, which are now accepted by most botanists as the basis for nomenclature. The last edition of these rules, the International Code of Botanical Nomenclature, was published in 1961.

Botanical nomenclature aims at fixity of names, lucidity and order, ideals which are often far from attainment. It is agreed that the starting point for nomenclature for flowering plants shall be the first edition of Linnaeus's *Species Plantarum*, 1753. Names established earlier are valid only if accepted by Linnaeus. It is laid down that the oldest name, with 1753 as the starting point, shall be accepted as the valid one, but since the rigid application of this principle might directly violate Article 4 of the rules by throwing "science into confusion," it is possible, by international consent, to "conserve" long-established and familiar generic names as the valid ones, even if, strictly, they have no claim to priority. Specific names cannot thus be conserved. A new name is recognised when it has been published in a book or periodical together with an adequate description of the plant, the description being in Latin. Generic names always begin with a capital letter; specific names never begin with a capital letter. Until quite recently it was customary to capitalise a specific name if it was derived from the name of a person, if it was a noun (e.g. the name of another plant), or if it was a name given by a pre-Linnaean author and adopted by Linnaeus; but the use of capitals for specific names has now been entirely discontinued.

No scientific name of a plant or animal can be considered complete unless it is accompanied by the name of its author. This condition is often disregarded but its importance must be stressed. The same name may have been used for different plants by two authors and unless it is known which plant is referred to, lucidity is not attained. For example, the name *Juniperus pseudosabina* is meaningless—it may refer to either of two species of juniper; but *Juniperus pseudosabina* Fischer et Meyer is the recognised name for a shrubby species of juniper from the Altai Mountains and Turkestan, and *Juniperus pseudosabina* Hook.f. is another name (synonym) for *Juniperus wallichiana* Hook.f. ex Brandis, a tree from the Himalayas and South Western China.

Where the author is a well-known botanist his name is often abbreviated, e.g. *Pinus sylvestris* L. (named by Linnaeus)

Ostrya japonica Sarg. (named by C. S. Sargent).

As knowledge of plants increases, conceptions of the limits of genera and species may alter. A plant originally in one genus may be transferred to another. In such an event the trivial name is retained, as well as that of the original author. For example, Eastern hemlock is known as *Tsuga canadensis* (L.) Carr. It was named *Pinus canadensis* by Linnaeus and later, when the concept of the genus *Pinus* became more circumscribed, was transferred to the genus *Tsuga* by Carrière.

Another similar example will illustrate why specific names appear to change. The alerce was for long known as *Fitzroya patagonica* Hook. f., the genus being created by the younger Hooker (f. = filius = son) for the reception of this species in 1851. In 1924 Johnston discovered that Molina had already described the tree as *Pinus cupressoides* in 1782. The plant clearly did not fit with *Pinus*, even in 1851, and was entitled to generic rank, but there was no reason why the specific name should be changed as well as that of the genus; *cupressoides* had priority and the name *Fitzroya cupressoides* (Molina) Johnston is the correct present name for the tree. "Correct present name" is used advisedly, for it does not follow that this name is not liable to further correction. It may be that the tree was given a different name by a botanist prior to Molina and that this name has so far been overlooked. In such an event two courses are open to taxonomists; either the present name must be changed to satisfy the priority rule or an attempt must be made, assuming that this change would be a generic one, to have the present name conserved. Even old-established and familiar names sometimes disappear because of the rule of priority. The common spruce was for a long time known as *Picea excelsa* Link, which name it received in 1841. Karsten corrected the name in 1881, because Linnaeus had called the tree *Pinus abies* in 1753, hence *abies* has priority over *excelsa* and the name must be *Picea abies* (L.) Karst.

One or two other abbreviations, sometimes met with in connection with the authorities for names, call for brief explanation. Such are the terms "*ex*," "*in*" and "*non*." *Ex* means that the plant was described in manuscript by one author but named by another, e.g. black juniper (*Juniperus wallichiana* Hook.f. ex Brandis) was described in manuscript notes by the younger Hooker but actually published by Brandis in one of the Forest Floras of India. *In* means that the name appeared, not in a publication by the authority for the name, but in a work by another author; e.g. Lebanon cedar (*Cedrus libani* G.Don in Loud.) was described by G. Don in Loudon's *Gardeners' Chronicle*. *Non* is sometimes used to indicate more emphatically to which plant reference is being made. In the example of the junipers referred to previously we may find the name written *Juniperus pseudosabina* Hook.f. non Fisch.et Mey., meaning the juniper named *pseudosabina* by the younger Hooker, and *not* the one so named by Fischer and Meyer.

Another abbreviation which is sometimes seen is ×, which indicates that the plant is, or is presumed to be, a hybrid. For example, the name of the hybrid Dunkeld larch might be rendered as *L. decidua* Mill. × *L. leptolepis* (Sieb. et Zucc.) Gord. but the tree is usually given a special name, its hybrid origin being indicated by × thus: × *Larix eurolepis* A.Henry.

To anyone using botanical literature it will occasion some surprise that botanical nomenclature aims at fixity of names, for specific names sometimes appear to change with bewildering frequency and even familiar generic names are not immutable. This, while regrettable, is unavoidable, for the nomenclature of plants is a very broad study which cannot be readily simplified if it is to be applied on an international basis. It seems logical to uphold the rule of priority in general, and in the enormous botanical literature it is not very difficult for names which have been given by older authors to be overlooked, at least temporarily. The priority rule can be waived for long-established names, but it does not follow that the desire to conserve a name will be world wide. Moreover, increasing knowledge may lead to the splitting of genera and consequent rearrangement of species, and concepts of the limits of certain species may also change. No hard and fast rules can be given for the limits in either case; they must remain a matter of opinion and, it is to be hoped, experience. Thus, Buchholz (1939) concluded that the two species of redwood (*Sequoia*) are generically distinct and he renamed the wellingtonia (*S. gigantea* Decaisne), *Sequoiadendron giganteum*. Buchholz' view did not however find universal acceptance; thus while Rehder (1940) accepted it, Dallimore and Jackson (1948) did not; they retained the old name. But in the revision of their work by Harrison (1966), *Sequoiadendron* is adopted. Similarly, such a well-known name as that used for English elm, *Ulmus campestris*, has disappeared from the newer works on British trees and timbers, for it is probable that the English elm does not occur outside the British Isles, and the name *campestris*, formerly applied to it, also includes other elms (now considered to be distinct species) growing in continental Europe. The only thing to do, therefore, is to give the English species a name of its own, viz. *U. procera* Salisbury.

It sometimes happens, that within a group of plants accepted as a species, several sub-groups, differing only in minor details, can be detected. Depending on how distinct such sub-groups are held to be, they are distinguished as sub-species, varieties or forms. Thus the copper beech, which is regarded as a variety of the common beech, and not as a distinct species, is known as *Fagus sylvatica* L. var. *cuprea* Loud. Concerning Japanese beech, however, opinion is divided as to whether it should be regarded as a distinct species, or as another variety of the common beech. Its name may thus appear as *Fagus sieboldii* Endl. or as *Fagus sylvatica* L. var. *asiatica* DC.

Since the number of plant species runs into hundreds of thousands it is necessary to have some system by which they can be classified in an orderly manner, plants which share certain features in common being grouped together in various ways. The grouping of species to form genera, as in the examples referred to earlier, is one step in this direction; according to their presumed relationships genera are in their turn associated in families, families in orders, orders in classes and classes in phyla.

Numerous systems of classification have been proposed, but a perfect "natural" classification, in which plants would be grouped entirely according to their relationships, remains to be devised. The various systems differ in the ways in which they make use of the features of plants to define their various groups: consequently the limits of a family, or a phylum, for example, may differ from one system to another. For our present purposes plants may conveniently be divided primarily into two groups; the lower plants, or cryptogams, which reproduce by spores (e.g. algae, fungi, mosses, ferns) and the higher plants, or phanerogams, which produce seeds and are hence commonly referred to as seed-plants or spermaphytes. These are the only ones which need concern us, as they are the only ones which produce timber.

The seed-plants fall into two distinct groups, those with naked seeds, the Gymnospermae, and those of which the seeds are enclosed within the ovary of the flower, the Angiospermae.

The Gymnospermae is not a big group. It is further divided into a number of orders, several of which contain only ancient, extinct plants. Only one order, the Coniferales, is of importance from the point of view of timber. The woods produced by members of the Coniferales are the softwoods, which differ considerably in their structure from hardwoods, that is, from woods produced by angiospermous plants.

It is unnecessary here to detail the characters which distinguish the Coniferales or conifers from other gymnosperms, but most conifers are cone-bearing plants with narrow, evergreen leaves; hence the term needle-leaved trees, which is sometimes applied to them. Nor is it necessary to give here the botanical characters by which the Coniferales are subdivided into half a dozen families or sub-families, including the yews and their allies (Taxaceae) and the pines, silver firs, hemlocks and others (Pinaceae).

The Angiospermae is a much bigger group than the Gymnospermae and is subdivided into many more orders and families. The first step is its subdivision into two classes, based on whether the embryo plant has a single cotyledon (first leaf) or two cotyledons. The members of the former (Monocotyledoneae) are mostly herbaceous, but include the bamboos, palms, screw pines and a few other arborescent plants. The latter class, the Dicotyledoneae, includes the trees from which the hardwoods are obtained. The manner in which the dicotyledons are subdivided depends on the system of classification adopted. The one outlined here, pp. 12–22, is that of Engler and Prantl (1897–1915) (see also Willis 6th ed., 1931, and 7th ed., 1966)[1] the system which is in

---

[1] Although the 6th edition is now somewhat out of date in matters of taxonomic detail, it contains a great deal of general information not included in the 7th edition.

B

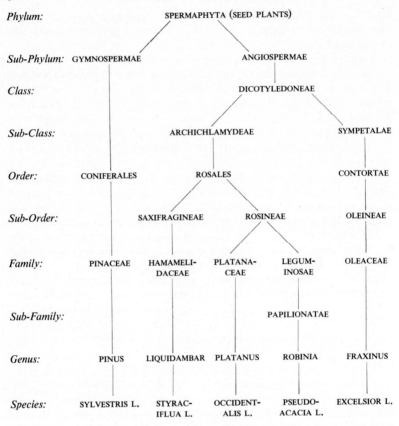

Phylum: SPERMAPHYTA (SEED PLANTS)

Sub-Phylum: GYMNOSPERMAE   ANGIOSPERMAE

Class: DICOTYLEDONEAE

Sub-Class: ARCHICHLAMYDEAE   SYMPETALAE

Order: CONIFERALES   ROSALES   CONTORTAE

Sub-Order: SAXIFRAGINEAE   ROSINEAE   OLEINEAE

Family: PINACEAE   HAMAMELI-DACEAE   PLATANA-CEAE   LEGUM-INOSAE   OLEACEAE

Sub-Family: PAPILIONATAE

Genus: PINUS   LIQUIDAMBAR   PLATANUS   ROBINIA   FRAXINUS

Species: SYLVESTRIS L.   STYRAC-IFLUA L.   OCCIDENT-ALIS L.   PSEUDO-ACACIA L.   EXCELSIOR L.

general use among wood anatomists. Here dicotyledonous plants fall into one of two sub-classes, depending in the main on whether the petals of the flowers are separate or joined together. These two sub-classes, the Archichlamydeae and the Sympetalae respectively, are split into a number of orders, each containing one or more families to which the numerous genera are assigned.

To illustrate the main divisions, the full classification of Scots pine (*Pinus sylvestris* L.), red gum (*Liquidambar styraciflua* L.), western plane or buttonwood (*Platanus occidentalis* L.), false acacia or black locust (*Robinia pseudoacacia* L.) and European ash (*Fraxinus excelsior* L.) is given above.

Families and orders vary much in size. Thus the maidenhair tree (*Ginkgo biloba* L.) is the only living representative of the Ginkgoales, an order considered to be of equivalent rank to the Coniferales: again the order Verticillatae contains only the family Casuarinaceae, which has a single genus, *Casuarina* (the Australian forest oaks) with fewer than forty species. On the other hand, the order Rosales contains eighteen families, of which half have at least some dendroid members: one family alone of this order, the Leguminosae, has over 600 genera and 12,000 species. Such numerical disparity between the different groups is to be expected in a natural classification, that is, in one which attempts to indicate relationships between plants, for the various groups have not all evolved at the same rate. It is unlikely that any proposed natural classification will meet with universal acceptance, for our knowledge of the evolution of plants is very fragmentary and it is hardly possible to decide with certainty what characters may be taken as being indicative of affinity; this is a matter of the judgement of those who have made a close study of the problems of the classification of plants (taxonomy). Two characters may be mentioned by way of illustration. The seed is a complicated structure and we can deduce, from the fossil evidence, probably with a fair degree of accuracy, the way in which it has evolved. The evidence would appear to be against the probability that the seed has arisen more than once in the course of evolution, hence there is reason to conclude that all seed plants are related by common ancestry and justification therefore, for assigning all of them to one major group. Moreover, other characteristics, besides the possession of seeds, are common to all seed plants and thus furnish corroborative evidence of common origin. On the contrary, there is ample evidence that the dendroid (or tree) habit has developed in a number of different plant groups and that it is, therefore, an unreliable guide to affinities. Nevertheless, in one recent system of classification (Hutchinson, 1959) the dendroid habit is regarded, in a more restricted way, as reliable for this purpose.

It is generally agreed that the reproductive parts of a plant, i.e., the flower and fruit, which are not so constantly exposed to environmental influences, are much more useful in indicating relationships than are vegetative parts, like leaves. Leaf characters are notoriously unreliable guides to relationships, although within a limited sphere they may sometimes be of service. In a similar way, characters of the wood, like those of the leaves, are of varied and limited taxonomic value.

Appendix to Chapter I

CLASSIFIED LIST OF SOME OF THE MORE IMPORTANT GENERA OF PLANTS WHICH PRODUCE WOOD OF ECONOMIC IMPORTANCE

This list is very far from complete: it has been estimated that there are over 20,000 species of woody plants in the world. The wood of some of these, by reason of its inherent properties, is of no value as timber; others, because of their scarcity or their inaccessibility, are, at most, only of local economic importance. A large number, of which the timber is, as yet, scarcely known, will no doubt appear in the world markets in the near future, as exploitation of tropical countries becomes more intense and better-known woods become scarcer.

The classification adopted here is that of Engler and Prantl.

GYMNOSPERMAE

CONIFERAE

TAXACEAE. *Taxus* (Yews): North Temperate. *T. baccata* L. (**Yew;** Europe, Asia, N. Africa).

PODOCARPACEAE. *Dacrydium:* South Temperate, East Tropical Asia. *D. colensoi* Hook. (New Zealand Silver Pine; New Zealand): *D. cupressinum* Soland. (**Rimu;** New Zealand): *D. elatum* Wall. (**Sempilor;** Eastern Tropical Asia): *D. franklinii* Hook.f. (**Huon Pine;** Tasmania).

Phyllocladus: Australasia, East Indies. *P. rhomboidalis* Rich. (**Celery-top Pine;** Tasmania).

Podocarpus: mostly Southern Hemisphere. *P. dacrydioides* A.Rich. (**New Zealand White Pine,** Kahikatea; New Zealand): *P. ferrugineus* D.Don. (**Miro;** New Zealand): *P. gracilior* Pilg., *P. milanjianus* Rendle and *P. usambarensis* Pilg. (**Podo,** Yellowwood; East Africa): *P.* spp. (Yellowwood; South Africa): *P. guatemalensis* Standl. (**British Honduras Yellowwood;** tropical America): *P. nubigenus* Lindl., *P. salignus* D.Don. and spp. (**Manio,** Maniu; S. America): *P. spicatus* R.Br. (**Matai;** New Zealand): *P. totara* D.Don. and *P. hallii* T.Kirk (**Totara;** New Zealand).

Saxegothaea: South America. *S. conspicua* Lindl. (Manio in part).

ARAUCARIACEAE. *Araucaria:* Southern Hemisphere (excluding Africa). *A. angustifolia* (Bert.) O.Kuntze (**Parana Pine;** Brazil and Argentine): *A. araucana* (Mol.) K.Koch (**Chile Pine;** S. America): *A. bidwillii* Hook. (**Bunya Pine;** Queensland): *A. cunninghamii* Sweet (**Hoop Pine;** Eastern Australia; New Guinea).

Agathis (Kauris): South Eastern Asia, Australasia. *A. alba* Foxw. (**East Indian Kauri;** East Indies): *A. australis* Salisb. (**New Zealand Kauri;** New Zealand): *A. palmerstonii* F.Muell. and spp. (**Queensland Kauri;** Queensland): *A. vitiensis* Benth. et Hook. (**Fijian Kauri;** Fiji).

PINACEAE. *Abies* (Silver Firs): North Temperate. *A. alba* Mill. (**Silver Fir, Whitewood** (in part); Europe): *A. amabilis* Forbes (**Amabilis Fir;** Western North America): *A. balsamea* Mill. (**Balsam Fir;** North America): *A. grandis* Lindl. (**Grand Fir,** Lowland Fir; Western North America): *A. lasiocarpa* (Hook.) Nutt. (**Alpine Fir;** Western North America): *A. procera* Rehder (**Noble Fir;** Western U.S.A.).

Pseudotsuga: Western North America, Eastern Asia. *P. taxifolia* (Pior.) Britt. (**Douglas Fir,** Columbian Pine, British Columbia Pine, Oregon Pine; Western North America).

Tsuga (Hemlocks): North America, Eastern Asia. *T. canadensis* (L.) Carr. (**Eastern Hemlock;** Eastern North America). *T. heterophylla* Sarg. and *T. mertensiana* (Bog.) Carr. (**Western Hemlock;** Western North America).

Picea (Spruces): North Temperate. *P. abies* Karst. (**European Spruce, Whitewood** (in part), White Deal; Europe): *P. engelmannii* (Parry) Engelm. (**Engelmann Spruce;** Western North America): *P. glauca*

(Moench) Voss. and *P.* spp.[1] (**Eastern Canadian Spruce;** North America):
P. glauca (Moench) Voss. var. *albertiana* Sarg. (**Western White Spruce;**
Western North America): *P. sitchensis* Carr. (**Sitka Spruce,** Silver Spruce;
Western North America).

Larix (Larches): Northern Hemisphere. *L. decidua* Mill. (**European Larch;**
Europe): *L.* × *eurolepis* A.Henry = *L. decidua* × *L. leptolepis* (**Dunkeld
Larch**): *L. laricina* K.Koch (**Tamarack Larch;** Tamarack, North
America): *L. leptolepis* Gord. (**Japanese Larch;** Japan): *L. occidentalis*
Nutt. (**Western Larch;** Western North America): *L. sibirica* Ledeb.
(**Siberian Larch;** North East Russia and Western Siberia).

Cedrus (True Cedars): North Africa, Asia Minor, Himalayas. *C. deodara*
(Roxb.) Loud. (Deodar; Northern India).

Pinus (True Pines): Northern Hemisphere. *P. banksiana* Lamb. (**Jack Pine;**
North America): *P. caribaea* Morelet and *P. oocarpa* Schiede (**Caribbean
Pitch Pine;** Central America and Caribbean): *P. cembra* L. v. *sibirica*
Loud. and *P. koraiensis* Sieb. et Zucc. (**Siberian Yellow Pine,** Siberian
Pine, Korean Pine, Manchurian Pine; Siberia and Eastern Asia): *P.
contorta* Dougl. v. *latifolia* S.Watson (**Lodgepole Pine;** Western North
America): *P. lambertiana* Dougl. (**Sugar Pine;** Western North America):
P. monticola Dougl. ex Lamb. (**Western White Pine;** Western North
America): *P. nigra* Arnold v. *calabrica* Schneid. (**Corsican Pine;** Europe):
P. palustris Mill. and *P. elliottii* Engelm. (**American Pitch Pine,** Longleaf
Pitch Pine; Southern North America): *P. pinaster* Ait. (**Maritime Pine;**
Mediterranean): *P. ponderosa* Laws and *P. jeffreyi* A.Murr. (**Ponderosa
Pine,** Western Yellow Pine; Western North America): *P. radiata* D.Don.
(**Radiata Pine,** Monterey Pine, Insignis Pine; Western North America;
now extensively planted in Australasia and South Africa): *P. resinosa*
Ait. (**Canadian Red Pine,** Norway Pine; Eastern North America): *P.
strobus* L. (**Yellow Pine,** White Pine, Weymouth Pine; Eastern North
America): *P. sylvestris* L. (**Scots Pine, Redwood,** Red Deal, Yellow
Deal; Europe).

TAXODIACEAE. *Sequoia:* Western U.S.A. *S. sempervirens* Endl. (**Sequoia,**
Californian Redwood).

Taxodium (Swamp Cypresses): Southern North America. *T. distichum*
Rich. (**Southern Cypress,** Bald Cypress, Red Cypress, Yellow Cypress).

Cryptomeria: Eastern Asia. *C. japonica* (L.f.) D.Don (**Sugi;** Japan).

CUPRESSACEAE. *Callitris* (Cypress Pines): Australia and New Caledonia.
C. glauca R.Br. (White Cypress Pine, Murray Pine; Australia).

Tetraclinis: North Africa and Malta. *T. articulata* (Vahl) Masters (**Thuya**).

Widdringtonia: South and East Africa. *W. whytei* Rendle (Milanji Cedar,
Milanji Cypress; East Africa).

Fitzroya: Southern Chile. *F. cupressoides* (Mol.) Johnston (**Alerce**).

Thuja (Arbor Vitae): North America, Eastern Asia. *T. occidentalis* L.
(**White Cedar,** Northern White Cedar; Eastern North America): *T.
plicata* D.Don (**Western Red Cedar;** Western North America).

Cupressus (True Cypresses): Northern Hemisphere. *C. macrocarpa* Gord.
(Monterey Cypress; Western North America).

Chamaecyparis (False Cypresses): North America, Eastern Asia. *C.*

---

[1] *P. glauca* (White Spruce); *P. rubens* Sarg. (Red Spruce); *P. mariana* B.S. et P.
(Black Spruce).

lawsoniana Parl. (**Port Orford Cedar,** Lawson's Cypress; Western North America): *C. nootkatensis* Spach. (**Yellow Cedar,** Alaska Cedar; Western North America). *C. thyoides* (L.) B.S.P. (**Southern White Cedar;** Eastern North America).

Juniperus (Junipers, Pencil Cedars): Northern Hemisphere. *J. procera* Hochst. (**African Pencil Cedar;** East Africa): *J. virginiana* L.[1] (**Virginian Pencil Cedar,** Red Cedar; North America).

ANGIOSPERMAE
DICOTYLEDONEAE
ARCHICHLAMYDEAE
VERTICILLATAE

CASUARINACEAE.   *Casuarina:* Australia, Polynesia. *Casuarina* spp. (She Oak, Forest Oak; Australia).

SALICALES

SALICACEAE.   *Populus* (Poplars, Cottonwood, Aspens): mostly North Temperate. *P. alba* L. (**White Poplar,** Abele; Eurasia): *P. balsamifera* L. (**Canadian Poplar,** Cottonwood; North America): *P.* × *canadensis* Moench v. *serotina* Rehd. (**Black Poplar,**[2] Black Italian Poplar): *P. canescens* Sm. (**Grey Poplar;** Europe, Western Asia): *P. deltoides* Bartr. ex Marsh. (**Eastern Cottonwood;** Eastern North America): *P. grandidentata* Michx. (**Canadian Poplar,** Largetooth Aspen; North America): *P. tremula* L. (**European Aspen;** Temperate Old World): *P. tremuloides* Michx. (**Canadian Aspen,** White Poplar; North America): *P. trichocarpa* Hook. (**Black Cottonwood;** Western North America).

Salix (Willows): mostly North Temperate. *S. alba* L. and *S. viridis* Fr. (**White Willow;** Temperate Old World): *S. alba* L. v. *coerulea* Sm. (**Cricket-bat Willow**): *S. nigra* Marsh. (**Black Willow;** North America).

JUGLANDALES

JUGLANDACEAE.   *Juglans* (Walnuts): mostly Northern Hemisphere. *J. cinerea* L. (Butternut; Eastern North America): *J. nigra* L. (**American Walnut,** American Black Walnut; Eastern North America): *J. regia* L. (**European Walnut;** Europe, Asia): *J. sieboldiana* Maxim. (**Japanese Walnut;** Japan).

Carya (Hickories): Eastern North America, Eastern Asia. *C. glabra* Sweet, *C. ovata* K.Koch and spp. (**Hickory;** Eastern North America): *C. illinoensis* K.Koch, *C. aquatica* Nutt. and spp. (**Pecan;** Eastern North America).

FAGALES

BETULACEAE.   *Carpinus:* Northern Hemisphere. *C. betulus* L. (**Hornbeam;** Europe).

Ostrya: North Temperate. *O. carpinifolia* Scop. (**European Hop-hornbeam;** Southern Europe and Asia Minor): *O. virginiana* K.Koch (**American Hop-hornbeam;** North America).

---

[1] *J. lucayana* Britt. (Red Cedar; West Indies) also furnishes Pencil Cedar.
[2] Also used for *P. nigra* L. and *P. robusta* Schneid.

Betula (Birches): Northern Hemisphere. *B. alleghaniensis* Britt. = *B. lutea* Michx. (**Yellow Birch;** Eastern North America): *B. papyrifera* Marsh. (**Paper Birch;** North America): *B. papyrifera* Marsh. var. *occidentalis* Sarg. (**Western Paper Birch;** Western North America): *B. pendula* Roth. = *B. verrucosa* Ehrh. and *B. pubescens* Ehrh. (**European Birch;** Europe).

Alnus (Alders): mostly Northern Hemisphere. *A. glutinosa* Gaertn. (**Common Alder;** Europe): *A. incana* Moench (**Grey Alder;** Northern Europe): *A. rubra* Bong. (Red Alder; Western North America).

FAGACEAE. *Nothofagus:* Australasia, South America. *N. cunninghamii* Oerst. (**Tasmanian Myrtle;** Australia): *N. dombeyi* Bl. (**Coigue,** Chilean Beech; Chile): *N. menziesii* Oerst. (**Silver Beech,** Southland Beech; New Zealand): *N. moorei* Maid. (**Negro-head Beech;** Australia): *N. obliqua* Mirb. (**Roble;** Chile): *N. procera* Oerst. (**Rauli,** Chilean Beech; Chile).

Fagus (Beeches): North Temperate. *F. crenata* Bl. and spp. (**Japanese Beech,** Buna; Japan): *F. grandifolia* Ehrh. (**American Beech;** Eastern North America): *F. sylvatica* L. (**European Beech;** Europe).

Castanea (Chestnuts): North Temperate. *C. dentata* Borkh. (**American Chestnut;** North America): *C. sativa* Mill. (**Sweet Chestnut;** Europe).

Quercus (True Oaks): Northern Hemisphere. *Q. alba* L. and *Q.* spp. (**American White Oak;** North America): *Q. castaneaefolia* C.A.Mey. (**Persian Oak;** Caucasus, Iran): *Q. cerris* L. (**Turkey Oak;** Southern Europe, Western Asia): *Q. ilex* L. (**Holm Oak,** Evergreen Oak; Mediterranean region): *Q. mongolica* Fisch. ex Turcz. var. *grosseserrata* Rehd. et Wils. and *Q.* spp. (**Japanese Oak;** Japan): *Q. robur* and *Q. petraea* Liebl. (**European Oak;** Europe): *Q. rubra* L. emend. Du Roi and *Q.* spp. (**American Red Oak;** North America).

URTICALES

ULMACEAE.   *Ulmus* (Elms): Northern Hemisphere. *U. americana* L. (**White Elm;** Eastern North America): *U. carpinifolia* Gleditsch (**Smooth-leaved Elm,** European Elm; Europe): *U. glabra* Huds. non Mill. (**Wych Elm;** Europe, Western Asia): *U.* × *hollandica* Mill. var. *hollandica* (**Dutch Elm**): *U. procera* Salisb. (**English Elm;** Britain): *U. thomasii* Sarg. (**Rock Elm;** Eastern North America): *U.* spp. (**Japanese Elm;** Japan).

Phyllostylon: Tropical America. *P. brasiliensis* Cap. (**San Domingo Boxwood,** Baitoa).

Celtis: Northern Hemisphere, South Africa. *Celtis occidentalis* L. (**Hackberry;** North America): *Celtis* spp. (especially *C. adolfi-frederici* Engl., *C. soyauxii* Engl. and *C. zenkeri* Engl.) (**African Celtis,** Esa; Tropical Africa).

MORACEAE. *Morus* (Mulberries): Northern Hemisphere. *M. nigra* L. (Blackor Common Mulberry; Western Asia).

Chlorophora: Tropical America and Africa. *C. excelsa* Benth. et Hook.f. and *C. regia* A.Chev. (**Iroko,** Odum, Mvule; Tropical Africa): *C. tinctoria* (L.) Gaud. (**Fustic,** Old Fustic; Tropical America).

Artocarpus: Eastern Asia. *A. integrifolia* L. (Jak Wood).

Antiaris: Indomalaya, Tropical Africa. *A. africana* Engl. and *A. welwitschii* Engl. (**Antiaris,** Chenchen, Oro, Kirundu; West Africa).

Brosimum: Tropical and South America. *B. paraense* Hub. (**Satiné;** Tropical America).
Piratinera: Tropical America. *P. guianensis* Aubl. and *P.* spp. (**Snakewood,** Letterwood).

PROTEALES

PROTEACEAE. *Grevillea:* Australia. *G. robusta* A.Cunn. (**Grevillea,** African Silky-Oak; East Africa (planted)).
Knightia: New Zealand, New Caledonia. *K. excelsa* R.Br. (Rewarewa, New Zealand Honeysuckle; New Zealand).
Cardwellia: Northern Queensland. *C. sublimis* F.Muell. (**Australian Silky-Oak).**

SANTALALES

SANTALACEAE. *Santalum:* Indomalaya. *S. album* L. (**Sandalwood;** Southern India).

RANALES

CERCIDIPHYLLACEAE. *Cercidiphyllum:* Japan and China. *C. japonicum* Sieb. et Zucc. (**Katsura).**
MAGNOLIACEAE. *Magnolia:* Asia and North America. *Magnolia* spp. (**Magnolia;** North America).
Liriodendron: North America and China. *L. tulipifera* L. (**American Whitewood,** Canary Whitewood, Yellow Poplar; North America).
ANONACEAE. *Oxandra:* Tropical America. *O. lanceolata* Baill. (**Lancewood).**
Cleistopholis: Tropical Africa. *C. patens* Engl. et Diels (**Otu).**
MYRISTICACEAE. *Virola:* Tropical America. *V. bicuhyba* Warb. (**Bicuiba):** *V. koschnyi* Warb. (**Banak):** *V. surinamensis* Warb. and *V.* spp. (**Dalli).**
Pycnanthus: Tropical Africa. *P. angolensis* Warb. (**Ilomba,** Pycnanthus, Akomu; West Africa).
MONIMIACEAE. *Laurelia:* Chile, New Zealand. *L. aromatica* Juss. (**Chilean Laurel;** Chile): *L. serrata* Ph. (**Tepa;** Chile).
Persea: Tropics. *P. lingue* Nees (**Lingue;** Chile).
LAURACEAE. *Phoebe:* Tropical America and Asia. *P. porosa* Mez. (**Imbuya,** Embuia, Brazilian Walnut; Southern Brazil).
Ocotea: Tropics and sub-tropics. *O. barcellensis* Mez. (**Louro inamui;** Brazil): *O. bullata* E.Mey. (Stinkwood; South Africa): *O. rodiaei* Mez (**Greenheart;** British Guiana): *O. rubra* Mez. (**Red Louro,** Determa, Wana; Tropical America): *O. usambarensis* Engl. (**East African Camphorwood;** East Africa).
Eusideroxylon: East Indies. *E. zwageri* Teijsm. et Binn. (**Billian,** Belian, Borneo Ironwood).
Beilschmiedia: Tropics and Australasia. *B. tawa* B. et H.f. (Tawa; New Zealand).
Endiandra: Asia and Australia. *E. palmerstonii* C.T.White (**Queensland Walnut;** Northern Queensland).

ROSALES

CUNONIACEAE. *Ceratopetalum:* Eastern Australia. *C. apetalum* D.Don (**Coachwood).**
HAMAMELIDACEAE. *Liquidambar:* America and Asia. *L. styraciflua* L.

(**American Red Gum,** Satin Walnut, Hazel Pine; South Eastern United States).

PLATANACEAE. *Platanus* (Planes): North Temperate. *P. acerifolia* Willd. (**European Plane,** London Plane, Lacewood; Europe): *P. occidentalis* L. (**American Plane,** Buttonwood; Eastern North America).

ROSACEAE. *Malus* (Apples): North Temperate. *M. sylvestris* Mill. (**Apple;** Europe, Eastern Asia).

Pyrus (Pears): Europe, Asia, North Africa. *P. communis* L. (**Pear**).

Sorbus: North Temperate. *S. aria* Crantz (**Whitebeam;** Europe).

Prunus: North Temperate. *P. avium* L. and *P.* spp. (**European Cherry**): *P. serotina* Ehrh. (**American Cherry,** Black Cherry; Eastern North America).

LEGUMINOSAE. (It is impossible here to give anything like a representative list of the genera of dendroid plants in this enormous family. An attempt has been made to note some of the more important genera, but the choice has been, of necessity, somewhat arbitrary.)

I. MIMOSOIDEAE. *Albizzia:* Warm regions, Old World. *A. lebbeck* Benth. (**Kokko,** Siris, East Indian Walnut; India, Burma): *A.* spp. (**Nongo,** Red Nongo; East Africa): *A.* spp. (**West African Albizzia;** West Africa).

Acacia: Warm regions, Old World. *A. aneura* F.Muell. (**Mulga;** Australia): *A. melanoxylon* R.Br. (**Australian Blackwood;** Australia).

Xylia: Tropical Asia and Africa. *X. dolabriformis* Benth. (**Pyinkado;** Tropical Asia).

Piptadenia: Tropics. *P. africana* Hook.f. (= *Piptadeniastrum africanum* (Hook.f.) Brenan) (**Dahoma,** Ekhimi, Dabema; Tropical Africa): *P. buchananii* Bak. and *P.* spp. (Mpewere, Mkufi; East Africa).

Plathymenia: Brazil. *P. reticulata* Benth. (**Vinhatico**).

Cylicodiscus: West Africa. *C. gabunensis* Harms (**Okan,** Denya).

II. CAESALPINIOIDEAE. *Erythrophleum:* Africa, N. Australia, China. *E. guineense* G.Don (**Missanda,** Tali, Erun, Sasswood, Mauve; Tropical Africa): *E. ivorense* A.Chev. (**Missanda,** Tali, Erun, Sasswood, Potrodom; Tropical Africa).

Mora: Tropical America. *M. excelsa* Benth. (**Mora**).

Cynometra: Tropics. *C. alexandri* C.H.Wright (**Muhimbi;** Uganda).

Prioria: West Indies, Central America. *P. copaifera* Griseb. (**Cativo**).

Guibourtia: Tropical America and Africa. *G. coleosperma* J.Léon. (**Rhodesian Copalwood,** Rhodesian Mahogany, Muzaule; Rhodesia): *G.* spp. (**Bubinga;** West Africa).

Pseudosindora and *Sindora:* East Tropical Asia (**Sepetir,** Makatu).

Hymenaea: Tropical America. *H. courbaril* L. (**Courbaril,** West Indian Locust).

Peltogyne: Tropical America. *P.* spp. (**Purpleheart,** Amaranth).

Brachystegia: Tropical Africa. *B.* spp. (**Okwen;** West Africa).

Microberlinia: Tropical Africa. *M. brazzavillensis* A.Chev. and *M. bisculcata* A.Chev. (**Zebrano**).

Baikiaea: Tropical Africa. *B. plurijuga* Harms. (**Rhodesian Teak;** Rhodesia).

Intsia: Tropics, Old World. *I. bijuga* O.Ktze. and *I. palembanica* Miq. (**Merbau;** Eastern Asia).

Afzelia: Tropical Africa and Asia. *A.* spp. (**Afzelia,** Apa, Aligna, Doussié; Africa): *A. quanzensis* Welw. (**Afzelia,** Chanfuta, Mkora; East Africa).

Daniellia: West Africa. *D. ogea* Rolfe ex Holl. and *D. thurifera* Bennett (**Ogea,** Daniellia).

Eperua: Tropical America. *E. falcata* Aubl. and *E. grandiflora* Benth. (**Wallaba**).

Berlinia: Tropical Africa. *B. grandiflora* Hutch. et Dalz. and *B.* spp. (**Berlinia**, Ekpogoi; West Africa).

Koompassia: Malaya. *K. malaccensis* Maing. (**Kempas**).

Distemonanthus: West Africa. *D. benthamianus* Baill. (**Ayan**, Anyaran, Movingui).

Dicorynia: Tropical America. *D. paraensis* Benth. (**Basralocus**, Angelique).

Caesalpinia: Tropical and Sub-tropical. *C. echinata* Lam. (**Brazilwood**; Brazil): *C. granadillo* Pitt. and *C.* spp. (**Partridgewood**; Venezuela).

III. PAPILIONATAE. *Afrormosia:* Tropical Africa. *A. elata* Harms. (= *Pericopsis elata* van Neeuwen) (**Afrormosia**, Kokrodua; West Africa).

Bowdichia: Tropical South America. *B.* spp. (**Sucupira**, Black Sucupira).

Castanospermum: Australia. *C. australe* A.Cunn. (**Black Bean**).

Baphia: Tropical Africa. *B. nitida* Lodd. (**Camwood**; West Africa).

Laburnum: Southern Europe and Western Asia. *L. anagyroides* Medic. (**Laburnum**; Southern Europe).

Millettia: Tropical and Sub-tropical. *M. laurentii* De Wild. (**Wenge**; Congo): *M. stuhlmannii* Taub. (**Panga panga**; East Africa).

Robinia: North America. *R. pseudoacacia* L. (**Robinia**, False Acacia, Black Locust).

Brya: Tropical America. *B. ebenus* DC. (**Cocuswood**, Cocoswood, Cocus, Green Ebony).

Dalbergia: Warm regions. *D. cearensis* Ducke? (**Kingwood**, Violet Wood; Brazil): *D. frutescens* Britton var. *tomentosa* Standl. (**Brazilian Tulip Wood**): *D. latifolia* Roxb. (**Indian Rosewood**): *D. melanoxylon* Guill. et Perr. (**African Blackwood**; East Africa): *D. nigra* Fr.All. and *D.* spp. (**Brazilian Rosewood**, Rio Rosewood, Jacaranda; Brazil): *D. oliveri* Gamb. (**Burma Tulip Wood**; Burma): *D. retusa* Hemsl. and *D.* spp. (**Cocobolo**; Central America): *D. sissoo* Roxb. (**Sissoo**, Shisham; Northern India and Pakistan): *D. stevensonii* Standl. (**Honduras Rosewood**; British Honduras).

Pterocarpus: Tropics. *P. angolensis* DC. (**Muninga**, Ambila; South and East Africa): *P. dalbergioides* Roxb. (**Andaman Padauk**; Andaman Islands): *P. indicus* Willd. and *P.* spp. (**Amboyna**, Narra; East Indies): *P. macrocarpus* Kurz (**Burma Padauk**, Pradoo; Burma, Thailand): *P. pedatus* Pierre (**Maidu**, False Amboyna; East Asia): *P. soyauxii* Taub. (**African Padauk**, Barwood; West Africa).

Gossweilerodendron: West Africa. *G. balsamiferum* Harms. (**Agba**).

Andira: Tropical America and Africa. *A. inermis* H.B. et K. (**Angelin**; Tropical America).

Pterygopodium: West Africa. *P. oxyphyllum* Harms. (**Lolagbola**).

GERANIALES

ERYTHROXYLACEAE. *Erythroxylum:* Warm regions. *E. mannii* Oliv. (**Landa**; West Africa).

ZYGOPHYLLACEAE. *Guaiacum:* Central America. *G. officinale* L., *G. sanctum* L. and *G.* spp. (**Lignum Vitae**).

Bulnesia: South America. *B. arborea* Engl. (**Verawood**, Maracaibo Lignum Vitae; Venezuela, Colombia).

RUTACEAE.   *Fagara:* Tropics. *F. flava* Krug. et Urb. (= *Zanthoxylum flavum* Vahl.) (**West Indian Satinwood**, Jamaica Satinwood; West Indies): *F. macrophylla* Engl. (**African Satinwood**, Olon; Tropical Africa).

Fagaropsis: East Africa. *F. angolensis* Dale (**Mafu**).

Flindersia: Malaya, Australia. *F. brayleyana* F.Muell. and *F. pimenteliana* F.Muell. (**Queensland Maple**, Maple Silkwood; Queensland).

Chloroxylon: India and Ceylon. *C. swietenia* DC. (**Ceylon Satinwood,** East Indian Satinwood).

Amyris: Tropical America. *A. balsamifera* L. (Amyris Wood, Torchwood).

SIMARUBACEAE.   *Simaruba:* Tropical America. *S. amara* Aubl. (**Simaruba**).

Ailanthus: Eastern Asia, North Australia. *A. altissima* (Mill.) Swingle (Tree of Heaven; China).

BURSERACEAE.   *Canarium:* Tropical Africa and Asia. *C. euphyllum* Kurz. (**Indian Canarium,** Dhup, White Dhup, Indian White Mahogany; Andaman Islands): *C. schweinfurthii* Engl. (**African Canarium;** Tropical Africa): *C.* spp. (**Malayan Canarium;** Malaya).

Aucoumea: West Africa. *A. klaineana* Pierre (**Gaboon,** Okoumé).

MELIACEAE.   *Cedrela:* Tropics, except Africa. *C. fissilis* Vell. and *C.* spp. (**South American Cedar,** Cigar-box Cedar, Cedar, Cedro; Tropical South America): *C. mexicana* Roem. and *C.* spp. (**Central American Cedar,** Cigar-box Cedar, Cedar; Central America, West Indies): *C. toona* Roxb. (**Burma Cedar,** Toon, Yomhom; Tropical Asia): *C. toona* Roxb. var. *australis* C.DC. (**Australian Cedar;** Eastern Australia).

Khaya: Tropical Africa. *K. ivorensis* A.Chev. and *K.* spp. (**African Mahogany**).

Chukrasia: Tropical Asia. *C. tabularis* A.Juss. (**Chickrassy,** Chittagong Wood): *C. velutina* W. & A. (**Yom hin**).

Entandrophragma: Tropical Africa. *E. angolense* C.DC. and *C.* spp. (**Gedu Nohor**): *E. candollei* Harms. (**Omu,** Heavy Sapele): *E. cylindricum* Sprague (**Sapele,** Aboudikro): *E. utile* Sprague (**Utile,** Assié, Sipo).

Swietenia: **American Mahogany;** Tropical America. *S. candollei* Pitt. (Venezuelan Mahogany): *S. macrophylla* King (Honduras Mahogany, Central American Mahogany, Baywood; Central America): *S. mahagoni* Jacq. (Cuban Mahogany, Spanish Mahogany; West Indies).

Carapa: Tropics. *C. guianensis* Aubl. (**Crabwood,** Andiroba; Tropical America).

Melia: Palaeotropical and sub-tropical. *M. composita* Willd. (**Lunumidella;** Ceylon).

Sandoricum: Tropical Asia and Africa. *S. indicum* Cav. (**Katon;** Indomalaya).

Dysoxylum: Tropical Asia, Australia. *D. fraseranum* Benth. (Australian Mahogany, Rose Mahogany; Eastern Australia).

Turraeanthus: West Africa. *T. africanus* Pellegr. and *T. vignei* Hutch. et J.M. Dalz. (**Avodiré**).

Amoora: Tropical Asia. *A. polystachya* Hook.f. et Jackson and *A. cucullata* Roxb. (**Tasua;** Thailand).

Guarea: Tropical America and Africa. *G. cedrata* Pellegr. and *G. thompsonii* Sprague et Hutch. (**Guarea,** Bossé, Obobo; West Africa).

Lovoa: Tropical Africa. *L. brownii* Sprague (Nkoba, Uganda Walnut; Uganda): *L. klaineana* Pierre ex Sprague (= *L. trichilioides* Harms.) (**African Walnut,** Dibétou, Sida; West Africa).

VOCHYSIACEAE. *Vochysia:* Tropical America. *V.* spp. (**Quaruba,** Yemeri; Tropical America).
Qualea: Tropical America. *Q.* spp. (Mandio, Mandioqueira).
EUPHORBIACEAE. *Aextoxicon:* Chile. *A. punctatum* Ruiz et Pav. (**Olivillo**).
Croton: Tropical and sub-tropical. *C. megalocarpus* Hutch. (**Musine;** East Africa).
Ricinodendron: Tropical Africa. *R. heudelotii* Pierre ex Pax (**Erimado;** West Africa): *R. rautanenii* Schinz (**Mugongo;** South Tropical Africa, Rhodesia).
Hura: Tropical America. *H. crepitans* L. (**Hura,** Sandbox, Assacu).

SAPINDALES

BUXACEAE. *Buxus* (Box): Europe, Asia, Central America. *B. macowani* Oliv. (**East London Boxwood,** Cape Box; South Africa): *B. sempervirens* L. (**European Boxwood;** Mediterranean, Western Asia).
ANACARDIACEAE. *Dracontomelum:* Malaya, Melanesia. *D. dao* Merr.et Rolfe (**Paldao,** Dao; Philippines): *D.* spp. (**New Guinea Walnut;** New Guinea).
Parishia: Tropical Asia. *P. insignis* Hook.f. (**Red Dhup;** Andaman Islands).
Campnosperma: Tropics. *C.* spp. (Terentang; Malaya).
Astronium: South America. *A. fraxinifolium* Schott and *A. graveolens* Jacq. (**Gonçalo alves,** Zebra Wood).
Schinopsis: South America. *S. lorentzii* Engl. and *S. balansae* Engl. (Quebracho).
AQUIFOLIACEAE. *Ilex* (Hollies): Temperate and Tropical. *I. aquifolium* L. (**Holly,** European Holly; Eurasia, North Africa): *I. opaca* Ait. (American Holly; North America).
CELASTRACEAE. *Euonymus:* North and Central America, Eurasia, Australia. *E. europaeus* L. (Spindle Tree; Europe, Western Asia).
Goupia: Central and Tropical South America. *G. glabra* Aubl. (Kabukalli, Goupi).
ACERACEAE. *Acer* (Maples): North Temperate. *A. campestre* L. (**Field Maple;** Europe, Western Asia): *A. macrophyllum* Pursh (**Pacific Maple,** Oregon Maple; Western North America): *A. platanoides* L. (**Norway Maple,** European Maple; Europe): *A. pseudoplatanus* L. (**Sycamore;** Europe, Western Asia): *A. saccharinum* L. and *A. rubrum* L. (**Soft Maple;** Eastern North America): *A. saccharum* Marsh. and *A. nigrum* Michx.f. (**Rock Maple,** Hard Maple; Eastern North America): *A.* spp. (**Japanese Maple**).
HIPPOCASTANACEAE. *Aesculus* (Horse Chestnuts, Buckeyes): North Temperate, South America. *A. glabra* Willd. (Ohio Buckeye; North America): *A. hippocastanum* L. (**European Horse-chestnut;** Europe): *A. octandra* Marsh. (Yellow Buckeye; Eastern North America): *A. turbinata* Bl. (**Japanese Horse-chestnut;** Japan).
SAPINDACEAE. *Harpullia:* Palaeotropical. *H. pendula* Planch. (Tulipwood; Eastern Australia).
RHAMNACEAE. *Rhamnus:* Most North Temperate. *R. purshiana* DC. (Cascara; Western North America): *R. zeyheri* Sond. (Pink or Red Ivory Wood; South Africa).
Maesopsis: Tropical East Africa. *M. eminii* Engl. (**Musizi**).

MALVALES

GONYSTYLACEAE.   *Gonystylus:* Indomalaya. *G. bancanus* Baill. and *G.* spp. (**Ramin**, Melawis; Malaya, Sarawak).

TILIACEAE.   *Pentace:* Eastern Tropical Asia. *P. burmanica* Kurz (**Thitka,** Burma Mahogany; Burma).

Nesogordonia: Tropical Africa. *N. papaverifera* Capuron (= *Cistanthera papaverifera* A.Chev.) (**Danta;** West Africa).

Tilia (Limes): North Temperate. *T. americana* L. and *T.* spp. (**Basswood;** Eastern North America): *T. japonica* Simpk. and *T.* spp. (**Japanese Lime;** Japan): *T. vulgaris* Hayne and *T.* spp. (**European Lime;** Europe).

TRIPLOCHITONACEAE.   *Triplochiton:* West Africa. *T. scleroxylon* K.Schum. (**Obeche, Wawa,** Ayous, Samba, Arere).

Mansonia: Tropical Africa and Asia. *M. altissima* A.Chev. (**Mansonia,** African Black Walnut; West Africa).

BOMBACACEAE.   *Bombax:* Tropical. *B. buonopozense* P.Beauv. and ?*B.* spp. (**West African Bombax;** West Africa): *B. malabaricum* DC. (Cotton Tree; India).

Ceiba: Tropical America. *C. pentandra* Gaertn. (**Ceiba,** Silk Cotton; naturalised in Old World Tropics): *C. occidentalis* Burk. (**Ceiba;** Tropical America).

Ochroma: Tropical America. *O. lagopus* Sw. (**Balsa,** Polak).

STERCULIACEAE.   *Sterculia:* Tropical. *S. oblonga* Mast. and ?*S.* spp. (**Yellow Sterculia,** Okoko; West Africa): *S. rhinopetala* K.Schum. (**Brown Sterculia;** West Africa).

Tarrietia: Palaeotropical. *T. actinophylla* Bail. (**Tulip Oak;** Eastern Australia): *T. argyrodendron* Benth. (**Tulip Oak,** Crowsfoot Elm; Eastern Australia): *T. cochinchinensis* Pierre (**Chumprak,** Champrag; Thailand): *T. utilis* Sprague (**Niangon,** Nyankom; West Africa): *T.* spp. (**Mengkulang;** Malaya).

PARIETALES

EUCRYPHIACEAE.   *Eucryphia:* Australia, South America. *E. cordifolia* Cav. (**Ulmo;** Chile).

OCHNACEAE.   *Lophira:* Tropical Africa. *L. alata* Banks ex Gaertn. (**Ekki,** Azobé, Bongossi; West Africa).

THEACEAE.   *Tetramerista:* Malaya. *T. glabra* Miq. (**Punah**).

GUTTIFERAE.   *Cratoxylon:* Indomalaya. *C. arborescens* (Vahl.) Bl. (**Gerong- gang;** Malaya).

Mesua: Tropical Asia. *M. ferrea* L. (Ironwood; India and Burma).

Calophyllum: Tropics. *C. brasiliense* Camb. (**Jacareuba;** Tropical America): *C. brasiliense* Camb. var. *rekoi* Standl. (**Santa Maria;** Central America): *C. tomentosum* Wight (**Poon;** India): *C.* spp. (**Bintangor;** Malaya).

Symphonia: Tropical Africa and America. *S. gabonensis* Pierre (Osol; West Africa): *S. globulifera* L.f. (Manni, Matakki, Boarwood, Chewstick; Tropical America).

DIPTEROCARPACEAE.   Chiefly Eastern Tropics. It is not possible to deal with this family in the same way as others in this list. Timbers derived from more than one species, and even from species of more than one genus, may be marketed together under one trade name.

Dipterocarpus: Tropical Asia. *D. tuberculatus* Roxb. chiefly (**Eng, In;**

Burma, Thailand): *D. zeylanicus* Thw. (**Hora**; Ceylon): *D.* spp. give **Apitong** or **Bagac, Keruing** or **Kruen, Gurjun, Yang, Dau.**

Anisoptera: Tropical Asia. *A.* spp. (**Mersawa, Krabak, Kaunghmu, Palosapis**).

Dryobalanops: Eastern Tropical Asia. *D.* spp. (**Kapur,** Borneo Camphorwood, **Keladen**).

Hopea: Tropical Asia. *H. odorata* Roxb. (**Thingan**; India, Tropical East Asia): *H.* spp. (**Selangan Batu;**[1] North Borneo, Sarawak, Brunei; **Merawan**; Malaya: cf. also *Shorea* spp.).

Pentacme: Eastern Tropical Asia. *P.* spp. (**White Lauan**; Philippines: cf. also *Parashorea* spp. and *Shorea* spp.).

Shorea: Eastern Tropical Asia. *S.* spp. (**Light Red-, Dark Red-, Yellow-, White Meranti, Light Red-, Dark Red-, Yellow Seraya, Selangan Batu,**[2] **Red-, White Lauan, Alan, Red Selangan, Balau, Red Balau, Sal, Chan**: cf. also *Hopea* spp., *Parashorea* spp. and *Pentacme* spp.).

Parashorea: Eastern Tropical Asia. *P. stellata* Kurz. (**Thingadu**; Burma): *P.* spp. (**White Seraya, White Lauan**: cf. also *Pentacme* spp. and *Shorea* spp.).

FLACOURTIACEAE.   *Scottellia:* West Africa. *S. coriacea* A.Chev. (**Odoko**).

Gossypiospermum: Central and South America. *G. praecox* P.Wils. (= *Casearia praecox* Griseb.) (**Maracaibo Boxwood,** West Indian Boxwood, Zapatero).

DATISCACEAE.   *Tetrameles:* Tropical Asia. *T. nudiflora* R.Br. (**Kapong**).

Octomeles: South East Asia. *O. sumatrana* Miq. (**Binuang**).

MYRTIFLORAE

LYTHRACEAE.   *Lagerstroemia:* Palaeotropical. *L. hypoleuca* Kurz. (**Andaman Pyinma**; Andaman Islands): *L. speciosa* Pers. (**Pyinma**; Tropical Asia).

LECYTHIDACEAE.   *Cariniana:* Tropical America. *C.* sp. (**Jequitiba**; Brazil).

RHIZOPHORACEAE.   *Cassipourea:* Tropical America and Africa. *C. elliottii* Alston (**Pillarwood**; East Africa).

Poga: West Africa. *P. oleosa* Pierre (**Poga**).

NYSSACEAE.   *Nyssa:* North America and Asia. *N. aquatica* L. and *N. ogeche* Bartr. (**Tupelo**; U.S.A.): *N. sylvatica* Marsh. (**Tupelo,** Black Gum; U.S.A.).

COMBRETACEAE.   *Terminalia:* Tropics. *T. alata* Roth., *T. crenulata* Roth. and *T. coriacea* W.et A. (**Indian Laurel**; India, Burma): *T. amazonia* Exell (Nargusta; British Honduras, Trinidad): *T. arjuna* Bedd. (**Kumbuk**; India, Ceylon): *T. bialata* Steud. (**White Chuglam, Indian Silver-grey Wood**; Andaman Islands): *T. ivorensis* A.Chev. (**Idigbo,** Framiré, Emeri, Black Afara; West Africa): *T. procera* Roxb. (**White Bombway**; Andaman Islands): *T. superba* Engl. et Diels (**Afara, Limba**; West Africa).

Anogeissus: Tropical Africa and Asia. *A. acuminata* Wall. (**Yon**; Burma, India, Thailand): *A. latifolia* Wall. (Axle-wood; India).

MYRTACEAE.   *Eugenia:* Tropics. *E. gustavioides* Bailey (Grey Satinash; Eastern Australia).

Syncarpia: Eastern Australia. *S. glomulifera* Niedenzu (**Turpentine,** Luster): *S. hillii* Bailey (Red Satinay).

Tristania: Eastern Asia, Australia. *T. conferta* R.Br. (**Brush Box**; Eastern Australia).

---

[1] Also includes species of *Shorea*.   [2] Also includes species of *Hopea*.

Eucalyptus: nearly all, Australia. A large genus, furnishing many valuable timbers. *E. acmenioides* Schau. and *E. carnea* R.T.Bak. (**Yellow stringybark**); *E. crebra* F.Muell. and *E.* spp. (**Ironbark**): *E. diversicolor* F.Muell. (**Karri**; Western Australia): *E. fraxinoides* Deane et Maid. (**Australian White Ash**): *E. gigantea* Hook.f., *E. obliqua* L'Hérit., and *E. regnans* F.Muell. (**Tasmanian Oak**; *E. regnans* is also Mountain Ash, Victorian Oak): *E. globulus* Labill. and *E. bicostata* Maid., Blakely et Simmonds (**Southern Blue Gum**, Blue Gum): *E. maculata* Hook. and *E. citriodora* Hook. (**Spotted Gum**): *E. marginata* Sm. (**Jarrah**; Western Australia): *E. microcorys* F.Muell. (**Tallowwood**): *E. pilularis* Sm. (**Blackbutt**): *E. redunca* Schau. var. *elata* Benth. (**Wandoo**; Western Australia): *E. saligna* Sm. (**Saligna Gum**).

MELASTOMACEAE. *Dactylocladus:* Sarawak. *D. stenostachys* Oliv. (**Jongkong**).

UMBELLIFLORAE

ARALIACEAE. *Acanthopanax:* Asia. *A. ricinifolius* Seem. (**Sen**; Japan).

CORNACEAE. *Cornus:* North Temperate, Tropics (Mountains). *C. florida* L. (**Dogwood**, Cornel; U.S.A.).

SYMPETALAE

ERICALES

ERICACEAE. *Arbutus:* North and Central America, Mediterranean. *A. menziesii* Pursh (Madroña, Manzanita; Western North America). *Erica:* Africa, Europe. *E. arborea* L. (Giant Heath, Bruyère; Africa, Mediterranean).

PRIMULALES

MYRSINACEAE. *Rapanea:* Africa, Asia. *R.* (*Myrsine*) *melanophloeos* (L.) Mez (Beukenhout, Cape Beech; South Africa): *R.* spp. (**Rapanea**; East Africa).

EBENALES

SAPOTACEAE. *Palaquium:* Indomalaya. *P.* spp. and other trees of the family (**Nyatoh**; South East Asia). *Achras:* West Indies. *A. sapota* L. (**Sapodilla**). *Mimusops:* Tropics. *M. djave* Engl. (**Moabi**, Djave; West Africa): *M.* (*Dumoria*) *heckelii* Hutch. et Dalz. (= *Tieghemella heckelii* Pierre ex A.Chev.) (**Makoré**, Baku, Cherry Mahogany; West Africa): *M. hexandra* Roxb. (Palu; Ceylon, India): *M.* spp. (**Massaranduba**; Brazil).

EBENACEAE. *Diospyros:* Warm regions. *D. ebenum* Koen (**Ceylon Ebony**, East Indian Ebony; Ceylon, India): *D. celebica* Bakh. (**Macassar Ebony**; Celebes): *D. marmorata* Park. (**Andaman Marblewood**, Zebrawood; Andaman Islands): *D. virginiana* L. (**Persimmon**; U.S.A.): *D.* spp. (**African Ebony**; Tropical Africa).

CONTORTAE

OLEACEAE. *Fraxinus* (Ashes): Northern Hemisphere. *F. americana* L. (**American Ash**, White Ash) and *F.* spp. (**American Ash**; North America): *F. excelsior* L. (**European Ash**; Europe, Asia Minor, India): *F. mand-*

schurica Rupr. (**Japanese Ash,** Tamo; Japan): *F. nigra* Marsh. (**American Ash,** Black Ash, Brown Ash; North America).

Olea: Warm regions, Old World. *O. europaea* L. (Olive; Mediterranean): *O. hochstetteri* Bak. (**East African Olive,** Musheragi; East Africa): *O. laurifolia* Lam. (Black Ironwood; South Africa): *O. welwitschii* Gilg.et Schellenb. (**Loliondo,** Elgon Olive; East Africa).

APOCYNACEAE. *Gonioma:* South Africa. *G. kamassi* E.Mey. (**Knysna Box-wood,** Cape Boxwood, Kamassi Boxwood).

Alstonia: Old World Tropics. *A. congoensis* Engl. and *A. boonei* De Wild. (**Alstonia,** Patternwood, Stoolwood, Emien; Tropical Africa).

Dyera: South East Asia. *D. costulata* Hook.f. (**Jelutong**).

Aspidosperma: Tropical and South America. *A. desmanthum* Benth. (Araracangan, Aracan; Brazil): *A. peroba* Fr.All. and *A.* spp. (**Peroba Rosa,** Red Peroba; Brazil).

TUBIFLORAE

BORAGINACEAE. *Cordia:* Warm regions. *C. abyssinica* R.Br. (**Mukumari;** East Africa): *C. alliodora* Cham. (**Salmwood,** Ecuador Laurel; Tropical America): *C. goeldiana* Hub. (**Freijo;** Brazil).

VERBENACEAE. *Tectona:* Tropical Asia. *T. grandis* L.f. (**Teak**).

Gmelina: Tropical Asia, Australia. *G. arborea* Roxb. (Gamari; Burma, India): *G. leichardtii* F.v.M. (White Beech, Grey Teak; Eastern Australia).

SCROPHULARIACEAE. *Paulownia:* Eastern Asia. *P. tomentosa* Steud. (Kiri; Japan).

BIGNONIACEAE. *Jacaranda:* Tropical America. *J. copaia* D.Don (**Futui**).

Catalpa: America, Eastern Asia. *C. speciosa* Ward. (Catalpa, Hardy Catalpa; U.S.A.).

Tabebuia: Tropical America. *T. donnellsmithii* Rose (**Prima Vera;** Mexico, Central America).

Paratecoma: Brazil. *P. peroba* Kuhlm. (**White Peroba,** Ipé Peroba).

RUBIALES

RUBIACEAE. *Calycophyllum:* Tropical and South America. *C. candidissimum* DC. (**Degame,** Lemonwood; Tropical America).

Adina: Tropical Asia and Africa. *A. cordifolia* Benth. et Hook. (**Haldu,** Kwao, Kwow, Hnaw; Burma, Thailand, India).

Mitragyna: Tropical Africa and Asia. *M. ciliata* Aubrev.et Pellegr. (= *M. stipulosa* Kuntze) (**Abura;** West Africa): *M.* spp. (**Nazingu;** Uganda).

Sarcocephalus: Palaeotropical. *S. cordatus* Miq. (**Kanluang;** Thailand, Burma): *S. diderrichii* De Wild. (= *Nauclea diderrichii* De Wild.et Th.) (**Opepe,** Bilinga, Kusia; West Africa).

Gardenia: Palaeotropical. *G. latifolia* Ait. (Gardenia, Indian Boxwood; India).

Canthium: Palaeotropical. *C. dicoccum* Merr. (Ceylon Boxwood; India, Ceylon, Burma).

COMPOSITAE. *Brachylaena:* Tropical and South Africa. *B. hutchinsii* Hutch. (**Muhuhu;** East Africa).

CHAPTER 2

THE HISTOLOGY OF WOOD

It is well known that wood is not a solid, homogeneous substance, but a porous one composed of large numbers of very small elements or cells, the cavities of which, in the dry condition at least, are largely occupied by air. Practically all of the cells of which wood is composed are derived from the layer that, in the tree, lies immediately outside the wood and which is known as the vascular cambium (Fig. 1). The cells of this cambium are of two kinds; spindle-shaped, axially elongated cells, the fusiform initials, and the ray initials, which are cells about as broad as they are high. Both are much flattened in a radial direction, i.e. along a radius of the trunk.

The cells of the cambium are living cells, each consisting of a protoplast enclosed in a cell wall. The term cell is used, correctly, for the living substance, since many cells have no cell walls. In plants however, the cells are walled, the walls remain after the death of the protoplast and commonly continue to serve a function in the plant. In the study of plant anatomy these dead remains, the cell walls, are also called cells. Nevertheless, it is important to appreciate that these dead remains are totally different from the living cells which gave rise to them and which are able to carry out certain vital functions. Living cells can, for example, add new material to their walls, they can use, store or pass on food material and they can, at least when young, divide, increase in size and change in shape. Dead cells, on the other hand, are mere boxes and are, of course, unable to carry out such functions, any more than can an empty matchbox; nearly all the functions which they perform in the plant are dependent on the activity of living cells.

Each cell of the vascular cambium possesses a thin wall of its own, and adjacent cells are united by a thin layer of intercellular substance, the middle lamella. When a cell divides into two cells, this middle lamella is formed first as the common dividing wall and upon it the new wall of each cell is deposited. The first-formed wall of any cell is called the primary wall. Very frequently this wall is indistinguishable from the middle lamella, except by the application of stains or by the use of special techniques, and the true middle lamella (or intercellular substance) and the primary walls of the contiguous cells, are together loosely referred to as middle lamella. The primary wall is rarely deposited evenly over the middle lamella; usually certain areas remain very thin and constitute the primary pit-fields. Through minute pores in these areas there are submicroscopic protoplasmic connections (plasmadesmata) between adjacent cells.

C

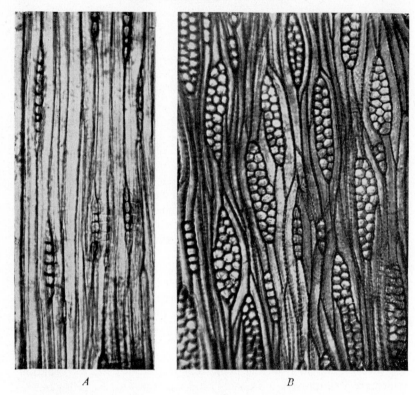

A   B

Fig. 1.—Vascular cambium or its immediate derivatives as seen in tangential longitudinal view. *A*, Scots Pine (*Pinus sylvestris*); *B*, Ash (*Fraxinus excelsior*). The vertically elongated cells are fusiform initials; in the Pine they are too long to be completely included in the figure but the pointed ends of some of them can be seen; in the Ash these cells are much shorter and complete initials are seen in the section; in some the pitted walls are well shown. In the Pine the ray initials are seen as axial chains of cells, while in the Ash similar chains, which will give rise to uniseriate rays, are present, as well as more or less fusiform clusters from which the multiseriate rays will be formed. (Both × 180.)

The cells of the vascular cambium do not themselves form new elements of the wood, but during the growing season they divide, the two daughter cells being separated by a tangential wall (Fig. 2). One of these cells remains as a cambial initial: if it is the outer one, then the inner cell is added to the wood; if the inner cell is destined to continue as the cambial initial, then the outer one becomes a cell of the phloem. With certain exceptions the vascular cambium, once formed, remains and continues its activity throughout the life of the tree.

The process of differentiation in a cell cut off by the cambium and added to the wood generally involves a change of shape and often an increase in size; it may also involve further cell divisions, e.g. by the

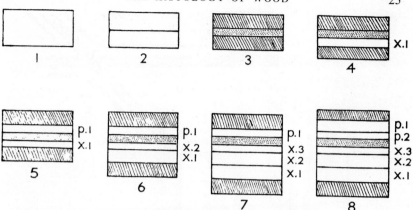

Fig. 2.—Diagrams to illustrate the initiation of a cell of interfascicular cambium and its subsequent activity, as seen in transverse section. (1) Parenchyma cell, which (2) divides by a tangential wall and (3) a second tangential wall to cut out a cambial initial (stippled). This cambial initial divides (4), cutting off an inner cell which is added to the xylem (x.1); successive divisions of this initial 5–8, cut off cells towards the centre (x), which form secondary xylem and cells toward the periphery (p) which form secondary phloem.

laying down of horizontal cell-walls, for an axial strand of parenchyma cells may be formed in this way from a single derivative of the vascular cambium. It is important to realise that these cells are living; only in such cells can growth and differentiation occur. The middle lamella and primary wall are extensible, so that the cell can expand as new material is added to the wall during growth.

As the growing cell approaches its full size the deposition of the much stiffer secondary wall takes place (Fig. 3) (Kerr and Bailey, 1934; Wardrop and Harada, 1965). This wall may be thin or extremely thick, and it is deposited on the primary wall in layers. Three main layers are usually recognised, a thin outer layer, which is the oldest, and which, of course, comes next to the primary wall; a thicker middle layer and a thin inner layer which forms the wall surface bounding the cell cavity or, in the living cell, the protoplasm. These several layers are now conveniently designated P, the primary wall, and S_1, S_2 and S_3, respectively the outer, middle and inner layers of the secondary wall. Sometimes yet another layer is deposited, not regularly over the cell, but in the form of thin, spiral bands, which give the spiral thickening found in some cells. Such spiral thickening and sometimes, indeed, the whole of S_3, has been termed the tertiary wall, but there is no justification for this usage and the term should be avoided (see Wardrop and Dadswell, 1957). There is every reason for regarding the S_3 as the innermost and youngest layer of the secondary wall.

The middle lamella is at first composed largely of pectic materials, and the primary wall consists mainly of cellulose and pectic substances.

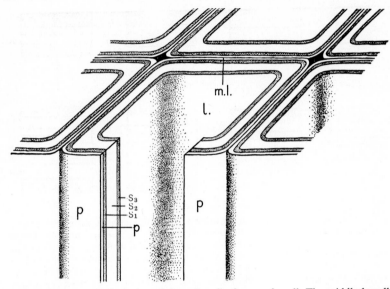

Fig. 3.—Diagram of the layers of the cell wall of a woody cell. The middle lamella is shown in black, followed by the primary wall (white), the outer layer (s_1) of the secondary wall (stippled), the middle layer (s_2) of the secondary wall (white) and the inner layer (s_3) of the secondary wall (stippled), which surrounds the lumen of the cell. *m.l.*, middle lamella; *p.*, primary wall; s_1, s_2, s_3, successive layers of the secondary wall; *l.*, lumen of cell.

The secondary wall, at its inception, consists of cellulose, or of cellulose and related compounds. Thus, to begin with, the cell wall is not woody or lignified. Lignin, a complex substance whose chemical composition has yet to be fully determined, is deposited later, among the substances which formed the original wall (Thornber and Northcote, 1961, 1962; Freudenberg, 1964). The middle lamella and primary wall become strongly lignified, and the primary wall often becomes indurated with mineral substances as well. Lignin is also deposited in the secondary wall, but here, even in the fully differentiated cell, it is relatively less abundant than in the primary wall and the middle lamella.

Investigations during the last thirty-five years or so have yielded a good deal of information on the detailed structure of the cell wall. It is now known how the actual molecules of cellulose, which form the basic framework of the wall, are arranged and how lignin, water and other substances occur in the walls. This aspect of wall structure is dealt with in a subsequent chapter (Chapter 8).

The secondary wall is not deposited evenly over the whole of the primary wall, for it is usually interrupted over the primary pit-fields, or elsewhere over the primary wall, and consequently pit-like structures are built up in the wall in these regions. These pits may remain of equal size from their base or floor, at the middle lamella or primary

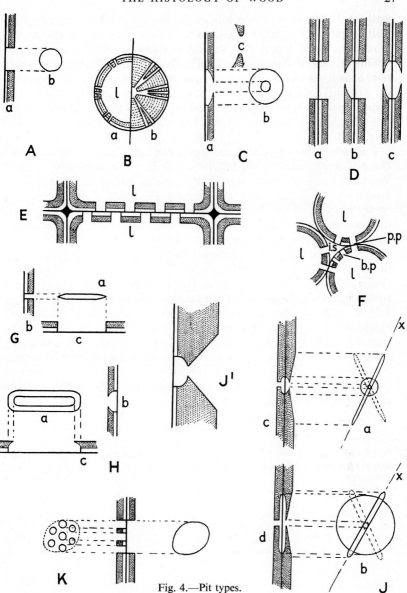

Fig. 4.—Pit types.

A. Simple pit in vertical section *a* and surface view *b*.

B. Ramiform pits; in the half *a*, the cell wall is relatively thin and there are three groups of simple pits; in the half *b*, the pits of each group have coalesced, due to thickening of the wall, forming ramiform or branched pits.

C. Bordered pit in vertical section *a* and surface view *b*; the typical, somewhat rounded margin of the aperture of such a pit is shown (in section), at *c*.

[continued overleaf

wall, to their mouth or aperture at the inner surface of the secondary wall: a pit of this shape is known as a simple pit and is shown diagrammatically in Fig. 4 *A*, in section at *a* and in surface view at *b*.

Simple pits in very thick-walled cells sometimes appear to branch outwards from the cell lumen and are then called ramiform pits. They do not, of course, arise as branching structures; their appearance results from the coalescence of several pits as the inner area of the cell wall surface decreases with increasing thickening of the wall (Fig. 4 *B*).

Frequently, however, the secondary wall develops so as to over-arch the pit cavity, which thus becomes a domed structure with a small aperture (Fig. 4 *C*). When such a pit is seen in surface view the aperture appears to lie in the centre of a larger area, which is the pit floor, or pit membrane, visible through the transparent wall (Fig. 4 *C, b*). Since the aperture thus appears to be surrounded by a border, a pit of this type is known as a bordered pit.

A pit in one cell is usually opposite to one in the contiguous cell, the two forming a pit-pair (Fig. 4 *D*). A pit-pair may be composed of two simple pits (Fig. 4 *D, a*) or of two bordered pits (Fig. 4 *D, c*) but sometimes a simple pit and a bordered pit make up the pit-pair (Fig. 4 *D, b*), which is then termed half-bordered. Sometimes several small pits in the wall of one cell may abut on to a large pit in a neighbouring element, such an arrangement being known as unilaterally compound pitting (Fig. 4 *K*). Pits on the walls of adjacent cells do not invariably coincide however (Fig. 4 *E*), and occasionally a pit may abut on to an intercellular space and not on to the wall of a contiguous cell; such pits are known as blind pits (Fig. 4 *E, F*).

Fig. 4.—*continued*

D. Pit-pairs, such as might be found between a vessel element or tracheid and a parenchyma cell; *a*, both pits simple; *b*, one pit simple, the other bordered; *c*, both pits bordered.

E. Blind pits; the pits on contiguous walls do not form pairs.

F. Blind pits; portions of three contiguous cells surrounding an intercellular space; typical pit-pairs occur between adjacent cells, as well as blind pits, which abut on to the intercellular space; in one of these latter the middle lamella has disappeared.

G. *a*, a very elongate simple pit, surface view; *b*, showing its appearance in vertical section when the section passes along the short axis of the pit; *c*, in vertical section when the section passes parallel to the long axis.

H. As *G*, but pit bordered.

J. Bordered pits with extended apertures; *a* and *b* in surface view, *c* and *d* in a vertical section along the plane marked *x*. *J'* is an enlarged view of the wall in *J* to show the primary and secondary layers.

K. Unilaterally compound pitting; on the right a single large simple pit has developed in the primary pit-field; on the left several small simple pits have developed in this field.

b.p., blind pit; *i.s.*, intercellular space; *l.*, cell lumen. Where the wall is shown differentiated into layers, the middle lamella is shown as a black line, the primary wall white and the secondary wall stippled.

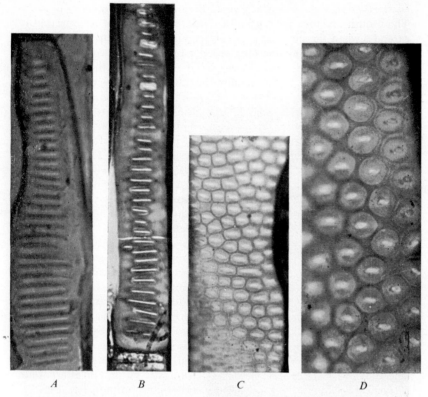

A	*B*	*C*	*D*

Fig. 5.—Types of pit arrangement : *A*. Scalariform, Magnolia (*Magnolia* sp.) (× 350). *B*. Scalariform, Chilean Laurel (*Laurelia aromatica*) (× 320). *C*. Opposite, Alder (*Alnus glutinosa*) (× 725). *D*. Alternate, Poplar (*Populus* sp.) (× 725). In *C* the opposite arrangement is not qute regular and in the centre of the figure a few of the pits are alternate.

Pits vary much in shape and size. Simple pits may appear circular or elliptical in surface view; they may be slit-like or rhombic. Depending on the direction in which it has been sectioned, a slit-like pit may appear large or small in sectional view (Fig. 4 *G*). Pits are sometimes very small, but in rare instances a simple pit may occupy most of the width of a cell. Bordered pits may have an elliptical outline, sometimes markedly so (Fig. 4 *H*). Deposition of secondary wall material may be more irregular than has just been indicated. Thus it will be noticed in Fig. 4 *C* that the aperture of the bordered pit is actually rather rounded, i.e. it narrows somewhat from the surface of the lumen, before widening into the pit chamber. In thick-walled cells the aperture may lead into a canal before opening into the pit cavity, this canal often having the shape of a flattened funnel (Fig. 4 *J, J'*): the aperture is thus slit-like and, in a pit pair, the two apertures are commonly set at an angle to each other so that, in surface view, they appear as a cross (Fig. 4 *J*). The mouth or inner aperture of a bordered pit may be so long that it extends, when the pit is seen in surface view, beyond the boundary of the pit border, such an aperture being termed an extended pit aperture. Frequently, however, it does not extend so far and is then termed an included pit aperture. Sometimes the pit chamber is very small or virtually non-existent, so that the pit appears to be a slit-like simple pit: a continuous range of pit structure, from the obviously bordered to the simple, may be seen in wood cells.

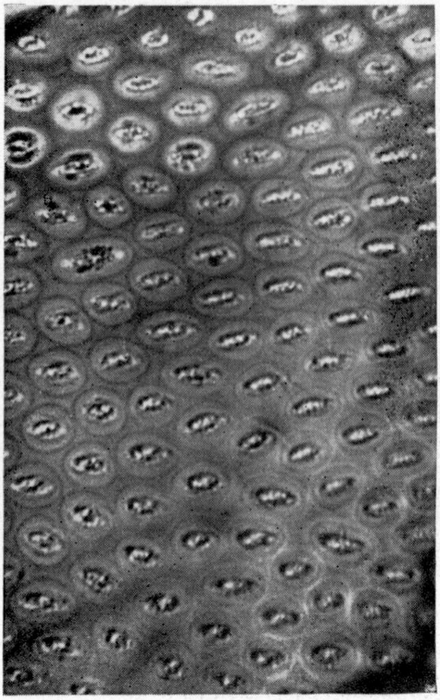

The distribution of pits in an element is sometimes an important feature in the diagnosis or identification of wood. Very elongated bordered pits may stretch across the width of a cell and occur regularly one above another, so that the wall has a ladder-like appearance (scalariform pitting). Pits may occur in two or more regular vertical rows, with the members of adjacent rows opposite one another (opposite pitting) or alternating (alternate pitting) (cf. Figs. 5 and 7). Crowded pits having the alternate arrangement commonly have a more or less hexagonal outline in surface view, while where the arrangement is opposite, the outline in surface view is often more or less rectangular. Nor are pits always regularly distributed; small pits may occur in clusters and give the appearance of a sieve in surface view (cribriform or sieve pitting), and sometimes several pits develop in one primary pit-field.

Fig. 6.—Vestured pits in a vessel of Afrormosia (*Afrormosia elata*) (× 420). The pit arrangement is alternate.

Sometimes the membrane of a pit is perforated by minute pores, a fact which has been demonstrated by the passage of Indian ink (a liquid suspension of extremely fine particles of carbon) through the membrane between two cells (Bailey, 1958). It was formerly thought that such perforations were of frequent occurrence but many of these apparent "perforations" have been shown in fact to be small, sometimes branched, highly refractive outgrowths from the secondary wall. Pits with these outgrowths are said to be vestured (Fig. 6); they are encountered in certain dicotyledonous families (e.g. Dipterocarpaceae,

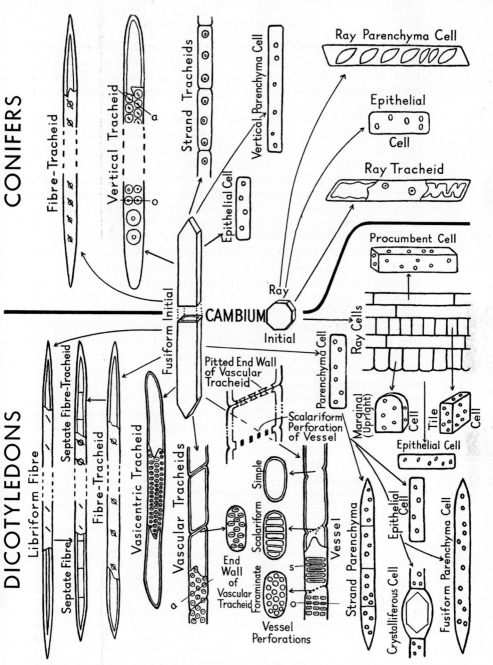

Fig. 7.—Diagram to show types of elements of secondary wood and the cambial initials from which they arise. The cambial initials are shown from approximately the tangential aspect. The several types of pit arrangement are shown in the tracheids and vessels, viz.: alternate (*a*), opposite (*o*) and scalariform (*s*).

many Leguminosae) and their presence or absence is fairly constant in certain families or genera (Bailey, 1932, 1933; Schmid and Machado, 1964; Schmid, 1965). On occasion granular precipitates in the heartwood may simulate this type of pit, but they are clearly artifacts and must not be confused with vestured pits.

Reference has been made to the thin areas in the walls of the cells of the vascular cambium, the primary pit-fields. Similar pit-fields may occur in any cells which, like those of the vascular cambium, do not possess a secondary wall. In general botanical usage such areas are commonly referred to as pits, but the wood anatomist reserves this term for spaces in the secondary wall. Pits, in this stricter sense, may form over primary pit-fields or over parts of them; but they may form elsewhere, while primary pit-fields may be covered over by the secondary wall.

A cell cut off from the vascular cambium, toward the wood, may differentiate into one of the four types of xylem element, that is, parenchyma cell, fibre, tracheid or vessel element (Fig. 7). Not all types of element necessarily occur in every wood but the parenchyma cell is invariably present, although in some conifers it is confined to the rays. Each type of element serves one or more special functions in the tree. Parenchyma cells serve for storage of food reserves and as depositories for waste materials. They may also pass on food and water to other parts of the wood. Parenchyma, usually alone among the other wood elements, remains alive, at least in the functional wood or sapwood (but see Fahn and Arnon, 1963). Parenchyma cells may also have a supporting function. Vessels and tracheids are conducting elements, serving to convey water and dissolved mineral salts from the

Fig. 8.—Tracheids, parenchyma and fibres.

A. Sugi (*Cryptomeria japonica*); T.L.S. (× 110) showing square-ended axial parenchyma cells, some of which contain resin, showing as black masses: the remaining cells, apart from the rays (the vertical rows of rounded cells), are the elongated axial tracheids, some of which show the characteristic pointed ends.

B and *C.* Alder (*Alnus glutinosa*); in *B* (T.S.), most of the cells are rather thin-walled fibres; the large element at the top is a vessel; almost central is a small cell with a thick, dark outline; this is a parenchyma cell with gummy contents; a second one lies above and slightly to the right of it and a third, also above and to the right, shows a horizontal wall, with simple pits, which appear as dark dots because they are filled with gummy material (× 510): in *C* (R.L.S.), square-ended parenchyma cells and fibres with pointed ends can be seen (× 215).

D. Rewarewa (*Knightia excelsa*); T.S. (× 215); thin-walled parenchyma cells, lined with dark, gummy material, form a horizontal band across the centre of the figure; fairly thick-walled fibres are seen on either side of this band; the larger fibres are those which have been cut across the middle, while in the smaller ones the section has passed through the tapering ends; the dark, vertical line on the left is part of a uniseriate ray.

E. Andaman padauk (*Pterocarpus dalbergioides*); T.S. (× 215); a band of parenchyma cell passes horizontally across the centre and there are fibres above and below. In none of these examples are the fibres very thick-walled.

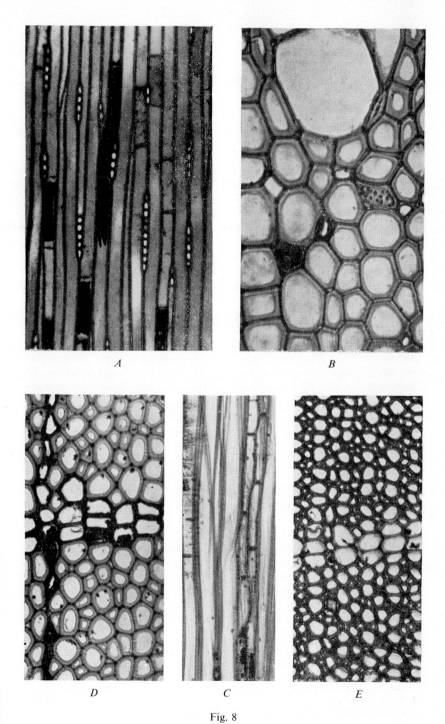

A   B

D   C   E

Fig. 8

roots to the leaves. Fibres are purely mechanical elements, concerned with support; to them, the rigidity of many woods is mainly due. In hardwoods, tracheids, and even vessels, may have a supporting function, but this is very subsidiary to that of conduction. In softwoods the function of support, as well as of conduction, devolves upon the tracheids.

The parenchyma cell in wood (Figs. 7, 8) is more or less brick-shaped, but it may be squatter, or alternatively, much more elongated. At maturity its walls may be thin or thick, but its pits are simple. Sometimes its walls thicken very markedly and its protoplasm soon dies. Such thick-walled parenchyma cells, which often show ramiform pits, are known as stone cells; their function is purely that of support.

The tracheid (Fig. 7) is commonly an elongated element with pointed or rounded or chisel-shaped ends, and with rather thin walls perforated by bordered pits. Tracheids may, however, be quite short: some may have fairly thick walls: the end walls may be horizontal or oblique. All, however, are characterised, in secondary wood, by possessing bordered pits.

The fibre (Fig. 7) is a long, pointed element in which the pits are simple and slit-like. It is commonly described as thick-walled, but this is a poor criterion for the identification of fibres. In heavy woods, the walls of the fibres are thick, so thick sometimes, that little remains of the original lumina of the cells. The fibre wall may, however, be very thin: in very light-weight woods the fibres may have thinner walls than the parenchyma cells of most timbers.

A thick-walled fibre with slit-like simple pits is termed a libriform fibre: its function is principally one of support. There are, however, all stages of gradation between libriform fibres, with slit-like pits, and tracheids, with characteristic bordered pits. These intermediate elements (Fig. 7) are called fibre-tracheids and are both conducting and supporting in function. In a typical fibre-tracheid the bordered pits are small, with slit-like apertures which often extend beyond the pit borders. There is considerable difficulty in defining a fibre-tracheid precisely: the definition proposed in the glossary of the International Association of Wood Anatomists (1957) limits it to fibre-like tracheids commonly having pointed ends, and bordered pits with lenticular to slit-like apertures. Brazier and Franklin (1961), however, define fibre-tracheids as "fibres with distinctly bordered pits".

Fig. 9.—Vessels. *A*. Avodiré (*Turraeanthus africanus*); T.S., showing a number of vessels, which are many times larger than the fibres; the fibres form the bulk of the section; the vertical lines are the rays (× 39). *B*. Part of a vessel of English Oak (*Quercus* sp.); R.L.S., showing two complete vessel elements and simple perforations (× 120). *C*. American Red Gum or Satin Walnut (*Liquidambar styraciflua*); a nearly complete scalariform perforation in a vessel, seen in face view; R.L.S. (× 725). *D and E*. Scalariform perforations, *D*, in Cape Box (*Buxus macowani*) and *E*, in Common Box (*Buxus sempervirens*); both R.L.S. (× 600).

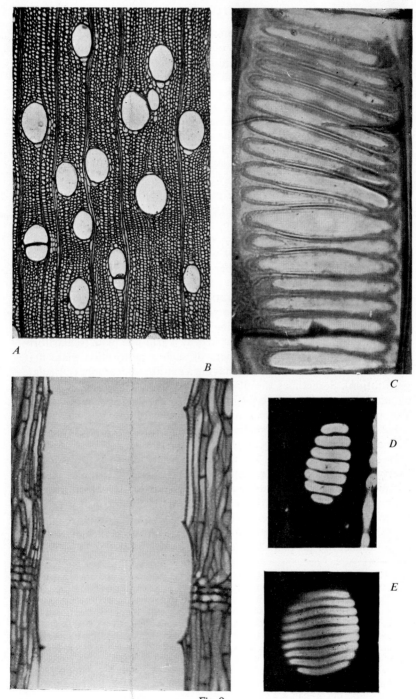

A

B

C

D

E

Fig. 9

The vessel (Figs. 7, 9), is primarily a water-conducting structure. It differs from the other elements of the wood in its origin, which is not from a single cell, but from a number of cells; hence it is really a compound structure. It is formed, in secondary xylem, from an axial row of cells, from which the end walls have disappeared, more or less completely; it is, in fact, a pipe, perhaps sometimes a few metres in length. Normally its wall, which has bordered pits, is not very thick, although in some heavy woods the vessels are thick-walled.

The individual components of a vessel are spoken of as vessel elements, vessel members or vessel segments. The end walls of these elements are often very oblique in woods of primitive families and more or less transverse in those of the more advanced families. Where two vessel elements adjoin, there are, of course, two end walls, one belonging to each member, and separated by the middle lamella. End walls and intervening middle lamella may disappear completely, or all but completely, leaving a narrower or wider rim of wall material and thus placing the lumina of the members in free communication with one another (Fig. 9 *B*); a perforation of this type between adjacent vessel members is called a simple perforation. Alternatively, only parts of the walls may disappear and when the perforated end wall has two or more openings it is described as having a multiple perforation. Adjacent elements are then commonly separated by a grid-like plate (scalariform perforation) (Figs. 9, 10). The bars of such a perforation plate may sometimes branch, the plate then having a net-like appearance (reticulate perforation). Sometimes the plate is perforated by a number of small circular or polygonal holes (foraminate or ephedroid perforation). The perforations of the two apposed end walls are not necessarily coincident, for it may happen that a large opening in one wall coincides with a number of small openings in the other.

In some woods, during the period of transition from sapwood to heartwood, ray or axial parenchyma cells adjacent to vessels may resume growth in an unusual way. The pit membranes which separate their protoplasts from the vessel lumen may grow out into the vessel in the form of little bladders. This may occur quite normally, or as a result of mechanical injury or fungal attack. Growth takes place from large numbers of pit-pairs so that the vessel may become filled with a

Fig. 10.—Vessel perforations. *A* and *B*. Alder (*Alnus glutinosa*); *A*. Scalariform perforation plate seen in face view; R.L.S. (× 290). *B*. Scalariform perforation plate, in section (edge-on view); the bordered pits of the vessel wall are clearly seen; T.L.S. (× 725). *C*. Lime (*Tilia* sp.) showing vessels with simple perforations, seen in face view; note also spiral thickening on vessel walls; R.L.S. (× 290). *D*. Olivillo (*Aextoxicon punctatum*); part of a very long scalariform perforation plate; note forking of some of the bars; R.L.S. (× 320). *E*. *Vaccinium leschenaultii*; perforation plate with thick, forked bars, a type of reticulate perforation plate; note the apparently cross-shaped mouth of uppermost bordered pit; this is due to the photograph having been taken in the plane of the pit membrane so that both apertures of the pit-pair are seen, somewhat out of focus (× 970).

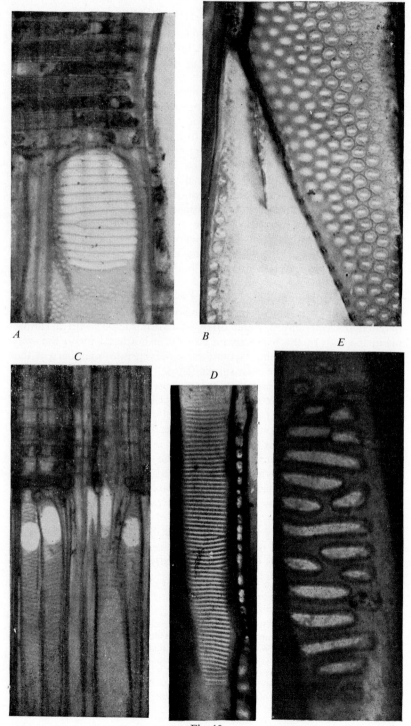

A

B

C

D

E

Fig. 10

parenchyma-like mass of these ingrowths from the walls, which are termed tyloses (Fig. 11, A and B). A tylosis is thus an extension of a living parenchyma cell, containing protoplasm and sometimes also the nucleus of the parent cell, which may pass into it. Its wall may become thickened or lignified, forming a sclerotic or stone-cell tylosis (Fig. 11 D). After the death of their protoplasts the remaining walls of tyloses may significantly affect the penetrability of the timbers in which they occur. Similar types of growth, from parenchyma cells into inter-cellular spaces rather than into vessel elements, are termed tylosoids (Fig. 11 E).

Chattaway (1949) investigated the development of tyloses and the secretion of gum in heartwood formation and found the processes to be conditioned by the size of the pit apertures. According to her findings, tyloses are formed where the width of the aperture of the pits between vessels and ray cells exceeds about 10 μ,[1] while in woods with these pit apertures of smaller dimensions, gum is secreted into the vessels. The fine structure of tyloses is described by Kórán and Côté (1965).

Where two different types of cell are apposed, the composition of the pit-pairs varies. Thus a pit-pair between a vessel or tracheid and a parenchyma cell may be, and often is, half-bordered, with a simple pit in the wall of the parenchyma cell and a bordered pit in the wall of the conducting element. Sometimes, however, both members of the pit-pair are bordered, or both simple (Frost, 1930).

Although a piece of wood consists largely of vertical or axial elements, i.e. elements normally extending longitudinally in the wood parallel to the vertical axis of the trunk, sheets of cells also extend through the wood in a radial direction. Such sheets of cells constitute the rays, and in them most of the cells have their longer axes horizontal and radial. The cells of the rays are derived from the squat ray initials of the cambium, while those which form the axial elements come from the fusiform initials. Rays usually consist of parenchyma cells exclusively, but they may contain ray tracheids or may even be composed entirely of these elements.

Rays vary enormously in size and shape. Sometimes they are com-posed of a sheet of cells no more than one cell wide (uniseriate) and a few cells high, sometimes they are massive structures, hundreds of cells

---

[1] μ (pronounced *mew*) is a unit of measurement commonly used for objects of microscopic dimensions; 1 μ =0·001 millimetre.

Fig. 11.—Tyloses. A and B. Thin-walled type, in vessels of Robinia (*Robinia pseudo-acacia*). A in T.S. (× 60), B in T.L.S. (× 60). C. Thick-walled type in Queensland Walnut (*Endiandra palmerstonii*); a single vessel, filled with four tyloses, is shown; T.S. (× 290). D. Sclerotic type in Greenheart (*Ocotea rodiaei*); three very thick-walled tyloses fill the upper vessel; T.S. (× 170). E. Tylosoids in a radial resin canal in a fusiform ray of Scots Pine (*Pinus sylvestris*); the canal, in the centre of the ray, contains three, possibly four, tylosoids; T.L.S. (× 305).

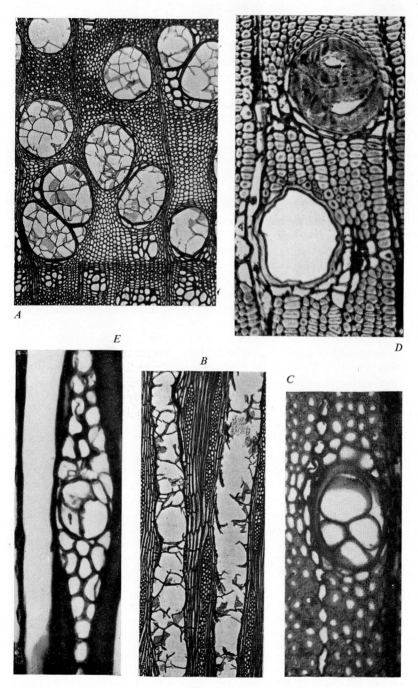

Fig. 11

high and twenty or more cells wide (multiseriate). A ray more than one cell wide is usually rather boat-shaped in section (i.e. as seen in a tangential longitudinal section of the wood) but rays exhibit great variety of form (Fig. 12) and are of considerable value in the identification of timbers.

Though the elements of wood are so small that a microscope must be used to study them, it is impossible to see them under the microscope as solid objects in a piece of wood. A three-dimensional picture of them must be built up from the study of a series of flat, two-dimensional sections, cut in different planes in the wood. Three planes are selected for study; that which represents the horizontal plane in the. trunk (transverse section) and two longitudinal planes, one passing along a radius of the trunk (radial longitudinal section) and one at right angles to this (tangential longitudinal section). It will be realised that a tangential longitudinal section can be strictly at right angles to one radial plane only, but the size of the sections used is so small in relation to the size of the trunk that this limitation is rarely a serious matter Truly tangential sections can be obtained by peeling a trunk, as is done when making rotary-cut veneers. In these the faces are everywhere tangential. Such a method of cutting is, however, not practicable for microscope sections.

The transverse section will enable the axial elements of the wood to be studied in transverse sectional view, but the rays will be cut along their length. Care must be exercised in interpreting the width of the rays—other than uniseriate ones—from this section, for they may be cut near their upper or lower margins, when they will appear narrow, or through their broader middle region. Both longitudinal sections will give a longitudinal view of the axial elements. From the radial section it will be possible to study the rays along their length, while from the tangential section the rays can be examined end on, in effect, since their elements extend horizontally. Perforations in vessels must generally be studied in the radial section, if the original end walls were other than nearly transverse, for the end walls of the component cells, and consequently the perforations, are seen most nearly in face view in this section. In tangential sections these perforations are viewed edge on, and even a simple perforation, seen thus, may appear to be an end wall, so that a vessel may be mistaken for a row of short tracheids (cf. Fig. 14 B).

Fig. 12.—Rays in T.L.S. A. American Beech (Fagus grandifolia); in the centre note the small, uniseriate rays; to the left, small multiseriate rays and on the right, part of a large multiseriate ray. B. Lignum Vitae (Guaiacum sp.); here the rays are small, almost entirely uniseriate, and regularly storeyed. C. Deodar (Cedrus deodara); the rays, as in most softwoods, are uniseriate, although a partially biseriate ray is seen on the extreme right: the rays are tall. D. Douglas Fir (Pseudotsuga taxifolia); the rays are low and mostly uniseriate; in the centre there is a broadly fusiform ray with a horizontal resin canal in its centre. (A, C and D × 110, B × 150.)

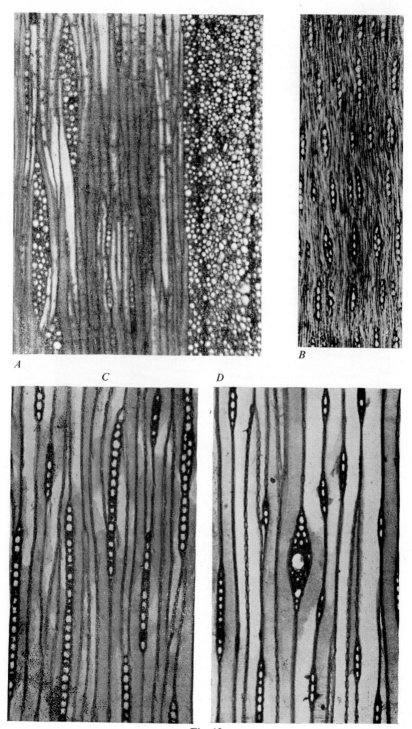

A

C

D

B

Fig. 12

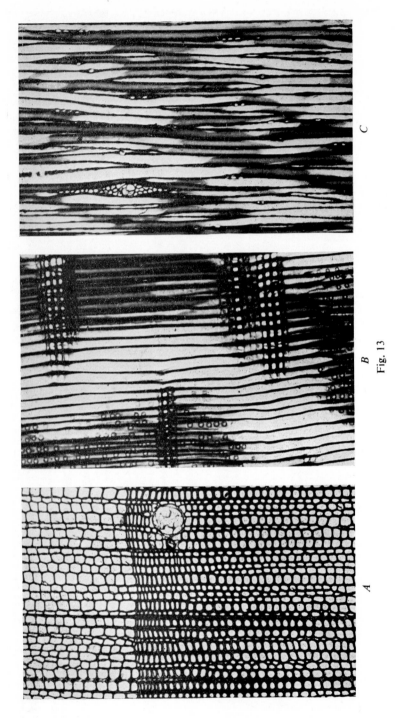

A   B   C

Fig. 13

Fig. 13.—Transverse, radial longitudinal and tangential longitudinal sections of a coniferous wood (softwood), Scots Pine (*Pinus sylvestris*). In *A* (T.S.), the vertical or axial tracheids, which form the bulk of the wood, are seen in transverse section; the larger tracheids at the top of the illustration are those of the early wood, at the beginning of a growth ring; in the lower part of the illustration the tracheids are rather smaller and thicker walled, as they pass into the denser late wood, which ends about two-thirds of the way up the figure; the thin vertical lines are rays, while on the right-hand side there is an axial resin canal in the late wood. In *B* (R.L.S.) the vertical lines are the tangential walls of the axial tracheids; where the section includes their radial walls, the characteristic coniferous bordered pits are seen; running horizontally are parts of three rays; the white areas in these are the large simple pits of the ray parenchyma; the ray tracheids are not very distinct at this magnification; in the bottom right-hand ray the two uppermost rows of cells are ray tracheids; then follows a row of ray parenchyma, three rows of ray tracheids, three rows of ray parenchyma and the lowermost row of ray tracheids. In *C* (T.L.S.), the vertical lines are the radial walls of the axial tracheids; the dark areas on them are regions where the section has included their tangential walls, the pale areas where it has passed through the lumina; several uniseriate rays, showing as short vertical rows of cells, can be seen and towards the top left-hand corner is a larger, fusiform ray, with a radial resin canal containing tylosoids. (All × 70.) Cf. also Fig. 52, and, for details of the ray, as seen in R.L.S. Fig. 43 *A*.

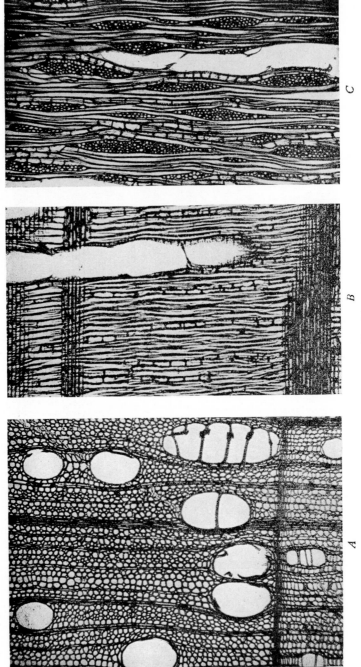

Fig. 14

Fig. 14.—Transverse, radial longitudinal, and tangential longitudinal sections of a dicotyledonous wood (hardwood), European Walnut (*Juglans regia*). In *A* (T.S.) the fibres, which form the bulk of the wood, are seen cut transversely; axial parenchyma occurs in very short tangential chains of two or three cells; though they are not very distinct in the figure a few of these chains may be seen, running horizontally, at the bottom of the figure; the vessels are much larger than the fibres and are solitary or in radial chains; those in the lower part are smaller and are at the end of the late wood; the early wood begins above the dark horizontal line which is the termination of the growth ring, formed by flattened cells; the dark vertical lines are the rays. In *B* (R.L.S.), the fibres run vertically and between them are chains of square-ended axial parenchyma cells; part of a vessel, showing several elements, is seen on the right, its lowermost element apparently separated from the next by a nearly transverse wall, but this is merely the rim of a simple perforation, viewed edge on; running horizontally are parts of three rays. In *C* (T.L.S.), the fibres run vertically and are interspersed with vertical rows of square-ended axial parenchyma cells; there is part of a vessel just to the right of the centre line; there are numerous more or less boat-shaped rays ranging from one to about five cells wide. (All × 60.)

Another very useful method for studying wood structure is by the examination of isolated wood elements. These may be separated by macerating small chips of the wood with certain strong oxidising agents, which break down the less resistant middle lamellae so that the elements fall apart and can be studied individually as solid structures. This method is the only one by which the lengths of the longer wood elements can be determined.

Although wood consists almost entirely of cellulose and related substances, and lignin, it often contains a variety of other substances, referred to as extractives or extraneous substances—gums, resins, tannins, oils, colouring matters, latex, starch, inorganic salts and other materials.

Much work remains to be done on these extraneous substances, for at present the wood anatomist's methods of dealing with them are slip-shod and casual in the extreme. Mineral deposits, whatever their nature, are usually referred to as white deposits, while any gummy material in a softwood is a resin, and in a hardwood, a gum, although the two groups of substances are by no means so sharply distinguished. Similarly a wood is said to contain oil if it has an oily feel, e.g. teak, although the so-called oil in this wood is an oleo-resin.

The inorganic materials in wood consist chiefly of silica and salts of calcium, and occur mainly in the lumina of the cells. Crystals, probably of calcium salts, are of common occurrence (Fig. 70), as are white chalky deposits in vessels.

Starch is formed exclusively in living cells, and hence in parenchyma, both axial and ray parenchyma, where it is stored as a reserve food material. Oils, which less commonly occupy these cells, may be stored for the same purpose.

Essential oils and tannins are sometimes found in special paren-chyma cells. Gums, resins and other materials of this type may occur in vessels, tracheids and parenchyma and even in the fibres. These substances are sometimes found in special cavities in the wood, which are described below.

True gums are carbohydrate substances, soluble in water but not in alcohol, and are usually formed by the breakdown and degradation of

Fig. 15.—A. Schizogenous duct: a radial resin canal in a ray of European Spruce (*Picea abies*); note that the duct is lined with an epithelium. This is from a T.L.S. so that the duct is cut transversely (× 580).

B. Lysigenous duct and vessel of *Shorea bracteolata*; the duct, an axial gum duct, is the lower of the two large cavities and has no lining epithelium; there are the remains of one or two cells around its margin; the upper one is a vessel and its wall is clearly seen; T.S. (× 170).

C. Lysigenous ducts; two axial gum ducts of African Walnut (*Lovoa klaineana*) filled with dark gum; note that there is no lining epithelium and that the cells around the margins of the ducts are somewhat irregularly disposed; the other large cavities are vessels; the two ducts are separated by a ray and there is another ray to the right of the right-hand duct; T.S. (× 175).

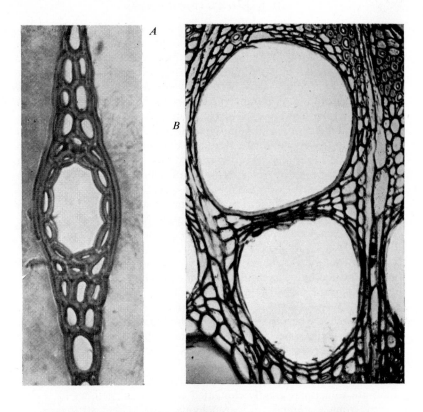

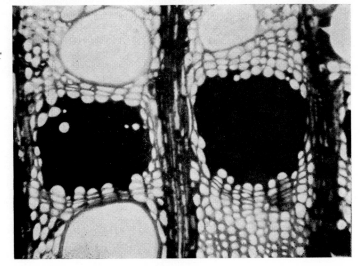

Fig. 15

the cell walls of the wood. Examples are gum arabic, found in *Acacia senegal* (L.) Willd., and cherry gum, obtained from species of *Prunus*. The resins, which are oxidation products of certain essential oils, are complex substances of varied chemical composition, insoluble in water but soluble in alcohol; they occur, for example, in members of the Dipterocarpaceae (gum dammar), the Leguminosae and the Pinaceae. The hard resins, like the copals, from such widely different genera as *Copaifera* and *Agathis*, and gum dammar, contain little or no essential oil. The oleo-resins contain a considerable quantity of oil and are more or less liquid; examples are the turpentines, like the resin or pitch from various species of *Pinus*, venetian turpentine from the European larch and copaiba balsam from species of *Copaifera*. The gum resins are mixtures of true gum and resin; examples are gum guaiacum from lignum vitae, and gamboge, a yellow dyestuff, from species of *Garcinia*.

Some of these extraneous materials, as has been noted, are deposited in special cavities or ducts. These ducts, which are found among the axial elements and in the rays, arise in one of two ways. Sometimes they are formed by the splitting apart of contiguous cells (schizogenous ducts) or sometimes by the breakdown of cells, so that a cavity is left (lysigenous ducts) (Fig. 15). Large ducts may originate schizogenously, and subsequently become enlarged by breakdown of the surrounding cells (schizo-lysigenous). Schizogenous ducts, but not lysigenous ones, are lined with parenchyma cells, which, like any cells which line a cavity, are called epithelial cells.

Latex and, much more rarely, tannin, may occur in special tubes which are sometimes greatly elongated cells, and sometimes in vessels formed from a number of parenchyma cells. These structures are readily distinguished from ducts because they possess a wall of their own. A fuller account of ducts and latex tubes is reserved for subsequent chapters (cf. Chapters 5 and 6).

CHAPTER 3

THE TRUNK OF THE LIVING TREE

In considering the structure and origin of wood, which have been described in the previous chapter, it is important to keep in mind that man's use of wood is a secondary one. Wood has evolved in trees in response to their mechanical and physiological needs. It serves principally to support the leaves, flowers and fruits, so that the tree may obtain the necessary energy for its growth and secure the formation and dispersal of its seeds, and also to conduct from the roots, to these centres of growth and activity, the water and mineral ions absorbed from the soil which are necessary for their formation and continued functioning. It is pertinent therefore to consider the structure of the tree, and that of the wood which constitutes a major part of its bulk, in relation to the way in which it grows.

The phloem, or inner bark, which is closely associated with the wood in its origins, does not fall within our immediate field of study, but in a general view of the tree as a whole it cannot be ignored. Like the wood, it has essential conducting functions and furthermore is commonly concerned in the formation of the true bark which encases and protects all but the youngest parts of the tree.

Like other vascular plants, trees grow by the activity of permanently embryonic tissues at the apices of their shoots and roots. Whereas in herbaceous perennial plants the aerial shoots die back each year with the onset of the unfavourable season, and are renewed by the activity of buds at or below ground level, in the tree there is a permanent and expanding framework of aerial shoots which carry the apical buds upwards and outwards. The buds of trees are thus commonly much more obviously protected against desiccation and mechanical damage during the unfavourable season, by closely overlapping, relatively impervious and mechanically tough bud scales.

At the beginning of each growing season, "triggered" by increasing day-length, the apical buds break into growth. The bud-scales separate slightly and eventually drop off, and the new growth emerges, slowly at first and then at an increasing rate. Later in the year the rate of extension growth decreases and towards the end of the growing season a new dormant bud is organized at its apex. The origin and early development of the new growth can be followed anatomically by the study of sections of buds at various stages of their expansion.

The growing point or primary meristem at the tip of a shoot consists of a small but highly organized mass of tightly-packed, more or less cubical cells with abundant protoplasm. These, by active growth and division, give rise to new cells which enlarge and differentiate into the mature tissues of the young shoot. Not only does the apex produce the tissues of the stem, but it also initiates the formation of new leaves and axillary buds in the pattern characteristic of the species. Fig 16 shows a median longitudinal section of the growing point or apical meristem of a Sycamore shoot, in which young leaf primordia may be seen arising from the sides of the apex: only a small part of the whole bud is represented here: the older leaves of the bud and the bud-scales lie wholly outside the area of the photomicrograph.

As new tissue arises behind it therefore, the apex is carried upwards, giving rise to the growth in length (extension growth) of the shoot. This bears new leaves at intervals, which in sycamore would be arranged decussately. Of the cells produced by the apical meristem those in the centre of the stem become parenchymatous, forming the pith; the outermost layer forms the skin, or epidermis, of closely fitting cells, while those immediately within this form the cortex. In the region between the future cortex and pith the procambium, or provascular tissue, becomes recognizable closely behind the apex and its cells subsequently become differentiated into xylem (or wood) and phloem (or bast), characteristic of the vascular tissues of the new young growth. Provascular strands also differentiate in the leaf primordia and axillary buds so that the vascular system of the new shoot eventually becomes a unified whole.

The first formed xylem (termed protoxylem) consisting of tracheids, vessels and parenchyma (vessels would of course not be formed in most gymnosperms) arises in small groups in the inner side of the provascular tissue, closely behind the stem apex, i.e. in a region where growth in length is still very rapid. The primary walls of these elements, like those of other cells, are extensible, and thus keep pace in their growth with the elongation of the stem as a whole. Secondary walls, however, of a kind normal in later wood, would be out of place here since they are relatively very inextensible; in the protoxylem the secondary walls of tracheids and vessels take the form of rings or spiral bands which allow continued stretching of these elements even after the death of their protoplasts. It is instructive in this connection to note that in newly-formed protoxylem the spiral or annular thickenings are closely packed: only later do they become stretched out or separated in the way commonly seen in mature stems. The secondary walls of protoxylem elements are thus characterised by this spiral or annular structure and the absence of bordered pits.

Correspondingly, the first formed phloem, the protophloem, differentiates in the outer region of the provascular tissue, protoxylem and protophloem groups lying on the same radius. From the protoxylem, differentiation proceeds outwards, and the metaxylem is produced, while metaphloem differentiates in an inward direction from the protophloem. In the metaxylem, formed at a time when extension growth

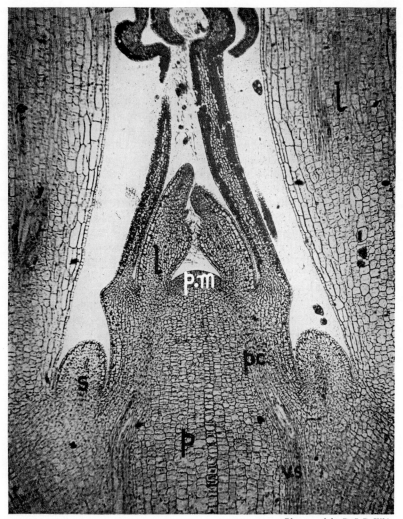

Photograph by D. J. B. White

Fig. 16.—Median longitudinal section of the middle part of a terminal bud of Sycamore (*Acer pseudoplatanus*), showing the shoot apex flanked by leaf primordia: *l.*, leaf; *p.*, pith; *pc.*, provascular tissue; *p.m.*, promeristem (apical meristem); *s.*, provascular strand of axillary bud; *v.s.*, vascular strand of main axis.

has come to an end, the secondary walls of tracheids and vessels are much better developed than in the protoxylem, being laid down as more or less transverse interconnecting bars (scalariform thickening) or as a network (reticulate thickening). Later formed metaxylem elements commonly show continuous secondary walls perforated only by bordered pits.

In many herbaceous plants, and in some trees (e.g. *Pinus* and *Acer*) the provascular tissue is in the form of a number of separate strands, so that in transverse section the vascular tissues of the young extension growth appear as a ring of separate vascular bundles: often, however, in trees, the provascular tissue and hence also the early xylem and phloem, form a complete cylinder.

In some herbaceous plants differentiation of xylem and phloem within the provascular strands continues until the whole of this is converted into these mature tissues. But in many herbaceous plants, and in trees, a zone of undifferentiated meristematic cells remains between the metaxylem and metaphloem. This forms the vascular cambium, which as has already been explained, gives rise to new xylem and new phloem during the subsequent life of the plant. The vascular cambium is often referred to as *the* cambium, but since it is not the only one, the qualifying adjective should be used.

In plants in which the provascular tissue (and hence therefore the proto- and meta- xylem and the phloem together) form discrete bundles, the zones of vascular cambium in adjacent bundles normally become connected by the cutting out of cambial cells in the relatively undifferentiated parenchyma between the bundles (Figs. 2 and 17). A complete cylinder of vascular cambium is thus established.

It must be emphasized that proto- and meta- xylem and phloem thus arise directly from cells formed from the apical meristem, and are hence termed primary, while xylem and phloem formed later owe their origin to the activity of the vascular cambium and are referred to as secondary. The distinction, though useful in practice, is however not an absolute one; there is commonly a transition region between primary and secondary tissues within which it is impossible with any certainty to assign any one particular element to either category.

The extension growth of young shoots can thus be referred to the activity of their apical meristems, while their increase in bulk, mainly of secondary xylem, results from the activity of the vascular cambium. Thus as the shoot increases in length the older parts increase in girth, so acquiring the necessary mechanical strength and increasing conductive capacity to maintain the extending shoot system which they carry. Although the secondary phloem is relatively slight in bulk it is of equal importance, in the growing twig or tree, to the xylem, serving principally to transport food substances, synthesized in the leaves, upwards to the growing points and downwards to the root. Thus if a tree is "ringed" by the complete removal of a strip of bark all round the trunk, death of the overground parts ensues sooner or later, brought about through the death of the root system.

The root of the tree, though largely out of sight and thus only too easily underestimated, grows in essentially the same way as the shoot, by the activity of primary apical root meristems and a secondary vascular cambium, and so comes to form a very extensive system ramifying throughout a considerable volume of soil. Its conducting tissues are of course in anatomical continuity with those of the stem.

The increasing girth of the vascular system, both in stem and root, brought about by the onset of activity of the vascular cambium, tends of course to split the cortex and epidermis of the young twig, and so to

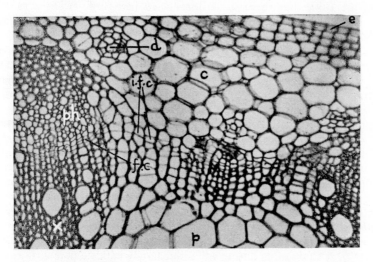

Fig. 17.—Transverse section of a small portion of a stem of Dahlia, showing vascular cambium (× 110). *c.*, cortex; *d.*, duct; *e.*, epidermis; *f.c.*, intrafascicular cambium; *i.f.c.*, beginnings of interfascicular cambium, the left-hand index lines pointing to a cell in which only a single wall has been formed; in that to which the right-hand index line leads, the two tangential walls have formed, cutting out the cambial initial. *p.*, pith; *ph.*, phloem (primary); *x.*, xylem (primary).

expose the inner tissues to desiccation and fungal attack. A new protective layer is formed to replace the ruptured epidermis. This is the cork or phellem, the outer bark of the tree, which like the secondary wood, arises from a secondary meristem, the cork cambium or phellogen.

When it is fully established, the cells which constitute the vascular cambium are, as we have seen (p. 24) of two kinds, fusiform initials and ray initials. The fusiform initials which produce the axial elements of the xylem and phloem are axially elongated cells with wedge-shaped ends (Fig. 7). In conifers and the more primitive dicotyledons these cells are many times longer than wide: in yellow pine (*Pinus strobus* L.) a fusiform initial may be 4 mm. long, while in transverse section it would measure about 0·040 × 0·012 mm. In more advanced dicotyledonous families, such cells tend to be shorter and sometimes, e.g. in ebonies (*Diospyros*), they are arranged in regular horizontal layers, and are said to be storeyed, an arrangement which is reflected in the gross structure of the wood (cf. pp. 127–30). The false acacia or black locust (*Robinia pseudoacacia* L.) possesses a storeyed or stratified cambium in which the fusiform initials are about 0·17 mm. long, less than one-twentieth the length of the yellow pine fusiform initial. The ray initials, as seen in tangential view, are no longer than they are wide, and are somewhat squarish or lozenge-shaped (Fig. 7); in a radial direction they are somewhat narrower. It is from these cells that the cells of the rays are formed.

The types of wood cells to which the vascular cambium can give rise have already been considered. Axial parenchyma cells usually arise in vertical rows, each row a derivative of a fusiform initial which has divided into a number of cells by transverse walls, Bearing in mind the shape of the fusiform initial, it might be expected that the axial parenchyma of the xylem would occur in strands, terminated at either end by a cell with one wedge-shaped end, i.e. of the same shape as the ends of the fusiform initial. This does sometimes happen, such rows of cells being termed strand parenchyma (Fig. 7), but the regular arrangement is often lost during the process of differentiation, by changes in size and shape of individual xylem cells and consequent adjustments in their relative positions. Sometimes only a single parenchyma cell is differentiated from a fusiform initial: such a cell has considerable resemblance to a fibre, so much so that it was formerly called a substitute fibre (Fig. 7). A study of its pitting will immediately indicate that such a cel is parenchymatous, and it is now distinguished as a fusiform parenchyma cell, in preference to the old and misleading term substitute fibre.

Where an axial file of cells, cut off from the vascular cambium, forms a vessel, there is a process of lateral enlargement, as a result of which the surrounding cells become disarranged so that the regular radial arrangement of the cambial products is soon lost. The constituent vessel elements may decrease in length during the process of vessel formation; when they become mature the end walls disappear, partially or completely, so that a tube is formed. Disappearance of these end walls appears to be due to a gradual dissolution associated with a breaking-up into several layers and not a sudden bursting, as has been suggested (Esau and Hewitt, 1940). The protoplasts of the young vessel elements gradually disorganise and the mature vessel remains as a dead tube or pipe. Vessels, formed in this way, may range in length, in different species, from a few centimetres up to a metre or more.

There is a close resemblance between the vascular tracheid of hardwoods, and a vessel element. Such tracheids may be regarded as incompletely developed vessel elements. They develop from axial rows of cambial derivatives, but the end walls are retained. So similar is a row of vascular tracheids to a vessel that, because of the constant orientation of the end walls, it may often be impossible to judge, in a tangential section, in which the end walls or perforations are seen edge on, whether a particular structure is a vessel or a column of vascular tracheids. In a radial section the difference is at once apparent, for the end walls of the vascular tracheids, seen more or less in surface view, will show characteristic bordered pits, which are quite different from the end perforations of vessel elements. Rather short and irregularly shaped vasicentric tracheids are sometimes found associated with vessels in hardwoods (e.g. oak); their original shape is often distorted and flattened, owing to the expansion of the associated vessels during differentiation.

The axial tracheid of softwoods is more comparable with the fibre of hardwoods in its differentiation. Both types of element are commonly much longer than the fusiform initial from which they were derived, so that elongation of these cells occurs during differentiation in a region of the trunk or branch which is not growing in length (Bailey, 1920; Bannan, 1956; Wardrop, 1964a). The differentiating fibres or tracheids elongate principally by growth at their tips, which in consequence are pushed between adjacent elements, a process known as intrusive growth. Thus in such a growing fibre the middle part may be mature with a secondary wall, while the end regions still possess only a primary wall. As tip-growth ceases, deposition of the secondary wall proceeds from the middle of the cell towards the newly extended tips (Wardrop and Harada, 1965).

The ray initials of the vascular cambium give rise exclusively to ray cells, which are nearly always parenchymatous; tracheids are formed in the rays of a few conifers and are recorded in at least one dicotyledon. In dicotyledons the ray parenchyma cells may differentiate into several types, but these are best left for consideration until the detailed histology of dicotyledonous wood is dealt with.

Cells of ray parenchyma, like those of the axial parenchyma, retain their living contents, at least in the sapwood (Nečesaný, 1966), and in some instances even in the heartwood. It has been found for instance (MacDougal and Smith, 1927) that in the redwood *Sequoia sempervirens* (Lamb) Endl., ray parenchyma cells may remain alive for a hundred years, during about seventy of which they were part of the heartwood. It is through the activity of the protoplasts of such living cells that food is transported through or stored in wood parenchyma. They play no direct part in the conduction of water in the wood.

Consideration of the fate of the cambial products cut off to the outer side of the vascular cambium is scarcely within the province of a book on wood structure, but brief reference may be made here to the phloem.

The axial elements of the phloem are of four kinds. The sieve-tube of angiosperms may be likened to a vessel in that it is formed from an axial row of cells (sieve-tube elements) and in that the end walls of these cells become perforated. The perforations take the form of numerous minute holes, so that the end walls appear finally as sieves—hence the

E

name, sieve-plate, which is applied to them. Sieve-plates may be transverse or oblique; they may include one or up to several distinct sieve areas and in the latter case are then said to be compound. Apart from the fact that the walls of sieve-tubes are not lignified, another fundamental difference between sieve-tubes and vessels is that sieve-tubes retain their living protoplasts, at least in part, during the functional period of their existence. In dicotyledons the young elements of a sieve-tube divide by longitudinal walls, each cutting off one or more cells, normally smaller than the sieve-tube elements themselves and known as companion-cells. The nucleus of the sieve-tube element then disintegrates, so that a sieve-tube is without nuclei. In conifers, sieve-tubes are not formed, but the sieve elements are single cells, with oblique, or nearly vertical sieve-plates, or rather, sieve-areas, on their radial walls. These cells are known as sieve-cells and are comparable not to a vessel, but rather to a softwood tracheid. Companion cells are not formed in the phloem of conifers. The sieve-cells, or sieve-tubes and companion cells, are concerned with transport of elaborated food materials from the leaves. Another axial element of the phloem is the parenchyma cell, commonly concerned with food storage, while a fourth type of element, the fibre, may be present. Phloem fibres are well seen in lime (*Tilia*) (Fig. 18 *C*), where they form tangential bands (hard bast) alternating with bands of soft bast (sieve-tubes, companion cells and parenchyma). The stringyness of the inner bark of lime is due to the hard bast, which originally produced the bass (corruption of bast) of commerce. The inner bark of other trees, e.g. the cloth-bark tree (*Antiaris*) of Africa and the lace-bark tree (*Lagetta*) of tropical America, likewise owe their use as primitive textiles to the presence of bast fibres in their phloem.

The rays extend through, or partly through, the phloem, and their parenchymatous cells are formed by the ray initials in the same manner as are the ray cells of the wood.

The activity of the vascular cambium leads to an increasing girth of the wood, so that the cambium itself (and of course the phloem as well) are moved further and further away from the pith. Consequently the

---

Fig. 18.—*A*. Cross-section of part of the trunk of a self-climbing Virginia Creeper (*Parthenocissus tricuspidata*). The soft cells of the phloem (sieve-tubes, companion cells and parenchyma), have disappeared, and only the hard fibres remain. Some of these fibres are visible in the bark, evidence that it has been formed in the phloem. *B*. L.S. of part of the trunk of *Parthenocissus tricuspidata*; the large rays of the wood extend into the bark, in which the white quill-like phloem fibres may be seen, both of which indicate that the bark has formed in the phloem. *A* and *B* are approximately natural size. *C*. T.S. of the phloem of Lime (*Tilia vulgaris*); bands of small thick-walled fibres alternate with bands of larger, thin-walled cells (sieve-tubes, companion cells and parenchyma); thin rays run vertically in the figure, the one on the left flaring out towards the top. The lowest thin white band is the vascular cambium and its immediate derivatives; below this is the last-formed wood (× 170). *b.*, bark; *ph.*, phloem region.

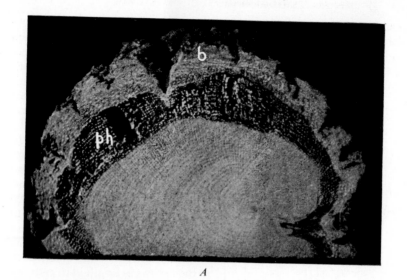

A

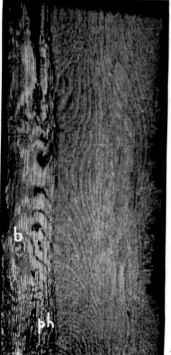

B

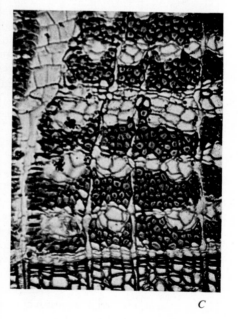

C

Fig. 18

cambium must extend tangentially over the increasingly large circumference of the wood to maintain its continuity. This tangential extension is brought about principally by a continued increase in the number of fusiform initials, some of which are further converted, by transverse divisions, into ray initials.

In storeyed cambia the fusiform initials divide longitudinally by anti-clinal (i.e. radial) walls. In non-storeyed cambia, however, the division process is more complex (Fig. 19). The fusiform initials divide by oblique, nearly transverse, walls (often referred to as "pseudo-transverse" walls), so that the resulting daughter cells lie axially one above the other. Each then grows in length at its ends, by apical intrusive growth, so becoming as long or longer than the parent cell from which it arose. The initially pseudo-transverse wall thus becomes tilted into the axial direction, so that the daughter cells come to lie largely side by side. The necessary tangential extension of the cambium is thus brought about (Bailey, 1923; Bannan, 1950; Esau, 1965).

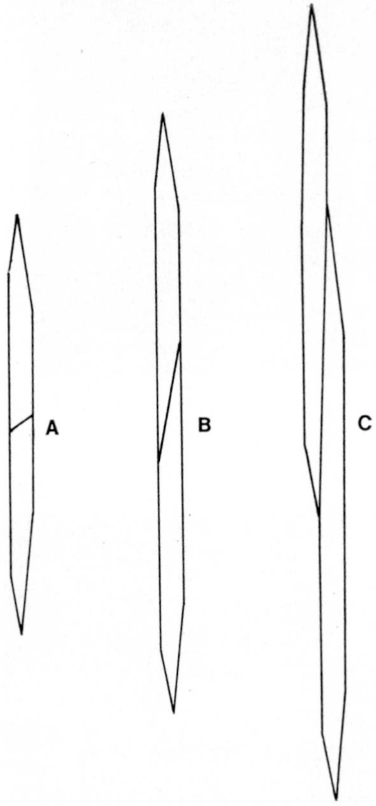

The number of divisions of this kind occurring in the cambium is, in many softwoods at least, far more than is needed to keep pace with the increasing cambial girth, and a considerable proportion of the initials so formed soon cease to act as cambial cells: they die or become differentiated into mature xylem elements (Bannan, 1950). The increasing girth of the cambium is then the result of a dynamic equilibrium between the production and elongation of new fusiform initials on the one hand and their limited activity and death on the other.

Fig. 19.—Diagrams illustrating the mode of radial longitudinal division of a fusiform initial of the vascular cambium, as it would be seen in T.L.S. The cell divides by a "pseudo-transverse" wall (A), but subsequently localised growth of the daughter cells tilts the new wall towards the axial position, and the two cells come to lie largely side by side (after Bailey, 1923).

Examination of transverse sections of woody stems reveals that the amount of phloem is very much less than that of the xylem and moreover that the phloem zone does not appear to increase greatly in width during the life of the tree. While it is true that the cambium cuts off many more xylem elements than phloem elements—some eight times as many in some instances (Bannan, 1962)—this does not wholly explain the disproportionately small amount of phloem in an old tree. The outer part of the phloem is commonly lost as bark, as is explained below; it is this continual "wastage" of the phloem that keeps it down to small proportions.

The effect of the increasing girth of a twig or sapling, in tending to cause splitting of its epidermis and underlying cortex, has already been referred to. These tissues are capable of some tangential expansion, by cell enlargement and even some cell division, but their potential here is limited, and they are gradually replaced by the formation of cork, a tissue which is almost water-proof and gas-proof, and is resistant to mechanical damage and to attack by micro-organisms.

The cork-cambium, or phellogen, which produces the cork, may arise in different positions in different species. In most trees it is formed initially in the outer part of the cortex, but it may be deep-seated, arising just outside the phloem, as in the barberries (*Berberis*), or superficial, arising in the epidermis, as in the willows (*Salix*). As in the formation of interfascicular cambium, the parenchyma cells in which the cork cambium arises divide twice, forming two tangential walls, thus cutting out a central cell which is the cork-cambial cell (Fig. 20 *A*).

Commonly the cork cambium cuts off cells to the outside only, although in some plants, for example the currants (*Ribes*), cells are also cut off internally, forming a tissue called the phelloderm or secondary cortex, which is thus added to the existing primary cortex.

The cells which are cut off externally are the cork cells. They are closely fitting, without intercellular spaces, and at first they are of course living cells. Soon after their formation, however, a fatty substance (suberin) is deposited on their walls rendering them highly resistant to the movement of water and gases. The protoplasts, thus cut off from water and nutrients, die, and the cell cavities gradually dry out and become filled with air.

This tightly packed layer of impervious cells forms the outer bark of the tree. Apart from the protective functions already mentioned, it forms, with its air-filled cells, a heat-insulating layer which effectively checks rapid fluctuations in temperature in the tissues which it ensheaths. It is essential that some gaseous exchange take place between the internal tissues and the exterior, but this cannot happen through the impervious cork. The cork is, however, perforated by lenticels, which act as vents and allow the necessary gaseous exchange to occur. In a lenticel (Figs. 20 *B*, 21) the cork cells are different from those in other parts of the cork in that they are not closely packed without intercellular spaces: on the contrary they are rounded, often loose and powdery and there are plenty of air spaces between them. Lenticels are well seen, in a piece of bottle cork, as dark areas filled with loose, dusty

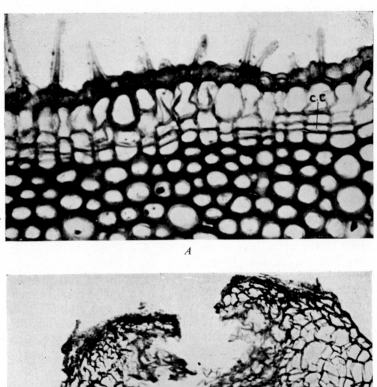

A

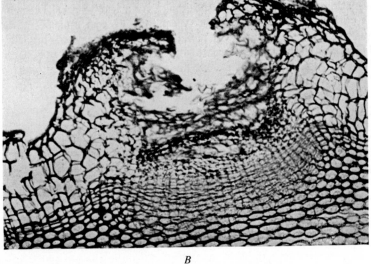

B

Fig. 20.—*A*. T.S. of the outer part of a young stem of Elder (*Sambucus nigra*) showing the formation of the cork cambium; the cork cambium (*c.c.*) lies in the cortex. To the right of the figure the cork cambium has been cut out but some of the cells in the centre show an earlier stage, only one tangential wall having been formed so far. Below the cork cambium is a fibrous region of the cortex (× 305).

B. T.S. of the outer part of a young stem of Hungarian Lilac (*Syringa josikaea*) showing cork cambium and lenticel in section (× 110). The cork cambium and its immediate derivatives are seen on the left as axial rows of radially flattened cells; these dip below the lenticel and here the cells are not very clear.

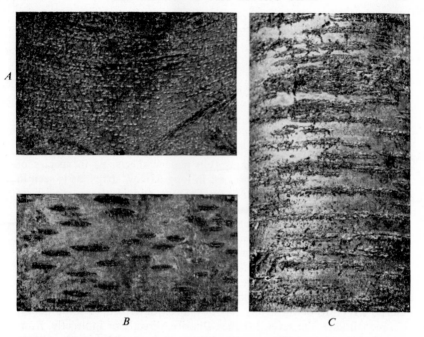

Fig. 21.—Bark showing lenticels. *A.* Holly (*Ilex aquifolium*); the lenticels show as small, pale dots. *B.* European Birch (*Betula* sp.) here the lenticels are the darker, horizontally elongated areas. *C.* Cherry (*Prunus* sp.); the lenticels are the horizontal, very elongated areas.

material. In many trees they occur as small, slightly raised dots on the surface of the bark, but they may be quite large, as in cherry and birch, where they are narrow, transversely elongated structures perhaps many centimetres in length (Fig. 21).

In some trees the cork cambium is able to expand tangentially and so to keep pace with the increasing girth of the trunk, remaining active throughout the life of the tree. Birch starts in this way, but later, as in most trees, the first cork cambium ceases to function and successive cork cambia arise, deeper and deeper in the cortex. Often, these new cork cambia are not continuous sheets, but arise as curved "shells," so that the bark is actually formed in patches or scales. Clearly, since the cortex, which is a primary tissue, does not normally increase in amount, it will soon be used up, as successive cork cambia form deeper and deeper within it. Subsequently, cork cambia are formed in the outer part of the secondary phloem, and it is in this tissue that cork formation occurs in the older parts of most trees. While there can be no replacement of the primary cortex, the phloem is, of course, being added to, throughout the life of the tree, by the activity of the vascular cambium, so that this loss of phloem is made good (Esau, 1964). In fact, but for the presence of this secondary tissue, which is itself being regularly replaced, the formation of successive cork cambia, after the primary cortex had been used up, could not occur.

The outer layers of bark are gradually shed. The dead cork, of course, cannot expand tangentially as the circumference of the bole increases, and unless it peels or rubs off, it cracks and gives rise to the fissured bark characteristic of some trees, like oak and elm. Sometimes, as in beech and spruce, the outer cork rubs off in minute powdery fragments and the bark remains smooth, or there may be special weak zones which permit of the bark flaking off in patches, as in plane (*Platanus*) and strawberry tree (*Arbutus*), or as thin papery sheets, as in species of birch. Again, the bark may peel off in long narrow strips, as is seen in Western red cedar (*Thuya plicata* D.Don) and in those species of *Eucalyptus* known as stringybarks (Figs. 22, 23).

Despite shedding of the bark, this tissue may attain to considerable thickness. In the Douglas fir it is usually 12–25 cms. thick and near the butt may be as much as 50 cms.; on the other hand in silver spruce it rarely exceeds a centimetre or so in thickness, while it is but little thicker in Western red cedar. Schwankl (1956) gives brief descriptions of a considerable variety of barks.

The structure of the trunk has now been described in some detail. To recapitulate, the several tissues all arise, directly or indirectly, from the apical meristem. The centre of the trunk is occupied by the pith, a primary tissue which does not increase in diameter after it is laid down by the apical meristem. The pith cells may disappear, when the non-existent pith is said to be fistular, but it normally remains, occupying a small and decreasing percentage of the trunk, as this increases in size. But the pith does not become squashed out of existence by the increasing secondary wood; this does not press inwards, but expands outwards. The pith is surrounded by a larger or smaller zone of wood, which has the primary xylem on its inner side and is encased externally in a sheath of living cells, the vascular cambium. The cells of the vascular cambium divide repeatedly during the growing season and remain more or less dormant at other times: even in the most favoured tropical climates, the activity of the vascular cambium shows marked periodical fluctuation. External to the cambium is the phloem or, as it is sometimes called, the inner bark. Beyond the phloem is the cork or outer bark, possibly separated from the phloem by a little primary cortex. The outer bark also is a secondary tissue, increasing internally by the activity of a secondary meristem, the cork cambium, and shedding the older cork from its external surface.

The pith is probably functionless, although it may contain a certain amount of water, as well as waste materials. The wood is a supporting tissue as well as being concerned with upward conduction of sap, and in its ray parenchyma, with food storage. The function of conduction falls upon the outer zone of the wood (the sapwood). The more central

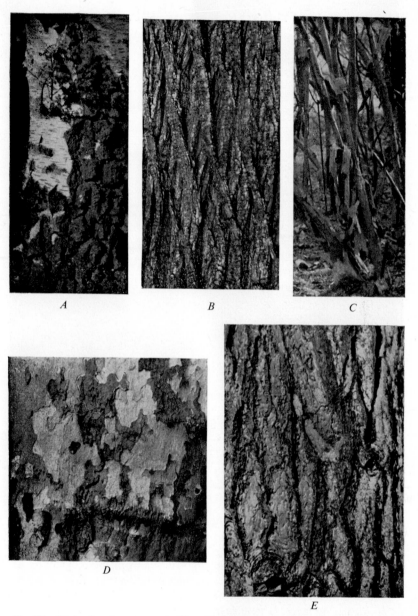

Fig. 22.—Bark of various trees. *A*. Silver Birch (*Betula pendula*), showing transition from the smooth, silvery bark with prominent horizontal lenticels, characteristic of the young tree, to the very rugged bark of the older tree. *B*. Sweet Chestnut (*Castanea sativa*). *C*. *Dipelta floribunda*, a shrub in which the bark is shed in long paper-like strips. *D*. London Plane (*Platanus acerifolia*); a tree in which the bark is shed in large flakes; the pale areas are regions where the bark has recently fallen and the dark areas where flakes are nearly ready to be shed. *E*. Scots Pine (*Pinus sylvestris*); somewhat rough, flakey or scaly bark.

Fig. 23.—Bark of various trees (in section). *A*. Holly (*Ilex aquifolium*); very thin bark. *B*. European Birch (*Betula* sp.); in the young bark (cf. Fig. 22 *A*) there are alternating layers of larger, thin-walled cells, and thick-walled cells which are radially flattened; breaks in the walls of the former cause the bark to peel in thin, horizontal strips: the figure shows peeling of part of the outer layer. *C*. Deodar (*Cedrus deodara*); thick rough bark; the shell bark is well shown in the outer layers, the shells being demarcated by the thin white lines which mark the positions of old cork cambia (all about natural size).

region, the heartwood, is probably usually completely dead, serving as a repository for waste materials and possibly, at certain times of the year, as a water store. The inner, younger phloem is concerned with the transport of elaborated materials from the leaves and in the older parts of trees the older, outer phloem has a second, if indirect function, in acting as the seat of cork cambium formation. The outermost covering or cork is an insulating layer, largely gasproof, waterproof and fungus proof.

Finally, brief mention must be made of two further functions of the cork. Where leaves and branches fall naturally, the exposed surface becomes sealed with a thin layer of cork cells. Again, where a tree is wounded, cork formation becomes specially active and, at least in small wounds, cork gradually covers the exposed area, thus, in time, sealing off a vulnerable spot from the attacks of parasites (Fig. 24).

A

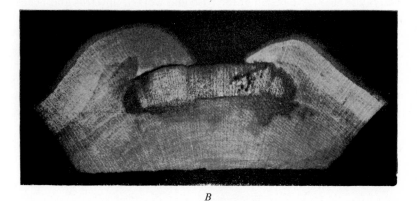

B

Fig. 24.—*A*. Bole of Cherry (*Prunus* sp.) with a large wound which has calloused over except in the centre. *B*. Transverse section across a partially healed wound in an Oak trunk. The wood in the region of the wound has become rotten. The darker areas around the rotten wood are due to wound gum, which forms a barrier to the invading fungal hyphae. Development of new wood and bark has resulted in the covering of over half the exposed wound.

CHAPTER 4

THE GROSS STRUCTURE OF WOOD

Since the gross features of wood are more obvious than its microscopic structure, it might appear more logical to treat the gross features first; but as these are determined by the minutiae of structure, there is sufficient justification for reversing the order of treatment.

In temperate climates, at least, the growth of a tree, and the addition of new wood and other tissues, takes place only during the favourable season of the year and for the rest of the year the tree remains dormant. Even in warm climates growth may be periodic; this is certainly so when there is an adverse period of the year, in the form of a dry season, but even where equable conditions prevail throughout the year the annual life cycle of at least some trees includes a resting period.

At the end of its first season's growth a tree is a small plant, consisting, above ground, of a vertical axis or main stem which terminates in a bud, in which is situated the apical growing point. Along this axis are borne a number of lateral buds, some of which will probably have developed into lateral branches. Since the tip is the youngest part of the stem, it might be expected that the stem will be tapered, for cambial activity should have begun at the base and worked upwards and hence, having been active for longer in the basal zone, should have resulted in a greater increase in diameter here than higher up. This, in fact, is what does happen—the stem or trunk is a very elongated cone, not a cylinder.

TABLE 1

Diameter of stem in successive internodes of a one-year sycamore (*Acer pseudoplatanus*) seedling, from measurements made by D. J. B. White. (Diameter of wood excludes diameter of pith.)

Internode	Diameter of stem (mm.)	Diameter of wood (mm.)	Diameter of pith (mm.)
1 (lowest)	5·80	3·96	0·84
2	5·72	4·00	0·80
3	5·20	3·28	1·04
4	4·80	2·96	1·12
5	4·56	2·56	1·20
6	4·32	2·20	1·40
7	4·12	1·56	1·92
8	3·96	0·96	2·24
9	3·88	0·56	2·56
10	3·68	0·44	2·60
11	———→ not measured ←———		

A   B

Fig. 25.—*A*. Giant Redwood (*Sequoia wellingtonia*) showing the tapered trunk of a fairly young tree. *B*. Beech (*Fagus sylvatica*) showing a virtually cylindrical bole.

During succeeding growing seasons the young stem will increase in height by means of its growing point (cf. Chapter 3), and in girth by the activity of its vascular cambium. After a number of years the tree trunk may be visualised as containing a number of greatly elongated and closely fitting hollow cones of wood, one produced each year, rather like a pile of pierrots' caps. The comparison is not, however, entirely apt, for the woody cones are not complete at the apex: here, each year, the growing point has been active in producing further extension growth. In some trees the conical form of the trunk is more marked than in others. Western red cedar and the redwoods (*Sequoia*) (Fig. 25 *A*) furnish excellent examples of tapered trunks, with flared butts which tend to exaggerate the taper. Sometimes, as in beech, in many of the Dipterocarpaceae and in the New Zealand kauri (*Agathis australis* Salisb.), the trunk is practically columnar (Fig. 25 *B*), the more apically placed vascular cambium having, by its greater activity, produced almost as much wood as the cambium of the basal parts, and in a shorter time.

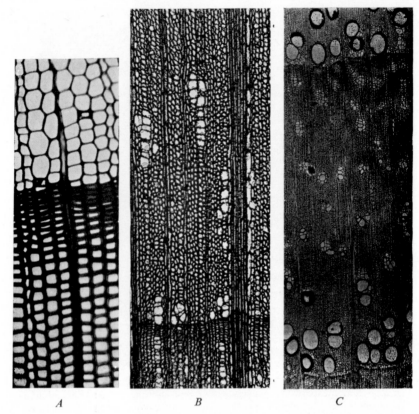

A   *B*   *C*

Fig. 26.—Growth rings. *A*. Western Red Cedar (*Thuja plicata*); the end of the growth ring is marked by thick-walled tracheids (T.S., × 135). *B*. Holly (*Ilex aquifolium*); the end of the growth ring is marked by a narrow zone of denser fibrous tissue (T.S., × 60). *C*. Tree of Heaven (*Ailanthus altissima*); the beginning of the growth ring is marked by a pore ring of large vessels (T.S., × 16).

At least in temperate trees, the wood formed late in the growing season often differs from that produced earlier. In softwoods this difference may be in the production of tracheids with thicker walls and often of smaller dimensions later in the year (Fig. 26 *A*). In hardwoods the vessels formed early in the growing season may be larger and more numerous than the later formed ones (Fig. 26 *C*), or the fibres in the later formed wood may be thicker-walled and perhaps smaller than those formed earlier. Again, the end of a seasonal increment may be marked by the formation of parenchyma, or of radially flattened fibres, so that the limits of each season's growth can usually be readily determined (Fig. 26 *B*). The first-formed wood each season is termed spring wood, or better, early wood, the wood formed later in the year being known as summer wood, or preferably, late wood. When a trunk is cut transversely, these increments appear as a series of more or less concentric circles about the pith. They are often referred to as growth rings, a very convenient term, although not strictly correct, for if the trunk is considered, as it should be, as a solid object, the rings are merely transverse sections of growth cones. However, the term growth ring is unlikely to pass into disuse and it is certainly to be preferred to "annual ring"[1] which implies that each growth ring is formed during a year. While this is normally true for north temperate trees, knowledge of the growth of tropical trees is so limited that it would be rash to assert that in these a growth ring is formed within a year or, alternatively, that only one growth ring is formed each twelve months (Alvim, 1964).

It is common knowledge, although it is not quite true, that the age of a tree can be determined by counting its growth rings. In the first place, it is necessary to ensure that the ring count be made very low down in the trunk, i.e. below the height which the apical growing point reached during the first year of growth, for if the count be made at a higher level the oldest growth rings will not be included. It has also to be borne in mind that a tree, even in a temperate climate, may form more than one growth ring during a growing season. The tree may suffer a check in its growth, perhaps because of drought, or perhaps because it has been defoliated by late frosts, or by a caterpillar plague. Although the cessation of growth will be temporary, it may be marked by some change in the wood elements, with the consequent formation of a growth ring. Such a ring is termed a false growth ring (Fig. 27 A). It might well deceive an inexperienced observer, counting the rings on a stump, although such a ring is usually less sharply defined than a true growth ring, the elements on its outer side gradually merging into those formed later in the year. In a seasonal growth ring the elements immediately external to its boundary—the first of the next growing season—are generally sharply differentiated from the last formed elements of the previous season. Another curious type of growth ring is sometimes encountered in old trees where one or more growth rings are not continuous, but merge into an older ring (Fig. 27 B). Such interruptions, producing discontinuous growth rings, result from the vascular cambium in localised areas remaining inactive for one or more seasons, although its normal activity is usually resumed. In such areas, of course, no new wood is produced during the period of inactivity, consequently the rings here appear to fuse with the one formed when the cambium was last active.

A detailed study of growth increments in a number of species has been made by Glock, Studhalter and Agerter (1960); forest-grown trees were avoided, since these might be expected to have grown under favourable conditions. They found eight growth rings in one branch

---

[1] A frequent verbal variant is "annular ring", which would seem to imply that rings may be other than annular, so that it is therefore necessary to emphasise that the growth ring is a ring-shaped ring!

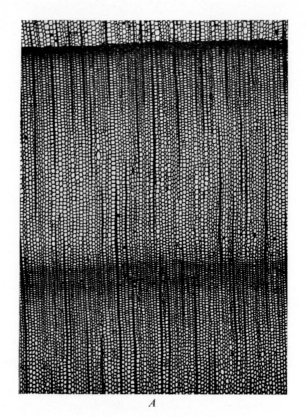

A

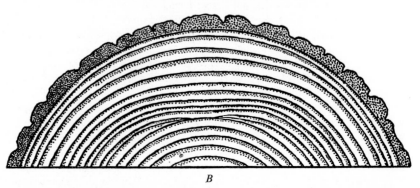

B

Fig. 27.—*A.* False growth ring in Western Red Cedar (*Thuja plicata*); the boundary of a true growth ring lies almost at the top of the illustration and above this is the beginning of the ring of the succeeding year: the false growth ring is seen just below the middle of the figure: it is rather paler than the ring which marks the boundary, for its cells are not so thick-walled, nor is its outer margin as distinct as that which marks the end of the season's growth; T.S. (× 27). *B.* Diagram of discontinuous growth rings in a cross-section of a log.

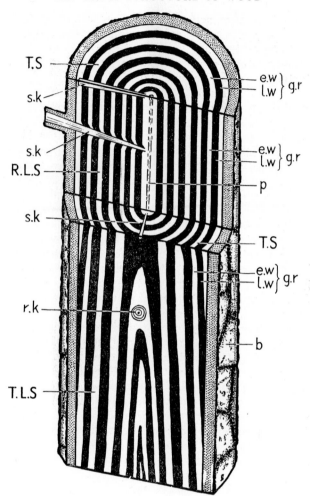

Fig. 28.—Diagram of a log cut in different planes. T.S., transverse surface (cross-cut or end-grain). R.L.S., radial longitudinal surface (quarter-sawn). T.L.S., tangential longitudinal surface (plain-sawn). *b.*, bark; *e.w.*, early wood; *g.r.*, growth ring; *l.w.*, late wood; *p.*, pith; *r.k.*, round knot; *s.k.*, spike knot.

known to be only four years old and they mention trees which had formed 15 sharply bordered growth layers in four years. They could discover no criterion by which a false growth ring could be distinguished with absolute certainty from a normal seasonal one. Moreover, growth layers might be incomplete and not extend over the whole tree.

Growth increments are often to be seen on the longitudinal surfaces of wood. A radial surface, which is exposed in quarter-sawn timber, will reveal them as a series of more or less parallel lines, while on

F

tangential surfaces these increments will show as a series of cones one within the other and with the apices pointing towards the top of the tree (Fig. 28) (Jane, 1951).

The thickness of each growth cone is partly an inherent character of the species but is also very dependent on various factors of the environment of the individual tree and is very sensitive to differences or changes in this environment. Some trees, like yew and box, grow slowly; others, like balsa, extremely rapidly; but there is an enormous range in the growth rate of a species, dependent upon external conditions. MacMillan (1904) has recorded naturally dwarfed conifers growing in rock crevices on Vancouver Island. Among them were two silver spruces (*Picea sitchensis* Carr.) of which one, less than 30 cm. high and with a trunk 2 cm. in diameter, was 98 years old, and another, slightly shorter and 1·8 cm. in diameter, was 86 years old. Assuming growth to have been uniform over the 98 years, the former tree would have had growth rings about 0·1 mm. wide. In contrast, English-grown silver spruce may have growth rings up to 12 mm. wide, an increment in the order of 100 times greater than that of the Vancouver Island dwarfs.

Nor is the annual increment always of the same size all round the tree; sometimes the pith of the trunk is excentric, with much wider growth rings on one side than upon the other.

From the foregoing it may appear that there is so much variation in ring width and so many factors influencing the size of a growth increment, that any attempt to correlate ring width with rainfall, temperature and other climatic features would be doomed to failure. Careful examination of the growth rings of one species of tree, growing in a limited area, coupled with statistical analyses of the data, have been used, nevertheless, as a means of obtaining information of this sort and for the determination of the incidence of climatic cycles (Douglas, 1919, 1928, 1936; Glock, 1941; Dobbs, 1951; Giddings, 1962). It will be apparent that the use of trees for such a purpose calls for great care, since the sizes of the rings in an individual tree are influenced, not only by the general climate, but also by the much more local factors like shading, water supply, temperature and soil conditions, which form part of the immediate environment of that particular tree. Clearly, ring counts and measurements of a single tree will not suffice for this purpose, although it has been found in some instances that a surprisingly small number of individuals will furnish reliable data on the past climate of a district. The period of the past which can be probed depends on the age of the trees which can be used. In the case of such long-lived plants as the Californian Big Trees or Wellingtonias, this period may exceed 3,000 years. In this work features of the wood other than the thickness of the growth ring may be valuable. Injury to the vascular cambium and young unlignified cells of the xylem by frost may result in the temporary formation of abnormal tissue revealed to the unaided eye as discoloured, tangentially running lines and microscopically by collapsed cells, excessive quantities of parenchyma and wide rays. Glock, Studhalter and Agerter (1960) regard such frost rings as more reliable guides to absolute dating, while more normal growth rings may be less reliable.

Conduction of water in the wood is limited to its outer layers. The more centrally situated wood is generally held to be non-functional as far as water movement is concerned, although it has been suggested that it acts as a reservoir from which, at certain times, water may be drawn by the peripheral layers of the wood. It is in the central part of the wood that materials like tannins, resins, colouring matters and so on tend to be deposited and frequently, as a result, this wood becomes darker than that at the periphery. The contrast is often marked: thus in walnut the purplish or grey-brown wood of the centre is quite distinct from the pale peripheral wood, and in some of the ebonies the outer wood is oatmeal coloured, the older wood being black or dark brown. The more central wood, which becomes coloured in this way, forms the heartwood; the younger, paler coloured wood is the sapwood. Some trees, like the spruces and most poplars, do not show this colour change, the wood remaining of a uniform hue throughout the trunk; such trees are referred to as sapwood trees. There is no functional difference between the older wood of such trees and that of heartwood trees; physiologically these sapwood trees possess heartwood, although its limits are not made visible by differences of colour.

In the heartwood, the parenchyma cells, both axial and ray, are, it is believed, generally dead—the heartwood containing no living cells (Frey-Wyssling and Bosshard, 1959; Fahn and Arnon, 1963). Neverthe-less, living parenchyma cells have been found in heartwood, which was presumed to be 70 years old, in Californian redwood (cf. p. 55), and further investigation may show that the heartwood does not always consist entirely of dead cells.

Histologically, heartwood and sapwood elements are identical. The only change which may take place in the transformation from sapwood to heartwood is that the vessels may become blocked with tyloses, a feature well shown by English oak and robinia, or with gummy material (cf. p. 36). Nevertheless, because of the deposition of extraneous materials in the walls and lumina of its elements, heartwood may be appreciably heavier than sapwood from the same tree.

The extent of the heartwood relative to the whole woody cylinder is generally fairly constant in any species, although it sometimes shows considerable variation, as in Western yellow pine (*Pinus ponderosa* Dougl.). The sapwood may be very narrow, e.g. in larch, sweet chestnut and robinia, and even limited to one or two of the youngest growth rings, but it may be wide, as in Turkey oak (*Quercus cerris* L.), the hickories and the maples. Sometimes the sapwood is so regular in thickness that it must be concluded that one growth ring of the sapwood is added to the heartwood each year, although whether heartwood

Fig. 29.—Sapwood and heartwood in *Gymnanthes lucida*. The sapwood is white and the heartwood is olive to dark brown and attractively marked (about natural size).

formation is, in fact, as regular as this is not certainly known. In other species the heartwood is less regular and the sapwood may vary considerably in thickness in different parts of a transverse section; sometimes the outline of the heartwood is convoluted so that there are alternating wider and narrower zones of sapwood around the section (Fig. 29). In some species the heartwood gradually merges into the sapwood and there is no clear-cut demarcation between the two.

In sapwood trees, and in trees with normally light-coloured heartwood, a definite heartwood may sometimes form. Thus European ash, in which heartwood and sapwood are not normally sharply defined, may develop a black or dark brown heartwood (false heartwood) the presence of which does not appear to affect the strength properties of the wood. How this happens is not known, but a very slight difference in the nature or amount of one or more of the extraneous substances normally present in the wood might be quite sufficient to bring about the development of colour, so that some quite minor differences in the metabolism of the tree might induce the development of such a heartwood. Sometimes development of colour in the older wood of a sapwood tree is due to the early stages of fungal infection. Thus, spruce wood, which normally undergoes no heartwood colour change, becomes a pale bluish-purple in the incipient stages of infection by *Fomes annosus* Fr. and reddish-brown when attacked by *Trametes pini* (Thore) Fr.

Sometimes patches of light-coloured wood, which look like sapwood, are found in the heartwood and the term included- or internal-sapwood is used to describe them. How this happens is not clear; it has been suggested that premature death of the parenchyma cells of a portion of the sapwood, caused, for example, by low temperatures, may prevent

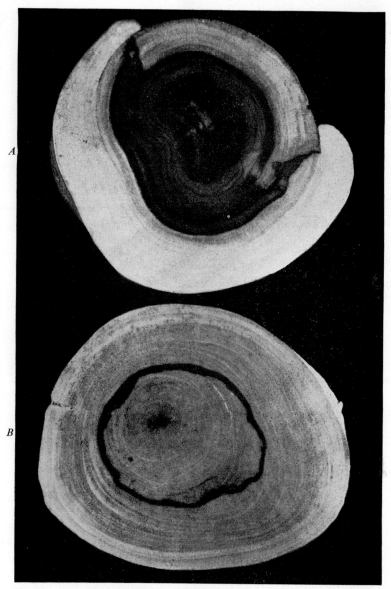

Fig. 30.—Irregular formation of heartwood. *A*. Lignum Vitae (*Guaiacum* sp.). This is a section from the bole of a tree which has been severely damaged, probably by the tearing away of a branch. The wounded area at the top had been partially covered with new tissue. Heartwood formation has proceeded more rapidly on the lower, sound side and the outer rings of heartwood on this side are sapwood in the region of the wound. *B*. In this section, also Lignum Vitae, the visible heartwood forms a very small and irregular zone round the pith and also a thin annular zone about midway between the pith and the periphery.

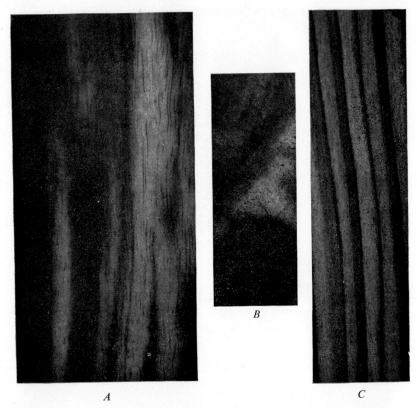

Fig. 31.—Included sapwood in species of Ebony (*Diospyros*). *A*. Marble wood, longitudinal surface; *B*. Marble wood, end-grain; in these, the included sapwood is irregular. *C*. Zebra wood, in which zones of sapwood and heartwood alternate.

such parts from being transformed into heartwood. On the other hand, there seems to be no reason why the colour change from sapwood to heartwood should always take place regularly. From what has just been said in reference to false heartwood, it is possible that slight chemical differences in different parts of the wood may account for included sapwood. Perhaps the most striking examples of variations in colour are seen in some of the ebonies, where patches of black and oatmeal-coloured wood alternate, sometimes regularly, so that the wood is striped (zebra wood) and sometimes irregularly, so that the wood looks rather like marble (marble wood) (Fig. 31).

Apparent heartwood may also develop, sporadically, in the sapwood. This wound heartwood is said to be a pathological development and to be caused when the living cells of the sapwood are injured, as in the region of wounds. Where wounds occur, degradation of the cell walls may take place and one of the resulting products is known as wound

Fig. 32.—Bark pockets. *A*. Deodar (*Cedrus deodara*); a small lenticular bark pocket (*b.p*) lies in the wood just below the bark (*b*) in which bark shells are conspicuous: the darker parts of this pocket are due to resin, the pale area is cork: this is a radial longitudinal surface and the rays show as small, horizontal streaks (about natural size). *B*. Cedar (*Cedrus* sp.); part of a transverse section of a trunk; three bark ingrowths (*i*) are shown, and two others in which the bark has been cut off from the exterior, forming bark pockets (*b.p*) (about ¼ natural size).

gum. The formation of wound heartwood may perhaps be due, in part at least, to wound gum.

In the tree trunk, of course, there are other tissues besides the wood. The centre is occupied by the pith, normally a very thin core of paren-chymatous cells. The pith may be distinctive: thus in oak it has, in cross-section, the shape of a five-rayed star, in beech it is triangular, in ash ellipsoidal and in teak squarish. In walnut the pith is septate, consisting of transverse plates of tissue (septa), separated by spaces.

It is usual to refer to all tissues outside the wood as bark, distinguish-ing between the soft and sometimes stringy inner bark (bast) and the corky outer bark (cork). An account of the structure and development of the bark is given in Chapter 3 (pp. 59–65) where some of its more outstanding morphological characteristics are also described.

Pockets of bark are sometimes found buried in the wood when a log is cut up. This seemingly improbable condition is brought about by the death of an area of vascular cambium. Clearly, wood cannot continue to be formed within this dead area, although it continues to be formed by the surrounding living cambium; thus gradually the dead cambium and the bark outside it become surrounded by newer wood. In time the adjacent living cambium extends laterally, and so reforms over the dead area; the continuity of the cambial sheath is thus restored. Wood can then be formed over the embedded bark, which subsequently becomes buried deeper and deeper in the wood as the trunk increases in girth (Fig. 32).

The young tree has a number of branches growing from its trunk, though in older trees these are often entirely absent from the lower part of the trunk. Thus in some tropical trees the first branches may be 80 feet (25m.) or more above ground level.

As the trunk of the young tree forms new layers of wood, the bases of any branches growing from it will gradually become embedded, forming knots. If the branches are living they, like the trunk, will undergo a seasonal increase in length and thickness, so that although their bases become embedded in the bole, their length and thickness can increase by the activity of their apical growing points and vascular cambia. If, as often happens, a branch dies, its more distal parts will probably become brittle or rotten, and will eventually break off; the remaining snag will finally become completely embedded in the trunk, forming a knot.

In a living branch the vascular cambium is continuous with that of the trunk and new wood is added as a continuous layer over both trunk and branch. Knot and surrounding wood are thus in organic continuity and when a board is cut out of this region the knot will be found to be tightly fixed in the wood. This is a live knot (Figs. 33, 34). In a dead branch there is, of course, no cambial activity and thus the knot formed when the basal part of a dead branch is engulfed by the enlarging trunk is not in organic continuity with the wood of the trunk. A dead branch may lose its bark, but if this remains it will also be enclosed with the wood and form part of the knot. These dead knots, therefore, are loose and may drop out of a plank. Sometimes pre- and post-mortem changes in the wood of a dead branch may lead to the formation of a copious quantity of resin and other materials, so that such a knot may become very resinous and sometimes extremely hard. The small black knots of spruce are of this type and may play havoc with hand tools when the wood is worked.

The knots or buried branches will lie within the trunk in the same position as the bases of the branches from which they were formed. Where the branches were more or less horizontal, a transverse section of

A

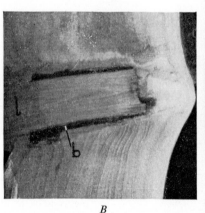

B

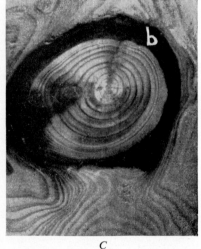

C

Fig. 33.—Knots. *A*. Cross-section of a trunk of Chile Pine (*Araucaria araucana*) showing five spike knots. *B*. Spike knot on a quarter-sawn surface of Spruce (*Picea* sp.); to the left the knot is a live knot (*l*), but farther out the branch died and appears to have been cut off some way from the trunk; this snag, with its bark (*b*), has been covered over and buried by the wood of the trunk, forming a dead knot. *C*. Round knot on a plain-sawn surface of Silver Fir (*Abies* sp.); this is a dead knot, surrounded by bark (*b*), the whole having become enclosed in the wood of the trunk. In both *B* and *C* note the distortion of the growth rings of the wood of the trunk in the region of the knot.

Fig. 34.—Spike knot in Elm (*Ulmus* sp.), seen in R.L.S. The branch which formed the knot had been carefully pruned off and has subsequently become enclosed in the wood of the bole. The distortion of the growth rings in the region of the knot is marked. Note that, although the branch had been carefully pruned, there is no continuity between its cut transverse surface and the enveloping wood of the trunk.

From a photograph by
Mr. B. A. Jay

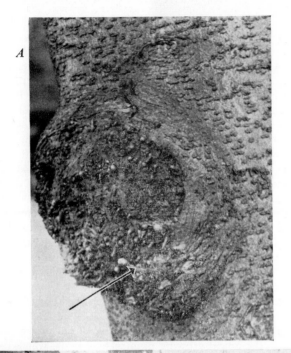

Fig. 35.—*A*. Burr in Red Horse Chestnut (*Aesculus carnea*). On this burr there are numerous buds, although only one (arrowed) has developed into a short branch: lenticels are well shown on the bark surrounding the burr. *B*. Burrs in Horse Chestnut (*Aesculus hippocastanum*): here numerous branches have arisen from the buds on the burrs; some of the new branches near the cut surfaces are shoots which have probably formed from adventitious buds in the region of the wound.

a log will show the knots cut longitudinally, while, if the branches were ascending, the knots will be cut through obliquely in such a section. In a radially cut surface of the trunk all the knots will be cut through longitudinally; such knots are known as spike-knots. A tangential surface will show knots cut through transversely if the branches were horizontal, or more or less obliquely if the branches were ascending. It is only on tangential surfaces that these round knots occur (Fig. 122 *B*).

The buds which were present on the stem or branches of the sapling tree, but which failed to develop into shoots, have yet to be considered. Such buds often grow very slowly, just keeping pace with the increasing girth of the stem or branch, so that they remain at its surface. They may continue thus for years until, for some reason, they develop into shoots—or die. Such buds, or the shoots into which they have developed, are termed epicormic. An epicormic bud was originally connected with the vascular system of its parent shoot by a vascular strand, and this connection must remain if the bud is to survive. Its vascular strand consequently lengthens year by year, although it does not increase appreciably in thickness. In a radial section of the parent member this strand will show as a very slim spike knot, while on a tangential surface it will be cut more or less transversely and form a very small round knot, usually referred to as a pin-knot.

Other buds may arise, irregularly as it were, and not as epicormic buds do from the apical growing point. These buds, which frequently arise on wounds, are called adventitious buds: where they are numerous, they may give rise to burrs. Damage to the trunk, causing a wound, may stimulate adventitious buds to grow into shoots. These adventitious buds do not, of course, have vascular strands extending to the centre of the trunk, although as the parent member increases in girth their proximal parts become embedded and form knots in the wood which has arisen subsequent to their initiation. Clusters of such small knots, or of those formed by epicormic branches, often associated with burrs, are frequently seen in the wood of yew and common elm. Again, according to the direction in which the wood has been cut, they will appear in prepared timber as clusters of spike- or pin-knots (Figs. 35, 132 *A–C*).

In good timber trees the knots are confined to the middle of the trunk, for as a result of natural crowding of the trees, or their controlled adjacent planting by the forester, the lower branches are shaded and so die at an early stage. The snags which are the remains of them gradually become wholly enclosed in the trunk, so that subsequent growth produces clean, knot-free timber. Thus the prime grades of timber are found in the outer part of the trunk. When a big log is converted into lumber the larger-sized timbers, for use as beams and bressummers (where the presence of knots, within limits, is relatively unimportant), are cut from the centre of the log, while the smaller sizes, in which knots might prove detrimental to the wood in use, are obtained from the outer parts.

CHAPTER 5

THE HISTOLOGY OF CONIFEROUS WOODS (SOFTWOODS)

A general account of the minute structure of wood has been given in Chapter 2. There are, however, considerable differences between the structure of coniferous woods (softwoods) and those derived from dicotyledonous trees (hardwoods) (cf. Figs. 13,14), so that it will be necessary to give a more detailed account of the histology of each of these principal types of wood.

Softwoods are of simpler structure than hardwoods. The greater part of the wood consists of tracheids, which are both water-conducting and supporting elements; axial (vertical) parenchyma is never abundant and is sometimes altogether absent; neither vessels nor fibres are present. In hardwoods, on the other hand, the axial elements include parenchyma, fibres, vessels and sometimes tracheids, together with a type of cell intermediate between fibre and tracheid, the fibre-tracheid; the wood is more complex in structure. Because they possess vessels (or pores), hardwoods are sometimes called porous woods and softwoods non-porous woods; pored and non-pored are preferable terms, which avoid any implication that dicotyledonous woods are, necessarily, more porous, physically, than softwoods.

The axial (vertical) tracheids of softwoods are often very long: extreme lengths of nearly 11 mm. are recorded for hoop pine (*Araucaria cunninghamii* Ait.), while lengths of under a millimetre are uncommon: transverse measurements range between 15 and 80 μ (0·015–0·080 mm.). Hence the axial tracheid is a very tenuous structure indeed, perhaps 100 or more times longer than broad. Seen in radial section, it usually has rather rounded ends, while in tangential section the ends appear more pointed: thus, considered in three dimensions, the ends are approximately wedge-shaped. In transverse section, these tracheids are usually square or polygonal and the thickness of the wall varies considerably, depending largely on its position in the growth ring. Tracheids of the early wood are often relatively large, thin-walled and somewhat hexagonal in outline, and those of contiguous radial rows tend to alternate. Towards the end of the growth increment the tracheids are commonly rectangular and often radially flattened, and those of adjacent radial rows are opposite to one another (cf. Californian redwood, Fig. 158 *B*). In some softwoods, like Douglas fir and European larch, this change in wall thickness is very sudden, but the transition may be more gradual, as in the spruces (Fig. 152). Further, the proportion of the growth ring occupied by thick-walled tracheids is very small in some softwoods, e.g. pencil cedars (*Juniperus*) and false cypresses (*Chamaecyparis*); in others, like Douglas fir, it may be considerable. In a few

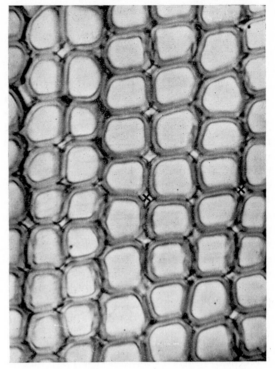

Fig. 36.—Black Juniper (*Juniperus wallichiana*); T.S. (× 530), showing intercellular
spaces (×) between axial tracheids.

conifers, e.g. pencil cedar (*Juniperus virginiana* L.) and hoop pine, the
tracheids tend to be somewhat rounded in section and thus do not fit
closely together at all points, so that intercellular spaces are left between
them (Fig. 36); but in nearly all softwoods the tracheids fit closely and

---

Fig. 37.—Bordered pits in axial tracheids of coniferous wood. *A–C*. Sitka Spruce
(*Picea sitchensis*). *A*. Pit-pairs in surface view (from R.L.S.). *B*. Pit-pair in section
(from T.S.); the pit apertures are not distinct because they are included in the thickness of the section and hence covered by wall material above and below; the torus
between the two pits is clearly shown. *C*. Pit-pairs in section (from T.L.S.); some pit
apertures distinct, others blocked by tori (all × 425). *D*. Deodar (*Cedrus deodara*);
pit-pairs in section (from T.L.S.), showing tori (× 295). *E*. Douglas Fir (*Pseudotsuga
taxifolia*); pit-pairs in section (from T.L.S.); in each pair one of the apertures is
blocked by the torus (× 425). *F*. Western Red Cedar (*Thuja plicata*); pit-pairs in
surface view (from R.L.S.); the dark horizontal lines between some of the pits are
the bars of Sanio or crassulae; in some pits three concentric rings are visible, the
innermost of which is the pit aperture, the next the margin of the torus and the outermost the border, i.e. the outer boundary of the pit membrane (× 295). *G*. Swamp
Cypress (*Taxodium distichum*); pit-pairs in surface view (from T.L.S.); these pits
are in an early wood tracheid and are smaller than those which occur on the radial
walls; part of a ray is visible in the top left-hand corner (× 425).

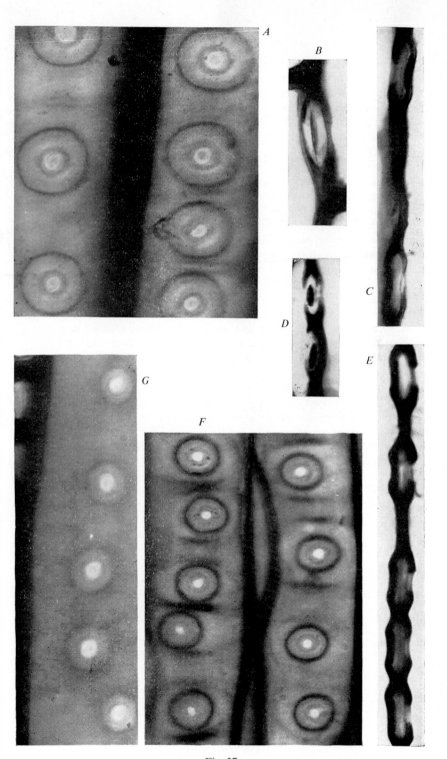

Fig. 37

intercellular spaces are not seen, except in that type of wood known as compression wood (see Chapter 9).

The axial tracheids originate from fusiform initials of the vascular cambium, and during differentiation increase considerably in radial diameter but not tangentially. Consequently they retain their alignment with the cambium cells from which they are derived. For this reason the tracheids in softwoods, seen in transverse section, tend to be in rather regular radial files.

Pits are present in the axial tracheids and are, of course, of the bordered type. They are very characteristic structures and their relatively large size and the ease with which they may be examined have led to their adoption, in some botanical textbooks, as the "typical bordered pit". They are far from typical, except of conifers: the bordered pit in hardwoods is usually much smaller and often rather simpler in structure.

In conifer tracheids the bordered pit is usually circular in surface view, with a small, circular mouth or aperture. The pit membrane is not of equal thickness throughout, for a circular thickened area occupies the centre and is surrounded by a thinner zone. The thicker region is the torus; it is bi-convex in section and usually of somewhat greater diameter than the pit aperture: the thin peripheral zone, often minutely perforated, is known as the annulus. In face view the pit may appear as three concentric rings, for the boundary of the torus may show as a third ring between mouth and border (Fig. 37). The bordered pits of some hardwoods are said to possess a torus, but it is certainly far less conspicuous than that of softwoods, partly, no doubt, by reason of the smaller size of the pits. In the cedars (*Cedrus*) the margin of the torus is indented or scalloped and in face view this structure has almost the appearance of a small circular saw (Figs. 38 *A* and 100 *A*, *B*). In *Tsuga* more or less radial bands often run from the torus to the pit border (Fig. 38 *B*).

Tori in softwood pits vary considerably in thickness; in *Thuja plicata*, at least, there is no torus. The pit membrane, with its torus, may be centrally placed between the borders of a pit-pair, but sometimes it is displaced to one side so that the torus blocks one of the pit apertures (Fig. 37 *B* and *E*). The pit is then said to be aspirated.

Fig. 38.—Bordered pits in axial tracheids of coniferous wood. *A*. Cedar of Lebanon (*Cedrus libani*); pits in surface view showing uniseriate and biseriate arrangement, the latter both alternate and opposite; pits show scalloped torus margins; R.L.S. (× 860). *B*. Western Hemlock (*Tsuga heterophylla*); pits in surface view showing the characteristic irregular margin of the tori; R.L.S. (× 860). *C*. Californian Redwood (*Sequoia sempervirens*); opposite biseriate pitting; each set of pits has formed in a primary pit-field and is separated from its upper and lower neighbours by bars of Sanio or crassulae; R.L.S. (× 295). *D*. Swamp Cypress (*Taxodium distichum*); multiseriate pitting; R.L.S. (× 330). *E*. Queensland Kauri (*Agathis palmerstonii*); alternate biseriate pitting, the pits having slit-like apertures; R.L.S. (× 330). *F*. Parana Pine (*Araucaria angustifolia*); multiseriate alternate pitting; the pit borders are somewhat hexagonal in outline; R.L.S. (× 330).

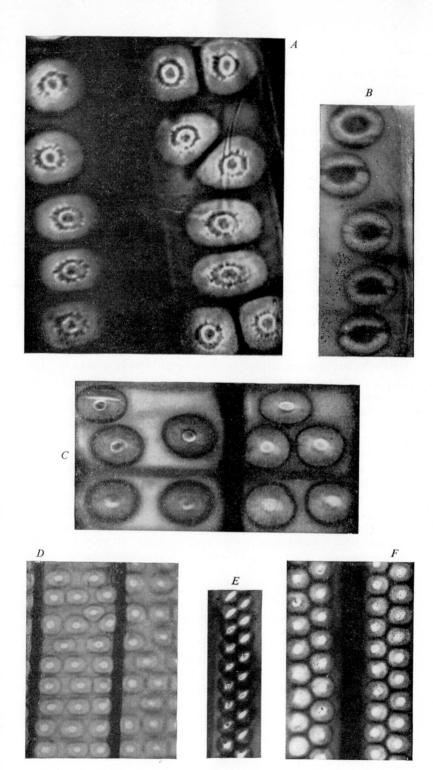

Fig. 38

In axial tracheids the bordered pits occur principally on the radial walls. Their diameter may be nearly as great as the radial diameter of the tracheid, so that a pit occupies almost the whole width of the radial wall, as is often seen in the true pines (Fig. 13 *B*); here, of course, the pits are in a single axial row (uniseriate). In some woods (e.g. Western red cedar) the pits are relatively smaller (Fig. 37 *F*), with a diameter appreciably less than that of the tracheid in which they occur. Such smaller pits may occur in two rows, either sporadically or fairly consistently: biseriate pitting is frequently seen in Californian redwood (Fig. 38 *C*), and in swamp cypress (*Taxodium distichum* (L.) Rich.) three rows of pits are not uncommon and four rows may sometimes be seen (Fig. 38 *D*).

Where multiseriate pitting occurs in conifer wood, the arrangement of the pits is nearly always opposite, but in *Agathis* and *Araucaria* the alternate arrangement is the rule and opposite pitting is rarely seen (Fig. 38 *E, F*). In these two genera the pits may be so crowded that their normally circular outlines become somewhat flattened and the pit borders may appear more or less hexagonal in surface view. Alternate pitting may be seen in the cedars (Fig. 38 *A*), but it is not frequent.

Bordered pits are not entirely confined to the radial walls of the axial tracheids, but their occurrence on the tangential walls is often sporadic, tending to be confined to tracheids of the outer part of the growth ring, and sometimes to the first few rows of tracheids in the ring. In some softwoods, for example, Californian redwood and swamp cypress, pits are frequent on the tangential walls of the axial tracheids (Fig. 37 *G*). Pits on tangential walls of axial tracheids are usually smaller than those on the radial walls of the same cells.

Although the pit aperture is commonly circular in outline, it may sometimes be elliptical and then it commonly happens that the long axes of the apertures of the two members of a pit-pair lie at a fairly constant angle to one another: when seen in face view slightly out of focus (i.e. when the plane of focus is that of the pit membrane), the tracheid then appears to have a number of crosses on its walls, formed by the apertures of pit-pairs. This feature is sometimes said to be diagnostic for the araucarian type of wood, but it may be found in genera other than *Agathis* and *Araucaria* and, moreover, it does not invariably occur in wood of these two genera.

Certain irregularities in wall thickness, other than pitting, may occur in softwood tracheids. In two well-known timbers, Douglas fir and yew, fine spiral thickening is present (Fig. 39 *A, B*). In Douglas fir spiral thickening is seen best in the tracheids of the early wood, and is less well developed, or even absent, in those of the late wood, while in yew all the tracheids show it. Spiral thickening is also a regular feature of the axial tracheids in *Torreya* and *Cephalotaxus*, genera allied to the yews, while in some spruces and larches it may be found occasionally, chiefly in the late wood.

In most of the cypress pines (*Callitris*) localised thickening of the secondary wall occurs on the radial walls in the form of transverse bars which overhang the bordered pits (Fig. 39 *C, D*). This type of thickening, which is known as callitroid thickening, appears to be restricted almost entirely to species of *Callitris*, but it has been noted occasionally in woods of one or two other genera.

Of entirely different origin from callitroid thickening are the transverse bars known as bars of Sanio, or, more correctly, as rims of Sanio, which are found exclusively on the radial walls of the axial tracheids (Figs. 37 *F*, 38 *C*). They are formed by a localised thickening of the middle lamella and primary wall in the neighbourhood of the pits Because there has been some confusion in the use of the term "bars of Sanio", the structures under discussion are now often referred to as crassulae. They are of frequent occurrence in softwoods (except in *Agathis* and *Araucaria*) and may form a sort of boundary, not only to single pits, but to a group of two or more which have developed in one primary pit-field.

It is also desirable to draw attention here to a feature which is sometimes seen in softwood tracheids but which can scarcely be considered as a structural feature. This is the spiral cracking or checking, which is found especially in thick-walled tracheids (Fig. 39 *E*). These cracks occur in a regular series, and are probably not present in the living tree, but arise during drying of the wood (but cf. compression wood, p. 216). While such checking is fairly distinctive, it is easily confused, on superficial examination, with spiral thickening. Checking of this sort is often associated with the bordered pits, and in a radial section showing it the pit aperture often appears to be greatly extended as an oblique slit in the wall However, the true circular aperture occupies the centre of this slit-like check, which passes through it. In this checking the pit appears to constitute a point of weakness in the wall.

Radially aligned bars, termed trabeculae, which pass across the lumina of axial tracheids, occur sporadically in coniferous wood. Usually a line of these trabeculae occurs, passing through a number of tracheids (Fig. 41). Trabeculae appear to develop as thin threads, which become coated with secondary-wall material. They do not seem to have any function It has been suggested (McElhanney *et al.*, 1935) that the original "thin thread" is a fungus hypha, formed in a fusiform initial and perpetuated in its derivatives, on which secondary-wall material is deposited. Such trabeculae are commonly cylindrical, and hollow, as might be expected if they are formed in the manner suggested. There is some evidence in favour of this suggestion but, at the same time, if this is the true explanation, the undeviating radial horizontal direction of the hypha is very striking.

Record (1934) has pointed out that the axial tracheids of the late wood of many conifers are to be identified with fibre-tracheids (cf. p. 34) rather than tracheids. He bases this view on the type of bordered

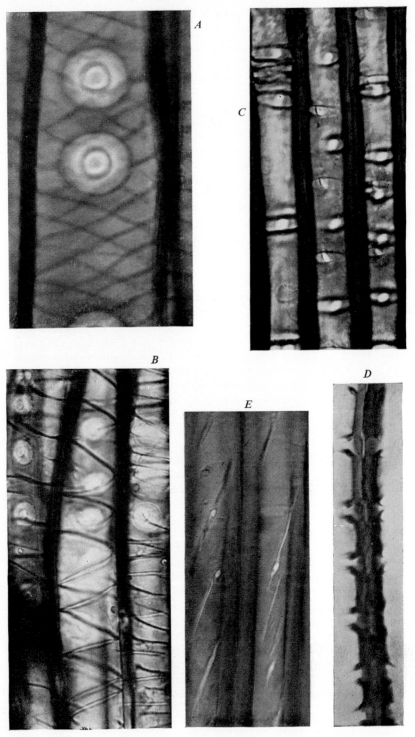

Fig. 39

Fig. 39 (*opposite*).—Wall features in axial tracheids of coniferous wood. *A.* Douglas Fir (*Pseudotsuga taxifolia*); spiral thickening on wall of axial tracheid; R.L.S. (× 425). *B.* Yew (*Taxus baccata*); spiral thickening on walls of axial tracheids; R.L.S. (× 295). *C* and *D.* White Cypress Pine (*Callitris glauca*); axial tracheids showing callitroid thickening i.e. bars of thickening on inner surface of wall; in *C* (R.L.S.) these are seen in surface view, in *D* (T.L.S.) in section (× 530). *E.* Californian Redwood; (*Sequoia sempervirens*) oblique cracks (checking) in walls of axial tracheids (× 295).

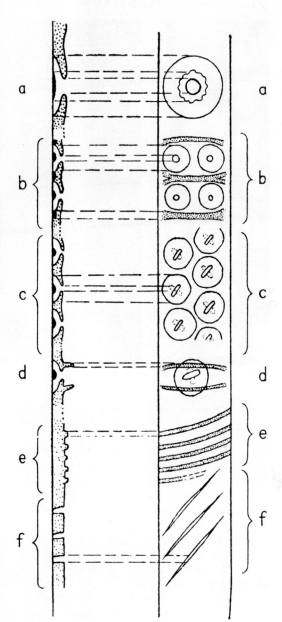

Fig. 40 (*right*).—Diagram of wall features of axial tracheids of coniferous wood. On the left, one wall of a tracheid is shown in tangential longitudinal section and on the right, a tracheid wall in surface view (radial longitudinal face). Sectional and surface views of the same feature are connected by broken lines. *a*, a large bordered pit with scalloped torus: *b*, biseriate pitting (opposite) and bars of Sanio or crassulae: *c*, biseriate pitting (alternate); pits with elongated apertures; the aperture of the other member of each pit-pair is shown by a dotted line: *d*, callitroid thickening: *e*, spiral thickening: *f*, checking of wall.

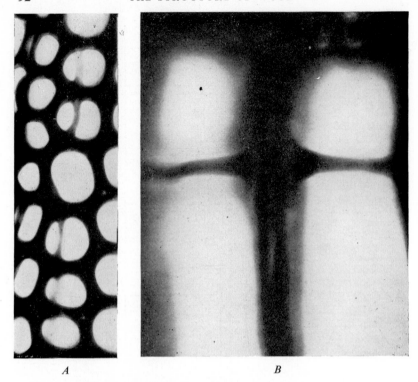

Fig. 41.—Trabeculae in White Cypress Pine (*Callitris glauca*). *A*. The trabeculae show as rather pale bars or rods in several of the tracheids; T.S. (× 430). *B*. The trabeculae are the radial rods passing across each tracheid; R.L.S. (× 860).

pit often found in these cells, in which the aperture is more or less slit-like and is sometimes extended beyond the border; on the occurrence of these pits on the tangential as well as on the radial walls; and on the gradually tapering and pointed ends of the cells, as compared with the rounded ends commonly found in the axial tracheids of softwoods.

Two other types of tracheid occur in coniferous wood, although unlike the axial tracheid, neither type is of regular occurrence. Strand tracheids are formed from fusiform initials of the cambium, but these cells, by transverse septation, each form several such tracheids. Strand tracheids (Fig. 42) resemble typical parenchyma cells in form, being more or less brick-shaped, but their walls possess bordered pits; hence these cells are readily distinguished from parenchyma cells. Strand tracheids are found associated with vertical resin canals and also with wounds and are sometimes mixed with parenchyma cells (mixed strands). in a few woods, like Douglas fir and the larches, strand tracheids sometimes occur in the outer limits of the growth rings.

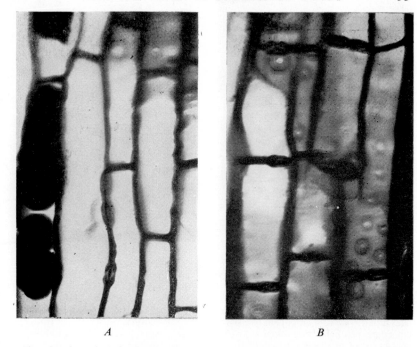

A   B

Fig. 42.—Strand tracheids in *Sequoia sempervirens* in R.L.S. In *A*, bordered pits in section are well shown in the axial walls between the lower central tracheid and the one to its left; on the extreme left is part of an axial parenchyma strand, the cells containing resin. In *B*, bordered pits (in section) can be seen on the end walls of the strand tracheids, while on the right, bordered pits are seen in surface view (both × 440).

Ray tracheids (Fig 43), which are developed, of course, from ray initials of the vascular cambium, are regularly present in the rays of *Pinus, Picea, Larix, Pseudotsuga, Cedrus, Tsuga* and yellow cedar (*Chamaecyparis nootkatensis* (Lamb.) Spach.), and are found occasionally in other genera such as *Abies, Sequoia* and *Thuja*. Like strand tracheids, ray tracheids are distinguished from parenchyma cells by their bordered pits, which may occur on all walls of the cells Unlike axial tracheids, ray tracheids have their longest axes lying in the radial plane of the wood and their tangential walls may be somewhat obliquely placed.

Ray tracheids often form the upper and lower marginal cells of the rays and there may be more than one row present; they may sometimes be interspersed among the ray parenchyma or they may constitute an entire ray, a feature sometimes seen in the pines, especially in juvenile wood In yellow cedar, ray tracheids and ray parenchyma are commonly segregated, a ray consisting wholly of one or the other type of cell.

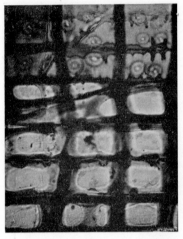

A   *B*

Fig. 43.—*A*. Part of a ray of Scots Pine (*Pinus sylvestris*) in R.L.S. Two rows of ray tracheids are seen along the top of the ray; in the upper row, two of the bordered pits have been outlined in black; in the lower of the two rows the peg-like dentations of the horizontal walls are seen. The ray parenchyma cells contain large window-like pits, usually one to a cross-field (a cross-field has been outlined in white and two of the simple pits have been outlined in black) (× abt. 190). *B*. A small part of a ray of Scots Pine in R.L.S., showing parts of two rows of dentate ray tracheids with bordered pits (top) and parts of four rows of ray parenchyma with large, simple pits; each of these, in most instances, occupies the whole of a cross-field (× 400).

The bordered pits of the ray tracheids are smaller than those of the axial tracheids Sometimes, in the spruces, minute peg-like outgrowths of the horizontal and end walls of the ray tracheids project into the lumina, especially in the late wood; such dentate tracheids may also be found in larch, while they are also characteristic of some of the pines. Of the commercially important species of pine, those with their leaves in bundles of five—the soft pines—exemplified by sugar pine (*Pinus lambertiana* Dougl.) and yellow pine (*P. strobus* L.), have smooth walls in their ray tracheids, while nearly all the two- and three-needle pines have ray tracheids with well-developed dentations In some of the hard pines like the longleaf pine (*P. palustris* Mill.), these teeth are very strongly developed, and those from the upper and lower walls of the cell may meet, forming reticulate ray tracheids. The ray tracheids of Douglas fir may possess spiral thickening, and this feature has also been observed in some of the spruces.

Softwoods may possess both axial and radial parenchyma, the latter, the parenchyma of the rays, being present invariably. Axial and radial parenchyma may line resin cavities, but consideration of these cells (epithelial cells) will be deferred until resin is dealt with.

Axial parenchyma is never as abundant in softwoods as in some hardwoods. Phillips (1948) calls parenchyma abundant when there are "five or more cells per sq. mm. of transverse section in that portion of the ring containing most parenchyma." It is usually found in strands, the cells of which are generally conspicuous by reason of their dark-coloured contents. It is rare in the pines and other members of the Pinaceae, and is absent in the yews and other Taxaceae and in *Agathis* and *Araucaria*. In *Sequoia*, *Taxodium* and other members of the Taxodiaceae, and in the Cupressaceae (e.g. *Cupressus*, *Thuja*) axial parenchyma is relatively abundant (Fig. 49). The cells are often scattered, but they may occur in concentric bands (zonate arrangement), and in some members of the Pinaceae they may occupy the outer margin of the growth ring. The pitting in the walls of these cells is, of course, simple. The pits sometimes

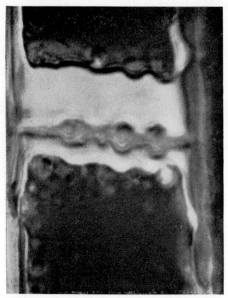

Fig. 44.—Sugi (*Cryptomeria japonica*); nodular end wall between two cells of axial parenchyma. The dark masses in the two cells are resin (× 1510).

give the end walls a beaded appearance (nodular end walls), and a similar appearance may be produced by localised thickening of the primary wall and not by real pitting (Fig. 44).

The softwood ray is usually wholly parenchymatous; the exceptions to this generalisation, which happen to occur in some of the commonest and most important commercial softwoods, have already been mentioned (p. 93). The detailed morphology of these ray parenchyma cells is varied, and in the identification of wood use must be made of apparently trivial details, like the location of the pits, the thickness of the horizontal and end walls, the presence or absence of nodular end walls and other minor features: for fuller details Phillips' (1948) paper should be consulted.

There is considerable variation in the pits which occur on the radial walls of the ray parenchyma, i.e. pits which form pit-pairs with the pits of the contiguous axial tracheids, and these pits, and their arrangement, are of great value in the identification of softwoods. For this purpose it is not the arrangement of the pits over the radial wall as a whole to which attention is paid, but their distribution in a cross-field, a cross-field being that area of a radial section bounded by the upper and lower horizontal walls of a ray parenchyma cell and the walls of an axial tracheid (Fig. 43 *A*). Moreover, it is to the pits in the early wood that attention is directed.

Phillips (1948) classifies these pits into five types (Fig. 45):—

1. *Fenestriform:* large simple, or almost simple, window-like pits which occupy most of the cross-field. Such pits are found in the two-needle and five-needle pines, in *Dacrydium, Phyllocladus* and matai (*Podocarpus spicatus* R.Br.).
2. *Pinoid:* fairly small pits, simple, or at most, very narrowly bordered, and variable in shape. Such pits are found in some of the pines, e.g. the pitch pines.
3. *Piceoid:* small bordered pits with a narrow, often somewhat extended aperture. Pits of this type are found in spruces (*Picea*), larches (*Larix*) and Douglas fir (*Pseudotsuga*) and in certain other genera or species.
4. *Cupressoid:* small bordered, or partially bordered pits with a fairly elliptical, wide aperture which is included, but which may extend to the border along its long axis. Examples of genera with pits of this type are *Cupressus, Taxus* and *Araucaria*.
5. *Taxodioid:* small pits which superficially may resemble the cupressoid or pinoid type: here, however, the aperture is larger than the border in most parts of the pit, i.e. the walls slope outwards to the aperture, not inwards as in the cupressoid type. Taxodioid pits are found, among other genera, in *Taxodium, Sequoia, Cedrus* and *Thuja*.

Some of these pits have been referred to as bordered and it may well be objected that great stress has already been laid on the rule that pits in parenchyma cells are simple. The exception, as has been mentioned, occurs when a parenchyma cell abuts on to a tracheid or vessel, as happens here. In such a position both members of a pit-pair may be either bordered, or simple, or the pair may be half-bordered.

Epithelial parenchyma is most conveniently considered in connection with resin, to which attention may now be given. It has already been pointed out (pp. 46, 48) that the term resin is used for any dark, gummy or resinous substance found in softwoods, whatever its chemical nature, and it is in this loose sense that the term is used here; no attempt is made to differentiate between the different sorts of material, superficially of this type, that occur in the conifers.

Resin occurs in most softwoods in cells, but in some well-known genera it is found in special cavities. It may also occur as a result of injury to the tree, in which instance it will, of course, be found sporadically, and not constantly, in the species.

Intracellular resin may be found in the axial tracheids but it does not occur in the ray tracheids. It is commonly found in parenchyma cells,

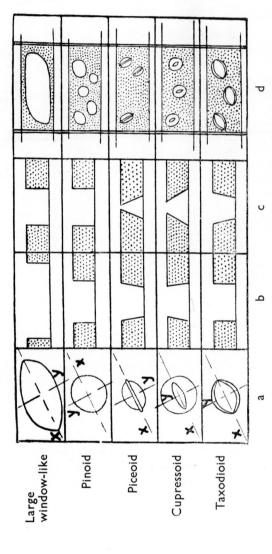

Fig. 45.—Diagrammatic representations of pitting on radial walls of ray parenchyma cells in coniferous wood. Column *a*, pits in surface view; column *b*, pits in section, cut along the axis marked *x* in column *a*; column *c*, pits in section, cut along the axis marked *y* in column *a*; column *d*, pits as seen in surface view in a cross-field (R.L.S.); the double vertical lines in *d* are the walls of an axial tracheid. N.B.—The pinoid pit may be slightly or partially bordered.

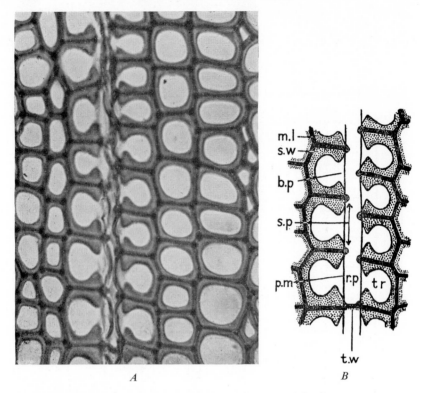

A   *B*

Fig. 46.—*A*. T.S. Scots Pine (*Pinus sylvestris*); just to the left of centre a ray runs through the section and the walls of the axial tracheids adjoining it appear to be incomplete; the gap in each is a bordered pit, one of a pit-pair, of which a large, eye-shaped pit of the ray parenchyma cell forms the other member; the separating pit membrane curves into the ray parenchyma (× 370). *B* is a diagrammatic representation of the lower part of this ray and the contiguous axial tracheids. *b.p.*, bordered pit; *m.l.*, middle lamella and primary wall; *p.m.*, pit membrane; *r.p.*, ray parenchyma cell; *s.p.*, simple (large, eye-shaped) pit; *s.w.*, secondary wall; *tr.*, axial tracheid; *t.w.*, tangential wall of ray cell.

which might be expected, for resin can only be produced by living cells and the parenchyma cells are the only living cells of the wood. It does not necessarily follow, however, that resin is wholly produced by these wood parenchyma cells, for it is conceivable that the resin, or some precursor of it, might be produced elsewhere and only deposited in the wood parenchyma cells.

Resin occurs in the axial tracheids in woods of several softwood genera, where it may appear as lumps on the walls, although it often occurs as transverse, biconcave discs known as resin plates. These plates, from a superficial examination, might easily be confused with end walls, or, in a radial section, with trabeculae. A transverse section

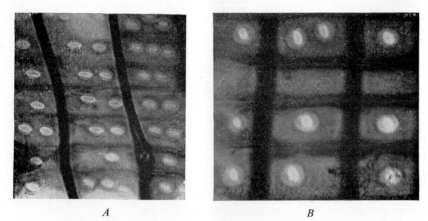

A   B

Fig. 47.—Pitting in ray parenchyma: *A*. Californian Redwood (*Sequoia semper-virens*); R.L.S. of a small part of a ray (× 330); one or two taxodioid pits occupy each cross-field. *B*. Yellow Cedar (*Chamaecyparis nootkatensis*); R.L.S. of a small part of a ray (× 860); one or two cupressoid pits occupy each cross-field.

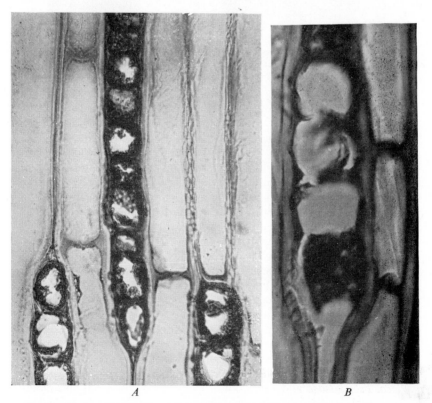

A   B

Fig. 48.—Resin plugs in New Zealand Kauri (*Agathis australis*). In *A* there are three plugs, looking like transverse walls, in the axial tracheids, one on each side of the central ray and one immediately above the right-hand ray. In *B* there are two resin plugs in the tracheid immediately to the right of the ray. Resin is also seen in the ray cells. Both T.L.S. (*A* × 370, *B* × 530).

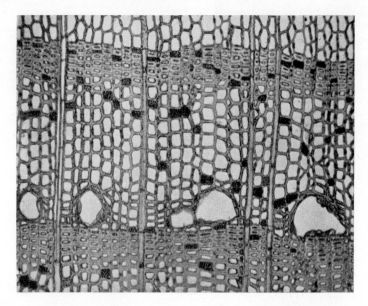

Fig. 49.—Californian Redwood (*Sequoia sempervirens*); T.S. showing traumatic resin ducts in the early wood of a growth ring and numerous axial parenchyma cells containing dark resinous contents (resin cells) (× 70).

cut through one of these resin plates may of course pass through its median plane, or near its upper or lower boundary. If the former, the tracheid will appear in the section to be full of resin: if the latter, its lumen will seem to have a resinous lining. Tracheids which contain resin are distinguished by the name resinous tracheids (Fig. 48); such tracheids are characteristic of the genera *Agathis* and *Araucaria*, where they are found in the vicinity of the rays.

The ray parenchyma cells of softwoods often contain dark-coloured resin, which may occur in discrete masses on the walls or, alternatively, may line the lumen of the cell (Fig. 161 *A*). Resin is also commonly found in the axial parenchyma cells, which, with their dark contents, are a prominent feature of some coniferous woods, like *Sequoia* (Figs. 42 *A*, 49). For this reason axial parenchyma cells are often termed resin cells. It is important to appreciate, however, that these axial parenchyma cells do not invariably contain resin.

Intercellular resin occurs, as a normal feature of the wood, in special schizogenous ducts known as resin canals or resin ducts, which run axially between the axial tracheids and radially in the rays. Resin ducts (Figs. 13 *A*, 50) are found in four important commercial genera, *Pinus*, *Picea*, *Pseudotsuga* and *Larix*, all of which have both axial and radial resin canals. In the Eastern Asiatic genus *Keeteleria*, only the axial ones occur and it is not certain that even these are a constant feature of the

Fig. 50.—Radial longitudinal section of Scots Pine (*Pinus sylvestris*) containing both axial and radial resin canals. The large axial canal is towards the right and in its lower part some of its epithelial cells may be seen. Only a very small piece of the radial canal is visible, immediately to the left of the axial canal, but its epithelium can be seen, approximately in the middle of the ray, on the left-hand side of the figure (× 70).

wood. Seen in transverse section, the axial canals are usually more or less circular and usually occur singly, although in Douglas fir they are not uncommonly found in pairs. Radial resin canals are more or less circular in cross-section in the pines, oval in the spruces and larches, and either round or somewhat angular in Douglas fir. The epithelial cells which line the canals remain thin-walled in the pines, and are often not distinct in a section, either because of damage in section cutting or because of their collapse. In *Picea*, *Pseudotsuga* and *Larix* the epithelial cells become thick-walled, although in the sapwood some thin-walled cells may be found which are, it may be presumed, the ones which are actively secreting resin into the canal (Figs. 51, 52).

A resin canal forms from a parenchymatous group of cells, derived from cambial initials. These cells are formed, as concerns the axial canals, from derivatives of the fusiform initials which divide up into strands in the same manner as when axial parenchyma is produced. Sooner or later some of the middle lamellae between the centrally placed cells disappear and the contiguous cells enlarge and separate, leaving the resin canal in their midst. The radial resin canals form in a similar way, their epithelia being produced by ray parenchyma and thus, ultimately, from the ray initials of the vascular cambium.

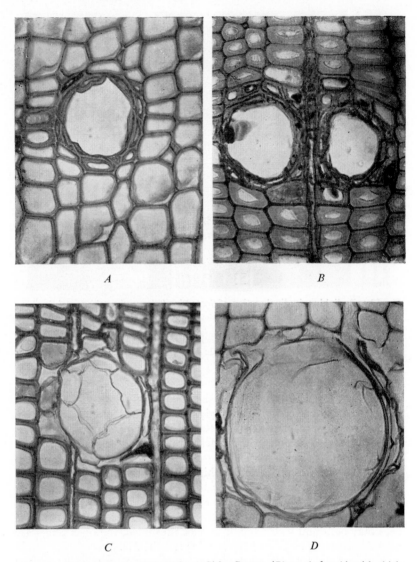

A   B

C   D

Fig. 51.—Axial resin canals in T.S. *A*. Sitka Spruce (*Picea sitchensis*) with thick-walled epithelial cells. *B*. Douglas Fir (*Pseudotsuga taxifolia*) with thick-walled epithelial cells; the paired canals, as seen in the figure, are characteristic of Douglas Fir, although its axial canals are not invariably paired. *C*. Scots Pine (*Pinus sylvestris*) with thin-walled epithelial cells. *D*. Yellow Pine (*Pinus strobus*); the thin-walled epithelial cells have collapsed; only remnants of them are to be seen. (*A*, *B* and *C* × 245, *D* × 220.)

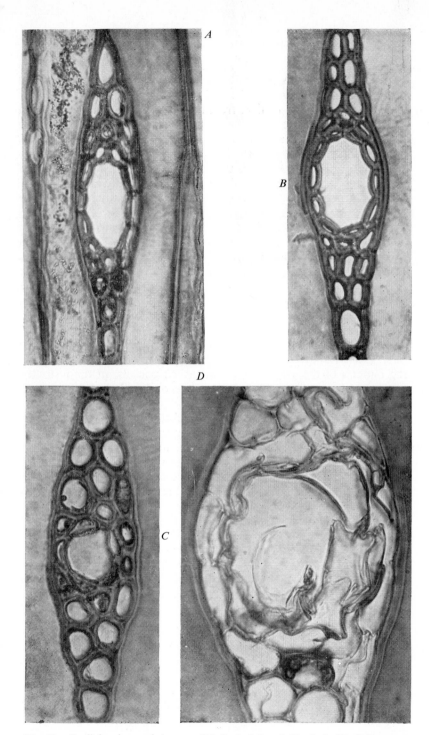

Fig. 52.—Radial resin canals in rays; T.L.S. *A.* A Larch (*Larix lyalii*). *B.* European Spruce (*Picea abies*). *C.* Douglas Fir (*Pseudotsuga taxifolia*). In *A, B* and *C* the epithelial cells are thick-walled and retain their shape. *D.* Yellow Pine (*Pinus strobus*); the epithelial cells are thin-walled and most of them have collapsed (all × 580).

H

Resin canals which appear sporadically in softwoods are thought to be due to injury and are consequently referred to as traumatic. Axial resin canals of this type tend to be close together in tangential lines (Fig. 49) and are thus distinct from the normal canals: they also tend to vary in size. Apart from their occurrence in softwoods possessing normal canals, they are known in *Cedrus*, *Sequoia*, *Abies* and *Tsuga*. Such traumatic axial ducts are often short and cyst-like: hence the term resin cysts which is sometimes used to describe them. Radial ducts of traumatic origin are found in the rays and are usually immediately to be distinguished from the normal radial ducts by reason of their large size.

Resin canals may become filled with tylosis-like structures, which because they occur in a canal (i.e. in an intercellular space and not in a vessel), are sometimes known by the special term "tylosoids" (Fig. 11 E). Tylosoids may occasionally become thick-walled and sclerotic.

Where splits or shakes occur in the living coniferous tree, these cavities often become repositories for resin in a solid or liquid form. Such cavities are referred to as pitch pockets (Fig. 53). Pitch pockets may be large, it being recorded that they have yielded as much as 40 gallons of resin in Douglas fir. Eades (1932) differentiates between pitch seams or pitch shakes, which are openings in the grain following the outlines of the growth rings, and pitch pockets, in the restricted sense, which are larger cavities or more or less lens-shaped cracks crossing the growth rings.

The causes of the formation of pitch pockets are not fully understood. They are, undoubtedly, often due to injury and hence must be regarded as traumatic structures. Forsaith (1926), however, indicates that at times they are really very large schizogenous resin cysts, formed in the same manner as resin canals, except that the vascular cambium forms very much more parenchyma than in the production of a normal axial resin canal.

In yew the wood normally is not only devoid of resin structures of any sort, but contains no resin.

The rays of conifers (Figs. 155, 160) do not show as much variety of shape as do those of dicotyledonous woods. As seen in tangential longitudinal section they are usually uniseriate, although individual rays may be biseriate in part (e.g. in *Taxus*, *Abies*, *Sequoia*), while wholly biseriate rays of fusiform outline have been recorded in Californian redwood, Monterey cypress (*Cupressus macrocarpa* Gord.) and in one or two other softwoods.

Some species have a proportion of tall rays (exceeding a height of thirty cells), examples being silver fir (*Abies alba* Mill.), and species of *Podocarpus*. Again, in some softwoods there appear to be no high rays; Phillips (1948) records sugi (*Cryptomeria japonica* (L.f.) D.Don.) and southern white cedar (*Chamaecyparis thyoides* (L.) B.S.P.) as among species in which the rays are rarely more than fifteen cells high, while

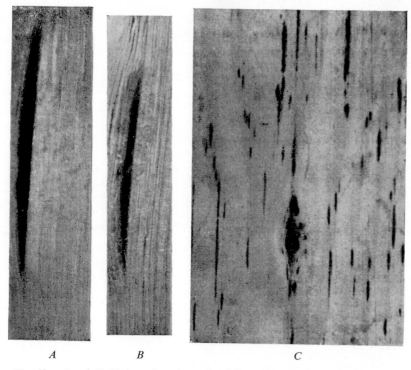

A   B   C

Fig. 53.—*A* and *B*. Pitch pockets in a pine, ? Scots Pine (*Pinus sylvestris*), a little under natural size; the surfaces are almost radial. *C*. Resin canals in Western White Pine (*Pinus monticola*), tangential longitudinal surface, about natural size; the resin canals are not as large as the dark streaks might suggest, as these are produced by resin oozing out of the canals; the round, dark area near the bottom, almost in the centre line, is a small round knot.

in the junipers the rays are conspicuously low. The general impression gained by an experienced observer from inspection of a tangential section of a softwood gives a much better idea of the height of the rays than an inadequate numerical treatment. Thus, in deodar cedar (*Cedrus deodara* (Roxb.) Loud.) and *Abies alba* Mill. the rays, in general, appear high, although no difficulty will arise in discovering rays only two cells high. Similarly, the rays of Douglas fir look low, as do those of Californian redwood; yet in the latter species rays as many as forty cells high may be found, although on an average the height varies between ten and fifteen cells (Bailey and Faull, 1934).

In genera in which radial resin canals occur, the shape of some of the rays is considerably altered by the formation of these canals (Fig. 154). Such canals are usually solitary and occupy the centre of the ray, but they may be excentric and a ray may contain two canals. Excentrically placed canals are frequent in larch (Fig. 154 *B*) and give the ray a "tailed" appearance in tangential section; similar rays sometimes occur in spruces. The ray commonly bulges abruptly round the canal so that in a tangential longitudinal section it appears to be shouldered, but the bulge may be more gradual, as is often seen in the pitch pines; in Douglas fir a ray containing a resin canal is characteristically broadly fusiform. A radial resin canal in Douglas fir is usually small, occupying a relatively small part of the width of the ray, but in the pines, spruces and larches these resin canals are larger. In the pines they may appear to occupy the entire width of the ray, because in the mature wood the thin-walled epithelial cells become squashed.

From these brief descriptions it might appear that those rays which contain resin canals are of considerable value in the identification of woods. This is true as long as it is kept in mind that they are subject to a good deal of variation and that examination of a single ray, or of its shape alone, may mislead rather than help.

CHAPTER 6

THE HISTOLOGY OF DICOTYLEDONOUS WOODS
(HARDWOODS)

The wood of dicotyledons is considerably more complex than that of conifers. In softwoods, the bulk of the woody tissue consists of axial tracheids which are relatively small as seen in transverse section and which, except in detail, are similar in all softwoods; the rays are narrow —commonly uniseriate—and in most genera are wholly parenchymatous; axial parenchyma, if present, is sparse. Thus, there is relatively little difference in general structure between various coniferous timbers; a few are sufficiently distinctive to be recognisable by the unaided eye, but in general, identification demands attention to detail, and often, at that, to detail which calls for the use of the higher powers of the microscope.

In hardwoods, the axial elements are more varied. The vessels differ enormously in size in different woods and may be large enough to be visible to the unaided eye. Parenchyma may be abundant and distributed in characteristic and definite ways, sometimes in large and conspicuous masses, while rays may be uniseriate and only a few cells high or, at the other extreme, large multiseriate structures perhaps 2–3 cm. high and many cells wide. Moreover, although hardwood rays are exclusively parenchymatous, several distinct types of cell may contribute to their make-up. It is not surprising, therefore, that many hardwoods are distinctive enough to be recognisable with the unaided eye or, at most, with a hand-lens. Nevertheless, the microscope, and even its high powers, is often needed for the certain identification of hardwoods.

Hardwoods almost invariably consist of four or five types of element —vessel element, parenchyma cell, libriform fibre, tracheid and fibre-tracheid. All these types, except cells which form the ray tissue, are related developmentally in that they all derive from the fusiform initials of the cambium. Differentiation of these cells derived from the fusiform initials seems to proceed along three lines, but it must be emphasised that these three lines are not clear cut and sharply separated. Along one line there is normally a phase of elongation in the process of differentiation, so that the definitive element is considerably longer than the initial from which it has developed. Elements of this type are the libriform fibres, the fibre-tracheids and one type of tracheid; the first two characteristically having pointed extremities. Along a second line of differentiation, which leads to the vessel element and to another type of tracheid, there is little or no elongation during development; in fact, in some more advanced woods the vessel element may be shorter than the initial from which it arose. Yet again, a cell cut off from a fusiform initial may divide into an axial row of two or more cells by means of transverse walls and so form an axial chain of parenchyma cells; such division does not, however, always occur, for sometimes such a cell gives rise to a single parenchyma cell (Fig. 7).

Differentiation of the derivatives of the fusiform initials of dicotyledons has led to specialisation in several directions and the tracheid, a sort of "general purposes" element in softwoods, becomes of less importance and is replaced by cells of other types. It is probably correct to regard the vasicentric tracheid of hardwoods as the cell which is equivalent to, or homologous with, the axial tracheid of the softwood, but it is not now a general purposes element, for it has lost, or largely lost, its function of support and is concerned mainly with water conduction. The vasicentric tracheid is not an invariable constituent of dicotyledonous wood; where it does occur it is often found associated with the large vessels (e.g. in some oaks). It is seldom very long and is rather irregular in outline, with rounded ends, a thin wall, and numerous small bordered pits. These are found over the whole surface of the walls, and not confined to the radial walls as so frequently happens in the softwood tracheid. Another distinction from the softwood tracheid shown by these cells is that they do not occur in radial files, for as the vessel with which they are associated expands laterally during the process of differentiation, the tracheids may become distorted and displaced and so lose any regular arrangement which they might once have possessed.

Water conduction, which is the function of the hardwood tracheid, is also the main, if not the only function, of the vessel, which as we have seen, is formed from an axial row of cells, by the partial or complete disappearance of their end walls. In more primitive hardwoods these vessel elements (each element being that unit of the vessel formed from a fusiform initial) are long, longer than the initials from which they have arisen, and their perforated end walls are decidedly oblique. In the more advanced types of wood the elements are shorter, sometimes even shorter than the initials from which they have been formed, and are often somewhat barrel-shaped, while their end perforations tend to be horizontal. The vascular tracheids formed in some woods, e.g. elm, resemble vessels in that they occur in axial rows, each member of which has differentiated from a cell cut off from a fusiform initial. These cells retain their end walls and at maturity are indeed no more than an axial row of empty cells, with bordered pits in their walls, carrying out the same functions as a vessel. We might, in fact, regard such a row of vascular tracheids as an incompletely developed vessel, the protoplasts of the cells having died before the end walls had become disrupted. It sometimes happens that an axial row of vascular elements consists in some parts of vascular tracheids and elsewhere of vessel elements.

The function of support in hardwoods falls mainly upon the libriform fibre, which is an elongate element, often, but not invariably thick-walled and with few often slit-like pits in its walls. This type of cell may exceed a length of five millimetres, but this is exceptional and those of yellow birch (*Betula lutea* Michx.) and of American whitewood (*Lirio-dendron tulipifera* L.), with lengths of about two millimetres or perhaps rather more, may be regarded as above average in length.

Between the vasicentric tracheid and the libriform fibre there are all stages of gradation; some of these cells of intermediate type are more tracheid-like and their conducting function is probably of greater importance than their supporting one, while others more nearly resemble the libriform fibre and in them the function of conduction is probably subservient to that of support. Such intermediate elements are called fibre-tracheids. They may be abundant, forming the bulk of the wood: to them the timber largely owes its strength; alternatively they may be few or absent. Fibre-tracheids may have thick walls and they possess small bordered pits, commonly with oblique slit-like apertures extending beyond the border. Like libriform fibres, they are usually regularly fusiform in shape. In both libriform fibres and fibre-tracheids the ends may be forked, or they may have a somewhat serrated appearance. Such irregularities are produced during growth, when the somewhat plastic wall has pressed against contiguous cells, usually ray paren-chyma, and become permanently distorted as a result.

In describing hardwoods, it is not often that much attention is paid to precise differentiation between libriform fibres and fibre-tracheids; it is more usual to refer quite loosely to all such cells as fibres. Moreover, tracheids of hardwoods normally receive scant attention. Generally, therefore, in descriptive work, we refer to three types of cells; fibres, parenchyma and vessel elements.

In a relatively small number of dicotyledons, vessels are absent and the function of conduction falls entirely upon tracheids (cf. p. 145).

Vessels may be distributed more or less evenly throughout the growth ring, thus producing a diffuse-porous wood. In diffuse-porous woods, however, it is not unusual to find a narrow zone at the end of each growth ring which is devoid of vessels, or at least, in which vessels are very sparse. An excellent example of this arrangement is seen in *Eucalyptus gigantea* Hook.f., one of the species yielding the so-called Tasmanian oak, in which the last-formed wood in the ring is dark coloured and nearly free of vessels; from a very superficial glance at an end grain surface, this wood might be mistaken for a softwood (Fig. 54). Another, and curious type of distribution of vessels is seen in the Dipterocarpaceae, where the spacing is very irregular. In transverse section the vessels are seen to be very patchily distributed, areas with

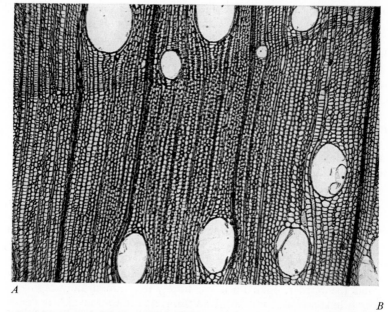

A

B

Fig. 54.—*A*. Australian "Mountain Ash" (*Eucalyptus regnans*), showing a zone at
the end of a growth ring free, or almost free, of vessels; T.S. (× 60). *B*. End-grain
view of Alpine Ash (*Eucalyptus gigantea*) showing several growth rings, the dark
areas being the vessel-free boundaries; a few gum galls are seen near the left-hand
margin of the figure (× about 2).

numerous vessels being interspersed with areas in which the vessels are
relatively sparse (Fig. 165 *A*).

In woods like beech and sycamore (*Acer pseudoplatanus* L.) the
vessels are of much the same size throughout the growth ring (Fig. 144),
but in some woods they are much larger at the beginning of the season's
growth and often more numerous as well. When the vessels of the early
wood are so close together that in transverse section they form more
or less a continuous ring, the wood is termed ring-porous (e.g. elms,
ashes, some oaks) (Fig. 142). In some woods, such as hickory and sometimes teak, the continuity of the ring is broken by the wider spacing of
the early wood vessels; such woods are termed semi-ring-porous.
Sometimes, as for example in black walnut (*Juglans nigra* L.) and

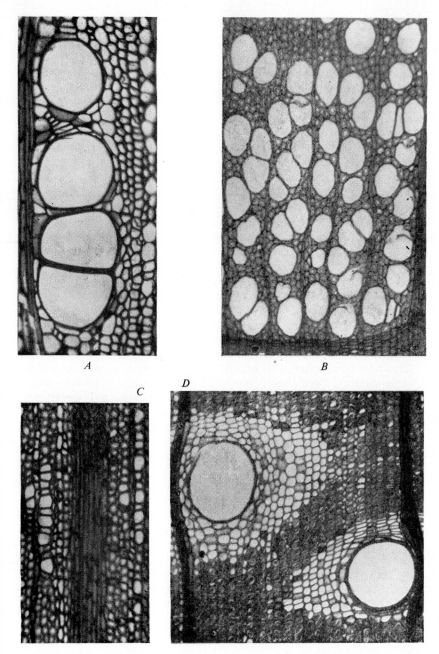

Fig. 55.—Vessel arrangement, size and shape. *A*. Cigarbox Cedar (*Cedrela* sp.); short radial chain of vessels. *B*. North American Beech (*Fagus grandifolia*); diffuse-porous; vessels angular, often in short, radial, oblique or tangential chains. *C*. Holly (*Ilex aquifolium*); very small, angular vessels in long, radial chains. *D*. Rain Tree (*Samanea saman*); solitary, round vessels (all T.S. × 130).

basswood (*Tilia americana* L.) the vessels of the early wood are not appreciably different in size from those which occur in the later formed wood, but they form, none the less, a distinct pore ring.

As seen in transverse section, vessels may be distinctly circular in outline, a feature especially well shown in kokko (*Albizzia lebbeck* Benth.) and in some maples (Figs. 174 *A*, 184 *A, B*); they may be decidedly oval, as in sweet chestnut, and the early wood vessels of ash (Fig. 56 *C*). A somewhat angular outline characterises the vessels of some woods, like hornbeam, willow and magnolia (Fig. 147 *C*).

Vessels vary enormously in size, the smallest being no more than 20 *μ* or so in diameter, the largest as much as half a millimetre (500 *μ*). In a section of one of the English oaks, the largest vessels (i.e. in the pore ring) had an average tangential diameter of 268 *μ*, the smallest vessels of the late wood measured, on average, no more than 34 *μ* along the same axis.

Vessels may occur singly (solitary) or in groups (multiple) (Figs. 55 *D*, 56 *A*). A frequent multiple arrangement is for the vessels, as seen in transverse section, to be disposed in short radial chains or groups of two to about half a dozen, flattened at their surfaces of contact (Fig. 55 *A*): such a chain has arisen from successive cells cut off by an axial line of cambium initials. More extensive radial groups, as seen, for example, in holly (Fig. 55 *C*) and olive, are termed vessel chains or pore chains, the term pore being often used in reference to vessels as viewed on transverse surfaces. Pore chains sometimes run obliquely, a feature sometimes shown by the willows, or more or less tangentially, as is sometimes seen in lime; in some of the Proteaceae these more or less tangential chains of vessels appear in transverse section as festoons between the large rays (Fig. 56 *A*). Vessel clusters are of frequent occurrence and are well shown in the limes and in the late wood of robinia and tree of heaven (Fig. 56 *B*), while more extensive clusters, in the form of sinuous, more or less tangential bands, are seen in the elms (Fig. 180).

Even when they are actually solitary, vessels may have a close topographical relationship. Thus groups of vessels often tend to run radially in the oaks (Fig. 177), obliquely in sweet chestnut (Fig. 142 *B*), or tangentially in some Proteaceae. Where the arrangement is oblique it sometimes changes direction periodically so that the vessels as seen in the transverse sections tend to lie in > -shaped lines, the arrangement so characteristic of the walnuts. A rather less regular and more localised arrangement of this type characterises some woods, especially the eucalyptus woods, in which the vessels, as seen on the end grain, have an arrangement somewhat reminiscent of flames; this arrangement is conveniently referred to as flame-like (Fig. 56 *C*).

On the longitudinal surfaces of a piece of hardwood the vessels are visible, if they are large enough, as longitudinal grooves which are termed vessel lines. If the vessels pursue a sinuous course such lines will appear short and where the undulations tend to be in one direction,

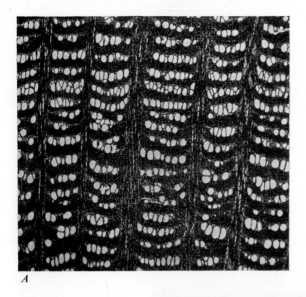

A

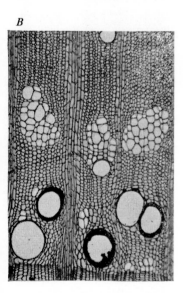

B

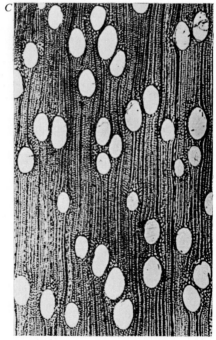

C

Fig. 56.—Vessel arrangement. *A.* Southern Silky Oak (*Orites excelsa*); vessels in tangential festoons between the large rays; T.S. (× 16). *B.* Tree of Heaven (*Ailanthus altissima*); in the lower part of the figure are large vessels of the early wood (the wood is nearly ring-porous); beyond these are large clusters containing numerous small vessels (× 38). *C.* Australian "Mountain Ash" (*Eucalyptus regnans*) showing oval vessels in oblique lines, an arrangement which gives the flame-like arrangement of vessels, so characteristic of eucalyptus woods seen at lower magnifications (× 27).

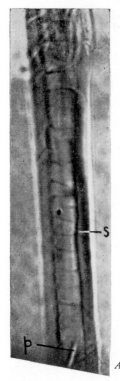

Fig. 57.—*A*. Spiral thickening in fibre of Holly (*Ilex aquifolium*) (× 860). A simple slit-like pit (*p*) is seen at the bottom of the section, in surface view, while one, cut across its long axis, is seen at *s*. *B*. Spiral thickening and pitting in vessels of Lime (*Tilia vulgaris*) (× 170).

as in wavy-grained woods, they will be shorter on one longitudinal surface than on that at right-angles to it. Long vessel lines may be regarded as indicative of a straight-grained wood. In a wood in which the vessels are of oval section the vessel lines will, on the whole, be wider on the radial than on the tangential face.

In some woods spiral thickening may be present on the vessel walls, similar to that of certain conifer tracheids (see p. 88). In some instances it occurs only in some of the vessels, in other woods in all of them. It is well shown in the limes (Fig. 57 *B*).

Little need be said here concerning libriform fibres and fibre-tracheids. They may be several times longer than the cambial initials from which they arise, although in light-weight woods especially, they sometimes do not increase in length in this way. They then resemble fusiform parenchyma cells, from which they may be distinguished by their pits; simple and slit-like in the libriform fibre and bordered in the fibre tracheid. Not infrequently, fibres and fibre-tracheids occur in

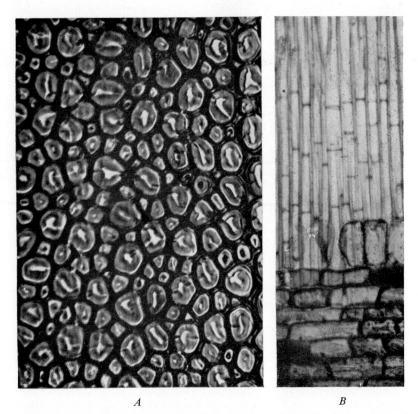

A   *B*

Fig. 58.—*A*. Gelatinous fibres in Robinia (*Robinia pseudoacacia*); the inner part of the secondary wall, which is not lignified, is shown here lighter in tone than the lignified outer parts; T.S. (× 530). *B*. Septate fibres in Crabwood (*Carapa guianensis*); the lower half of the figure is occupied by part of a ray, the upper half by septate fibres; R.L.S. (× 180).

regular radial files, and in most timbers they vary considerably in size as seen in transverse section, depending, of course, on whether they happen to have been cut through near their ends or through their wider, middle region. Since the latter region occupies more of the length than do the tapering ends, there is more likelihood that this region will be cut in any section and consequently small fibres seem to be less abundant in transverse sections than larger ones. Fibres may be distinctly flattened along their radial axes so that they appear oblong in transverse section: such flattened fibres may occupy the end of the growth ring (Fig. 147 *A*). It is not usual to find spiral thickening in fibrous elements, but it sometimes occurs, as for example, in the fibres of holly (Fig 57 *A*).

The inner part of the secondary wall of both libriform fibres and fibre-tracheids may be peculiarly modified, being very thick but containing little lignin. Such cells (Fig. 58 *A*) are known as gelatinous fibres (or fibre-tracheids). Gelatinous fibres are characteristic of a normal variant of wood structure known as tension wood, which is discussed further in Chapter 9.

Fibres or fibre-tracheids may contain a number of thin, transverse septa, which are formed by the subsequent division of the original protoplast into a number of cells and their separation by cell walls. Such septate fibres or fibre-tracheids are more frequently seen in tropical woods (Fig. 58 *B*).

The parenchyma in hardwoods is generally much more abundant than that of softwoods and its distribution is sometimes distinctive and of great value for diagnostic purposes, for which its appearance in transverse sections is used. Classification of parenchyma distribution is not easy and various modifications of the terminology and definitions given in the Glossary of the International Association of Wood Anatomists (1932) have been suggested by Chalk (1937); Kribs (1937, 1950); Bailey and Howard (1941); Hess (1950) and the International Association of Wood Anatomists (1957).

Apart from that which forms a boundary to the growth rings, two types are recognised, apotracheal parenchyma, which is not associated with the vessels or vascular tracheids, and paratracheal parenchyma, which is associated with vessels and vascular tracheids. Apotracheal parenchyma may occur as isolated strands of axial parenchyma cells which, of course, appear in transverse sections as isolated parenchyma cells scattered among the fibre tissue; or in tangentially arranged sheets of cells, which may be only a single cell thick in a radial direction and perhaps only two or three cells wide tangentially; or in more extensive tangential bands, with a radial depth of one to several cells and, in transverse section, appearing as tangential zones alternating with zones of fibres. The two latter types are sometimes referred to as metatracheal parenchyma but this term is better avoided.

Viewed in transverse section, regularly spaced tangential lines or bands of axial parenchyma form a distinct pattern with the rays. If the parenchyma and the rays are of about the same width and distance apart, a net-like pattern is formed (reticulate parenchyma) while when the parenchyma is distinctly narrower than the rays, a ladder-like pattern results (scalariform parenchyma).

Paratracheal parenchyma may consist of no more than isolated parenchyma cells associated with the vessels, but it may completely ensheath them, so that the parenchyma appears as haloes surrounding the vessels. These sheaths may be flanged on the radial sides of the vessels so that in a transverse section they appear to be drawn out into wings. These wings may connect up with those of neighbouring vessels or the vessels may be embedded in broad bands of parenchyma. Sometimes the sheath is incomplete and then it generally appears in a

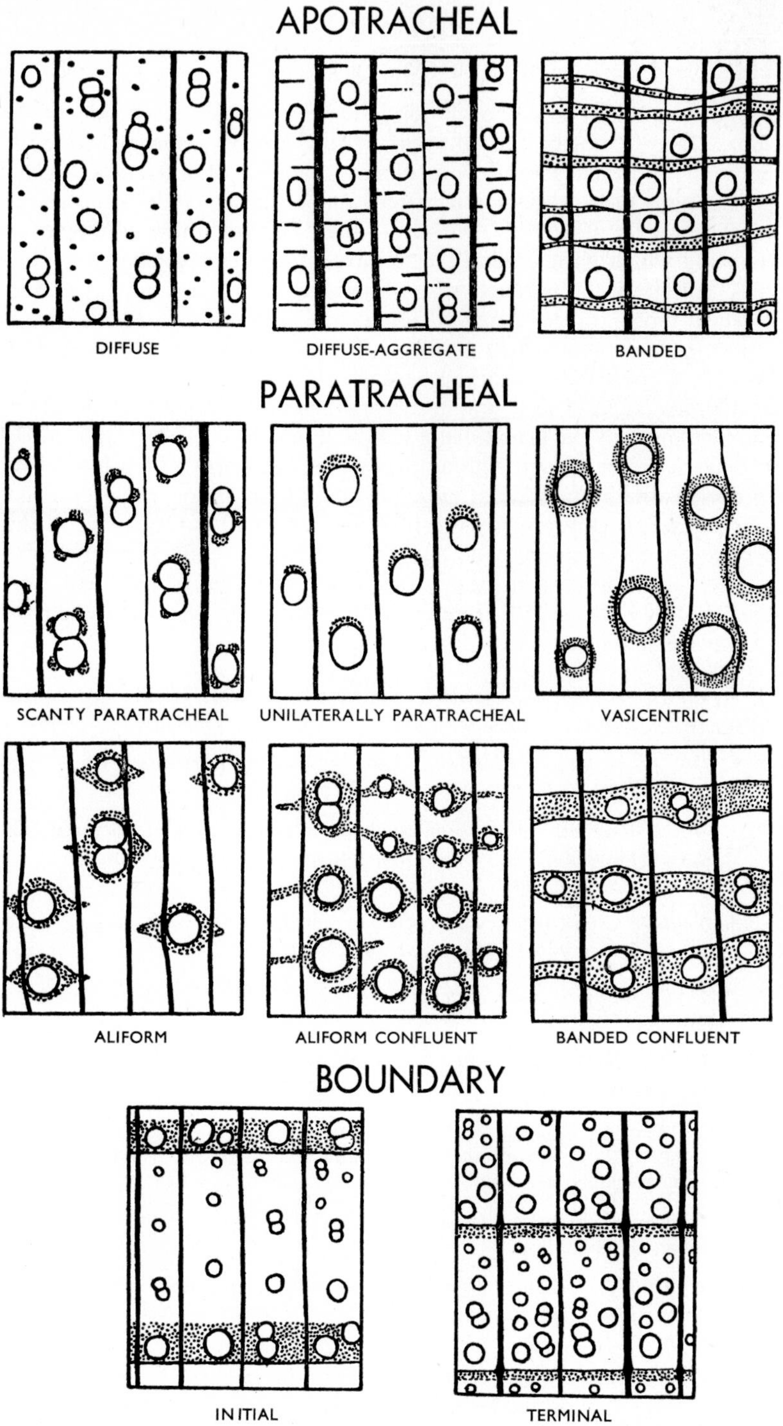

APOTRACHEAL

DIFFUSE

DIFFUSE-AGGREGATE

BANDED

PARATRACHEAL

SCANTY PARATRACHEAL

UNILATERALLY PARATRACHEAL

VASICENTRIC

ALIFORM

ALIFORM CONFLUENT

BANDED CONFLUENT

BOUNDARY

INITIAL

TERMINAL

Fig. 59.—Diagram of different types of distribution of parenchyma in hardwoods, as seen in transverse sections. (The parenchyma is shown as dotted areas, except in the first diagram, where it is represented by isolated dots and in the second, where it is shown as horizontal lines.)

transverse section as a cap or hood, usually on the outer side of the vessel. It must not be thought that there is always a sharp distinction between apotracheal and paratracheal parenchyma, for apotracheal parenchyma may on occasion include or partially include some vessels in its course. Generally, however, there is not much difficulty in deciding which parenchyma type is present in the specimen.

A third type of parenchyma, sometimes included among the apotracheal types, but here treated separately, is that which forms a zone at the end, or sometimes at the beginning, of the growth ring. It is usually referred to as terminal parenchyma, but this is an unfortunate term since, at least in a few timbers, a zone of parenchyma occurs at the beginning of the growth ring (Chowdhury, 1934, 1936; Jane, 1934). It is often difficult, even with a microscope, still more with a hand-lens, to decide whether a zone of parenchyma is terminal or initial, but that scarcely seems sufficient reason for referring to all parenchyma of this type as terminal parenchyma. Here it is termed boundary parenchyma.

The following classification of parenchyma types is modified from that used by Kribs (1950): it refers to the appearance of the parenchyma in transverse sections (Fig. 59: cf. also Figs. 60, 61):—

A. *APOTRACHEAL.* Parenchyma not associated with vessels or vascular tracheids.

   1. *Diffuse.* Isolated parenchyma cells among the fibre tissue: e.g. alder (*Alnus* spp.).

   2. *Diffuse-aggregate* [*Diffuse-in-aggregates, Diffuse-zonate*]. Isolated cells as in (1) and short tangential lines only a few cells long: e.g. mansonia (*Mansonia altissima* A.Chev.).

   3. *Banded.* Concentric bands, one to several cells wide radially: e.g. ekki (*Lophira alata* Banks v. *procera* Burtt Davy).

B. *PARATRACHEAL.* Parenchyma associated with vessels or vascular tracheids.

   1. *Scanty paratracheal.* Isolated parenchyma cells, or incomplete sheaths, associated with vessels: e.g. African walnut (*Lovoa klaineana* Pierre ex Sprague).

   2. *Unilaterally paratracheal.* Parenchyma forming caps, usually on outer side of vessels: e.g. idigbo (*Terminalia ivorensis* A.Chev.).

   3. *Vasicentric.* Forming an oval or circular halo round the vessels: e.g. ogea (*Daniellia* spp.).

   4. *Aliform.* Vasicentric parenchyma extending into tangential wings: e.g. satiné (*Brosimum paraense* Huber).

   5. *Confluent.* Parenchyma linking adjacent vessels:
      (a) *Aliform confluent.* The wings of aliform parenchyma connect with those of neighbouring vessels: e.g. Indian rosewood (*Dalbergia latifolia* Roxb.).

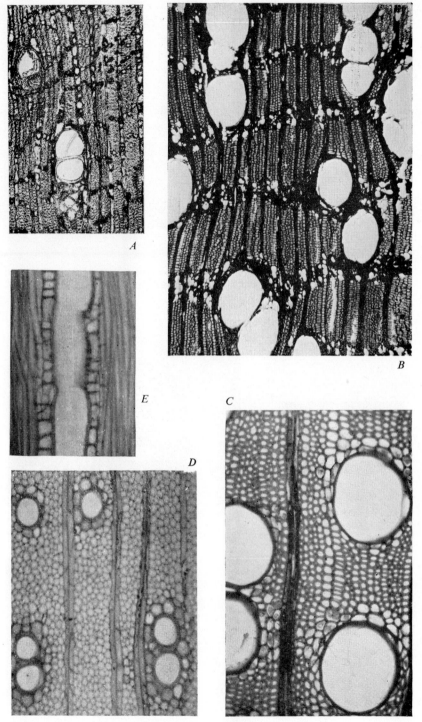

Fig. 60.—Parenchyma, as seen in transverse section. *A*. Indian Ebony (*Diospyros melanoxylon*): diffuse aggregate (× 55). *B*. Ekki (*Lophira alata* v. *procera*): concentric (× 40). *C*. African Walnut (*Lovoa klaineana*): paratracheal scanty (× 120). *D*. European Ash (*Fraxinus excelsior*): vasicentric (× 120). *E*, as *D*: vasicentric parenchyma in R.L.S. (× 120).

I

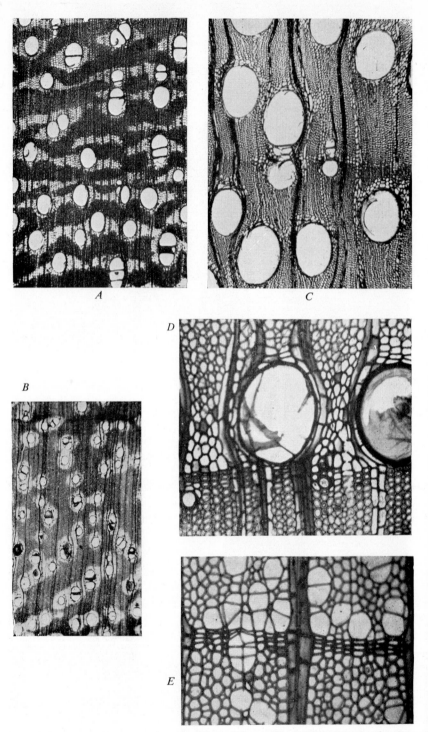

Fig. 61.—Parenchyma, as seen in transverse section. *A*. Ayan (*Distemonanthus bentham-ianus*): aliform confluent (× 20). *B*. Yellow Siris (*Albizzia xanthoxylon*): confluent (× 10). *C*. Idigbo (*Terminalia ivorensis*): unilaterally paratracheal (× 40). *D*. Teak (*Tectona grandis*): initial (× 120). *E*. Yulan (*Magnolia denudata*): terminal (× 120).

(*b*) *Banded confluent.* Adjacent vessels linked by bands of parenchyma; e.g. partridge wood (*Andira inermis* (Sw.) H.B.K.).

C. *BOUNDARY.* Parenchyma at beginning or end of growth ring.
1. *Initial.* At the beginning of the growth ring: e.g. teak (*Tectona grandis* L.f.).
2. *Terminal.* At the end of the growth ring: e.g. magnolia (*Magnolia* spp.).

This classification, like others which have been proposed, is at best a very broad summary of parenchyma types and, for purposes of identification, it may not be sufficiently detailed. Hess (1950) has attempted to meet this difficulty with a scheme which, while basically similar to that just outlined, is much more elaborate and detailed. Each detail in this classification is given a letter or symbol by the appropriate use of which it is possible to represent comprehensive descriptions of the parenchyma by means of fairly simple formulae.

In hardwoods, the cells derived from the ray initials of the vascular cambium differentiate into parenchyma. One or two exceptions have been recorded, e.g. the presence of ray tracheids in white oak and in Knysna boxwood (*Gonioma kamassi* E.Meyer) and of fibre-tracheids in *Neesia altissima* Blume; but these must be regarded as very rare exceptions which hardly invalidate the statement that the hardwood ray is exclusively parenchymatous. There is a very wide range of variation in hardwood rays (Figs. 62–65). They may be uniseriate as in willows and padauks (*Pterocarpus* spp.) and perhaps only a few cells high, as in lignum vitae (*Guaiacum*). At the other extreme are the relatively enormous rays, hundreds of cells (and many cms.) high, and many cells wide. Very large rays are seen in many casuarinas, in most oaks and in the Proteaceae. In some woods, the apparently large rays are, in fact, bundles of smaller rays, the individual rays being separated from one another by fibres belonging to the axial elements of the wood. Such a ray cluster, viewed with a lens on transverse and tangential surfaces, appears to be a single large ray but under the microscope its composite nature is apparent and the cluster may give the appearance of a large ray which is breaking up, or alternatively, of a number of small rays which are fusing to form a large one. Such ray clusters, in which individual rays are separated from one another solely by fibrous tissue, are called aggregate rays. They are found in alder (*Alnus*) and hornbeam (*Carpinus*) as well as in some evergreen oaks (*Quercus* spp.) and in some forest oaks (*Casuarina* spp.).

In some woods the rays are of two distinct sizes (Fig. 65 *D*): in most oaks there are large rays and small, uniseriate ones, while beech also has large and small rays, although here the two types are less distinct and tend to grade into one another. In Cape beech (*Rapanea melanophloeos* (L.) Mez), however, there are only large rays.

Although the rays of hardwoods consist exclusively of parenchyma cells, they are not necessarily composed of one kind of cell. Where

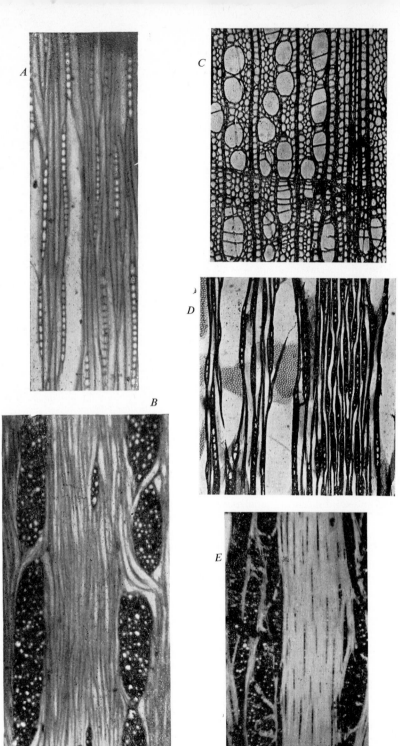

Fig. 62

there is only one type of cell, as in populars, the rays are called homogeneous, while the term heterogeneous is used to designate those which contain cells of more than one type, e.g. obeche (*Triplochiton scleroxylon* K.Schum.). The most frequent type of ray cell is the radially elongated procumbent cell. Not infrequently cells which are as tall, or often taller, than they are long, i.e. axially elongated, are found in rays and are known as upright cells. It is now customary to separate the upright cells into square cells (approximately square in radial section) and upright cells (ray cells in which the greatest length is axial); these two sorts of cells are, however, regarded as being of the same morphological type. Upright cells (in the wide sense) often occur along the upper and lower margins of the rays and are then called marginal cells, e.g. in the Meliaceae (Fig. 65 C). In holly (*Ilex aquifolium* L.) the centre part of the large rays is multiseriate and composed of procumbent cells, but there may be several rows of marginal cells arranged in a uniseriate manner, so that the rays may appear, in tangential section, to be tailed (Fig. 64 E, F). Upright cells may form a sheath, more or less complete, around the procumbent cells of the ray, and are then called sheath cells (Fig. 64 D).

Kribs (1935, 1950) has proposed a classification of rays based on their appearance in radial and tangential sections, which is often useful in descriptive work. The following scheme is based on Kribs' (1950) classification (Fig. 63).[1]

[1] This classification may cause some confusion since in Kribs' first classification (1935), homogeneous rays are classified as:—

Type I   Uniseriate rays rather low, numerous to scarce.
Multiseriate rays mostly fusiform with round or oval (T.L.S.) and radially elongated cells in multiseriate part, and with long or short uniseriate tips composed of cells identical with those of the multiseriate part.

Type II   Uniseriate rays scarce or absent; if present, low.
Multiseriate rays fusiform; composed entirely of small round (T.L.S.) radially elongated cells; uniseriate tips absent or very short.

Type III   Exclusively uniseriate.
Heterogeneous type II and Heterogeneous type III of the 1950 classification are Heterogeneous type IIA and type IIB respectively in the 1935 paper, in which Heterogeneous type III is reserved for exclusively uniseriate rays.
Thus any use of Kribs' terminology before 1950 will refer to that of the 1935 paper while that used after 1950 may refer to one or the other.
Brazier and Franklin (1961) use Kribs (1950) terminology, viz. Heterogeneous types I, II and III.

Fig. 62.—Types of rays in hardwoods. *A*. Horse-chestnut (*Aesculus hippocastanum*): uniseriate; T.L.S. (× 110). *B*. English Elm (*Ulmus procera*): multiseriate; T.L.S. (× 110): there is a biseriate ray nearly in the centre line. *C*. Alder (*Alnus glutinosa*): aggregate ray (on right); T.S. (× 75). *D*. Alder (*Alnus glutinosa*): aggregate ray (on right); T.L.S. (× 93). *E*. Rose She Oak (*Casuarina torulosa*): aggregate rays, left and right, uniseriate rays in centre; T.L.S .(× 40).

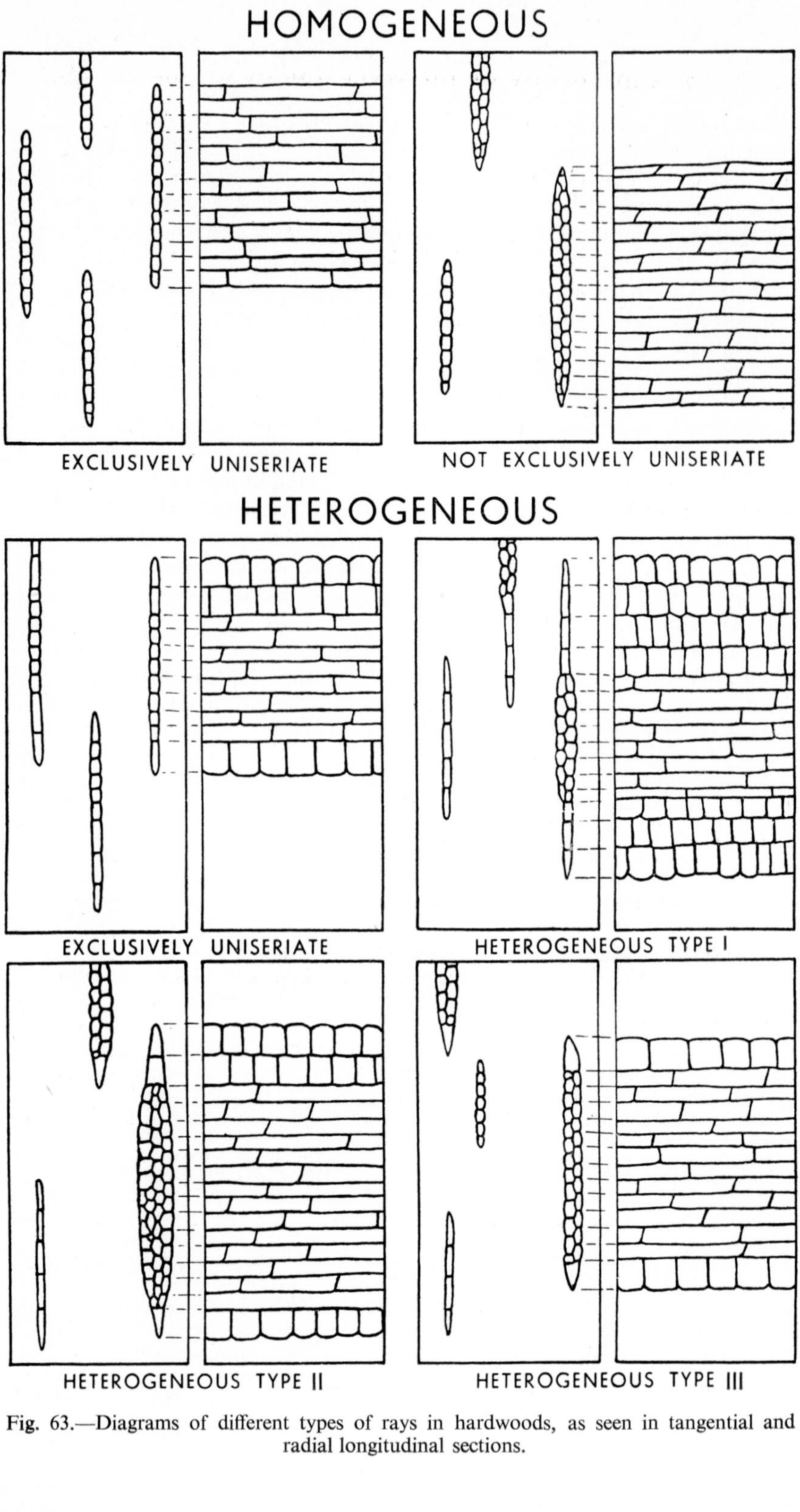

HOMOGENEOUS

EXCLUSIVELY UNISERIATE   NOT EXCLUSIVELY UNISERIATE

HETEROGENEOUS

EXCLUSIVELY UNISERIATE   HETEROGENEOUS TYPE I

HETEROGENEOUS TYPE II   HETEROGENEOUS TYPE III

Fig. 63.—Diagrams of different types of rays in hardwoods, as seen in tangential and radial longitudinal sections.

A. HOMOGENEOUS[1]

1. *Rays entirely uniseriate.* Composed of procumbent cells only.
2. *Rays not all uniseriate.* Composed of procumbent cells only.

B. HETEROGENEOUS

1. *Rays entirely uniseriate:* consisting of procumbent and upright cells.
2. *Rays not exclusively uniseriate:*
   (a) *Heterogeneous, type I. Uniseriate* rays composed of upright cells. *Multiseriate* rays with uniseriate tails as long as, or longer than, multiseriate part of ray. Uniseriate tails composed of upright (marginal) cells similar to those of uniseriate rays and taller than broad.
   (b) *Heterogeneous, type II. Uniseriate* rays composed of upright cells. *Multiseriate* rays with one row of large marginal cells or with uniseriate tails shorter than multiseriate part of ray. Uniseriate part of ray composed of marginal cells similar to those of uniseriate ray and taller than broad.
   (c) *Heterogeneous, type III. Uniseriate* rays usually of two sorts, some composed only of procumbent cells, some of upright cells. *Multiseriate* rays with square upright cells, usually in a single row: if tails occur, their cells are square.

The multiseriate part of the ray, referred to in the above classification, normally consists of procumbent cells, but there are exceptions, as, for example, when this part of the ray contains sheath cells or tile cells.

In the sapwood at least, the ray cells are living, and one of their functions is the storage of food materials; they are often packed with starch grains. One peculiar type of ray cell, found in the Sterculiaceae and certain allied families, is exceptional in losing its living contents at a very early stage. This is the tile cell (Fig. 64 *A–C*), so named because of its characteristic shape (Chattaway, 1933). When these cells are formed from the ray initials there is little radial elongation, so that tile cells are always squat in a radial direction. Rays of members of the Sterculiaceae are often very characteristic, for in transverse section they appear to consist of two distinct types of cells—the radially elongated procumbent cells and the short tile cells. In some woods (e.g. *Durio*) the tile cells are about the same height as the procumbent cells of the

[1] A *homogeneous* ray is defined as a xylem ray composed of radially elongated or procumbent cells, and a *heterogeneous* ray as one composed of morphologically different cells, commonly radially elongated and axially elongated or square cells.

No provision is thus made for rays composed exclusively of square or upright cells and there are objections to extending the term homogeneous to rays of this type. It is therefore recommended (International Association of Wood Anatomists, 1957) that the use of these terms shall be discontinued and that the following shall be used in reference to hardwoods:—

Heterogeneous ray tissue—Ray tissue in which the individual rays are composed wholly or in part of square or upright cells.

Homogeneous ray tissue—Ray tissue in which the individual rays are composed wholly of procumbent cells.

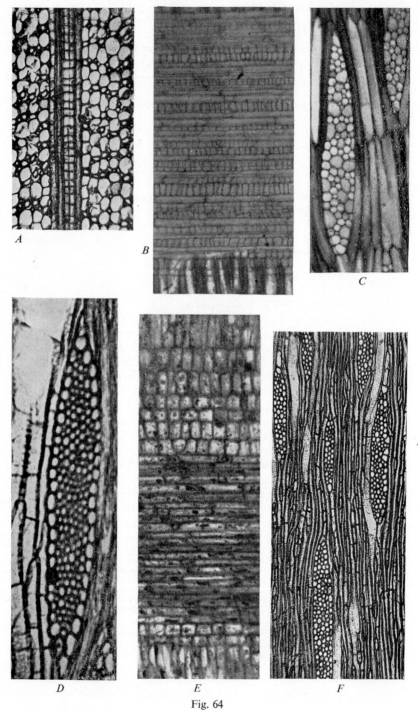

A

B

C

D

E

F

Fig. 64

ray, in others (e.g. *Pterospermum*) they may be twice as high or even more. When the height of the tile cells exceeds that of the procumbent cells the former, in a tangential section, will appear as large isolated cells among the normal ray cells; each, of course, is a member of a radial file of similar cells.

In transverse section the rays may be seen to be broader at the boundaries of the growth rings (e.g. the large rays of beech and maples) and are then said to be noded (Fig. 61 *E*). In transverse sections the rays may pursue very straight radial courses (Fig. 183 *A, B*), as in maples, or they may be more sinuous and bend around the larger vessels (Fig. 61 *C*). Rays of the latter type are sometimes termed weak, and the same term is sometimes used for rays which, in tangential section, have a somewhat irregular outline, e.g. teak, *Terminalia* spp. (Fig. 65 *A, B*). In mahogany (*Swietenia* spp.) and many other woods, the rays, as seen in this section, have a regular and symmetrical appearance (Fig. 65 *C*). While they may appear quite regular, rays are not necessarily symmetrical; the limes (*Tilia*) and American whitewood (*Liriodendron tulipifera* L.) show asymmetrical rays (Fig. 65 *B*), but the beginner will find that the asymmetry is far from obvious; for diagnoses, this feature may be of considerable value and is distinctive enough, once the eye has been trained to look for it.

Timbers of the more advanced families of dicotyledons may possess some form of storeyed structure, one or more of the axial types of element, or the rays, or both, being arranged in regular horizontal tiers. This tier-like arrangement is more frequent in tropical woods than in temperate ones, but it is not unrepresented in the latter, being found for example, in some horse chestnuts (especially the Japanese *Aesculus turbinata* Bl.) and in ebonies like the persimmons (cf. Fig. 67). Where rays alone are storeyed, the ray initials from which they arise are arranged in a like manner, and in some woods the same arrangement extends throughout the cambium, giving a storeyed or stratified cambium, a feature very often seen in certain families, like the Leguminosae, Sterculiaceae and Tiliaceae.

Storeyed structure gives the wood a very characteristic appearance if the height of the individual tiers is great enough to be visible to the

---

Fig. 64.—Rays in hardwoods. *A, B, C.* Obeche (*Triplochiton scleroxylon*), showing tile cells; in *A* (T.S.) the tile cells are the squarish cells in the centre of the ray: in *B* (R.L S.) most of the figure is occupied by part of a ray, in which several rows of radially flattened tile cells may be seen, interspersed among the rows of procumbent cells: in *C* (T.L.S.), the tile cells are the distinctly larger cells of the ray; note the short, storeyed fibres to the right (*A* × 120, *B* and *C* × 110). *D.* Mweye (*Celtis krausiana*) with ray in T.L.S. sheath cells (× 170). *E* and *F.* Holly (*Ilex aquifolium*); *E* (R.L.S.) showing part of a ray with procumbent cells in the lower half of the figure, and marginal (upright) cells, which form "tail," in the upper part; *F* (T.L.S.) showing large rays with uniseriate "tails" formed by marginal cells, and also uniseriate rays (*E* × 110, *F* × 60).

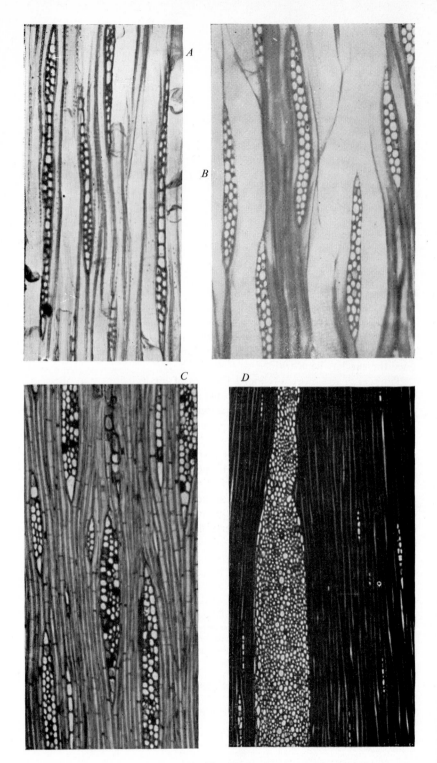

Fig. 65

unaided eye: in lignum vitae all the elements are storeyed but as the tiers are only 0·1 mm. high the storeyed arrangement is invisible without a hand-lens. The appearance is quite distinctive, resembling fine stippling, or, where it is prominent, the surfaces have an appearance which is reminiscent of a closely woven fabric, provided the illumination is correct (Fig. 66). To this "stippling" the term ripple marks is applied.

It is rare for the fibres or fibre-tracheids to have a tier-like arrangement, or perhaps, more correctly, the ends of such elements in a storeyed wood seldom coincide with those of the other elements, for they rarely remain the same length as the fusiform initials. During differentiation they normally increase in length, so that their tapered ends intrude between adjacent cells. Where this displacement is slight, a transverse section passing through the middle of a tier will show all the fibres to be about the same size and shape, while if it passes through the line of junction of two tiers, these elements should still be of the same shape but of smaller sectional area. A section passing near a line of junction of two tiers should show fibres of two distinct sizes, those which belong to the one tier being fairly large, the others, i.e. the tips of those of the adjacent tier which have intruded during differentiation, being much smaller. If the section passes very near their tips it will miss the extremities of their lumina so that they appear solid. In some woods, however, the fibres or fibre-tracheids retain the length of the fusiform initial, as is seen in obeche (Fig. 64 C).

Vessel elements and also parenchyma are sometimes storeyed. Clearly, in the parenchyma, it is an axial strand which occupies the length of a tier, and while occasionally such a strand consists of a single parenchyma cell (a so-called substitute fibre), it may be divided horizontally into two, four or more parenchyma cells (Fig. 67 A). Where these dividing walls are regularly disposed, they may produce subsidiary ripple marks lying within those caused by the main tiers.

Rays may be regularly storeyed, occupying the depth of one tier, but they may exceed this height, retaining, nevertheless, their regular horizontal alignment. Some woods having rays of two sizes may show the storeyed arrangement in the small rays while the large ones are irregularly disposed.

Hardwoods may contain many substances apart from the carbohydrates and lignin which make up the cell walls. Such substances are not an integral part of the wood, for its fundamental structure would

Fig. 65.—Rays in hardwoods. *A.* Katsura (*Cercidiphyllum japonicum*) with irregular (weak) rays; T.L.S. (× 115). *B.* American Whitewood (*Liriodendron tulipifera*) with asymmetrical rays; T.L.S. (× 110). *C.* Crabwood (*Carapa guianensis*), showing symmetrical multiseriate rays with distinct marginal (upright) cells and also uniseriate rays, some of which contain both procumbent and upright cells (top right) and others only upright cells (bottom left); T.L.S. (× 74). *D.* Northern Silky Oak (*Cardwellia sublimis*), showing part of one of the large rays and several small ones; the difference in size between the large and the small rays is striking; T.L.S. (× 38).

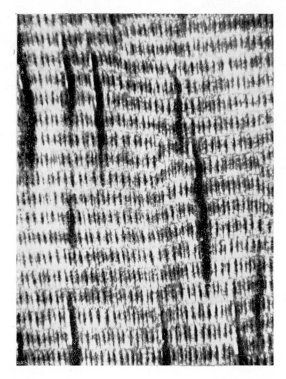

Fig. 66.—Storeyed rays in plain-sawn (tangentially cut) Ogea (*Daniellia thurifera*) (× 10); the rays are the small, dark flecks; the larger, dark streaks are parts of vessels. This is a photograph of the solid wood which, seen at natural size, would show the characteristic ripple marks, rather resembling stippling of the surface; such ripple marks would, however, be lost in reproduction from a half-tone block.

not be affected by their absence, and in consequence they are often referred to as extraneous materials or extractives.

The extraneous materials of wood range from simple substances like calcium salts and silica to carbohydrates like starch and sugars, tannins, saponins, gums, resins, essential oils, fats and fatty acids, latex, colouring matters and complex nitrogenous substances like alkaloids.

Present knowledge of these extraneous materials, as they occur in wood, is elementary or even sketchy. Reference has already been made to the almost casual manner in which they are treated by the wood anatomist (p. 46). The subject is largely unexplored, although even now, use is made of such substances indirectly, in that they may aid in identification, for the odour, taste and colour of wood, and sometimes its lustre, are due to them. They are also responsible for some special properties of wood extracts, like acidity, turbidity and fluorescence: the ash test (p. 300), again, depends upon the presence of extraneous

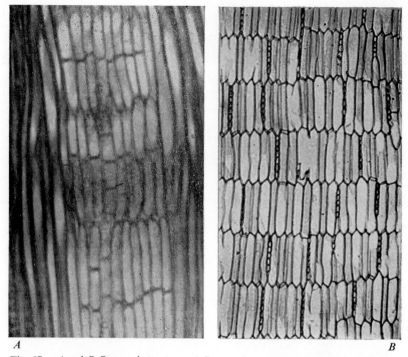

A   B

Fig. 67.—A and B. Storeyed structure. A. Storeyed parenchyma in Robinia (*Robinia pseudoacacia*); R.L.S. (× 170). B. Storeyed parenchyma and rays in Ambach (*Herminiera elaphroxylon*); T.L.S. (× 70).

substances. That more use will be made of these materials for identification as knowledge of them accumulates, is beyond reasonable doubt, but probably their utilisation for such a purpose will depend on the development of simple tests for their recognition. The wood anatomist is unlikely to have the time, even should he have the inclination and possess the necessary skill and knowledge, besides a sufficiency of material, to make elaborate chemical analyses for purposes of identification.

Here, these extraneous materials will be dealt with briefly and consideration will be confined largely to such substances as are readily seen in sections or in the solid wood, or whose presence affects the wood structure. Despite the obvious inaccuracy, it will be convenient to speak of gums and gummy materials, oils, white deposits and so on, in the same sense as these terms are used by the wood anatomist, and not with the precision of the chemist.

Silica may accumulate in the cells of wood, but it may also occur in the walls and is not then noted under the microscope. Amos (1952) tabulates over four hundred timbers in which silica occurs as visible

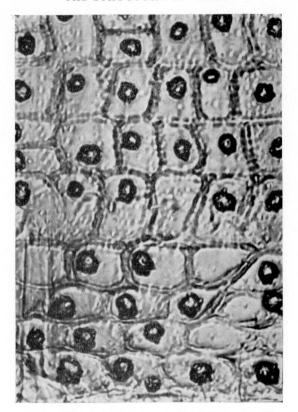

Fig. 68.—Silica inclusions in ray cells of *Parinari* sp. The
section was unstained and all other cell inclusions removed
by preliminary treatment in eau de javelle; R.L.S. (× 305).

cell inclusions, most commonly in ray cells, but sometimes in axial
parenchyma and other axial elements. Amos recognises two types of
siliceous inclusion, both of which consist of almost pure silicon dioxide.
The first type he calls silica inclusions. These have a wrinkled or uneven
surface and a refractive index of 1·434 and are smaller than the cell
lumina (Fig. 68). The second and rarer type is designated vitreous
silica; this has a vitreous appearance and a refractive index exceeding
1·5. Vitreous silica occurs as a lining on the cell walls or completely
fills the cell cavity and is usually found in vessels and other axial
elements; it may occur in ray cells.

Calcium salts are of very common occurrence and probably constitute
the bulk of the white deposits which occur in hardwoods. The white
deposits which occur in vessels, as in Cuban mahogany (*Swietenia
mahagoni* Jacq.) and teak—there are yellow ones in ekki—may be
calcium carbonate (Fig. 69 *C*); in teak they are said to be apatite, an

impure form of calcium phosphate. Sometimes, no doubt due to abnormal metabolism, these deposits are exceptionally abundant and may fill cracks or shakes which had arisen in the living tree (Fig. 69 *A*, *B*). The large, rock-like masses sometimes found in iroko (*Chlorophora excelsa* Benth. et Hook.f.) and appropriately known as stone (Fig. 70), furnish an excellent example.

Crystals consisting largely of calcium oxalate are frequently found in the parenchyma of hardwoods (Fig. 71) and may even occur in cells which contain silica inclusions. They are commonly rhomboidal. Cells in which they occur—crystalliferous cells—may be ray cells or axial parenchyma. In the rays they tend to be more common in certain horizontal rows of cells, and, when the ray is heterogeneous, are more likely to be found in upright cells than in procumbent ones. In axial parenchyma, crystals may occupy each cell of a strand or they may occur in some of the cells and not others. Cells containing crystals are frequently distended (Fig. 71 *A*). Sometimes one or more of the cells of an axial strand divide subsequently to the original division of the cambiform cell, and may then become repositories for crystals, forming what is called chambered parenchyma (Fig. 71 *C*).

Not all crystals have a rhomboidal shape; sometimes they are needle-like (acicular) and may then occur in bunches which are known as raphides, although crystals of this type are much more common in tissues other than wood. Crystals about four times as long as broad, and with pointed or square ends are termed styloids. Crystals are sometimes grouped in more or less spherical clusters (druses). A mass of very minute crystals, which has a granular appearance, is referred to as crystal sand. A peculiar type of crystal structure is the cystolith, which is a crystalline accretion around a projection from the cell wall; cystoliths are rare in wood but are known in woods of the family Opiliaceae (e.g. *Champereia manillana* Merrill, of the Indo-Malayan region) where they are found in the ray cells. Crystals are also found, very occasionally, in tyloses.

Gummy materials may occur in vessels, fibres or parenchyma; they are least common in fibres. They may, like other substances, also occur in special intercellular ducts and are sometimes found in large masses in shakes which have occurred in the living tree, a feature sometimes seen in agba (*Gossweilerodendron balsamiferum* Harms) (Fig. 72 *A*). These materials vary in consistency; they may be dry and gritty or more or less fluid, so that they tend to ooze out on to the surface of the wood and mar its appearance (Fig. 72 *B*), as sometimes happens in the

Fig. 69.—Calcium deposits. *A*, *B*. White deposits filling cracks or shakes in the wood of Fustic (*Chlorophora tinctoria*) (about natural size). *A* is an end-grain surface, *B* a tangential longitudinal surface: in *B* the confluent parenchyma is clearly shown. *C*. Deposits, of a pale yellow colour, in vessels of Ekki (*Lophira alata* var. *procera*); longitudinal surface (a little above natural size).

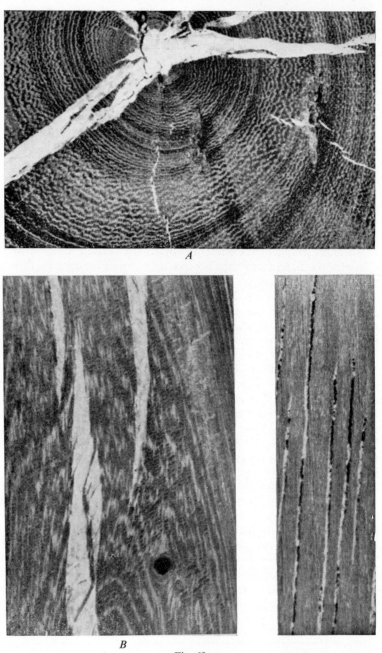

A

B

Fig. 69

Fig. 70.—Part of a large calcium deposit ("stone") taken from a log of Iroko (*Chlorophora excelsa*). The coin measures one inch (2·5 cm.) in diameter.

rose mahogany (*Dysoxylon fraseranum* Benth.) and in the African Copaiba balsam (*Daniellia oliveri* Hutch. et J.M.Dalz.). Where the more solid type of this material is found, it may occur as irregular lumps, as more extensive masses perhaps blocking up a vessel element, or may sometimes form septum-like plugs across a vessel. These materials are usually some shade of red or brown and may be very dark or even black; but yellow and white ones are known. The white and yellow deposits seen in some Dipterocarpaceae and so referred to, with the implication that they are mineral matter, are in fact very pale coloured gummy material (damar).

Distention of the parenchyma, both axial and of the rays, may occur, when certain parenchyma cells become repositories for oil (Fig. 73 *A–C*) as is well shown in the oil cells of the Lauraceae and Myristicaceae, while parenchyma may also contain tannin, resin, latex, mucilage and other substances. Sometimes such cells become enlarged and perhaps elongated (Fig. 73 *D*), as in the tanniniferous tubules seen in the Myristicaceae or in the latex tubes of the Euphorbiaceae and Apocynaceae, which are enormously elongated and branched cells.

Gums, mucilages and other materials may be deposited in intercellular canals which, like those of the conifers, may be either axial, when they occur between other axial elements, or radial, when they are found in the rays (Fig. 74 *A–C*). Such canals, by the separation or breakdown of cells, may thus be distinguished from the cellular canals and tubules just referred to.

K

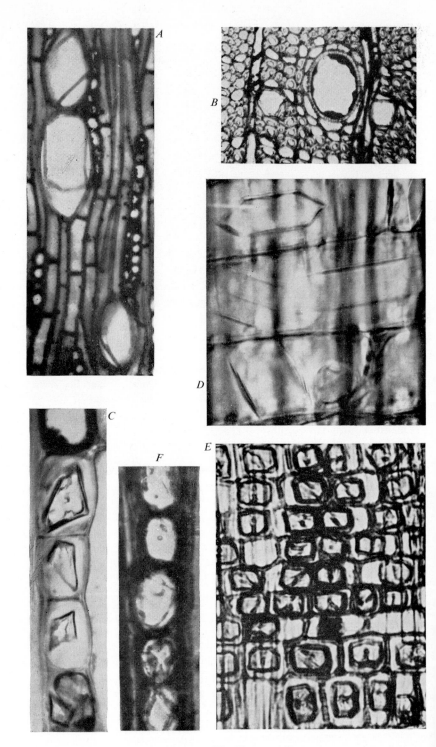

Fig. 71

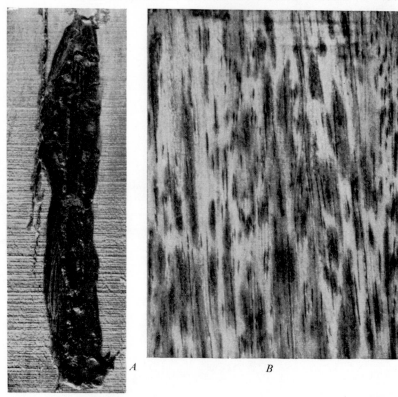

Fig. 72.—*A*. A piece of a board of Agba (*Gossweilerodendron balsamiferum*) with a large mass of gum which has oozed out on to the surface of the wood: this gum mass is about 40 cms. long. *B. Daniellia* sp.; the dark areas are caused by gum bleeding from the wood (a little above natural size).

[N.B.—Gum is here used in the wide sense, for any gummy material in hardwoods.]

Where the rays are very narrow, the presence of a canal may cause it to widen locally but the shape of the wider rays is not altered when canals occur in them. Several such canals may occur in a ray, and there seems to be no constancy of position as is found among coniferous

---

Fig. 71.—Crystals of calcium salts in cells of wood. *A, B*. Hickory (*Carya* sp.). *A*. (T.L.S.) showing distended parenchyma cells with crystals; two normal parenchyma cells lie almost in the centre, immediately below the two distended cells at the top left (× 175). *B*. (T.S.) shows a vessel, with a little gummy material, slightly to the right of the centre; somewhat to the left of this, and slightly below the horizontal central line, is a distended parenchyma cell with a crystal; two or three cells above this is a horizontal line of parenchyma with cells of normal size (× 175). *C*. Afrormosia (*Afrormosia elata*); chambered parenchyma, the cells containing crystals; L.S. (× 420). *D*. Parts of ray cells, with crystals, of *Gonystylus bacanus*; R.L.S. (× 860). *E*. Part of a ray of *Celtis philippinensis* with crystals in the cells; R.L.S. (× 305). *F*. Melawis (*Gonystylus warburgianus*); crystals in ray cells; T.L.S. (× 580).

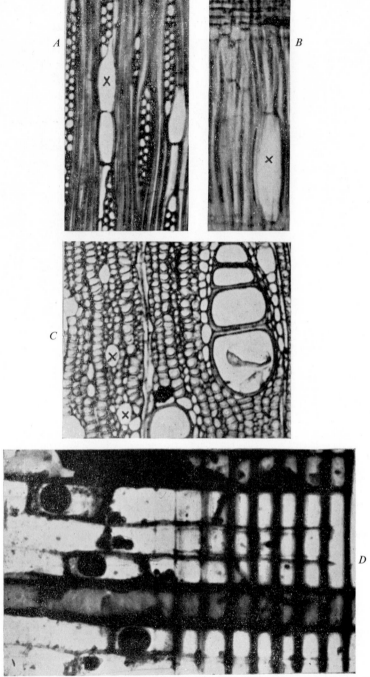

Fig. 73.—*A, B, C*. Oil cells (x) in Ramie (*Alseodaphne semicarpifolia*). *A*. T.L.S.
B. R.L.S., *C*. T.S. (all × 132). *D*. Pycnanthus (*Pycnanthus kombo*); part of a ray
showing two tanniniferous tubules, with dark contents, one at the extreme top, the
other just below centre; the other ray cells contain gummy or oily material; R.L.S.
(× 305).

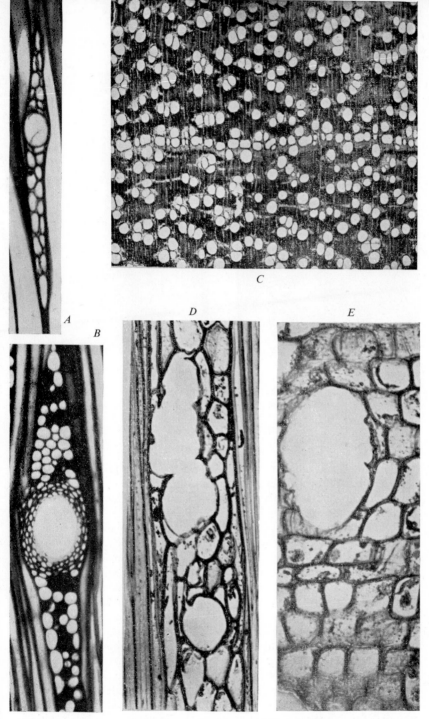

Fig. 74.—Gum ducts. *A*. Radial gum duct in a ray of Alstonia (*Alstonia congoensis*); T.L.S. (× 175). *B*. Radial gum duct in a ray of Blush Cudgerie (Pink "Poplar") (*Euroschinus falcatus*); the lysigenous nature of this duct is clearly shown; T.L.S. (× 175). *C*. Axial gum ducts in the wood of *Shorea bracteolata*; the gum ducts form a line across the centre of the figure; T.S. (× 11). *D, E*. Gum cysts in rays of *Ardisia barnesii*; *D*. T.L.S. (× 170), *E*. R.L.S. (× 170).

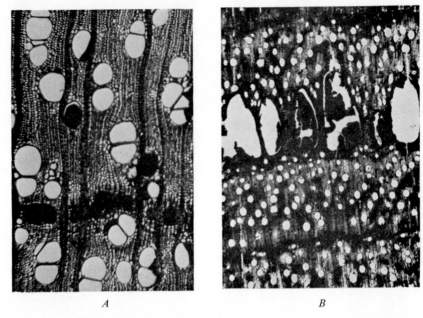

A   B

Fig. 75.—Traumatic gum ducts (gum galls). *A* in African Walnut (*Lovoa klaineana*);
the ducts, filled with dark gum, form a horizontal band a little below centre; note
that some of the vessels also contain dark, gummy material; T.S. (× 40). *B* in
White Sallee (*Eucalyptus paucifolia*); these large gum ducts are easily visible to the
unaided eye (cf. Fig. 76 *B*); T.S. (× 11).

genera in which radial resin canals occur. Among families in which
these canals occur are the Anacardiaceae, Burseraceae, Guttiferae and
Apocynaceae. Such canals often connect with axial ducts in the cortex
and sometimes with ducts in the pith.

Normally occurring axial canals appear to be of less frequent
occurrence than radial ones; it is rare for both types to be found in
the same wood, although this happens in the Dipterocarpaceae. The
axial canals are sometimes solitary, but they may be found in tangential
rows. They are found in a number of Leguminosae and as already
noted, in the Dipterocarpaceae, as well as in one or two genera of a
few other families. Traumatic axial canals are by no means uncommon
and are recorded for a number of families; radial canals of traumatic
origin, however, appear to be rare. Little is known about the origin of
these ducts; they appear to arise both schizogenously (p. 48) and
lysigenously (by breakdown of cells) but according to Solereder (1908,
p. 46) the presence of epithelium around an intercellular canal is not a
certain indication that it is schizogenous in origin, and developmental
studies furnish the only safe guide as to the nature of these cavities.
Some woods seem prone to develop traumatic axial ducts; they are seen

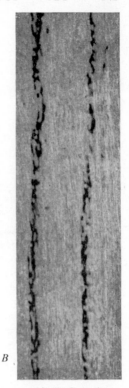

A

B

Fig. 76.—*A*. Latex traces in wood of Alstonia (*Alstonia congoensis*). *B*. Gum ducts (gum galls) in Blackwood (*Eucalyptus corymbosa*); (both about natural size).

in the gum canals which sometimes disfigure Tasmanian oak and other eucalypt woods (Figs. 75 *B*, 76 *B*) and also in those of African walnut (*Lovoa klaineana* Pierre ex Sprague) (Fig. 75 *A*) which are filled with a dark gummy material and which may improve the appearance of the wood. These last are believed to be schizo-lysigenous, that is, they arise schizogenously but later the cell walls around the canal become degraded into gum (gummosis) and thus enlarge the cavity (Groom, 1926). Woods of the family Myrsinaceae may show gum cysts or cavities of lysigenous origin in their rays (Fig. 74 *D*, *E*).

The latex tubes of the Euphorbiaceae and Apocynaceae have already been mentioned. In some Apocynaceae, for example, jelutong (*Dyera costulata* Hook.f.) and pattern wood (*Alstonia congoensis* Engl.), latex traces are found, which appear as short lenticular holes several milli-metres wide and a centimetre or more long, on the longitudinal surfaces. In the tree these holes are occupied by latex tubes embedded in thin-walled parenchyma, which pass from the xylem to the buds and leaves. By the uninitiated they might be identified as the galleries of a wood-boring insect in the timber (Fig. 76 *A*).

CHAPTER 7

SOME NON-TYPICAL TREES AND TIMBERS

The dendroid plants which have so far been considered are all conifers or dicotyledons and conform to a general plan. They are all large, with a trunk (or several trunks if they are shrubs) which is much branched; each branch terminates in a growing point. The bulk of the trunk is composed of secondary wood or xylem and, as seen in transverse section, consists of a small central pith surrounded successively by a broad ring of wood, a narrow zone of vascular cambium and a fairly narrow zone of phloem, followed by the cork cambium and outer bark. At least if the stem is young, there is nearly always a cortex between phloem and cork cambium.

Dendroid plants are, however, not confined to the conifers and dicotyledons, although in these two groups the tree habit is most prominent at the present day. Trees which belong to other groups of plants nearly always possess a different structure, while there are exceptions to the general plan even among the dicotyledons. It is with such non-typical trees that the present chapter is concerned. Considered as sources of timber these plants are of little importance, though they are of considerable botanical interest and for that reason deserve some consideration.

There are a number of arborescent ferns, notably the tree-ferns like *Dicksonia*, *Cyathea* and allied genera (Fig. 77). Some may attain a height of sixty to eighty feet (20–25 m.), consisting of a columnar trunk topped by a crown of huge leaves, in the centre of which lies the apical growing point of the stem. The trunk may fork into two equal branches and apparently this is not uncommon in some genera. These tree-ferns possess no vascular cambium and consequently have no secondary growth. The primary xylem forms a net-like cylinder, or more accurately a cone, completely surrounded on both sides by phloem. In transverse sections passing through such a cylinder, the xylem, with its surrounding phloem, may appear as a number of separate bundles; each represents a strand of the network and is termed a meristele. These meristeles, which may appear in the section to be wavy or corrugated, will be in the form of a broken ring. Other bundles may appear inside this ring, for sometimes the pith, which is large, contains additional strands of xylem and phloem.

These tree-ferns would seem to be, mechanically, of remarkably unstable construction, for the xylem is very much smaller at the base than higher up, having the form of an elongated, inverted cone. Nevertheless, outwardly the trunk may appear widest at the base, because

From a photograph by Dr. C. D. Adams

Fig. 77.—A tree fern, *Cyathea manniana*. Much of the trunk is hidden by the surrounding vegetation.

here there is an extensive outer region, composed of fine, closely compacted, interwoven adventitious roots, which lies outside the stem proper but which nevertheless adds considerably to its mechanical strength and rigidity. This structure serves to support a crown of very large leaves (each sometimes a few metres long) but it will be clear that it contains nothing to which the term timber might be applied (Fig. 78). The author has seen a section of one of these trunks converted into a handsome ash- or pin-tray but as far as he is aware that is the only type of use to which they are put.

Among the gymnosperms, the only class which is important in producing timber trees is the Coniferales, although the sole surviving

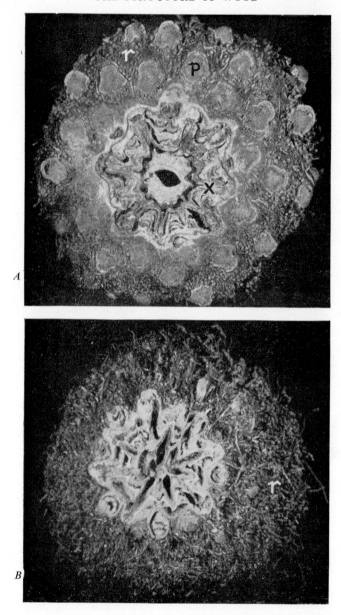

Fig. 78.—Transverse slices of a "trunk" of a tree fern (*Dicksonia* sp.). *A* was cut at a higher level than *B* and shows the xylem (×) which is entirely primary, surrounded by the bases of petioles of old leaves (p) and externally by a mass of adventitious roots (r). In *A* the bases of the leaf petioles are more numerous and are inter- mingled with adventitious roots (about natural size).

member of the order Ginkgoales, *Ginkgo biloba* L., the maidenhair tree of China and Japan, is a large tree which would probably pass, on casual inspection, as a broad-leaved tree. Its wood, however, is a typical softwood in appearance and structure (Fig. 79): it is light, rather brittle and too rare to be of commercial importance. The Cycadales, which are also gymnosperms, include plants with much the same appearance as tree ferns, i.e. with a columnar trunk capped by a crown of enormous, fern-like leaves (Fig. 80). These dendroid cycads are usually of short stature, but *Macrozamia hopei* T. Hill ex C. Moore may reach 20 m. and *Dioon spinulosum* Dyer sometimes exceeds 12 m. Cycad trunks contain little wood (Fig. 81): there is a large pith and a wide cortex. A specimen of *Dioon spinulosum* is recorded in which a trunk 33 cm. in diameter had about a third of its radius occupied by xylem, but this appears to be exceptional; normally less than a tenth of the radius consists of wood. Although a vascular cambium is present, secondary thickening takes place very slowly. In some cycads the first cambium dies and successive secondary cambia arise in the cortex, so that there is a series of concentric vascular zones, the outer ones taking the form of discrete bundles. In some cycads, tertiary cambia may arise, which form bundles between the secondary vascular zones. These tertiary bundles are remarkable for their inverse orientation, the phloem being toward the pith and the xylem toward the cortex.

In the remaining group of living gymnosperms, the Gnetales, *Ephedra* contains some shrubby species, while *Gnetum* is a genus of shrubs, climbers and small trees. The wood of these two genera contains vessels and is thus exceptional for gymnospermous wood. In *Ephedra* the wood is essentially a softwood, of which the bulk is composed of tracheids of the gymnosperm type, but it also contains numerous small, usually solitary vessels,, with foraminate (ephedroid) perforation plates. That of *Gnetum gnemon* L. (Fig. 82) with its vessels and conspicuous rays, might be taken for a hardwood (Maheshwari and Vasil, 1961).

There are a few genera of woody dicotyledons in which the wood possesses no vessels. Of such may be mentioned *Drimys*, a genus occurring mainly in South America and New Zealand (Fig. 83), and *Tetracentron* and *Trochodendron* from eastern Asia. In the wood of these plants, the function of water conduction falls entirely upon the tracheids. It might be thought that such woods would be easily confused with softwoods, but this, in fact, is unlikely, for although a transverse section will show, to some extent, a softwood-like regularity of the axial elements, most of these vesselless hardwoods have quite wide rays and, even in *Tetracentron*, where the rays are mostly fine, some are about four cells wide. Moreover, although the bordered pits of the tracheids may have a circular outline, they are quite different from the large circular pits so characteristic of softwoods (Fig. 84 *A*).

These vesselless hardwoods have given rise to controversy as to

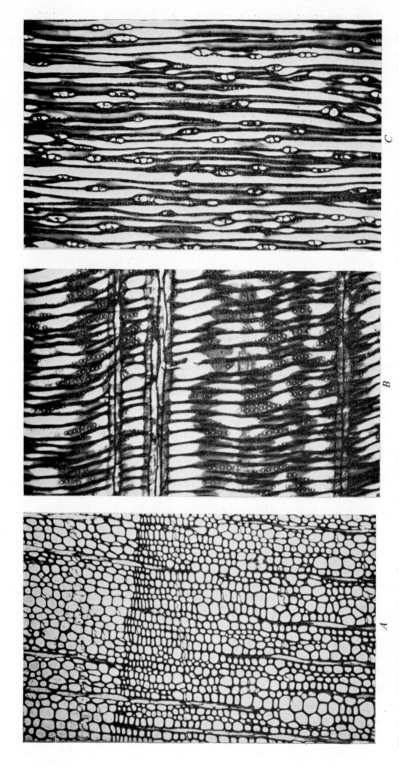

Fig. 79.—Maidenhair Tree (*Ginkgo biloba*). *A.* T.S., *B.* R.L.S. and *C.* T.L.S. of wood (× 170); the wood, which is of tracheidal structure, with bordered pits of the conifer type confined to the radial walls of the tracheids, and with uniseriate rays, resembles that of a conifer. In T.L.S. note the very low rays.

Fig. 80.—A cycad (*Cycas circinalis*) showing a short columnar trunk bearing a crown of large, fern-like leaves.

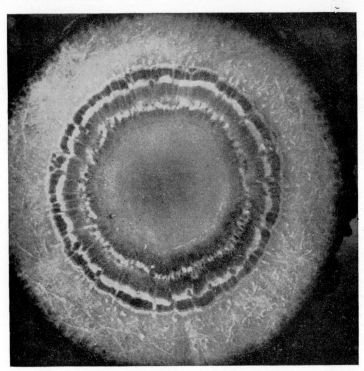

Fig. 81.—T.S. of a cycad trunk. There is a large pith in the centre, surrounded by three concentric rings of vascular tissue, then a wide cortex, in which the faint rings and lines are parts of leaf traces, while on the outside of the stem are leaf bases (showing black) (about one-third natural size).

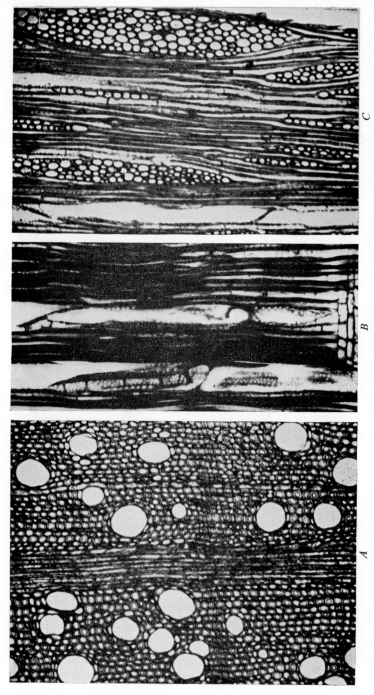

Fig. 82.—*Gnetum gnemon.* A. T.S., B. R.L.S., C. T.L.S. of wood (× 70). Although a gymnospermous plant, its wood, with numerous vessels and broad rays, has no resemblance to a softwood.

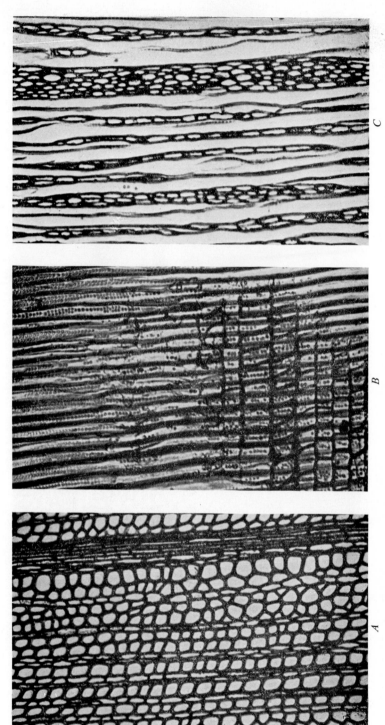

Fig. 83.—*Drimys winteri. A.* T.S., *B.* R.L.S., *C.* T.L.S. of wood (× 70). The tracheidal wood resembles that of a conifer, although the type of tracheidal pitting (cf. also Fig. 84 *A*) and the broad rays, are not softwood features but are typical of many dicotyledons.

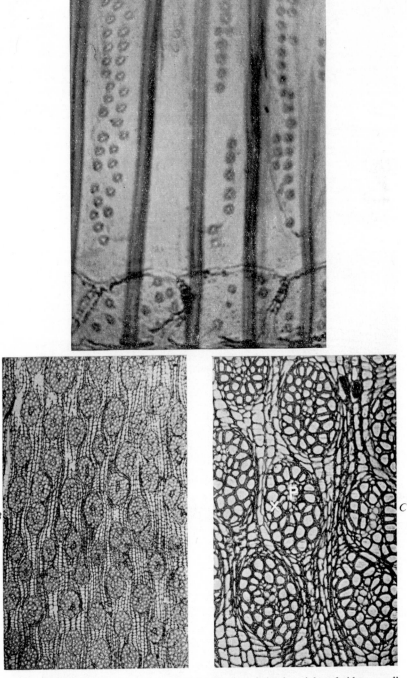

Fig. 84.—*A. Drimys winteri*, R.L.S. (× 305), showing pitting in axial tracheids ; a small portion of a ray is shown at the extreme bottom of the figure. *B, C. Dracaena* sp., T.S. of part of a stem (*B* × 16) (*C* × 52), showing separate vascular bundles embedded in lignified parenchyma. The bundle is the type in which the xylem (X) surrounds the phloem (P).

whether their vessels have been lost in the course of evolution, or whether they never possessed any (Bailey and Nast, 1944, 1945). If the latter, then there might appear to be some reason to regard them as more closely related to the conifers than are other dicotyledons. There is, however, good reason to believe that these plants never possessed vessels and little to support any relationship with gymnosperms. They may best be regarded as dicotyledons in which the structure of the wood does not conform to the basic dicotyledonous plan, i.e., as anomalies.

In the monocotyledons, which are usually herbaceous and without secondary thickening, the stem structure normally differs from that of dicotyledons. There is no clearly defined pith or cortex, but a parenchymatous ground tissue in which numerous vascular bundles are situated. In a transverse section these bundles may appear to be scattered throughout the stem, although they are more numerous in the more peripheral part. A few monocotyledons are trees: thus in the family Liliaceae there are, to mention three

Fig. 85.—A dendroid monocotyledon, *Cordyline australis*. The slender woody trunks are secondarily thickened, but in the monocotyledonous manner.

genera: *Dracaena*, the dragon's blood tree, of which one gigantic specimen of *D. draco* L. was 20 m. high and 14 m. in girth *Cordyline* (Fig. 85), and *Xanthorrhoea*, the grass trees or blackboys of Australia, which may be 3 m. or more high, while in the Palmae

L

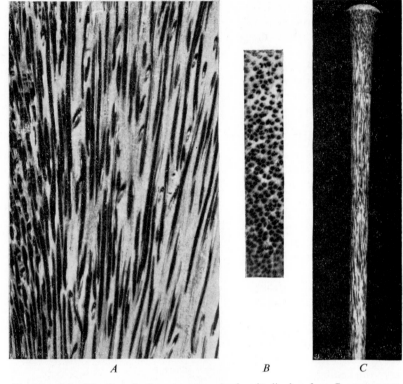

A   B   C

Fig. 86.—Palm Wood. *A, B. Caryota urens*; *A*, a longitudinal surface, *B*, a transverse surface (about natural size). *C*. Top of a walking-stick made of palm wood (porcupine wood); this stick is probably the wood of the Borassus or Fan palm (*Borassus aethenpium*). In all these figures the dark streaks or dots are the vascular bundles and the lighter parts are ground tissue.

(palms) there are many dendroid species, some of which may rise to 45 m.

Secondary thickening in monocotyledons is uncommon; where it occurs it differs from that in dicotyledons and conifers, for there is no vascular cambium between the xylem and phloem of the vascular bundles. A cambium arises in the ground tissue, outside the vascular bundles, and the cells which it cuts off toward the inner side develop

---

Fig. 87.—Diagrams of woody stems with non-typical structure, in T.S. (cf. classification, pp. 156–60).

A. Flattened stem (e.g. *Machaerium*)	*E*. Concentric stem (e.g. *Suaeda*)
B. Excentric stem	*F*. Disperse stem (e.g. *Bauhinia*)
C. Lobed stem (e.g. *Lantana*)	*G*. Divided stem (e.g. *Serjania*)
D. Interrupted stem (e.g. *Bignonia*)	*H*. Compound stem (e.g. *Thinouia*)

(Most of these diagrams are based on Schenck's figures.)

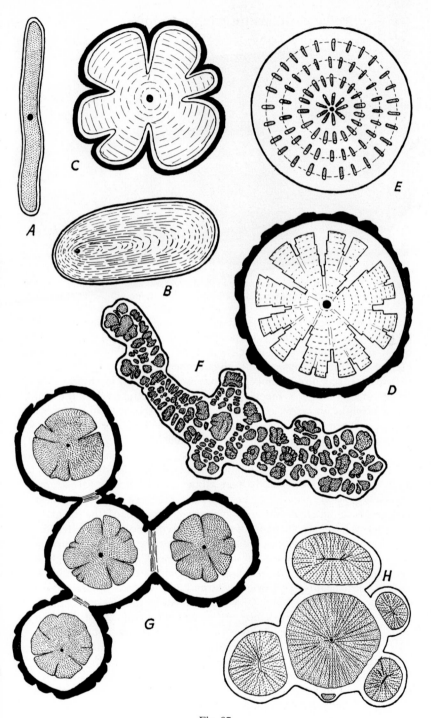

Fig. 87

Fig. 88.—T.S. of a trunk of Lignum Vitae (*Guaiacum* sp.) from which bark has been removed. This is an example of an excentric stem, the pith being at P.

into entire vascular bundles and ground tissue, while any cut off to its outer side are added to the peripheral ground tissue. That this can be an effective method of increase in girth is shown by the enormous diameter of the *Dracaena* trunk already mentioned.

In palms, secondary thickening may occur though in some of them no secondary tissue is formed, increase in the thickness of the trunk being brought about by cell enlargement. In others, although there is no discrete cambial region, cell division and cell enlargement occur in the ground tissue, particularly in that which is more centrally placed, while the fibres forming sheaths round the vascular bundles also increase in size. Thickening of the trunk may also be due, in part, to increase in the size of existing intercellular spaces and the formation of new spaces. The ground tissue may become very hard (Tomlinson, 1961). These unusual ways of increasing the size of the trunk are remarkable, and of all dendroid plants having non-typical structure, the palms are the most used as timber. They serve for constructional work, as whole trunks in house-building and piling, although the denser, outer part of the trunk may be cleft into pieces suitable for flooring and beams. The vascular strands are often a different colour from the ground tissue and on a longitudinal surface have the appearance of quills (Fig. 86), hence the name, porcupine wood, by which palm wood is sometimes known. It is because of this appearance and also because the wood takes a good finish, that it is also used at times for walking-sticks and umbrella handles, and for marquetry work.

Non-typical structure or, as it is usually called, anomalous structure, is also found in some dicotyledonous stems, although rarely in commercial timbers. It is very common in the stems of woody climbing

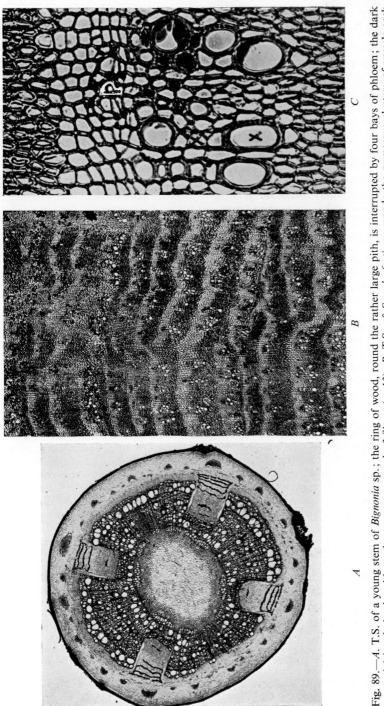

FIG. 89.—A. T.S. of a young stem of *Bignonia* sp.; the ring of wood, round the rather large pith, is interrupted by four bays of phloem; the dark tangential bands in the phloem bays are composed of fibres (× 13). *B*. T.S. of *Suaeda fruticosa* wood; the numerous clusters of vessels each form part of a vascular bundle of which the phloem is indistinct at the low magnification: each ring of bundles is formed by a different cambium (× 27). *C*. Enlarged view of a single bundle of *B*., *p*, phloem, ×, xylem (× 300).

156

plants or lianes, some of which may attain to large dimensions in tropical forests.

The following brief summary of these non-typical stems is based on that of Chalk and Chattaway (1937) which is, in turn, derived from Pfeiffer's (1926) monograph on abnormal secondary thickening. Other detailed accounts of these non-typical stems will be found in De Bary (1884), Schenck (1892), and in Solereder (1908) and Metcalfe and Chalk (1950). The anomalies may be classified thus:

A. DUE TO ABNORMAL GROWTH OF THE VASCULAR CAMBIUM

1. *The flattened or excentric stem:* caused by unequal production of secondary xylem and phloem in different parts. It is seen in any stem which has an excentric pith and is also responsible for the formation of flattened strap-like stems, of which an excellent example is seen in species of the leguminous liane *Machaerium* (Fig. 87 *A*) and in *Guaiacum*, a member of the Zygophyllaceae (Figs. 87 *B*, 88).

2. *The lobed stem:* here again, due to irregular formation of the secondary wood, the xylem is furrowed or, as seen in transverse section, lobed (Fig. 87 *C*). This type of stem is seen, although but slightly developed, in hornbeam, where the bole is commonly somewhat fluted and the growth rings, as seen in a transverse section, are rather wavy, and to a greater degree in the strongly fluted stems of the logwood, *Haemato-xylon campechianum* L.

3. *The interrupted stem:* this is essentially similar to the lobed stem in that xylem and phloem development is uneven, but here the vascular cambium is broken into strips, of which some are carried outward by the developing secondary xylem while alternate ones remain nearer the centre because xylem development is less rapid, although in these regions more phloem is formed. Thus the secondary wood is fluted, but there is cambium at the base of each furrow and on the crest of each ridge. Often secondary xylem begins to form, periodically, more rapidly along the margins of the furrows and thus a transverse section of the stem, instead of showing secondary wood in which there are deep, phloem filled bays with straight sides, will show these sides developed as a series of steps. This type of stem is well seen in species of *Bignonia* (Figs. 87 *D*, 89 *A*) and certain other members of the Bignoniaceae.

4. *The foraminate stem:* in the foraminate stem there are bands or islands of phloem in the secondary wood. Such phloem is termed interxylary or included phloem and the phloem groups are often called phloem islands. Phloem arises in this anomalous position in one of two ways:—
   (i) Localised areas of cambium stop growing; then, as the surrounding

---

Fig. 90.—Included phloem. *A.* Island type: *Strychnos nux-blanda*, T.S. (× 27); the phloem islands are the larger, dark areas; details of this tissue cannot be made out, because it collapses as the wood dries. *B.* Band type: *Cocculus laurifolius*, T.S. (× 27); the white areas across the centre of the figure are phloem; here also, the phloem has partially disintegrated. *C. Avicennia* ?*alba*; phloem of the band type, seen on a tangential longitudinal surface of a solid piece of wood; the bands of phloem have the appearance of growth rings (about natural size).

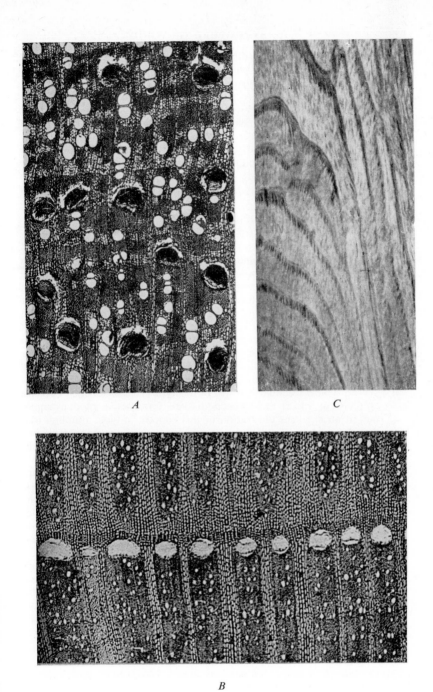

A

C

B

Fig. 90

cambium, which is still active, moves outward as it forms more secondary wood, the phloem outside the areas of inactive cambium gradually becomes surrounded by wood. In time, the active cambium heals over these phloem-filled gaps and functioning in the normal way, adds new wood in these areas. The result is that pockets of phloem become included in the secondary wood. This type of foraminate stem is seen in *Strychnos*.

(ii) Localised areas of the cambium cease to produce wood to the inner side and instead produce secondary phloem. After a time these areas revert to cutting off cells which differentiate into wood. In this way phloem islands are produced in the secondary wood, as in *Combretum*.

B. DUE TO ANOMALOUS LAYERS OF CAMBIUM

5. *The concentric stem:* here the initial vascular cambium is short-lived and is replaced by a new one developing in the cortex. The new cambium behaves like its predecessor and in its turn gives way to another. We have seen that this type of structure occurs in the stems of some cycads. Each cambial ring may form a vascular ring, with xylem to the inside and phloem externally, or separate vascular bundles may be formed, with intervening ground tissue (Fig. 87 E). Formation of bundles in this way must not be confused with that just described for certain monocotyledons, in which the cambium forms whole bundles to the inside. In the present instance xylem and phloem are formed on the inner and outer side of the cambium respectively.

Non-typical secondary growth of this type is characteristic of certain families, of which the Chenopodiaceae furnishes a good example: indeed an excellent illustration of this concentric type, although in a root, may be seen in a slice of beetroot. A good woody example is a small shrub of our southern and eastern coasts, *Suaeda fruticosa* Forsk (Fig. 89 B, C), which belongs to the Chenopodiaceae and in which a transverse section shows scattered vascular bundles embedded in a hard ground tissue, the whole making quite a hard, tough, "wood." Superficially, in this stem, we have an arrangement resembling that of the palms, with a hard ground tissue in which vascular bundles are embedded. In the palm stem, however, the structure may be primary, and if it has arisen by secondary thickening, it will be by secondary thickening of an unusual type (cf. pp. 151, 154).

Avicennia (Verbenaceae) has alternating zones of xylem and phloem, the latter being associated with parenchyma (conjunctive tissue) and sclerenchyma, and being in the form of discrete strands.

6. *The disperse stem:* in such stems there is, to begin with, the normal arrangement—central pith and xylem, cambium and phloem cylinders, but, by the growth of parenchyma cells of the wood, as well as those of the rays and pith, the xylem and phloem become cut up into irregular strands, which may be numerous, and so complex in their arrangement, that all traces of the original form is lost. This type of stem is seen in some species of *Bauhinia* (Fig. 87 F).

7. *The divided stem:* at first the stem contains a ring of vascular bundles. Each of these develops its own cambium or several adjacent ones may

Fig. 91.—A tree Lobelia (*Lobelia gibberoa*), in western Uganda.

form a common cambium. Each bundle, or group of bundles, develops as though it were a separate stem, even producing bark later. In time the original stem thus becomes a composite structure of several stems, rather like a rope with its several component strands. Growth of this type is seen in some species of *Serjania*, a genus of lianes belonging to the Sapindaceae (Fig. 87 *G*).

8. *The compound stem:* in which there is a central xylem and phloem mass, with its cambium, surrounded by a ring of woody cylinders each with its own cambium. *Thinouia*, another Sapindaceous genus, as well as some species of *Serjania*, possess this structure (Fig. 87 *H*).

Among these non-typical or anomalous stems it is only those which contain included phloem (i.e. the foraminate stem and the concentric stem), which are likely to be encountered by the student of wood structure, and included phloem is found but seldom in commercial timbers. Record (1934) recognised two types of included phloem, the island type, where the phloem occurs in scattered strands (Fig. 90 *A*), either standing in definite relation to the vessel groups or being independent of them, and the band type where the phloem strands form concentric series (Fig. 90 *B*). These types approximate to the foraminate

From a photograph by Professor A. S. Boughey

Fig. 92.—Pawpaw (*Carica papaya*); the tree-like habit is due to non-typical development of the phloem.

and concentric types of Chalk and Chattaway. Examples of the foraminate type are seen in *Neea* (Nyctaginaceae), *Avicennia* (Verbenaceae)
and *Erisma* (Vochysiaceae) as well as in the plants already mentioned,
while the concentric type is seen in *Simmondsia* (Buxaceae), *Dolio-
carpus* (Dilleniaceae), *Pueraria* and *Wistaria* (Leguminosae) and
elsewhere.

Finally, brief mention should be made of a few remarkable dicotyledons, dendroid in form, but in reality, probably little more than
gigantic herbs. Among such are the giant lobelias of East Africa
(Fig. 91), of which *L. gibberoa* Hemsl. may reach a height of 10 m.,
and the tree groundsels, from the same regions, of which *Senecio
gardnerii* Cotton rises to 8 m. In these plants there is a large pith
and relatively little xylem, so that the general plan is comparable to
that of some of the cycads, although this does not imply that there is
any relationship between these groups. Another remarkable tree is the
pawpaw (*Carica papaya* L.) (Fig. 91), much cultivated in the tropics
for its edible fruits. Although these trees may reach a height of 10 m.,
their boles are essentially herbaceous and non-woody and the chief
supporting tissue is the phloem (or bark) which contains thick-walled
fibres.

CHAPTER 8

THE ULTIMATE STRUCTURE OF WOOD

The structure of the walls of woody cells has already been touched upon briefly (pp. 25–26). Each cell has a primary wall, characteristic of the phase of cell expansion which follows its origin from the cambium, and a secondary wall, laid down inside the primary wall during the later stages of cellular differentiation. The thin "wall" to be seen between two young cambial derivatives has of course a tripartite organization, consisting of the middle lamella or intercellular layer, with a true primary wall (which it is convenient to refer to as P) on each side of it, formed by the respective protoplasts of the two cells. In mature wood the corresponding thin line, indicative of the boundary between contiguous cells, is often referred to loosely as the middle lamella, though in fact the middle lamella as seen in this sense commonly represents the same triple structure and is then more correctly referred to as the compound middle lamella. The secondary wall to be found within this structure commonly consists of three layers, the outer, middle and inner layers, laid down in that order and usually termed S_1, S_2 and S_3 respectively: spiral (or, more correctly, helical) thickening may be present on the inner surface of S_3, as in the tracheids of Douglas fir or in the vessel elements of lime and elm.

Examination of transverse sections of conifer tracheids or hardwood fibres under the high power of a microscope is, however, very unlikely to reveal this amount of detail in their walls. Indeed, apart from the distinction between the compound middle lamella and the secondary wall, and the presence of pits and spiral thickening, the wall commonly appears to be homogeneous. Sometimes however, owing to slight differences of refractive index, the several layers may be seen without recourse to special techniques (see Bailey, 1954, plate 4, Fig. 1), and if the section is stained for lignin with aniline sulphate or phloroglucinol and hydrochloric acid the compound middle lamella will probably be more densely stained than most of the secondary wall, while a narrow zone of the wall nearest the cell lumen may show less colour than the remainder. In some fibres a further layering or stratification of the wall may be visible, sometimes showing more layers than the four so far mentioned; however, all this fairly readily visible layering will be in the S_2 alone.

If longitudinal sections of tracheids and fibres are examined, their walls will again probably appear homogeneous, although occasionally they may show fine, oblique striations. If the pit apertures are elongated, it is probable that their long axes will be regularly oblique. Moreover where minute cracks or checks have formed in the wall, they will be found to be not randomly directed, but are most likely to have a similar fairly uniform oblique orientation (Figs. 39 *E*, 112 *B*). Furthermore, the elongated cavities in the wall produced by certain wood-rotting fungi, such as species of *Chaetomium*, invariably have an oblique orientation (Bailey and Vestal, 1937; Savory, 1954; Aaron and Wilson, 1955; Levy, 1965). Such features suggest that the wall is not homogeneous, but that some part of it, at least, has a structure with a helical organization in relation to the cell as a whole.

While normal visual examination is not a very successful way of showing the complex multi-layered structure of the wall, this feature can be clearly demonstrated by other methods. More than a century ago it was suggested that apparently homogeneous cell walls are built up of sub-microscopic crystalline particles or micelles, separated from one another by regions of looser construction, again implying an internal ordered structure concealed within an outward appearance of homogeneity. Since then, numerous techniques have been applied to the study of the walls of wood cells, and also to those of a wide range of other plant cells as well, and have yielded information on the chemical composition of cell walls, the ultimate arrangement of the molecules of which they are composed, and their multi-layered structure. More recently, the electron microscope has provided a most valuable additional tool in these investigations (see Liese and Côté, 1962; Côté, 1965; and references there cited). Elucidation of these problems, some of them very complex ones, has involved chemical and physical as well as botanical investigations, concerned not only with the mature structure of the cell wall, but also with the manner of its formation: see, for instance, Ott (1943), Wise (1946), Meyer (1950), Preston (1952), Roelofsen (1959), Thornber and Northcote (1961, 1962), Siegel (1962), Wardrop (1964), Côté (1965), Rogers and Perkins (1968). The subject is not only one of fundamental botanical interest, but is of great technical and commercial importance, for example in relation to the wood-pulp, paper-making and artificial silk industries.

The structural problem is a two-fold one, concerned on the one hand with the chemistry of the wall; that is, with the nature of the molecules of which it is composed, and on the other with their arrangement in the wall on a supra-molecular scale of organization.

In considering the chemistry of wood it must be remembered that wood is a very complex and stable material and the various chemical substances of which it is composed are very intimately associated in the walls of the wood cells. Consequently, methods of chemical analysis aimed at separating these substances, so that they may be studied in greater detail in a pure state, may lead to the unintentional breakdown of the very molecules it is desired to study. Thus there are still uncertainties in our knowledge of them, though great advances have been made in recent years, and their main features are well established.

Of the dry weight of wood, commonly about 99 per cent consists of two major components: cellulose and substances related to it, to which the general term holocellulose is applied, and lignin. Other substances, such as pigments, silica, resins and gums, make up the remaining 1 per cent or so of the dry wood substance, but these will not be considered in detail. They are the substances which the chemist tries to get rid of before making his analyses of the major components of the cell-wall and which he groups together under the vague term extractives. They are also sometimes referred to as extraneous materials. Though they normally form only a small proportion of the total dry weight of wood they may sometimes be of considerable importance in relation to its properties and uses as timber.

A first step in the chemical study of wood, after the removal of extractives, is thus the separation of the holocellulose and lignin fractions. It is chemically possible, though the procedures need not concern us here, either to dissolve away the lignin, leaving the holocellulose more or less intact, or alternatively, to extract the holocellulose and leave the lignin.

Some 70–80 per cent of the wood cell-wall is holocellulose, which consists of a variety of carbohydrates, together with certain related compounds.

Carbohydrates are a class of chemical compounds composed of carbon, hydrogen and oxygen, the last two elements being present in the same proportions as they are in water. Among the simplest of them are certain sugars, most of which have a molecule containing either five carbon atoms (e.g. xylose, arabinose) or six carbon atoms (e.g. glucose, galactose, mannose), and thus termed pentoses and hexoses respectively. These may be represented by the formulae $C_5H_{10}O_5$ (pentoses) and $C_6H_{12}O_6$ (hexoses), and are known as monosaccharides. Monosaccharides are soluble in water, sweet to the taste and, in the solid state, crystalline. Possessing similar properties, but having twelve carbon atoms in their molecule, are other sugars, the disaccharides, such as sucrose (cane sugar) with the formula $C_{12}H_{22}O_{11}$. Still more complex are the polysaccharides, many of which do not dissolve in water, and which are tasteless and, to all outward appearance, amorphous. Polysaccharides have large molecules, represented by such formulae as $(C_5H_8O_4)_n$ and $(C_6H_{10}O_5)_n$, these molecules being built up from a number (n) of monosaccharide units of either five- or six-carbon sugars. In a similar manner certain acidic derivatives of six-carbon sugars, collectively termed uronic acids (e.g. galacturonic acid derived from galactose) also form polymers, known as poly-uronides, which contribute to cell-wall structure.

In the analysis of holocellulose the wood chemist recognises certain principal fractions. About two-thirds of it, i.e. some 40–50 per cent of the whole wall, is insoluble in a 17·5 per cent solution of caustic soda; this, termed α-cellulose, has very large molecules. The remaining fractions, β- and γ-cellulose, are both soluble in 17·5 per cent caustic soda, although they may be separated chemically from each other in other ways. They consist of smaller polysaccharide molecules and polyuronides, as well as mixed polymers of monosaccharides and uronic acids. The β- and γ-fractions are often collectively referred to as hemicellulose. It must be emphasized that these α-, β- and γ-fractions do not precisely represent particular chemical substances. They are labels of convenience, and with our increasing knowledge of the chemistry of wood they are becoming less useful.

Lignin is not present in very young wood cells as they are cut off from the cambium, but is deposited in the wall in the later stages of cellular differentiation. It also is a compound of carbon, hydrogen and oxygen, but it is not a carbohydrate nor even related to this class of compound: it is essentially phenolic in nature. Nevertheless, like the polysaccharides, it is a polymer built up of relatively simple units. It is a stable, rather inert substance which has proved difficult to study, and its chemical composition and molecular structure are incompletely known (Baylis, 1960; Brauns and Brauns, 1960; Browning, 1963; Kratzl, 1965). In softwoods, the lignin content is commonly between about 25 and 30 per cent of the dry weight; in temperate hardwoods it is rather less, ranging from about 19 to 25 per cent, while in tropical hardwoods it may be higher; 30 per cent or more has been recorded.

In mature wood, lignin is most abundant in the middle lamella, where it may constitute 60 to 90 per cent of the dry weight. It is least abundant in the secondary wall where, in S_3, it often does not exceed 10 per cent of the dry weight. Correspondingly, the proportion of cellulose increases in the last formed part of the wall (Meier and Willkie, 1959; Meier, 1961). Analyses have shown that the early wood of a growth ring has a higher proportion of lignin in its cell walls than has the late wood. This is understandable, since the greater thickness of the walls of the late wood elements is due mainly to an increase in the thickness of S_2, so that the walls of the early wood have, in relation to their total thickness, a greater proportion of primary wall and middle lamella, where, as we have seen, the lignin content is higher.

The lignin and cellulosic components of the cell wall are very intimately related (Bolker, 1963), although the chemistry of this association is still imperfectly understood. The use of the term "ligno-cellulose," which implies a definite chemical compound, is best avoided in view of the incompleteness of present knowledge.

In the middle lamella, using the term in its strict sense, true cellulose is lacking. In the soft tissues of plants this layer consists mainly of pectic substances, which are essentially of a polyuronide nature, although in mature wood these are relatively less important as the middle lamella has then become heavily lignified.

α-cellulose can be broken down enzymically by wood-rotting fungi or chemically by suitable treatment with sulphuric acid. The principal product of such chemical treatment is β-glucose.[1] This breakdown involves the chemical addition of water to the cellulose molecule (i.e. hydrolysis) and may be represented by an equation such as:—

$$(C_6H_{10}O_5)_n + nH_2O = nC_6H_{12}O_6$$
Cellulose   Water   Glucose

However, this treatment produces smaller amounts of other sugars as well as glucose, an indication that the initial α-cellulose may have a variable composition and is not a single pure substance.

The reverse process, the synthesis of cellulose from glucose, is a more complex matter. Basically, however, the plant builds up the cellulose of its cell walls from numerous glucose units by an indirect sequence of enzymically controlled reactions which is not a mere reversal of hydrolytic breakdown (Colvin, 1964; Barber et al., 1964). Hence cellulose may be regarded as a polymer of β-glucose.

β-glucose is conventionally represented by its structural formula thus:

CH$_2$OH

the carbon atoms being numbered for reference according to the scheme:

This two-dimensional pattern is not an exact representation of the spatial arrangement of the atoms of the β-glucose molecule but it is a useful, conventional way of showing how the atoms are linked and their valencies satisfied. The atoms are, in fact, arranged in a three-dimensional pattern which is identical for each molecule and within which the spatial relationships of the atoms are known.

Two molecules of β-glucose can be visualised in a simple way as

[1] Glucose exists in α and β forms, which differ slightly in the configuration of their molecules and have different properties, although they are identical in chemical composition. The glucose obtained from α-cellulose has the β configuration, while the corresponding hydrolysis of starch yields α-glucose. Thus the very different properties and biological functions of cellulose and starch derive ultimately from a relatively minor difference between their constituent building units or monomers.

becoming linked by the elimination of a molecule of water between them, as indicated by the broken lines in the following formula:

$$CH_2OH \quad H \quad OH$$

The molecule so formed can thus be represented:

$$CH_2OH \quad H \quad OH$$

This is in fact the structural formula for a disaccharide, cellobiose, $C_{12}H_{22}O_{11}$.

A repetition of a process of this kind would result in the production of a long chain of linked glucose "units", the "units" being β-glucose residues, and the chemist has established that the cellulose molecule has a structure of this kind, as represented on the next page. Following the chemical convention of the numbering of the carbon atoms in the glucose molecule, cellulose is thus described as a $1:4$ polymer of β-glucose.

It is clear that the glucose residues are joined in a very precise and regular way and that in the formula alternate residues are, as it were, turned over, or rotated through 180°, with respect to their immediate neighbours. Hence a pair of such residues, rather than an individual one, might be considered as the building unit. Such a pair of β-glucose residues makes, as has been seen, a molecule of the disaccharide cellobiose, so that the cellulose chain might be regarded as built up of units of cellobiose. In this connection it may be noted that cellobiose can be obtained by controlled incomplete hydrolysis of cellulose, and moreover it represents a step in the pathway of the natural enzymic breakdown of cellulose by certain micro-organisms.

The "n" in the formula of the cellulose molecule stands, as we have seen, for the number of β-glucose residues of which it is made up. This number, commonly referred to as the "degree of polymerisation", (abbreviated to DP), is not a constant one and, on the basis of various analytical and physico-chemical studies, is now placed by most investigators between 5,000 and 10,000, although some believe it may be considerably greater. Estimates of the DP of cellulose have increased

M

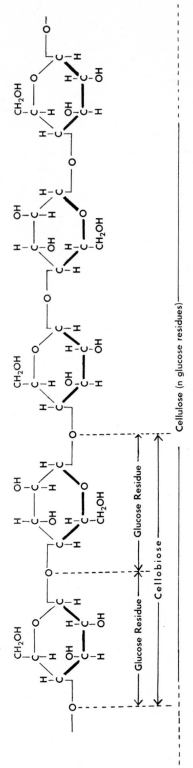

Diagram to illustrate the structure of the cellulose molecule.

steadily in the last 20–30 years, the increase arising from improvements in analytical techniques. It is now known that the earlier procedures led to some breakdown of the molecules of cellulose in the course of their separation from the other components of cell walls. Since a glucose unit is about 5 Å[1] in length, a molecule of cellulose might exceed 50,000 Å, i.e. 5 μ, in length: it is one of the many natural substances which form macro-molecules.

It has already been indicated that only some two-thirds of the holo-cellulose fraction is alkali resistant, and consists almost wholly of cellulose in the strict chemical sense, i.e. as the 1 : 4 polymer of β-glucose. The remaining one-third, soluble in alkali, yields on hydrolysis varying proportions of other six-carbon sugars, galactose and mannose, together with the very sweet, five-carbon sugar, xylose (wood sugar) and some uronic acid. It has therefore been inferred that polymers of these substances must exist in wood, and these are referred to respectively as galactan, mannan, xylan and polyuronide. Thus galacturonic acid, with the molecular structure thus:

```
                COOH
                 |
           OH    C ——— O   H
            |  /  H       \ |
            C             C
            |  \ OH    H  / |
           H   C ——— C   OH
                |       |
                H      OH
```

or xylose with the structure thus:

```
                 H
                 |
           H     C ——— O   OH
            |  /  H       \ |
            C             C
            |  \ OH    H  / |
          OH   C ——— C   H
                |       |
                H      OH
```

could both be visualized as giving rise to polymers in a way entirely analogous to that already outlined for glucose.

However, more recent detailed chemical investigations (see for instance Timell, 1964, 1965) have established that the principal non-cellulosic polymers are mixed ones, such as for example a glucurono-xylan characteristic of hardwoods and a galacto-gluco-mannan of softwoods. These are, moreover, not simply long, straight-chain 1 : 4 polymers like cellulose, but are smaller molecules, and bear side-branches; i.e. 1 : 2 or 1 : 6 linkages are also involved in their make-up. The DP values of their main "back-bones" are of the order of 200:

---

[1] Å (sometimes written A or AU) denotes Ångstrom unit. Å = 0·000,0001 mm. (one ten-millionth of a millimetre or one ten-thousandth of 1 μ).

the precise arrangement and structure of the side chains still present some chemical problems.

This complexity of the chemical composition of wood cell-walls is matched also by that of their physical structure, especially of the cellulose fraction. Much work has also been done in this field, for a knowledge of it has proved to be essential for understanding the behaviour of natural cellulose (Ott, 1943; Meyer, 1950; Preston, 1952, 1959). In this work attention has been directed especially to the problem of the organization of the cellulose molecules in natural fibres and in artificially regenerated cellulose like rayon (which is prepared from wood-pulp), and to the bearing of their arrangement on the strength and other properties of the fibre. The techniques used depend in great measure on the fact that natural cellulose is to a considerable extent crystalline: the size, form and arrangement of the crystalline components are of paramount importance.

In order to clarify the discussion it is convenient here to anticipate the evidence and firstly to indicate in outline the main conclusions to be drawn from it. Cellulose molecules do not exist in the cell wall as entirely discrete molecular chains; these chains are grouped together in bundles, or microfibrils, of fairly constant supra-molecular but sub-microscopic thickness, which form a fairly open framework of the wall (Fig. 99). The hemicelluloses play a less obvious, but no less important, part in wall structure, occupying, in part, the spaces between the microfibrils, and linking these together. Lignin is also deposited in the spaces, and those remaining are normally occupied by water; the permeability of the wall to water depends on the presence of inter-fibrillar spaces in which it is free to move.

The wall may thus be pictured as consisting of two continuous but inter-penetrating systems, that of the truly cellulosic microfibrils which are largely crystalline, and that of the spaces between them which are occupied by non-crystalline hemicelluloses, lignin and water. The basic physical structure of the wall may thus be described in terms of its microfibrillar framework. Although the direct study of this framework by electron microscopy has been possible only in the last 20 years or so, the largely crystalline nature of the microfibrils had enabled investigators, long before the advent of electron microscopy, to build up a considerable body of knowledge and understanding of cell wall structure, based on the application of well-established crystallographic methods of study.

In a crystalline substance the molecules have constant spatial relationships one to another, and so build up a regular, accurately repeated, three-dimensional pattern or "crystal lattice", the external form of the crystal being commonly determined by the pattern of the lattice. For example, the molecules of β-glucose build up this sugar in needle-shaped or, under some conditions, plate-shaped crystals. Alternatively, if a substance is non-crystalline, that is, amorphous, its

molecules are randomly arranged and the external form is correspondingly more variable.

To all normal outward appearances, cellulose is an amorphous, not
a crystalline, substance. Its appearance to the unaided eye, or even
under the high powers of the microscope, does not suggest that its
molecules are arranged in a regular pattern. This arises of course from
the fact that the dimensions of its crystalline regions are below the limit
of visibility of conventional microscopy: they lie, as we now know,
within the microfibrils revealed by electron microscopy. Following the
earlier recognition of these crystalline regions, within which the
cellulose molecules are regularly arranged, they were termed micelles or
crystallites. Though too small to be visible under the highest powers
of the light microscope, they could be studied by the methods of X-ray
diffraction and polarization microscopy. Thus the evidence derived
from these methods, revealing the existence and orientation of micelles,
may be closely correlated with the evidence of electron microscopy,
bearing upon the existence and orientation of microfibrils.

No more than brief mention can be made of X-ray diffraction
methods (Astbury, 1933; Bunn, 1945; Lonsdale, 1948; Roelofsen,
1959). In essentials, a single crystal or an aggregate of small crystals is
placed in an X-ray camera in the path of a beam of X-rays and these
rays are, in effect, "reflected" (strictly, they are diffracted) by the
planes of atoms and atomic groups of the crystal. The "reflected"
X-rays are allowed to fall on a photographic plate, where they produce
a symmetrical pattern of spots or arcs of circles, the forms and positions
of which, in relation to the central image of the undeflected beam,
correspond to the orientation and spacing of the regular layers of
atoms or atomic groups in the crystal. Amorphous substances do not
give these regular patterns when placed in the beam, for their atoms or
atomic groups lie at random and not in regular planes and in consequence the X-ray beam is scattered in a random manner. Given a
knowledge of the chemical composition of the crystal, X-ray diffraction
patterns can be used to estimate the arrangement of its atoms and, in
an aggregate of crystals, it is possible to determine whether the axes
of the individual crystals are parallel or scattered (Fig. 93).

While this X-ray diffraction technique has been used extensively for
studying cellulose, the use of polarization microscopy has a more
general application to wood. By its means, information on the crystalline structure of wood cell-walls can be obtained from the study of
ordinary wood sections. The method makes use of the peculiar optical
properties of crystals which again arise from the regular arrangement
of the atoms or atomic groups within them.

Although crystal optics is outside the field of study of most botanists
and timber technologists, nevertheless it is possible for the student,
especially if he has access to a polarizing microscope, to achieve some
understanding, in a general way, of the nature of the evidence bearing

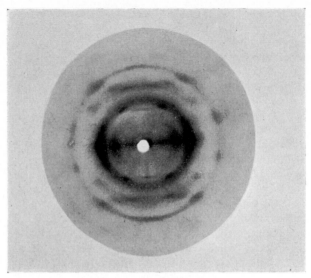

Fram a photograph by Prof. R. D. Preston

Fig. 93.—An X-ray diffraction photograph of Poplar wood. The regular pattern of rings and dots indicates crystalline structure of the cell walls: from such a pattern the spatial arrangement of the atoms in the cellulose molecule can be computed and the orientation of cellulose micellae in the cell walls can be inferred.

The white spot in the centre has nothing to do with the pattern; it is produced, for technical reasons, by a hole punched in the centre of the film, or a lead cup placed upon it.

on the fine structure of wood fibres which polarization microscopy can provide. As a first approach, however, the optical properties of crystals can perhaps be best appreciated by the examination of a large crystal of Iceland spar, a pure, transparent form of the mineral calcite, which occurs in the form of rhomboidal crystals. If a row of dots on a piece of white card is viewed through such a crystal, they appear double (Fig. 94 *A* and *B*) whereas, of course, when viewed through a piece of glass, no such double images are produced. Clearly, the ray of light from a dot to the eye of the observer passes through glass as a single entity, so that the visual image of the dot (assuming the surfaces of the glass to be flat and parallel) is unaffected by the presence of the glass. In the case of Iceland spar, however, where the image is a double one, two distinct rays, one more strongly refracted than the other, have travelled through the crystal along different paths and have thus given rise to two images of the dot.

If the Iceland spar crystal is rotated on the surface of the card as the dot is being viewed, it will be found that one image of the dot remains stationary, just as would happen to the image of the dot viewed through a similarly rotated piece of plate glass. The other image of the dot,

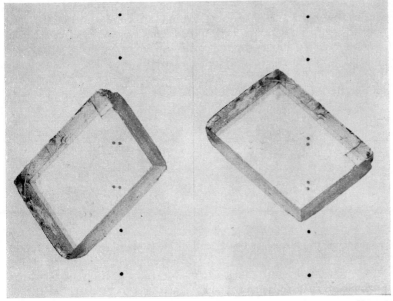

A

B

Fig. 94.—Birefringence in a crystal of Iceland spar. *A*, a row of black dots on a white background, as seen through a rhomb of Iceland spar (calcite). The crystal produces double images of the dots, and as it is rotated, (*B*), one image of each dot moves round the other (see text, p. 172).

however, moves in a circle round the stationary one. It would seem, therefore, that the ray which produces the stationary image obeys the laws of normal refraction: it is sometimes termed the "ordinary" ray. That producing the other image, because of its unusual behaviour, may be called the "extraordinary" ray and for this ray there is no single index of refraction, for it varies according to the direction in which the ray is propagated in the crystal. Iceland spar, then, has two indices of refraction, one, which is constant, for the "ordinary" ray, and one which varies according to the direction of propagation in the crystal, for the "extraordinary" ray. Iceland spar, in common with most crystalline substances, is consequently said to be birefringent, or doubly refracting. Furthermore, since there is a direct relation between the refractive index of a substance and the speed of light within it, the ray which suffers the greater refraction travels more slowly in the crystal than that which is refracted to a lesser degree, so that we may refer to "slow" and "fast" rays in a crystal.

Both the "slow" and the "fast" rays which emerge from the Iceland spar crystal differ in an important way from the ray which entered it, in that they are plane polarized. Light may be considered as being transmitted as a series of vibrations or oscillations and a normal ray of light may be pictured as consisting of a number of such vibrations, all occurring at right angles to the direction of propagation of the ray. Suppose that such a ray is being propagated towards the reader in a direction at right angles to this page, the direction of propagation could be represented as a dot, and the vibrations, since they occur in all possible directions, at right angles to the direction of propagation as a number of spokes of equal length, thus

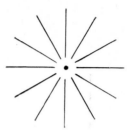

The rays which emerged from a slab of glass could be similarly represented, but those emerging from Iceland spar prove to be different, for both "slow" and "fast" rays each have the direction of vibration restricted to a single plane. Such rays are said to be plane-polarized. Moreover, the vibrations of the "slow" ray are in a plane at right-angles to those of the "fast" ray thus

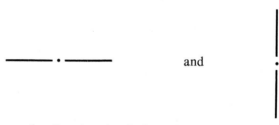

In some way, the vibrations in all planes but one, have, as it were, been "filtered off," although differently in the two rays, so that the crystal possesses two characteristic planes of polarization or, as they are often called, planes of vibration, and these are at right-angles to one another. With certain exceptions, which need not concern us here, crystalline substances behave optically like Iceland spar, so that, broadly speaking, birefringence or double refraction is characteristic of the crystalline state.

A single beam of plane polarized light, necessary for further study, may be produced by a crystal of Iceland spar which has been specially prepared, commonly in the form known as a Nicol prism, so that only the "fast" ray passes through it and the "slow" ray is totally reflected Nowadays, however, a transparent synthetic plastic sheet ("polaroid"), is more often used, which similarly produces a single plane-polarized beam. If the student can repeat the experiment illustrated in Fig. 94

and observe the images produced by the calcite through a sheet of polaroid, he will readily see, by rotating the polaroid, that the emergent rays from the calcite are polarized in planes at right-angles to each other: either image can be cut off at will, since, when the polarization plane of the ray is at right-angles to that of the polaroid, it is not transmitted to the eye.

If now two sheets of polaroid are mounted so that a ray of light passes sequentially through them, then if the polarization planes of the two polaroids are parallel, the light, plane polarized by the first, will pass through the second. If one of the polaroids is rotated, the amount of light which emerges from the second one gradually diminishes, until when the vibration planes of the two polaroids are at right-angles, the light transmitted is at a minimum. This is known as the "crossed" condition: ideally it should produce complete darkness, although because of imperfections in the polaroids, some light is usually transmitted. This arrangement is illustrated diagrammatically in Fig. 95 A where two square sheets of polaroid (their polarization planes indicated by arrows) are shown "crossed" to produce a dark field.

When a crystalline substance (e.g. the calcite crystal) is placed between the crossed polaroids it will in general (there are exceptions) appear illuminated in the otherwise dark field, Fig. 95 D, and if it is rotated it will become extinguished in four positions, one at each 90° of rotation. Two of these are shown in Fig. 95 B and C. Crystalline birefringent substances which behave in this way are said to be optically anisotropic. An arrangement of crossed polaroids thus provides a means of detecting crystalline structure. It is instructive to apply this test to a sheet of cellophane, which though of apparently uniform structure, nevertheless, like the natural cellulose from which it was prepared, contains more or less orientated submicroscopic crystals (known as micelles or crystallites) of cellulose, and it is "extinguished" when the mean orientation of these is parallel to the polarization plane of either polaroid.

The explanation of these phenomena is complex but need not concern us greatly here: they arise from the regularity of the arrangement of the atoms which characterises the crystalline state.

When the polaroids are in the crossed position, their polarization or vibration planes are at right-angles: they lie, let us say, N.–S. and E.–W. Suppose a crystalline birefringent substance is placed between them so that its vibration planes lie N.E.–S.W. and N.W.–S.E. The polarized ray from the first polaroid, vibrating N.–S., in passing through the crystal, is "resolved" into components along the vibration planes of the crystal, i.e. N.E.–S.W. and N.W.–S.E. These two rays, emerging from the crystal with these vibration planes, now have an E.–W. component and so, in part, are able to pass through the second polaroid. The extent to which they give rise to a visible image depends on the extent to which these two emergent rays have become "out of step" by

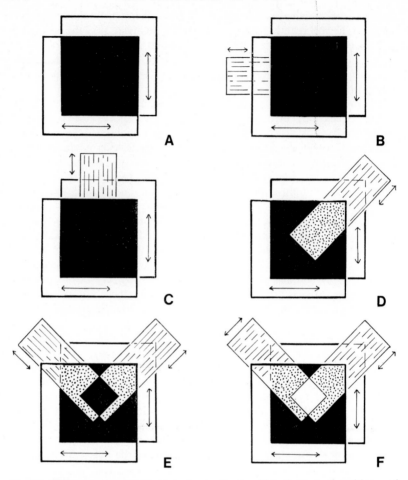

Fig. 95.—Diagrams representing two sheets of polaroid in the crossed position, and the optical properties shown by crystalline material inserted between them in various positions. A piece of cellophane may be used, representing, on a large scale, a cell wall. In *A* the polaroids are shown with their vibration planes (indicated by arrows) at right-angles, so producing a dark field. In *B* and *C* the cellophane is shown inserted with its mean crystalline direction parallel to either vibration plane; it is thus extinguished. At intermediate positions (*D*) it is visible against a dark field. In *E* a similar piece of cellophane is superimposed on the first with its micellae at right-angles to those of the first piece; darkness results, the two pieces being said to compensate each other. In *F*, where the two pieces have their micellar directions parallel, their optical effects are additive. Thus if the micellar orientation is known in one specimen, it may be determined in another by a comparison made in this way.

reason of their different velocities within the crystal: i.e. the so-called "path-difference". The net result is that the crystal is visible, although the brightness of the image and its colour depend on its thickness, as well as on the degree of birefringence of the crystal. The path-difference in the crystal is in fact equal to the thickness of the crystal multiplied by the difference between the refractive indices for the two rays.

Suppose now that the crystal lies instead with one of its vibration planes N.–S. and the other E.–W. Light emerging from the first polaroid and vibrating N.–S. will pass through the crystal still vibrating in this plane, and as it will have no component in the E.–W. direction it cannot now vibrate along this plane. Thus the E.–W. vibration plane in the crystal is now not operative. The total emergent light from the crystal is thus still only vibrating N.–S. and cannot pass through the vibration plane of the second polaroid, since it is vibrating in a plane at right-angles to it. Consequently the crystal will not appear illuminated. If the crystal is now rotated through 180° the same conditions apply. If instead it is rotated 90° in either direction, the other vibration plane of the crystal will be N.–S. and in the same way the ray will be prevented from passing through the second polaroid. There are thus four positions, 90° apart, in which the crystal is "extinguished", and when a crystal lies in these extinction positions its vibration planes are parallel to those of the polaroids and so can be found.

The importance of the determination of the direction of the polarization planes of a crystal lies in the fact that, for any given crystal, the orientation of these planes bears a constant relationship to the atomic arrangement of the crystal. Thus, in a cellulose crystal, the polarization planes of the "slow" and "fast" rays lie parallel and at right-angles respectively to the long axes of the cellulose molecules of which it is composed. If, therefore, the polarization planes are known, the molecular orientation of the crystal can be inferred. Clearly, however, there is an ambiguity here. In Fig. 95 B and C two extinction positions are shown, but the long axes of the crystals in the specimen are not necessarily as indicated by the arrows and shading in the specimen in these diagrams: they could equally well be at right-angles to these. In order to resolve this ambiguity it is necessary to compare the unknown specimen with a known one, as indicated in Fig. 95 E and F. If, as in E two crystals of equal path-difference are superposed at right-angles their birefringences cancel and darkness results. If, as in F, their crystal axes are parallel their birefringences are additive. The ambiguity can thus be resolved.

Although the optical anisotropy of a crystal, and the resulting extinction phenomena, are generally evident, this is not invariably so. Light which passes through the crystal along one particular direction, known as the optic axis of the crystal, is not doubly refracted, nor does it become polarized. Consequently, when a crystal is viewed between crossed polaroids, along a direction parallel to its optic axis, it appears to be isotropic and its true nature can be deduced only by viewing it in other directions. In crystalline cellulose, the optic axis is parallel to the long axis of the cellulose molecules, so that viewed along this direction its anisotropic nature is not evident.

These extinction phenomena, readily visible on a large scale, can be seen and made use of microscopically in a similar way. In a polarizing microscope one of the two polaroids (referred to as the polarizer) is mounted in the sub-stage and the other (the analyzer) in the body tube. These are normally set in the crossed position, and their planes of polarization are indicated by cross-wires in the eye-piece. The stage is made to rotate about the axis of the instrument so that a specimen may readily be viewed in different orientations between the crossed polaroids, and extinction thus occurs when the crystal axes of the specimen are parallel to the cross-wires. The microscope may also have ancillary fittings, which are beyond the scope of the present account: in particular a "compensator" by means of which the path-difference of a specimen may be measured. Thus if the thickness of the specimen is known its birefringence may be determined, or *vice versa*, and more precise conclusions can then be drawn about its crystalline properties than are evident from simple inspection. For further study the student is referred to Ambronn and Frey (1926), Anon. (1952), Hartshorne and Stuart (1960), and Preston (1965), or almost any textbook of optical mineralogy. Even at an elementary level, however, the examination of a thin wood section by polarizing microscope can be very informative. The section will be found to be optically anisotropic, for the cell walls appear illuminated, unless they happen to lie in one of the extinction positions, when, of course, they appear dark. It may, therefore, be inferred that the walls are crystalline, or at least, that they contain some crystalline material. It is clear, for various reasons to be discussed subsequently, that cell walls cannot be wholly crystalline, and moreover that the crystalline material they do contain must exist in the form of sub-microscopic micellar units. By observation of the extinction positions of the cell-wall material, the orientation of these micelles can be estimated. The extinction positions of cell-wall preparations can, however, give only an average estimate of the micellar orientation at the point under observation. Furthermore, it is found that the micelles in different layers of the wall may have quite different orientations and hence, if the wall is observed in surface view, so that these layers lie superimposed, they may neutralise or "compensate" each other's optical effects. Correct evaluation of the significance of extinction positions of cell walls seen in wood sections is thus often a matter of some complexity (Preston, 1952; Roelofsen, 1959).

In contrast to the cell wall, the middle lamella, no matter in what position it lies, always appears dark under the polarizing microscope and is thus optically isotropic. Consequently it is generally regarded as amorphous.

Since lignin occurs in the middle lamella, it must be assumed that lignin also is amorphous, and in support of this inference, it may be observed that lignin, and also the hemicelluloses, can be removed from the cell wall by appropriate chemical treatments without altering significantly the optical properties of the cellulose or its structure. Hence the conclusion that cellulose is the wall material which possesses the crystalline properties.

It was by means of the technique of polarization microscopy that an understanding of the layering or stratification of the wood cell wall was first obtained (Bailey and Vestal, 1937; Clarke, 1938a; Bailey and Berkeley, 1942; Wardrop and Preston, 1947, 1951), and it was established that the cellulose micelles are arranged helically round the wall. This recalls the orientation of pit-apertures, cracks (checks) and cavities produced by fungal decay, to which reference has already been made (p. 163). It was also established, from X-ray diffraction studies of cellulose, that the micelles are elongated in a direction parallel to the long-chain molecules of cellulose of which they are built up.

In the primary wall the pitch of the helices of the micelles is low, i.e. they lie nearly transversely. This is also the case in S_1, and often in S_3, but in S_2 the micelles are arranged in much steeper helices, more nearly parallel to the long axis of the cell (Fig. 96). The orientation of the micelles in any one layer, so far as this can be deduced from the extinction directions determined by the polarizing microscope, is however, only an average one. Even within a single layer of the wall, the micelles do not all have precisely the same orientation, for there is considerable angular dispersion of their axes about the mean, as given by the extinction positions. Preston (1949a) found this angular dispersion to be especially high in S_1. When a cell wall is viewed at right-angles to its surface, as seen for instance, in face view in a longitudinal section, so that the various layers are superimposed in the light path, the observed extinction directions will represent averages for all the layers together and thus are not accurately informative about any one layer. They usually approximate closely to the directions given by the S_2 alone (Preston, 1965).

Fig. 97 shows the appearance of a transverse section of softwood under the polarizing microscope; it illustrates some of the features referred to in the preceding paragraphs. The middle lamella (l) appears as a dark area between the walls of adjacent cells in accordance with its essentially optically isotropic nature, whereas the cell walls themselves appear illuminated. In the cell wall three layers are clearly shown (cf. Fig. 96); these are the outermost one (p) which is, in fact, probably the combined P and S_1 layers, the middle layer of the secondary wall (S_2) and the inner layer of the secondary wall (S_3). The outer layer (S_1) appears much brighter than the middle layer (S_2) because, both in the primary wall and in S_1, the micelles are more nearly transverse than longitudinal in their orientation and thus in a transverse section lie at

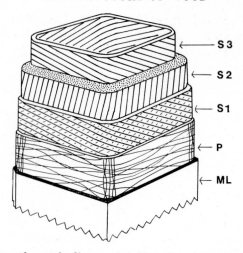

Fig. 96.—Diagram of part of a fibre or tracheid to show the usual orientation of the microfibrils in the various layers of the wall. There are no microfibrils in the middle lamella. In P they are sparse, and their orientation is rather irregular, but generally approximating to the transverse plane, except that some may be nearly axial. In S_1 the microfibrils lie mainly in rather flat "S" helices, though there are some lying in much less conspicuous "Z" helices. In S_2 the microfibrils lie in steeply pitched "Z" helices, while in S_3 they form flatter "S" helices. The transverse surface of the middle lamella is shown black, and that of S_2 is shaded, indicating their appearance as seen in the polarizing microscope. In contrast, P, S_1 and S_3 appear bright in transverse section.

(Because the terms "right-handed" and "left-handed", which have been used to define the direction of a helix, are ambiguous, the letters S and Z are often used instead. In an "S" helix the direction of the turns, on the side nearest the observer, is the same as the middle part of the capital S. A helix of the opposite sense is a "Z" helix.)

an angle approximating to 90° to the direction of observation, so that their birefringence is fully in evidence. In S_2, however, the micelles are more nearly parallel to the direction of observation, which thus approaches to that of their optic axes, so that their apparent birefringence is much less. In S_3, again, the micelles lie at an angle approaching 90° to the direction of observation, and hence appear bright. The indication given here of these differences in micellar orientation may be studied more precisely by examination and quantitative comparison, with the polarizing microscope, of oblique sections cut at different angles to the transverse plane (Wardrop and Preston, 1951; Mark, 1967); the relative brightness of the different layers of the wall changes with the obliquity of the section (Fig. 98). Although the general pattern of secondary wall structure so revealed (i.e. of rather flat micellar helices in S_1 and S_3 and steep ones in S_2) is a very basic and widespread one it is subject to a good deal of variation. For example, the actual angles of mean micellar orientation vary with the mean tracheid length

Fig. 97.—T.S. of wood of a Pine, photographed by polarizing microscope.
The middle lamella, being optically isotropic, shows as a thin dark line, not always visible between the cells. The thick white lines (p) represent the combined primary wall and outer layer of the secondary wall (S_1). The thick rather dark layer (m) is the middle layer of the secondary wall (S_2). The thin inner layer of the secondary wall (i) is the S_3. (Cf. Fig. 96.) The black horizontal and vertical lines are cross-wires in the eyepiece of the microscope, representing the planes of vibration of the polaroids. (× 600.)

(Preston, 1947, 1952, 1965) and so are determined to some extent by factors which influence tracheid length such as the position of the tracheid in the tree or in the growth ring (see Chapter 9).

Development of the electron microscope has provided a more recent method for investigating the structure of cell walls and since this instrument has become more widely available it has been used extensively for this purpose and has confirmed and extended the data obtained by the use of the older, more indirect techniques which have just been considered. A brief account of the *rationale* of this instrument and its contributions to knowledge of our subject is therefore necessary.

In the optical microscope, light rays are refracted and focused by glass lenses and this enables objects far smaller than those visible to the unaided eye to be seen. There is, however, a limit to the structural detail which can be seen with this instrument; that is, the ability of the lenses to differentiate clearly between two points close together. The limit of this resolving power, as it is called, depends, apart from the quality of manufacture of the lenses, on something other than mere magnification, for it is limited by the wave-length of the light used.

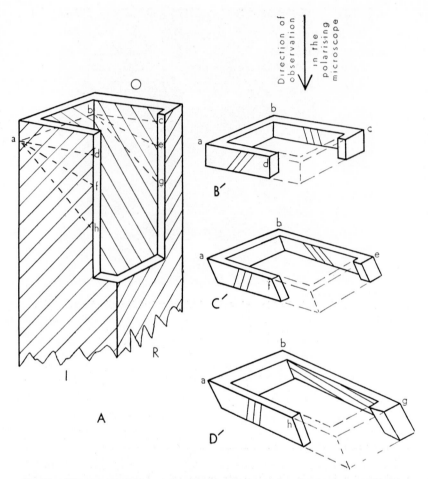

Fig. 98.—Diagrams and photomicrographs to illustrate the observations of Wardrop and Preston (1947, 1951) on micellar orientation in tracheid walls. The photomicrographs are of Port Orford Cedar (*Chamaecyparis lawsoniana*): *B*, a transverse section, *C*, a section cut at 20° to the transverse plane and *D*, cut at 40° to the transverse plane (all × 1010). In these sections the longer walls of the tracheids are tangential ones.

A is a diagrammatic representation of part of an axial tracheid, of which the upper, cut surface is truly transverse; the tracheid is viewed in such a way that the inner tangential wall, *I*, is on the left side, nearer the observer and the outer tangential wall, *O*, is at the back; the wall *R* is thus a radial one. Parts of the inner tangential and radial walls are shown cut away to reveal the inner surface of the outer tangential wall. The unbroken, oblique lines on the walls *I*, *O* and *R* represent the mean slope of the spirally arranged micelles in the middle layer (or S_2 layer) of these walls.

The broken lines *da*, *ab*, *bc*, define a transverse plane intersecting the tracheid: *fa*, *ab*, *be*, define a plane at 20° to this transverse plane, and *ha*, *ab*, *bg*, a plane at 40° to the transverse. If a transverse section is cut, as at *dabc*, the mean angles between the micelles in the tangential walls and the plane of the section will be numerically

B

C   D

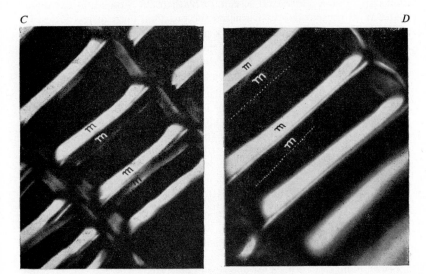

equal, though opposite in sense, on the two sides of the tracheid (*B'*). In a section
cut at 20° to the transverse plane (*fabe*) this numerical equality no longer exists (*C'*)
and in one cut at 40° to the transverse plane (*habg*) the inequality is more marked
(*D'*).

Correlated with this, a transverse section seen in a polarizing microscope (between
crossed polaroids) shows the middle layer of the wall *m* equally bright on both sides
of the cell (*B*), whereas in sections cut at 20° and 40° to the transverse (*C* and *D*)
there is a difference in the brightness of the middle layers of the two tangential walls,
which is specially marked in the 40° section. The explanation of this relationship is
that the apparent birefringence of cellulose varies according to the angle at which it

[*continued on p.* 184

N

Using blue light, i.e. light of short wave-length, and the best of modern lenses, it should be possible to see clearly two points lying about 0·15 μ or 1,500 Å apart. Resolution may be improved, but not very greatly, by using ultra-violet light, which has a still shorter wave-length, but since the image formed by ultra-violet light is not visible to the eye, it must be recorded on a photographic plate. The limit of useful magnification, using visible light, proves to be of the order of 2,000 times; that is to say, if a higher magnification is used, the image so produced, though larger, shows no more detail.

Resolution can be improved further, after this, only by using even shorter wavelengths. It is possible to use those of electron rays instead of light rays, which is the basis of the electron microscope. In this instrument (Wyckoff, 1949; Kay, 1965) a beam of high-velocity electrons *in vacuo* behaves as if it has a wave-motion of very short wave-length; this beam can be focused by electric or magnetic fields in broadly the same way as light rays in the optical microscope are focused by glass lenses. The images so produced by electron beams cannot be seen directly, but must be made visible to the eye either by their impact on a fluorescent screen, or by their effect on a photographic plate. With present-day instruments the practical limit of resolution is about 10 Å, although for some objects it may be as good as 2·5 Å. As an indication of the significance of these figures it may be recalled that a glucose molecule is about 5 Å in diameter.

Cell walls, like other biological materials, present special problems to the electron microscopist. His specimens must be very thin—about 250 Å or less—and are commonly prepared by fragmentation or by ultra-thin sectioning. Since the commoner biological substances are relatively transparent to electrons, specimens tend not to show much structural contrast unless this is artificially enhanced by the selective deposition of heavy metals in or on them. Moreover, for cell wall preparations to be fully informative, preliminary removal of some of the wall substances may be necessary. After appropriate chemical treatment

---

continued from p. 183]

is viewed, being greatest when the direction of observation is at right angles to the long axes of the micelles and zero when it is parallel to them.

The fact that the apparent birefringence of the outer layers of the tracheid walls shown in the photomicrographs behaves differently from that of the middle layers is evidence that the mean orientation of the crystallites in the outer and middle layers is different. The appearance of the outer layers in these photographs does not lend itself to the simple qualitative interpretation given for that of the middle layers and only precise birefringence measurements, of the kind made by Wardrop and Preston, can elucidate their micellar orientation.

[In *D* the limits of the outer tangential walls were shown so faintly in the photographs that they would not have reproduced in a block; their position, where visible has, for this reason, been indicated by the broken white lines.]

to remove the amorphous components of the wall (i.e. the hemi-celluloses and the lignin) the remaining cellulose fraction is found to have a microfibrillar structure: in the complete wall these microfibrils are more or less embedded in the amorphous matrix, which conceals them. After being exposed in this way the microfibrils are usually treated with a heavy metal, such as gold or palladium, which is deposited on them obliquely in such a way as to make them more readily distinguishable. This is the so-called "metal-shadowing" technique.

If a specimen is too thick to be examined directly in this way a "replica" of its surface may be made by pressing a suitable plastic material onto it. The replica is then stripped off and shadowed with metal, followed by a thicker carbon film. The plastic is then dissolved away, leaving a metal-shadowed carbon film which accurately repro-duces the original surface structure, and which may be electron-micrographed in its place (Robards, 1965b).

The type of structure revealed by these and other techniques, com-prising a system of microfibrils of indefinite length, and with a thickness of 50 to 250 Å, embedded in an amorphous matrix, is a virtually universal one in cell walls. It has been found not only in the cell walls of wood, but also in those of all other tissues of higher plants, and in algae and fungi. The proportions of the two components of the wall, as well as their respective chemical natures, may however differ very widely in different plants and different types of wall (Roelofsen, 1959). The whole structure may be thought of as resembling that of reinforced concrete on a sub-microscopic scale.

The first electronmicrographs of cell walls, showing their ultimate microfibrillar structure, were of algae and unthickened parenchyma cells (Preston, Nicolai, Reed and Millard, 1948; Frey-Wyssling, Mühlethaler and Wyckoff, 1948). Electronmicrographs of wood cells soon followed (Hodge and Wardrop, 1950), and since that work many investigators have prepared and studied them; see, for instance, Roelofsen (1959) and Côté (1965) and references cited by them.

Electronmicrographs of parts of the walls of conifer tracheids are shown in Figs. 99 and 100. In Fig. 99 the microfibrillar nature of the wall, revealed after delignification, can be seen, though the orientation of the microfibrils in relation to the cell as a whole is not shown in this figure. Figs. 100 A and B show bordered pits of Cedar of Lebanon (*Cedrus libani* Loud.), as seen in carbon replicas of radial longitudinal sections. In sectioning, the pit border nearer to the observer has been completely cut away, so that the scalloped torus and the whole of the pit membrane are visible, and the inner surface of the other pit border (to be visualized as lying below the plane of the paper) can be seen through the spaces between the microfibrils of the pit membrane. Comparison of these electronmicrographs with Fig. 38 A (a photo-micrograph of similar bordered pits) exemplifies the much higher resolution of structural detail afforded by electron microscopy, though still greater magnification and resolving power than are shown in Figs. 99 and 100 can be achieved.

Let us now consider the several wall layers in turn. In the study of the primary wall, electron microscopic examination presents difficulties, for the necessary preliminary extraction of lignin and other material may involve the removal of about 70 per cent of the dry substance of this part of the wall, or about 90 per cent of its fresh weight, since the water normally present must also be removed. This results in considerable shrinkage. Microfibrillar structure has nevertheless been demonstrated in the primary wall of tracheids and fibres by electron microscopy (Wardrop, 1954; Roelofsen, 1959; Cronshaw, 1965). The direction of the microfibrils is broadly transverse, although in the outer part of this layer some may be axially orientated. This is true as well of the fusiform initials of the vascular cambium, from which, of course, the axial elements of the secondary wood are derived (Bosshard, 1952, 1956; Preston and Ripley, 1954; Svenssen, 1956). It is probable that, during growth and differentiation, the microfibrils may suffer displacement from the positions in which they were originally laid down. It seems probable too, having regard to the small amount of fibrillar material in the primary wall, that the microfibrils are in reality relatively widely spaced, and that their apparent closeness, as shown in electronmicrographs, has been exaggerated by the inevitable shrinkage of this layer during the necessary preparative treatment.

In the outer layer of the secondary wall (S_1), which polarization microscopy shows to have a crystalline structure organized in the form of a rather flat helix, lying more or less transversely to the cell axis, it has for some time been suspected that there might be two sets of helices, of opposite sense. Wardrop's (1954) electronmicrographs of this layer revealed two such orientations, each at about 50° to the longitudinal axis of the cell, and Emerton (1957) was also able, by photomicrography at a magnification of less than 800 times, to show the existence of two sets of differently orientated fibrils, quite comparable in their arrangement with that of the microfibrils revealed by electron microscopy. Wardrop (1957a) also succeeded, by special methods, in demonstrating the same phenomenon with the optical microscope. The macrofibrils so revealed are, of course, aggregations of the much finer fundamental microfibrils which only electron microscopy can resolve. An electronmicrograph by Frei, Preston and Ripley (1957) of the S_1 layer of a conifer tracheid suggested that the microfibrils with different orientations are laid down in different lamellae and thus that they are not interwoven; electronmicrographs by Wardrop (1957a and 1964), confirm this arrangement.

Fig. 99.—An electronmicrograph of part of the secondary wall (probably the middle, or S_2 layer) of a tracheid of New Zealand Kauri (*Agathis australis*), after removal of the amorphous material of the wall, showing microfibrils ($\times$ 30,000).

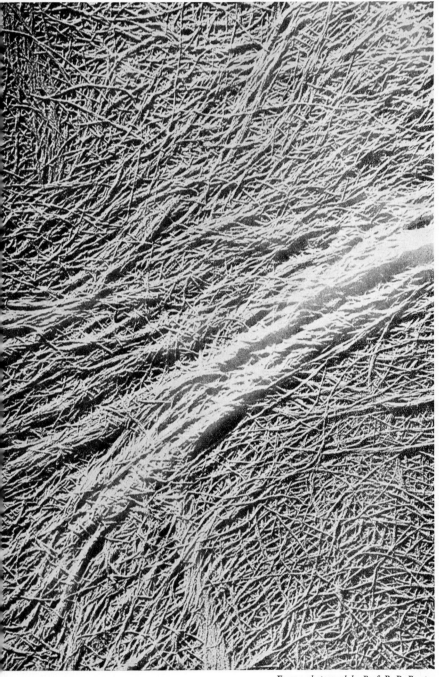

From a photograph by Prof. R. D. Preston

Fig. 99

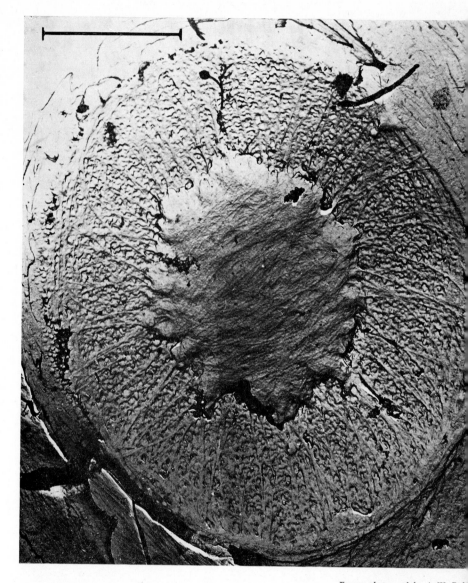

From a photograph by A. W. Rob

A

Fig. 100.—*A* and *B*: *Cedrus libani* (R.L.S.); electron-micrographs of carbon replicas of section bordered pits. The scalloped torus is seen supported centrally by the radially arranged bundle microfibrils of the pit membrane. In *A* the warty layer on the inner surface of the pit border text, p. 190) is visible through the gaps between these microfibrils. In *B*, the warty layer, some amorphous material of the wall, have been removed by suitable chemical treatment

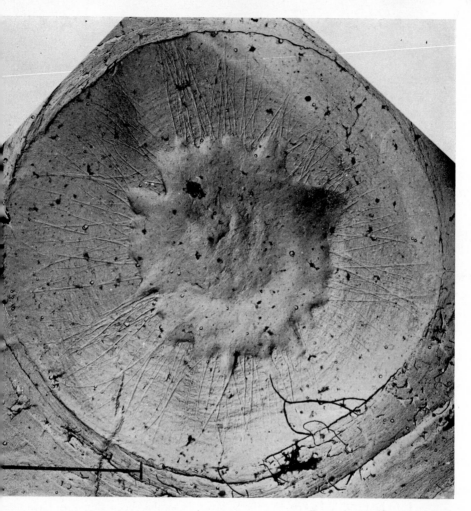

From a photograph by A. W. Robards

B

that the microfibrils show more clearly. The scale line on each figure represents 5 μ (cf. Fig. 38 A). C: *Pinus* sp. (R.L.S.). Parts of two tracheids, with bordered pits, as seen by polarizing microscope. The specimen is orientated so that the tracheid walls are almost extinguished except for the pits. Each pit appears as a bright circle with a dark centre spot and a dark cross. The centre spot is the pit aperture, and the dark cross is indicative of the circular arrangement of the microfibrils in the pit border. Where these lie parallel to the cross-wires of the microscope they are extinguished, but elsewhere they appear illuminated ($\times$ 450).

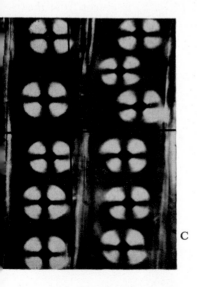

C

The evidence for the existence of these two helical systems of micro-fibrillar orientation also shows that one of them is more strongly developed than the other, and this may explain why one set eluded detection by the polarizing microscope for so long. In its application to the study of cell walls with various micellar orientations represented in them, the polarizing microscope tends to emphasize especially the best orientated systems: others which may nevertheless be present in the same material are far less readily detected.

Probably this double fibrillar arrangement is also present in hard-wood fibres, but it has been investigated, in the main, in conifer tracheids.

In S_2 the lignin content is lower than in S_1 and P, and the fibrillar material is relatively more abundant and more precisely orientated. It has for long been known that this layer may itself be lamellate (Bailey and Kerr, 1935). In some cells, numerous lamellae have been seen with the optical microscope and have also been shown in electronmicrographs (Frei, Preston and Ripley, 1957; Harada, 1965). The nature of this layering is uncertain, but alternate layers are probably richer in fibrillar material and poorer in lignin and other amorphous materials and *vice versa*. There may also be some slight differences in the direction of orientation of the fibrillar material in the different lamellae, although in all of them it is steeply inclined.

The S_3 is apparently a layer of somewhat variable structure, in which, generally, the microfibrils lie in rather flat helices, although at times they may be somewhat more steeply pitched. The fibrillar structure has been shown in electronmicrographs (e.g. by Liese and Hartmann-Fahnenbrock, 1953; and Harada, 1965), while Bucher (1957a and b) has made a very detailed study of this layer, after somewhat elaborate chemical treatment, with the aid of phase-contrast microscopy.

Spiral thickening, where it occurs, as for example in *Taxus* and *Tilia*, is to be regarded as part of the S_3 layer. It too has been shown to have microfibrillar structure (Liese and Côté, 1962).

Sometimes, e.g. in *Alnus*, *Betula* and *Picea*, S_3 is absent from the fibres or tracheids (Wardrop and Dadswell, 1957), and its absence is a usual feature of compression wood in conifers (see Chap. 9).

The inner surface of the tracheid wall is lined by a non-fibrillar film which sometimes has a warted surface (Liese, 1957). Subsequent investigations (Wardrop, Liese and Davies, 1959; Liese and Ledbetter, 1963; and Liese, 1965a) show that this lining membrane is to be regarded as the remains of the protoplast. There are pockets in it, containing minute spherical bodies, which protrude into the lumen of the tracheid and so give the warted appearance. Hence this "warty layer" is quite distinct from the secondary wall proper (see Fig. 100).

Electronmicroscopy has thus revealed microfibrillar structure in the primary wall and in all three secondary wall layers, the microfibrils lying in helices of varying pitch, flat in S_1 and S_3, and steep in S_2. This pattern is consistent with that of micellar orientations deduced from polarization studies, and it is clear that the microfibrils of electron-microscopy correspond, to a first approximation, with the micelles of polarization microscopy and X-ray diffraction methods. Ignoring the less prominent set of microfibrils present in S_1, it appears that the helices of the three layers of the secondary wall tend to alternate in direction, so that if in S_2 they are right-handed ("Z" helix), in S_1 and S_3 they are left-handed ("S" helix). The S, Z, S arrangement seems to be the more usual one, though the Z, S, Z order also occurs. The full significance of the rather precise helical orientations of the microfibrils in the secondary wall, and the mechanisms involved in the changes which occur as layer follows layer in the thickening process, are quite unknown, though it may be recognised in a general way that a hollow tubular structure like a tracheid, with a wall so constituted, will have a very high mechanical strength. Similar alternating helical patterns occur also in many other types of thick-walled cells.

In this summary account of the microfibrillar organization of the tracheid wall, the bordered pits, which are such conspicuous features of it, have not been referred to. As might perhaps be expected, however, the regularity of the helical systems of microfibrils in the wall is modified in and around the pits; the microfibrils are deflected from their helices and sweep around the pit borders in more or less circular courses (Harada, 1965; Liese, 1965b; and references cited by these authors). The details of structure in these regions are quite complex and need not concern us here. It is, however, noteworthy that the arrangement of the microfibrils in the pit border, like that in the other parts of the wall, can be deduced, in essentials, from polarization microscopy. As seen between crossed polaroids, a bordered pit appears as a bright circular area (representing the pit border) with a dark central spot (the pit aperture). The bright circle is divided into four quadrants by a dark cross, the arms of which lie parallel to the cross-wires of the microscope (Fig. 100 C). As the specimen is rotated, the cross remains stationary. This is because, in any circular arrangement of micelles, these must lie parallel to the cross-wires in four regions of the circle, independently of the rotation of the circular pattern. A fuller interpretation of this appearance is given by Preston (1952).

The close correspondence between microfibrillar and micellar arrangement in the tracheid wall brings us to another problem. From the X-ray diffraction data it is possible to estimate the dimensions of the micelles in cell walls, and on this basis they have been considered to be about 600 Å long, 50–100 Å wide and perhaps half this in thickness. In contrast, the microfibrils, while being of about the same thickness, or perhaps somewhat thicker, are of indefinite length. The cellulose molecules are also very much longer than the micelles, in wood cells probably some 10,000–50,000 Å.

The microfibrils may thus be visualized as being built up of smaller micelles, between which are regions where the molecular arrangement, though more or less parallel, is less regular than that of the crystal lattice of the micelles themselves. The links within a microfibril between micelles follow from the fact of the much greater length of the individual cellulose molecules, each of which, in different parts of its length, must pass through, and so contribute to the structure of, a large number of crystalline regions. The micelles are thus not discrete units of structure, but are linked by these regions of rather less than crystalline order. The surface regions of the micelles, and thus of the microfibrils, also represent transitional regions between the truly crystalline and the amorphous parts of the wall. They are described as being "para-crystalline", and it has been estimated that about one-third to one-half of the cellulose of cell-walls may be paracrystalline. In these para-crystalline regions other monomers may replace the glucose residues of the wall (Setterfield and Bayley, 1961). It is perhaps significant, in relation to this general picture, that if cellulose is treated with boiling dilute sulphuric acid its initial breakdown is into flat rod-like bodies some 200–1000 Å in length. It may be that these are the micelles, the paracrystalline regions which normally join them together having disappeared because their more open structure is more readily hydro-lysed by the acid.

Electronmicrographs show the microfibrils as quite distinct entities which, it appears, do not by themselves form a unified structure: they are believed to adhere by interaction with the amorphous hemi-cellulose matrix of the wall. Wardrop (1957a) has suggested that the superficial cellulose molecules of the paracrystalline zones may also be chemically united with the lignin of the matrix—see also Merewether (1957, 1960), Bolker (1963), Timell (1965)—so that, if this is so, then ligno-cellulose, for so long regarded as a compound of doubtful existence, may be a reality.

It is instructive also to consider the ultimate structure of the cell wall from another point of view, for the swelling and shrinking of wood, in relation to its gain or loss of water, is related to the sub-microscopic structure of its cell walls. It is significant, in this connection, that these dimensional changes do not greatly affect the crystalline structure of the wall; this has been demonstrated both by X-ray diffraction studies and by the polarizing microscope.

It has long been recognised that the crystallinity of cell walls on the one hand, and their dimensional instability on the other, can only be explained in terms of a structure which includes crystalline regions interspersed with regions which are non-crystalline and which can accommodate substances like lignin and water. Moreover, these different regions must be of a size too small to be resolved by the optical microscope.

An early view of this problem visualized the crystalline cellulose of the cell wall as existing in the form of minute particles, the micelles, elongated in the direction of the longitudinal axis of the cell and separated from one another by intermicellar spaces which contained lignin and other substances, and into which the water could penetrate, with resultant swelling of the wall (see, for instance, Seifriz (1936)). This postulated arrangement might be likened to that of a brick wall, with the bricks representing the micelles and the mortar representing the intermicellar substance: the latter would swell as water entered it, thus pushing the micelles farther apart, with a concomitant swelling of the wall as a whole, but without, however, altering the internal structure of the micelles themselves. The anisotropic swelling characteristic of wood and other natural fibrous materials might thus be related to the shape and orientation of the elongated micelles.

With increasing knowledge, however, this particular micellar hypothesis could no longer be accepted, for various reasons. Thus it does not accord with the observed very high tensile strength of cellulose. Moreover, in wood cells it is possible to remove either the crystalline cellulose or the amorphous lignin from the wall by chemical means without destroying the coherence and outward form of the cell wall as a whole. Thus it must be inferred that the two systems are interpenetrating. Nevertheless the fundamental concept of a wall consisting of two systems, one crystalline and the other amorphous, was sound.

Subsequently it was postulated (Frey-Wyssling, 1948; Hermans, 1949) that the micelles or crystallites are united into a meshwork by long-chain cellulose molecules extending from one to another, there being amorphous regions between them where these molecules are less regularly arranged. Spaces were visualized in the interstices of the meshwork, termed intermicellar spaces, which were considered to be occupied by water and the amorphous substances of the wall.

The development of electron microscopy has, however, necessitated a further revision of this hypothetical structure. As we have seen, the (mainly) crystalline microfibrils appear to be quite distinct features of the wall, which are structurally united only by the substances of the amorphous matrix: together these two very different components of the wall form a tough, elastic whole, the observed physical properties of which are interpretable in a general way in terms of its fine structure. There is, however, as yet no final word on these problems; though the broad features as we now understand them are probably not greatly in error, many lesser ones still require further study. There are also some very fundamental major problems still outstanding: for instance, in this account, the mature wood cell wall has been considered as an inert, static structure. We must not forget, however, that the cell wall is the product of a living protoplast, and that it grows both in area and thickness, maintaining at the same time its unity and coherence of form. How its growth is brought about raises problems of very diverse kinds. These involve not only problems of the biochemical pathways and enzymic "machinery" necessary for the synthesis of the whole range of cell wall substances, but also the problems of the means whereby cellulose is produced as microfibrils and by which these are orientated in the wall in the rather precise fashion described in this chapter. These are problems about which, as yet, our knowledge is only fragmentary.

CHAPTER 9

THE VARIABILITY OF WOOD: ABNORMAL WOOD: DISEASED WOOD

One of the drawbacks to the use of wood as a structural material is its variability. Not only is this variability characteristic of wood of the same kind which has been obtained from different trees, but also of pieces which have been derived from different parts of the same tree. Specimens of the same wood may vary in a number of ways: differences may be no more than those of colour; one piece may be knotty, another clear; growth rings may differ in width; grain and texture may vary in different specimens or there may be differences in density, hardness, toughness and other physical properties. The types of cells of which two pieces of the same wood are composed may be present in different proportions, their spatial relationships may differ (Fig. 101), so too may their sizes and the thickness and composition of their walls (cf. Bailey and Faull, 1934). Even within an individual tree, there may be important differences in the same type of element in different growth rings, or even in different parts of the same growth ring. Again, extractives (extraneous materials) may vary in quantity, if not in composition, in different specimens.

Variation in wood may be inherent. The individuals of a tree species, like those of any other species of living organisms, are not all alike; they vary within certain limits and it is to be expected that variation of this type may occur in the wood as well as in other parts of the plant. Apart from this individual variation, the wood may vary according to its age (i.e. according to the time in the life of the tree when it is formed), or to the age of the tree from which it is derived. Internal stresses in the growing tree may also produce an effect on the structure of the wood, such as brittle-heart in some trees.

Alternatively, variation may be the result of varied external factors, e.g. light, soil, water-supply and temperature (Richardson, 1964), as well as of competition with other organisms which form part of the environment of a living tree. Any of these may have their effects on the growth of a tree and may lead to variations in its wood, either at different times in the life of an individual tree or in different individuals of the same species.

An interesting series of observations by Liese and Dadswell (1959) suggests that insolation or perhaps temperature, may influence wood development. In *Populus robusta* and Douglas fir, grown in Germany, they found that fibres of the former and tracheids of the latter, taken from the north and south sides of corresponding parts of the same rings,

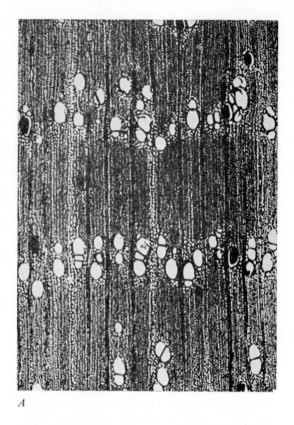

A

B

Fig. 101.—An atypical specimen of wood of African Walnut (*Lovoa* sp.). *A*. T.S. showing ring-porous structure (× 27) (cf. Fig. 173 *A*). *B*. Tangential longitudinal surface showing figure produced by the pore rings (a little under natural size).

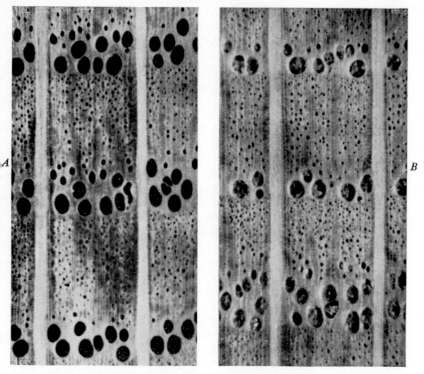

Fig. 102.—English Oak (*Quercus* sp.). *A*. Sapwood, with open vessels. *B*. Heartwood with vessels occluded by tyloses, T.S. (× 11).

differed in mean length, being consistently shorter on the south side by 3·3–8·1 per cent. In various tropical and temperate hardwoods, and in *Pinus radiata* grown south of the equator, there were differences of between 4·6 and 26·8 per cent, the elements on the north side being shorter. Within a growth ring these differences were greater in the late wood.

The changes in wood associated with ageing are primarily functional, for, after a time the parenchyma in any zone of wood in a tree lose their living protoplasts and the vessels and tracheids cease their conductive function. It is generally believed that, after these changes have taken place, the only functions of the wood are those of support and as a repository for waste materials, although it has been suggested that the wood may still serve as a water reservoir. In many trees the occurrence of these functional changes is rendered more obvious by a darkening of the wood, so that heartwood is visibly differentiated. In so-called sapwood trees no such readily visible differentiation takes place, but there is every reason to suppose that the more fundamental functional changes have occurred. As sapwood passes into heartwood, in many species a structural change may, however, occur, for tyloses may be formed in the vessels (Fig. 102). Commonly gums, tannins, colouring matters and other materials may be deposited in the cells, while food reserves, especially starch, disappear. In softwoods the bordered pits of the tracheids may become aspirated, that is, the torus is moved from its median position and comes to lie against the aperture of one member of the pit-pair. With these changes are associated differences in properties: apart from that of colour, sapwood in timber is usually more readily attacked by fungi and insects than is heartwood, while heartwood generally absorbs preservatives less readily than sapwood. On the other hand Koehler (1924) suggested that the reason why the heartwood of *living* trees may often be infected with fungi while the sapwood is not, may be because there is sufficient air in the heartwood for fungal growth, while the wetter sapwood does not contain enough air to make it a suitable substratum for wood-rotting fungi. Frey Wyssling (1964), however, regards the heartwood as being in an essentially anaerobic state; if this is so, then other factors must be involved in the distribution of fungal growth in the trunk.

Recent work on the chemistry of the cell wall (Thornber and Northcote, 1961a, 1961b, 1962) indicates that there are changes in its composition as sapwood passes into heartwood, the proportion of cellulosans increasing and that of pectic substances decreasing.

The distribution of knots in the bole of a tree illustrates one of the ways in which wood from different parts of it may vary. This variable feature, unlike the differences between heartwood and sapwood, is associated with the age of the tree, not with the age of a specific part of its wood. It is specially well illustrated by larger forest-grown trees, where shading results in the death of the oldest branches which originally clothed the young trunk: such branches decay or fall off. Their bases, and any snags which they leave, become buried in the wood of the trunk as it increases in girth, until finally all remains of these branches are engulfed and the subsequent wood is free from knots. In such trees, therefore, the older, more centrally placed wood of the trunk yields knotty timber, while the outer, younger layers give the clear or prime grades.

In temperate trees at least, the rate at which the wood is formed varies. Different species of trees differ considerably in this respect but in any species there is a maximum growth rate characteristic of optimum conditions and which may be regarded as inherent in that particular species. This rate is not however constant, but changes with age and, in general, the growth ring width increases rapidly for a relatively short period of years and then declines, rapidly at first and then much more slowly. Environmental factors, however, have a profound effect on the growth rate (Figs. 103, 104).

Wood from different parts of a tree may show marked differences (Fegel, 1941; Bannan, 1941–2, 1942, 1944, 1952). That from branches

is generally the densest wood in the tree, that of the roots the least dense, although in softwoods, rootwood may be denser than that from the trunk. Compared with wood from the bole, the cells in branch wood are generally smaller, and the growth rings are narrower, while in the root, fibres and tracheids have a greater diameter and vessels are larger, although in total they occupy a proportionately smaller volume. In roots also, growth rings tend to be narrower than those of the trunk, while in ring-porous woods the pore-rings in the roots are often less well-defined than are those in the aerial parts (Figs. 105, 106). It is, therefore, often more difficult to estimate the age of a root than that of a trunk or branch by a ring count.

The wood of spring twigs—on which the older anatomists often based their description of wood structure—is often different from that of the trunk and it is well known that such wood, like that derived from young trees, is to be avoided in making descriptions of wood structure. Such "juvenile" wood, that is, wood formed during the early life of a tree or branch, often has cells of much smaller dimensions than those of more "mature" wood, from which it may also differ in the distribution of its vessels, parenchyma and sometimes even, of its fibres. The vessels

Fig. 103.—Douglas Fir (*Pseudotsuga taxifolia*); transverse surface, showing variation in width of growth rings.

o

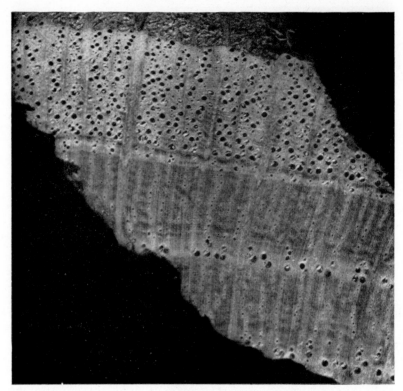

Fig. 104.—An Oak, ? Turkey Oak (*Quercus cerris*); a small piece of transverse surface showing an apparent change in structure from ring-porous to diffuse-porous wood. The lower two growth rings are relatively wide, the wood being fairly fast grown; the upper apparent ring is in fact about twenty rings of very slowly grown wood, in which late wood is, virtually, non-existent (× about 8).

may have a different shape, or their perforations may be scalariform, while in the vessels of the mature wood these are simple. In ring-porous woods juvenile wood may fail to develop a pore ring. It is recorded that barberry (*Berberis vulgaris* L.) has septate fibres in its first growth ring, although the fibres of succeeding rings are not septate. The fibres or tracheids are shorter than comparable tracheids of mature wood (cf. pp. 203–205). Juvenile wood is also less dense than mature wood. In softwoods it shows a less abrupt transition from early wood to late wood than in subsequent growth rings, while its late wood is less dense and occupies a smaller proportion of the ring. These differ-

Fig. 105.—Deodar (*Cedrus deodara*); transverse sections of wood from different parts of the same tree (all × 267). A. From the centre of the butt. B. From the edge of the butt. C. From a large branch. D. From a root.

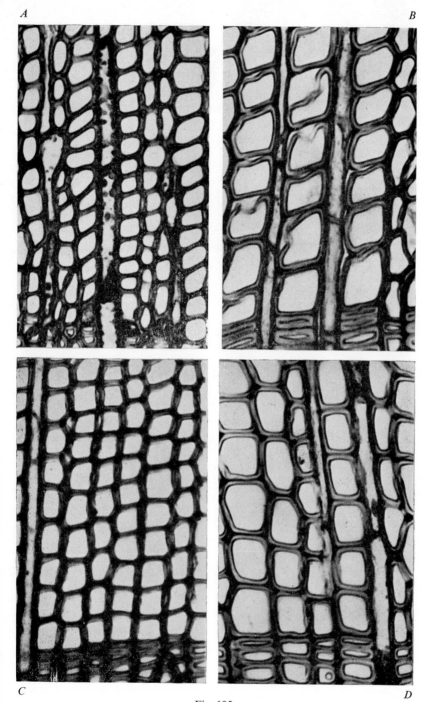

A   B

C   D

Fig. 105

A

B

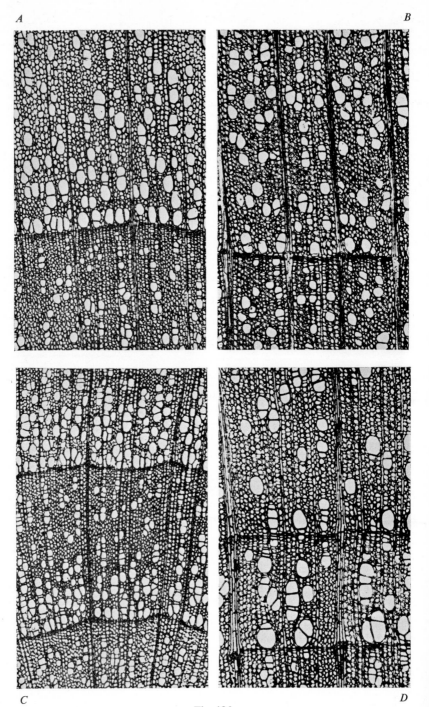

C

D

Fig. 106

ences have been shown to be related to changes in wall thickness and tracheid dimensions (Larsen, 1957; Rendle and Phillips, 1958; Zobel, Webb and Hensen, 1959). Other changes, recorded by Rendle (1960), are a decrease in the angle of spiral grain, should this be present; an increase, from the pith outwards, in the durability of durable heartwood; an increase in the cellulose content of the walls and a decrease in their lignin content.

Phillips (1941) noted that the pitch of the microfibrils in the secondary wall is lower near the pith than towards the periphery of the trunk, the helices steepening fairly rapidly and, after the first few rings, attaining a more or less constant angle. Subsequently, Preston (1948, 1949a) and Preston and Wardrop (1949) showed that there is a broad relationship between tracheid length and the angle of the microfibrils in the S_2 layer of the secondary wall, which is expressed in the form:

$$L = A + B \cot \theta$$

where L is the length of the tracheid, A and B are constants and θ is the mean angle of the helices of the microfibrils to the longitudinal axis of the cell. Since the cotangent of an angle decreases as the angle itself increases, this equation means that the longer the tracheid the steeper will be the pitch of the helices. A similar relationship also holds for the S_1 and there is reason to believe that it is also true for the secondary walls of other types of cells as well as softwood tracheids. It is to be expected therefore, since the tracheids and fibres of juvenile wood are shorter than comparable ones of mature wood, that the microfibrillar helices will be less steep in juvenile wood than in mature wood. The reason for this relationship between cell length and steepness of the microfibrillar helices of the secondary wall is not known. It may be added that it does not apply to the primary wall, where the microfibrils remain very nearly transverse whatever the length of the cell.

The period over which juvenile wood is produced seems to vary. It is often found in the first 20–25 growth rings, but may occupy only about 15 rings. In general terms, there seems to be some correspondence between this period of formation of juvenile wood and the duration of the juvenile phase in the tree, i.e. that period of the life-cycle prior to flowering (cf. Wareing, 1959). In the trees included in Wareing's table, the juvenile period varies between five and thirty years, except in beech where it is given as between thirty and forty years.

In old trees the last-formed wood may be overmature or "senescent", being characterised by narrow growth rings and often by its brittleness and low density. It is not, generally, of good quality.

Fig. 106.—Lime (*Tilia vulgaris*); transverse sections of wood from different parts of the same tree (all × 48). *A*. From the centre of the butt. *B*. From the edge of the butt. *C*. From a small branch. *D*. From a root.

The variation in the length of the cellular elements, and especially of tracheids and fibres, in different parts of the tree, has been the subject of numerous investigations since Sanio (1872) (cf. also De Bary, 1884) studied the problem in Scots pine. Sanio found that from the centre of the trunk outwards, at any given height, tracheid length tends to increase to a maximum, after which it remains constant; and that, in any one growth ring, tracheid length increases up the trunk for a certain height, and from there upwards, decreases again. (See Table 2, p. 294).

These generalizations have since been tested by numerous investigators: see for instance, Spurr and Hyvärinen (1954b), and Bannan (1960), who refer to much other work of this kind, and Schultze-Dewitz (1965). Though, broadly speaking, Sanio's findings have been substantiated, there seems to be considerable variability in matters of detail, and differences have been reported as between different specimens of the same species. Thus a decrease in mean tracheid length after the maximum had been reached has been reported both in long leaf pine (*Pinus palustris* Mill.) and in Douglas fir, but Gerry (1916) found, in a specimen of Douglas fir which she investigated, that maximum tracheid length had not been attained after 455 years. Dinwoodie's (1963) graphs for tracheid length in sitka spruce indicate that there is a rapid increase in tracheid length in the earliest rings and then a much slower increase, reaching a maximum between the 120th and 180th ring. He suggests that the rapid increase limited to the early years gives an impression of an apparent maximum which may have led a number of investigators to mistake this for the true maximum which is reached more slowly much later.

Similarly, in hardwoods, a decrease in mean fibre length after a maximum had been reached, has been found in European beech, and Bosshard (1951) found, in European ash, an increase in fibre length along a given radius in the first 30 growth rings and thereafter a decrease. Desch (1932), however, found an increase of fibre length in beech even at 129 years, and in poplar and alder after 100 years, although in the species which he investigated the most rapid increase occurred in the first five to ten years. Sundarasiva Rao (1959) found the most rapid increase in beech and robinia in about the first 15 rings and in oak and sycamore in about the first 25 rings, after which the increase was slight. He also observed that this increase was more gradual at the base of the bole than at higher levels. For Australian mountain ash (*Eucalyptus regnans*) Bisset and Dadswell (1949) found an increase in fibre length for about the first ten years, after which the length remained constant.

Again, a number of investigators have found that both in softwoods and hardwoods tracheid or fibre length increases upwards, to a certain height in the trunk, in any one growth ring, and then decreases, thus confirming Sanio's work. For some hardwoods, however, various trends in fibre length from the base of the trunk upwards have been reported; thus Bisset and Dadswell (1949) found that in *Eucalyptus regnans* the maximum fibre length increased up to a certain height (almost 50 ft. or 15 m.) in the trunk, after which it showed a gradual decrease. For individual growth rings they found that the maximum fibre length increased from the base of the trunk up to a certain height, after which it decreased, though while older growth rings showed another increase towards the top of the tree, a similar second increase was not found in the younger rings. In the shagbark hickory (*Carya ovata* (Mill.) K.Koch) Pritchard and Bailey (1916) found another pattern of variation; here fibre length decreased from the base of the trunk upward, while the length of the vessel elements increased from the base of the trunk to a certain height, at which the maximum was attained, after which there was a decrease in their length.

Chalk, Marstrand and Walsh (1955) found that, in certain leguminous woods with a storeyed or stratified vascular cambium, maximum fibre length was attained in a year or two. This does not, however, appear to hold for robinia, according to Hejnowicz and Hejnowicz (1959) and Sundarasiva Rao (1959). Thus the latter found that fibre length increased rapidly over about the first 15 growth rings, when there was a sudden change to a slow rate of increase up to at least 60 years, beyond which his measurements did not extend. The vessel elements, on the contrary, showed a remarkably uniform length from the pith outwards.

Other studies have been concerned with tracheid length in the early wood and late wood, and for a number of softwoods it has been found that the late wood tracheids are longer than those laid down earlier in the year, although in the Douglas fir examined by Gerry (1915) the reverse was found to hold. In Sitka spruce Chalk (1930) found an increase of up to 12 per cent in length in the late wood while, also in Sitka spruce, Dinwoodie (1963) found maximum tracheid length at the end of the growth ring and minimum length at the boundary between early wood and late wood.

A number of hardwood species have been similarly examined for seasonal variation in fibre length by Bisset and Dadswell (1949, 1950) and Bisset, Dadswell and Amos (1950). It was found that, in species possessing distinct growth rings, there was an increase in fibre length from the first- to the last-formed wood in a growth ring, at any one level in the ring. In species without growth rings, little or no variation was found. The variation in fibre length throughout a growth ring of *Eucalyptus regnans* in which the growth rings are not very distinct, is shown in Fig. 107. In softwoods, in most instances, a small increase in tracheid length was found from the early wood to the late wood of a ring, late wood tracheids being up to 11 per cent longer than those of the first-formed wood of the ring. In alpine ash (*Eucalyptus gigantea*) in which the wood has distinct growth rings, the late wood fibres of a ring were about 60 per cent longer than those of the early wood. Bosshard (1951) found a corresponding increase of up to 79 per cent

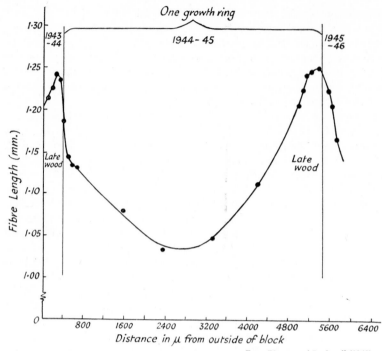

From Bissett and Dadswell (1949)

Fig. 107.—Graph showing variation in fibre length in one growth ring of Australian
"Mountain Ash" (*Eucalyptus regnans*).

in European ash, which is ring-porous, while Sundarasiva Rao (1959)
observed that, in several woods possessing distinct growth rings, both
fibres and vessel elements were longer in the late wood of a ring. In
oak (*Quercus robur*) the increase in fibre length was about 23 per cent,
in beech 21 per cent, in robinia 17 per cent and in sycamore only
9 per cent, whereas for the vessel elements it was approximately 50 per
cent in oak, about 20 per cent in beech and robinia and no more than
4 per cent in sycamore.

Apart from variation in fibre or tracheid length during a growing
season, Elliott's (1960) studies of tracheid length in Sitka spruce show
that length is affected by the rate of growth and that, early years apart,
the wider the growth ring the shorter the tracheid. While Echols'
(1958) measurements of tracheids of Scots pine and those of Bisset,
Dadswell and Wardrop (1951) for radiata pine and maritime pine
show the same relationship to ring width as Elliott found in Sitka
spruce, MacMillan (1925) found longer tracheids in free-growing trees
of *Picea rubens* than in suppressed ones. Elliott concluded that in
juvenile wood of Sitka spruce, where tracheid length is increasing
rapidly, it is more dependent on age than on the width of the growth

ring, although later, when the increase in tracheid length, if any, is slower, the growth rate has the stronger influence. Elliott points out, however, that his results were obtained from forest trees with wide growth rings at the centre and narrow ones nearer the periphery. Dinwoodie (1963) also concluded that age had a more important effect on tracheid length than ring width in the first 15 rings of the tree, but after the first 50 rings he regarded age as less important in this respect than ring width.

Anderson (1951) concluded that tracheid length in certain softwoods is related to distance from the pith and Hejnowicz and Hejnowicz (1958) found a similar relation for fibre length in *Populus tremula*, which also seems to indicate that tracheid and fibre length are related to the rate of incremental growth.

In the first growth ring Dinwoodie found that longer tracheids were associated with more rapid extension growth. The shortest tracheids, however, occurred in the widest ring. He considers therefore that tracheid variation is intimately connected with the activity of the vascular cambium which, in its turn, is strongly influenced by the activity of the apical meristem.

The inter-relationships of growth rate and tracheid length in a number of conifers have also been studied by Bannan (1960a, b, 1962b, 1963a, b, 1964, 1965). A feature of this work is that consideration is given not only to growth rate in the usual sense (i.e., in terms of ring width, which is a measure, of course, of the frequency of tangential divisions in cambial cells and their immediate derivatives) but also to the occurrence and frequency of anticlinal divisions in the cambium. Since these are initiated in a pseudo-transverse manner (see p. 58 and Fig. 19) they might be expected to influence the mean length of fusiform initials and hence of the tracheids arising from them.

In *Thuja occidentalis* L., in trees of similar diameter and varied growth rate, and showing transitions from wide to narrow rings and vice versa, there is in general an inverse relationship between tracheid length and ring width, the narrower rings having the longer tracheids, as indeed other workers have found in other species. The frequency of anticlinal divisions in cambial cells was found to be approximately constant in rings thicker than ca. 0·3 mm., at about two per cm. of growth increment, but it rises sharply in very narrow rings.

Similar relationships were found in species of *Pinus*, *Pícea*, *Pseudotsuga* and *Cupressus*, anticlinal divisions tending to occur at a constant rate in rings above a certain critical thickness, but increasing in very narrow rings. The result is that the usual inverse relationship between ring width and cell length tends to be reversed in very narrow rings, so that cell length reaches a maximum in rings of width about 1–2 mm. The importance of a full knowledge of cambial activity, in relation to a proper understanding of trends in tracheid length in the growing tree, is thus emphasised.

It has been pointed out, e.g. by Kennedy and Wilson (1954), Echols (1955, 1958) and de Zeeuw (1965) that genetic factors have to be considered, for tracheid length may be, at least in part, inherent. The problem of the determinant factors in tracheid length is thus a complex one and its analysis is beset with many difficulties, not the least of which, as de Zeeuw remarks, is that an enormous amount of labour is required to bring forth a few facts. The varied conclusions arrived at by some of the earlier workers may represent real differences, but it is also possible that they may arise from certain inadequacies of measurement. For instance, it is not always known if observations were made from one specific region of the growth rings, and it seems likely that some of the differences may be attributable to neglect of this important precaution. The great variability in tracheid length, even within one region of a growth ring, repeatedly emphasised by Bannan, is another factor. Investigations are necessary not only of a number of individuals of a species, but of individuals which have come from as widely different environments as possible, since there are obviously environmental as well as inherent variations. In Douglas fir for example, one investigation has shown that the late wood tracheids are shorter than those of the early wood, and a second that the early wood tracheids are shorter than those of the late wood. This contradiction may be due to variation of one or both of the types just mentioned; a third possible explanation is that the material in which the late wood tracheids were found to be shorter than those of the early wood contained compression wood, for Bisset and Dadswell (1950) found that where compression wood is present, late wood tracheids are shorter than those of early wood.

What does seem to be clear is that, in the present state of knowledge of this aspect of wood variability, it would be unwise to generalise in matters of detail. Broadly speaking, however, subsequent work tends to confirm that of Sanio.

Another type of variability of wood structure concerns the dimensions and frequency of the rays in relation to the growth rate of the wood.

Bannan (1937), in a study of the xylem ray-tissue of certain conifers, found that mean ray height at similar linear distances from the pith was greatest in specimens with the widest growth rings. In *Thuja occidentalis* (Bannan, 1954) and in some Pinaceae (Bannan, 1965) there is a positive correlation between ray volume or height and the width of the growth rings.

White and Robards (1966) have investigated the dimensions and frequency of rays in specimens of hardwoods with wide and narrow growth rings. In the species examined, ash, sweet chestnut and sassafras, there were significantly more rays per unit area of the transverse surface in wood with wide growth rings than in slower-grown wood. The three species studied are ring-porous ones, and growth ring width may be taken as a measure of the radial growth rate.

The faster growth rate also resulted in the production of wider rays (as observed in tangential longitudinal sections) and this extra ray width was a result both of increased cell number and cell size in ash and sassafras, but was due solely to increased cell number in sweet chestnut.

The ray width, expressed as number of cells, showed a striking increase in all the faster-grown specimens. In ash the change was essentially from 3- to 4-seriate. In chestnut, sometimes described as a wood with uniseriate rays, the increase in rate of growth resulted in the formation of almost equal numbers of uni- and bi-seriate rays.

It is well known that the density of wood may vary with the part of the trunk from which the wood has been derived (cf. Myer, 1930). Density tends to fluctuate with height, butt logs often being denser than those obtained from higher levels in the bole. In Scots pine, Fouarge and Sacré (1943) found that wood from the butt was generally stronger and nearly always harder and denser than wood taken from other parts of the bole. It is known, nevertheless, that wood from the swollen butts of some trees, particularly those grown under swamp conditions, e.g. tupelo (*Nyssa aquatica* L.), is less dense than wood from other parts of the trunk. In white ash, Paul (1924) found that while, in general, wood from the butt is denser than that higher up in the trunk, in trees from the Mississippi bottomlands (which are liable to flooding) the butt wood is of lower density than that from higher up the bole.

The density of a piece of wood depends largely, but not entirely, on the amount of wall material which it contains. This wall material, however, is not always distributed in the same way in different samples of wood from the same species of timber (p.165). In general, vessels and wood parenchyma cells are relatively thin-walled and it is the walls of the fibres which vary most in thickness; in dense woods their walls are thick and their lumina are small, while in light-weight woods thin-walled fibres with large cavities occur. Moreover, in light-weight woods the fibres are generally larger than those of heavy woods and, for a given volume of wood, more wall material would be required for a large number of small cells than for a small number of large ones, even if their walls were the same thickness. Thus an unusually high proportion of fibres, relative to vessels and parenchyma, or vice versa, might account for the "heaviness" or "lightness" of a piece of wood, by reason of variation not only in wall thickness but also in cell size.

Extraneous materials also play a part in determining the density of timber. A very resinous piece of softwood would probably be considerably denser than one with little resin, and similarly, a sample of iroko, containing heavy deposits of calcium salts, would probably have a greater density than one with only sparse white deposits.

Little is known regarding patterns of variation in the chemical and physical nature of the cell walls (but cf. Thornber and Northcote, 1961a, b and 1962) and also those associated with reaction wood (pp. 210–28). There is evidence that the wood substance may vary in composition in different parts of the trunk both in the chemical and physical structure of the cell walls and in the chemical composition of the middle lamellae.

In any tree, the wood of different parts would seem to be subject to stresses, either constant or intermittent. Jacobs (1945) considered that in hardwoods and in large conifers, the more peripheral wood is in longitudinal tension and the inner layers are in longitudinal compression, which at the centre may be of the order of 1,500 lbs. per square inch. (100 kg/cm²). In small coniferous trees, however, there is some variability, and the outer layers may be in compression and the inner ones in tension. These findings apply to erect trunks; in those which are inclined these stresses may well be increased and certainly altered in their distribution. It has been suggested that there may also be transverse stresses, both in the radial and tangential directions, of which the occurrence of shakes in living trees is evidence (Westing, 1965). In addition, the bending of trees by wind must temporarily impose varied additional stresses upon the trunk and branches.

Boyd (1950) also was of the opinion that great compression might exist in the centre of large trees. Although this is relieved by some adjustment of the cells in this region, numerous compression failures occur, which, where the walls have become distorted or broken, can readily be detected with the microscope. Such compression failures are most evident at the centre of the bole and are progressively less frequent towards the periphery. It is these failures which are associated with brittleheart (see p. 228).

It is not impossible that the defect of timber known as spiral grain (Misra, 1939; Priestley, 1945; Preston, 1949b), a structural peculiarity all too common in some species, is also associated with stresses to which the growing tree is subjected.

Another well-recognised variant of wood structure is characteristic of branches and leaning trunks. Generally, a cross-section of a trunk shows the pith placed centrally, with the growth rings forming concentric zones around it. This, however, does not hold for the trunks of leaning trees, nor for branches, where the pith is excentric, and where, associated with this excentricity, wood of a specialised kind, known as reaction wood, is formed.

A branch may be likened to a cantilever beam, i.e. a beam fixed at one end only. The weight of the beam acts downwards and exerts a pull on the upper side of the branch which consequently tends to be stretched, that is, to be in a state of tension; the lower side of the branch tends to be in a state of compression. The upper side of a branch (or the upper side of a leaning trunk) can therefore be referred to as the tension face, while the lower side (or the lower side of a leaning trunk) can be referred to as the compression face.

A cross-section of a branch of a softwood usually shows the pith nearer to the upper side and the reaction wood on the lower or compression side of the branch. The reaction wood of a soft-wood is therefore called *compression wood* (Figs. 108 *A* and 109). In a hardwood the reaction wood normally occurs on the upper (tension) side and is therefore called *tension wood* (Fig. 108 *B*). The term reaction wood is thus used generically to cover both the compression wood of a softwood and the tension wood of a hard-wood. It must be stressed, however, that the names compression wood and tension wood refer only to the *positions* in which the reaction wood is formed; they do *not* imply causality of stress in its formation. Indeed, as will be seen, all the evidence now available indicates that neither tension nor compression *as such* is responsible for the formation of reaction wood.

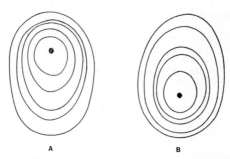

Fig. 108.—Diagrams of transverse sections of branches, showing the usual form of excentricity accompanying the formation of reaction wood. *A*, in a conifer; normal wood on the upper side and compression wood below. *B*, in a dicotyledon, normal wood on the lower side and tension wood above.

Well-developed compression wood in a softwood is quite conspicuous, especially on the end-grain, and may often be recognized by its reddish colour and rather dull, lifeless appearance, as well as by the excentric growth with the wider growth rings on the lower side (Figs. 109, 110). These wider growth rings appear to be composed mainly of late wood type tracheids so that the contrast between the early and the late wood is reduced.

When a transverse section of compression wood is examined under the microscope it will be seen that the tracheids are not close-fitting and angular in cross-section like those of normal wood, but that they are more rounded in cross-section and consequently there are intercellular spaces between them (Fig. 111). The presence of these intercellular spaces is one of the best diagnostic features of compression wood. Only one timber is likely to be misleading in this respect: African pencil cedar (*Juniperus procera*) has such intercellular spaces in its normal wood, so here other features must be used to determine whether or not compression wood is present (Phillips, 1937, 1940). In such timbers as kauri and Parana pine, where the growth rings are normally somewhat indistinct, compression wood may not be very obvious at first sight, but under the microscope the characteristically rounded compression wood tracheids will be evident.

In longitudinal sections, compression wood tracheids show oblique checking. These checks are often associated with the apertures of bordered pits. In addition to these checks, fine spiral striations are seen

212   THE STRUCTURE OF WOOD

Fig. 109.—Compression wood in a small branch of Deodar (*Cedrus deodara*). The growth rings are excentric, the pith lying nearer the upper side: the heartwood is rather irregularly developed. The somewhat darker coloured compression wood (sometimes called redwood) is seen on the lower side, especially at x (about natural size).

on the tracheid walls (Fig. 112). Both the checking and the striations, so characteristic of compression-wood tracheids, are to be found in wood taken straight from the growing tree. Although such checking may develop in normal wood tracheids as a result of drying from the green condition, the spiral striations are not produced in this way.

The greater width of the growth rings in compression wood derives from the larger number of cells in the radial direction than is present on the opposite side of the axis. This results from the more frequent division of the cells of the vascular cambium in the zone of compression wood than elsewhere. Compression wood commonly appears, in transverse section, in an arc, or a crescent-shaped patch. The frequency of cell division falls off from the two ends of the arc into the zones of normal wood. The wood formed in these two regions (sometimes known from their positions as side-wood) is often intermediate in appearance and properties between normal and compression wood.

Normal wood tracheids have a primary wall and a secondary wall in which the three layers, the S_1, S_2 and S_3 can usually be recognised (see p. 25). Compression wood tracheids, however, lack the S_3 layer (Onaka, 1949; Wardrop and Dadswell, 1950). The pitch of the microfibrils of the S_2 layer of compression wood tracheids is less steep than that in normal wood, viz. about 45° to the vertical as compared with 10–20° in normal wood, and the pitch of the checking seen in compression wood tracheids (which is limited to the S_2 layer) is an indicator of the pitch of the microfibrils of this layer. If the relationship indicated by Preston (see p. 203) as existing between fibrillar pitch and tracheid length holds for compression wood, it is to be expected that compression

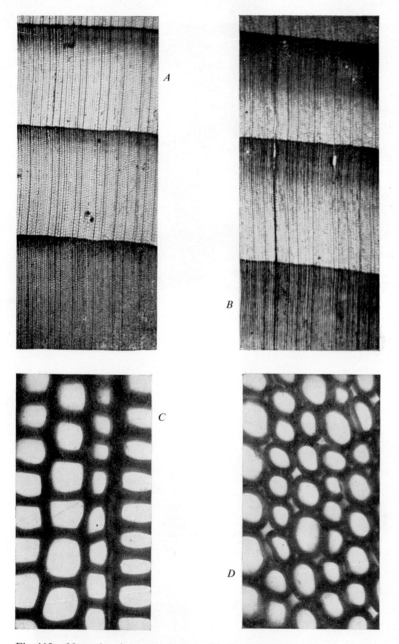

Fig. 110.—Normal and compression wood in Spruce (*Picea ?abies*). *A*. Normal wood. *B*. Compression wood. Note the larger proportion of late wood in the growth increments in *B*. *A* and *B* both T.S. (× 18). *C*. Normal wood. *D*. Compression wood. In *C* the tracheids fit closely together, in *D* they are rounded, with intervening intercellular spaces. *C* and *D* both T.S. (× 365).

A

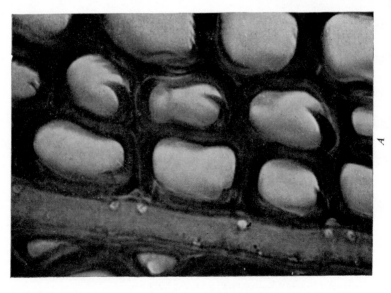

B

Fig. 111.—Transverse sections of compression wood in Cedar of Lebanon (*Cedrus libani*) (× 1060). *A*. Shows checking in the walls of the tracheids just to the right of centre. *B*. Shows, on the left, rounded tracheids and intercellular spaces.

wood tracheids will be shorter than normal ones. Dadswell and Wardrop (1949) and Wardrop and Dadswell (1950) point out, however, that this is a matter which it is extremely difficult to ascertain with certainty, because of the impossibility of comparing tracheid length in compression wood with that of exactly matched normal wood (i.e. wood occupying an exactly equivalent position in the growth ring). They have demonstrated, however, in Monterey pine (*Pinus radiata* D.Don.), that the tracheids of compression wood are shorter than would be expected for tracheids of normal wood occupying the same position in the same tree (Fig. 113). They (1952) find this reduction in length to result from an increased number of anticlinal divisions of the vascular cambium (cf. also Wardrop, 1948).

While the angle of orientation of the spiral thickenings, which are laid down in the tracheids of certain woods, does not necessarily coincide with that of the microfibrils of other parts of the wall, Patel (1962) found that in the normal wood of yew and of *Torreya californica* Torrey, the spiral thickening of the axial tracheids is almost transversely orientated, while in compression wood of the same species, where the S_3, with its low-pitched microfibrillar helices was absent, the spiral thickenings was orientated at about 45°, i.e. at about the angle which might be expected for the microfibrils of the S_2.

Compression wood tracheids have a lower cellulose content than those of normal wood but their lignin content is higher. The additional lignin appears to be deposited in the secondary wall.

Compression wood has been found in many genera of conifers (Westing, 1965, 1968) and it now seems certain that it may occur in any species. Pillow and Luxford (1937) recognised two broad classes of compression wood: *pronounced compression wood*, which is conspicuous and easily recognisable on sight, and *mild compression wood*, which is difficult to distinguish from normal wood, but which nevertheless can be recognised by microscopical examination. Pillow and Luxford pointed out that the structure of mild compression wood is intermediate between that of normal wood and pronounced compression wood, in the angle of the micellar spiral of its tracheid (and therefore presumably in its tracheid length) in the width of the growth rings and in the proportion of them occupied by latewood-type tracheids.

The distribution of compression wood within a growth ring seems to vary. Patel (1962) found that in eastern hemlock it generally occurred in the late wood and last formed early wood, although it was sometimes present throughout the thickness of the growth ring. In yew and in *Torreya californica* Torrey, compression wood was abundant throughout the growth ring, although less pronounced, and sometimes even absent from the last-formed late wood. In *Metasequoia glyptostroboides* Hu et Cheng it was common in the early wood.

It has long been recognised that the presence of compression wood

P

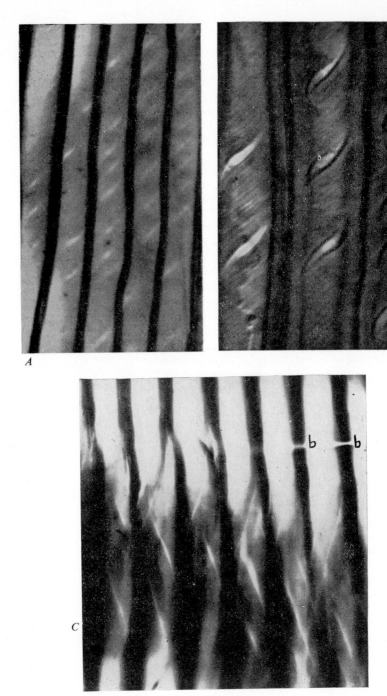

Fig. 112

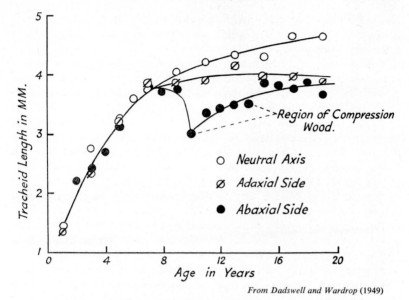

From Dadswell and Wardrop (1949)

Fig. 113.—Graph to show the change in tracheid length which accompanies compression wood formation in Monterey Pine (*Pinus radiata*).

in commercial timber can constitute a serious defect, because of its peculiar properties. It has been called *red wood*; in French, *bois rouge*; in German, *Rotholz* or *Druckholz* and in Swedish, *tenar*. Compression wood is very hard, and much denser than normal wood. It is also brittle, possibly because it contains less cellulose and more lignin than normal, and weight for weight it is lower in practically all its strength properties than normal wood. It breaks with a short, brash fracture, which resembles that of rotten wood. It also shrinks on drying in an anomalous manner: its longitudinal shrinkage is commonly of the order of ten times that of normal wood, though its transverse tangential shrinkage may be less than normal. Thus the presence of compression wood in a piece of sawn timber not only reduces its strength but may also result in warping or splitting as the timber dries.

Tension wood (*Zugholz* in German), is found commonly in branches and leaning trunks of hardwood trees: like compression wood, it is often associated with an excentric pith. In hardwoods, however, the excentric pith is nearer to the lower side, the tension wood occurring

Fig. 112.—Compression wood in longitudinal section. *A*. Cedar of Lebanon (*Cedrus libani*) showing oblique checking in the walls of axial tracheids (× 340). *B* as *A*, but more highly magnified; the slit-like checking is clearly shown; note also the oblique striations on the tracheids, evidence of obliquely orientated microfibrillar structure of the wall (× 1060). *C*. Spruce (*Picea ?abies*) longitudinal section showing checking in axial tracheids and, at b, failure of the tracheid walls (× 460).

above the pith where the growth rings are wider than elsewhere. This is a broad generalization, to which, as will be seen subsequently, there are many exceptions.

Tension wood may be harder and denser than normal wood and it is sometimes darker in colour. It may have a horny appearance but commonly it is not very conspicuous to the unaided eye. It can sometimes be detected by its lustrous, silvery appearance on a clean-cut end-grain surface, as Clarke (1937b) found in beech. It will sometimes show up as a darker band of tissue, and its presence will often be revealed, when the timber is sawn, by the extreme woolliness of the longitudinal sawn surfaces: see, for example, F.P.R.L. (1956). Jutte (1956) reported that when wet wood of *Ocotea rubra* is sawn, the zones of tension wood have a very woolly surface which in extreme cases can be brushed up like hair.

Tension wood usually shows a more compact structure than normal wood, with fewer and smaller vessels, but more fibres. Thus Chow (1946), in his study of tension wood in beech, found that the vessels were generally fewer than in normal wood, and of smaller radial (but not tangential) diameter, the total volume occupied by them being less than in normal wood; there was, of course, a correspondingly greater volume of fibres and parenchyma. Onaka (1949) recorded fewer vessels, of smaller diameter, and fewer parenchyma cells in tension wood, and Berlyn (1961) found fewer vessels in the tension wood of *Populus deltoides* Bartr. than in the normal wood.

Under the microscope, tension wood can readily be recognised because of the presence of gelatinous fibres, or as they were originally called, tension wood fibres. In these fibres, the innermost part of the wall is unlignified, and is relatively rather thick and gelatinous in appearance. This unlignified layer, called the gelatinous layer, or G layer, is of cellulose, and often pulls away from the remainder of the wall (Fig. 114). It may sometimes almost completely fill the cell lumen. The remainder of the wall may be normally lignified.

In sections the G layer can be readily differentiated from the rest of the wall by treatment with chlor-zinc-iodine, whch colours it violet and the rest of the wall yellow. Lacking lignin the G layer does not stain with phloroglucinol and hydrochloric acid, which colour the remainder of the wall (or at least its outermost layers) crimson. Gelatinous fibres can also be differentiated by double-staining techniques. Sections stained conventionally with safranin and counterstained with light-green show the gelatinous layer stained bright green. Better, chlorazol black E in methyl cellosolve, either on its own or as a counterstain to lignin pink, may be used (Robards and Purvis, 1964). The gelatinous layer then stains black, in contrast to the pink of lignified walls, and records well photographically. Jutte and Isings (1955) used phase-contrast microscopy to determine the presence of tension wood in ash (where it is not always easy to distinguish the

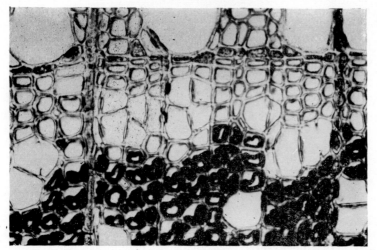

From a photomicrograph by A. W. Robards

Fig. 114.—*Salix fragilis*. T.S., showing normal wood above and tension wood below. In the tension wood fibres the G layer, densely stained, has pulled away from the outer layers of the wall (× 420).

G layer) although White and Robards (1965) did so by the use of chlorazol black E.

Wood fibres from normal wood usually have a secondary wall consisting of the S_1, S_2 and S_3 layers (pp. 25–26). Gelatinous fibres may have the G layer deposited immediately within the S_1, the S_2 and S_3 being absent, but sometimes the S_2 and the S_3 may be present (Wardrop and Dadswell, 1955; Robards, 1966). So the secondary wall of gelatinous fibres may have any of the following constitutions:—

$$S_1 + G$$
$$S_1 + S_2 + G$$
$$S_1 + S_2 + S_3 + G$$

The S_1 is always lignified, but the lignification of the S_2 and S_3, if they are present, seems rather variable. The G layer itself may be stratified and consist of two to four layers.

The G layer consists of exceptionally pure cellulose, which is more highly crystalline than the cellulose of the other wall layers. Its microfibrils are inclined at an angle of about 5° or less to the vertical axis of the cell; that is, they lie almost axially (Preston and Ranganathan 1947; Côté and Day, 1965; Norberg and Meier, 1966).

Chow (1946) found that the fibres of the tension wood of beech had a greater length, as well as thicker walls, than those of normal wood. Nečesaný (1960) also records that, in a number of temperate hardwoods,

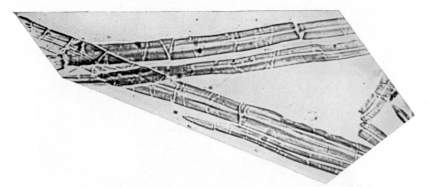

Fig. 115.—Isolated fibres from tension wood showing the characteristic spiral markings (slip planes) as well as transverse fractures (× 280).

the fibres of tension wood are longer than those of normal wood. Clarke (1937b), however, was unable to find longer fibres in beech tension wood, nor were Dadswell and Wardrop (1949) able to establish such a difference between tension wood and normal wood fibres in the Australian timbers they studied. Indeed, subsequently, Dadswell and Wardrop (1955) found that tension wood fibres might be either of the same length as those of normal wood, or longer, or shorter.

Both Onaka (1949) and Patel (1962) noted that gelatinous fibres have slit-like pits with their apertures parallel to the longitudinal axis of the cell; in normal fibres, of course, the pit apertures lie obliquely. Patel considers that the apertures are more slit-like than in normal fibres and he found that two or three of them may coalesce to form an abnormally long slit in the fibre wall. It is possible that the fibre figured by White (1962), as showing vertical checking, shows in fact coalescent pit apertures.

In longitudinal sections gelatinous fibres nearly always show oblique markings, and sometimes fractures in their walls. These are identified with incipient slip-planes and minute compression failures (Dadswell and Wardrop, 1946; Wardrop and Dadswell, 1947). Slip-planes are deformations in the walls of individual fibres, whereas compression failures extend, more or less in straight lines, across a number of fibres (Robinson, 1920; Rayne, 1945); see Figs. 115, 119 F. It may be that the microfibrils of the G layer, lacking the support of lignin in between them, are abnormally prone to buckling under compression.

Gelatinous fibres (which Dadswell and Wardrop (1949) preferred to call tension-wood fibres) are a common histological feature of some woods. Patel (1962) found them in a large number of plants, not only in the secondary wood, but also in primary structures like petioles and pedicels. In secondary wood of stems and roots of robinia he also found axial parenchyma with a G layer, in which the micellar orientation appeared to be similar to that of a G layer in a fibre. Such axial parenchyma cells sometimes also showed coalescent pit apertures, though slip-planes were not observed.

Patel was unable to find any differences among gelatinous fibres occurring in different parts of a bole or branch, and it seems reasonable to regard any zone of wood which contains gelatinous fibres as tension wood, regardless of its position in relation to the pith. Although in non-vertical trunks and branches it is usual for the pith to be excentric towards the lower side and for tension wood to develop in the wider growth rings above it, this is not invariable. Gelatinous fibres may be associated with a centric pith, or the pith may be excentric towards the upper side, tension wood then occurring in the narrower growth rings above it. This is well shown in a striking section of a branch of *Sassafras officinale* Nees et Eberm. figured by White (1962): (see also Jaccard, 1938; Onaka, 1949; and Wardrop, 1956). The distribution of tension wood in different parts of a tree may also vary: thus Kaeiser (1955) found gelatinous fibres mainly on the upper side of a leaning bole of *Populus deltoides* Bartr. at breast height, whereas at higher levels in the trunk they occurred on all radii. Tension wood has been recorded as particularly common in poor-quality top-logs (F.P.R.L., 1956).

On the other hand, tension wood is not invariably associated with non-vertical growth. Patel found it to be common in oak, beech, hornbeam, birch and horsechestnut, although he did not find it in lime. Moreover, Onaka (1949) records excentric growth without the presence of gelatinous fibres in a number of hardwoods.

Even within a growth ring the distribution of gelatinous fibres may vary. Patel (1962) found that, in non-vertical branches, they were more common in the early wood on the upper side of the branch and in the late wood on the lower side, although this was not invariable. In roots a uniform distribution of gelatinous fibres throughout a ring was found.

Like the compression wood of softwoods, tension wood has unusual shrinkage properties on drying compared with those of normal wood. It has exceptionally high longitudinal shrinkage, which is difficult to account for on present knowledge. Its tensile strength is normal, or even higher than normal, though its compression strength is low. The presence of tension wood in timber may lead to collapse during drying, which is irreversible and cannot be removed by reconditioning treatments. Such irreversible collapse associated with the presence of tension wood has been found in species of *Eucalyptus*.

Clarke (1935) studied the compressive strength and toughness of samples of English ash, some of which appear to have been tension wood. When treated with phloroglucinol and hydrochloric acid, wood which was weak in compression showed the middle lamellae stained pink and the secondary walls unstained, while wood of high compression strength showed the whole of the walls of the fibres, as well as the middle lamellae, stained pink to crimson. The initial failure, in tests of compression strength parallel to the grain, took the form of minute slip-planes in the secondary walls of the fibres. It thus appears that the lower compressive strength of tension wood is to be related to the lower lignin content of the cell walls. Clarke found, however, that the phloroglucinol test gave no clue to the toughness of his specimens. In the toughness test failures were found to occur nearly always between the primary and secondary walls of the fibres, or across the primary walls and middle lamellae; only rarely was the secondary wall itself fractured. This type of failure thus suggested that the property of toughness might depend on the nature of the primary wall and the middle lamella, and that the interface between the primary and secondary wall is a plane of weakness. It is interesting to note that in conifer wood failure under tension often occurs by separation between the S_1 and S_2 layers, an interface which seems similarly to be a plane of weakness (Mark, 1967).

In beech, as in ash, Clarke (1936, 1937) found tension wood to be weaker than normal wood in compression, but in tensile strength and toughness it was slightly stronger than normal wood. However, other data on the strength properties of tension wood seem to be limited and not always consistent (Panshin, de Zeeuw and Brown, 1964).

Nowadays it seems clear that the causes of the formation of compression wood in conifers and of tension wood in hardwoods are fundamentally similar. Various views have been put forward over the years to account for their formation, but it is now evident that gravity plays an important part (see reviews by White, 1965; Wardrop, 1964b, 1965; Westing, 1965, 1968).

Ewart and Mason-Jones (1906) bent stems of certain conifers into loops at the beginning of the growing season. When the loops were subsequently examined it was found that compression wood had developed on the lower side, although the bending of the stem to produce the loop must have put the wood on the lower side of the lower half of the loop in tension, not compression. Similar observations have been made by Jaccard (1938, 1940) and other investigators, both on coniferous and deciduous trees (Fig. 116 *A*, *B*). Burns (1920) grew potted white pine trees horizontally and bent the stems sideways, i.e. at right-angles to the force of gravity (Fig. 117). Thus one side of the stem was put under tension and the other side under compression. Yet, in the region of the bend in the stem, compression wood formed at the bottom, in a position quite unrelated to either the compression or the tension set up in the stem by the experimental bending. Wardrop (1964b, 1965) describes comparable experiments on artificial bending of shoots of *Tristania conferta* (a dicotyledon) and the consequent production of tension wood. If, however, the shoots were rotated on a klinostat, no tension wood was formed.

Robards (1965a) experimented with shoots of crack willow (*Salix fragilis* L.) bent into loops, and showed that there was a positive correlation between the degree of excentricity of the secondary growth of the wood and the quantity of gelatinous fibres formed. By growing straight one-year shoots of willow on suitable frames at various angles to the vertical he showed (1966) that the degree of excentricity and the production of gelatinous fibres were dependent upon the angular displacement of the stem from the vertical, and were greatest when the displacement was 120° (Fig. 118). This behaviour thus closely parallels the geotropic responses of growing roots (Audus, 1964).

There is increasing evidence that plant growth hormones play a part in the formation of reaction wood, as they do in the regulation of other growth processes. Gravity is known to affect the distribution of auxin (β-indolyl acetic acid, or IAA) in various plant organs, so it is perhaps not unexpected that the formation of reaction wood

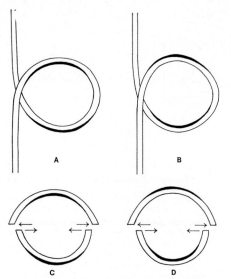

Fig. 116.—*A* and *B*: diagrams illustrating the formation of reaction wood (shaded) in growing stems bent into vertical loops; *A*, compression wood in a conifer, *B*, tension wood in a dicotyledon.

If the loops are cut into upper and lower halves, as indicated in *C* and *D*, in both cases the upper half of the loop tends to open, and the lower half to close slightly. Thus the different distributions of compression and tension wood are complementary to their different properties and produce similar effects [after Jaccard (1938)].

on the upper or lower side of a branch or leaning trunk should be related to the presence of more or less IAA in these regions. Thus Wershing and Bailey (1942) treated softwood seedlings with IAA, and found that the plants produced tracheids similar to those of compression wood. Wardrop and Davies (1964) have extended this type of experiment to the use of gibberellic acid (GA), another natural growth regulator, and also of IAA and GA in combination. They have further confirmed and extended the anatomical findings of Wershing and Bailey, showing that the compression wood so induced is identical with that arising naturally, even in fine details of structure visible only by electron microscopy. Onaka (1949) also induced the formation of compression wood, not only by the use of IAA, but also with naphthalene acetic acid (NAA), a synthetic auxin-like substance. He found, further, that auxin is naturally present in higher concentration on the lower side of leaning coniferous stems than on the upper side. Fraser (1952) has also used IAA to produce compression wood.

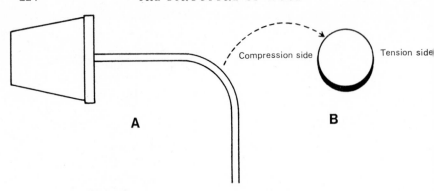

Fig. 117.—*A*, diagram (plan view) of a potted White Pine, grown horizontally, with its shoot bent, also horizontally, at right-angles, so that the compression and tension set up by the bending are lateral. *B*, transverse section of the stem in the region of the bend, showing that the formation of compression wood (shaded) is nevertheless on the lower side [after Burns (1920)].

Nečesaný (1958) similarly induced compression wood formation in upright stems of softwoods by the use of IAA, and found, further, that the normal formation of tension wood in bent hardwood stems could be suppressed by auxin treatment. That auxin treatment may cause the formation of compression wood and suppress that of tension wood suggests that compression wood is produced in regions of relatively high auxin concentration, and that tension wood is formed in circumstances of auxin deficiency. Additional evidence in support of this view comes from the work of Cronshaw and Morey (1965) and Kennedy and Farrar (1965), who showed that the application of 2-3-5-tri-iodobenzoic acid (known also as TIBA) which is a recognised anti-auxin (i.e. a substance which nullifies the effects of auxin) induces tension wood formation in hardwood stems.

Although the response of woody shoots to gravity, in producing reaction wood, may thus be governed by hormonal influences, and Wardrop (1960–61) associated the role of auxin in this context with the control of peripheral divisions in the vascular cambium, it is important to appreciate that the response has two quite different components. There is not only the response of the cambium in the changed rate of its tangential divisions, but also a response of the individual axial cells so produced (fibres in a hardwood and tracheids in a conifer) in the altered natures of their secondary walls (White, 1965). Normally the two responses occur on the same side of the shoot, but occasionally they may be spatially separated, as in the branch of *Sassafras* mentioned earlier (p. 221).

Of special interest is the work of Balch (1952) on the effects of attack by the aphid *Adelges piceae* (Ratz) on balsam fir. This stimulates the vascular cambium to produce an abnormal, reddish-brown, brittle

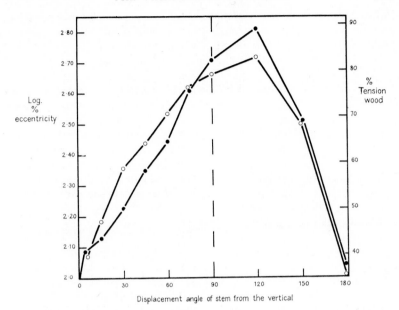

Fig. 118.—*Salix fragilis*. The production of tension wood in shoots in relation to their displacement from the vertical. ●————● The log. percentage excentricity of the stems. ○————○ The radial dimension of the zone of tension wood, expressed as a percentage of the year's total xylem diameter. Note that both graphs peak at 120° [Robards (1966)].

wood, in which the tracheids are similar to those of compression wood. Moreover, Balch was able to obtain similar wood by the application of IAA. Later workers (see Westing, 1968) have reported similar effects of other parasites.

Wind also can affect the production of reaction wood. Phillips (1940) related the development of compression wood in African pencil cedar (*Juniperus procera* Hochst.) chiefly to wind. He found, in forest-grown trees, that this tissue occurred mainly on the side of the tree away from the prevailing wind. It is, of course, towards this side that the tree might lean. Exposure to a prevailing wind is said sometimes to be the cause of both types of reaction wood (F.P.R.L., 1956).

Pillow (1931) reported that a hurricane which swept across Florida in 1926 was permanently recorded in a stand of longleaf pine (*Pinus palustris*) by the development of compression wood. Its formation began in the latter part of 1926 and continued during 1927, but had ceased by 1928 in some trees and had diminished in intensity in others. This was an evenly spaced stand of trees, and bending due to the hurricane was greatest in the upper parts of the trunks, which remained bent for some time.

Although the formation of reaction wood in a trunk or branch is induced by the orientation of that part of the tree in relation to gravity, and not by compression or tension forces as such, nevertheless there is good evidence that when reaction wood is formed it does itself give rise to bending forces within the trunk or branch.

Thus Jaccard (1938) bent young saplings of various species into loops and observed the subsequent production of reaction wood (Fig. 116 *A*, *B*). When the loops were cut from the tree and divided into upper and lower halves these tended to change their curvatures, as indicated in Fig. 116 *C*, *D*. It was thus evident that compression wood exerted longitudinal pressure and tension wood exerted longitudinal tension. Wardrop (1964b, 1965) also found, in experiments with saplings of *Liquidambar styraciflua* held in a bent position by a wire attached to a spring balance, that the tension in the wire increased as reaction wood was formed.

Sinnott (1952), following on the work of Hartmann cited by him, induced the formation of compression wood in vertical and lateral shoots of *Pinus strobus* by bending them into abnormal positions. The compression wood did not always appear on the lower side of the shoot, but was sometimes formed on the upper side. Sinnott emphasises that compression wood develops considerable longitudinal extension, thus tending, if present only on one side of a shoot, to bend it in the direction away from that side. He believes that compression wood is formed in displaced trunks or branches only in positions where it will tend to restore them to their original positions. It is thus an important regulatory agent in maintaining the growth pattern of the tree. Though gravity establishes the orientation of this pattern in relation to the earth, the inter-relations of the parts of the pattern, e.g. the angle between a lateral branch and the trunk, involve something more (Sinnott, 1960). Wardrop's (1956) experiments with *Eucalyptus* shoots also show that the location of tension wood in a displaced branch tends, by its longitudinal contraction, to result in the branch regaining its original position if it is free to do so.

The mechanisms involved in the production of the forces and curvatures observed by these and other investigators are not properly understood: neither is the significance, in relation to them, of the special structure of the tracheids or fibres of reaction wood. It seems most probable, however, that the forces are generated during the process of differentiation of fusiform initials into mature wood elements.

The capacity of reaction wood in conifers to develop longitudinal extension, and so, if present on one side of an axis, to cause bending away from that side, is discussed quantitatively by Westing (1965), who also considers possible mechanisms involved (1968).

There seems little doubt that the bending ought to be more properly considered not simply in terms of the behaviour of reaction wood alone, but rather in the balance of its behaviour in relation to that of normal wood which is formed on the opposite side to it.

In the course of its differentiation into a tracheid or fibre a fusiform initial changes from a thin-walled, turgid, living and growing cell into a thick-walled, dead cell, which is part of the wood and must therefore be subject to the normal hydrodynamic forces which transpiration from the leaves produces in the wood. In a transpiring tree the water in the wood is under tension or negative pressure, so that in the process of differentiation of a fusiform initial there is a change from a state of internal turgor or positive pressure, probably of several atmospheres, to one of internal negative pressure. It seems likely therefore, since wood is to some extent both elastic and plastic, that the fusiform initial must tend to shrink slightly during differentiation. This, of course, might be expected to be true of any fusiform initial, not merely those of reaction wood, and presumably contributes to the tensile state of the young wood and the compressed state of the older, more central wood of a tree.

As long as the tendency to shrinkage of the newly maturing wood is uniform and symmetrically distributed round a trunk or branch it will not tend to produce bending. If, however, the shrinkage was unsymmetrical for any reason, then bending would tend to occur. This suggests that an explanation of the effects of compression wood might not necessarily involve actual extension during differentiation, which is difficult to visualize physiologically, but might possibly be sought in its having a *lesser shrinkage* during differentiation than does normal wood. Correspondingly the contractional forces exerted by tension wood would be understandable if it had a *greater shrinkage* than normal wood. At first sight this approach to the problem seems an improbable one, since on drying both compression wood and tension wood are known to exhibit *greater* longitudinal shrinkage than normal wood. It must be remembered, however, that the wood of a living tree is never dry and shrinkage during cellular differentiation, if it occurs, is most probably quite a different matter from shrinkage in drying of felled timber.

At the present time, however, our knowledge of the structure of compression wood and tension wood cannot be interpreted simply in these mechanical terms. It may be that in compression wood the abnormally high deposition of lignin reduces shrinkage during differentiation. In tension wood, on the other hand, it would be natural to assume that the presence and specialised structure of the G layer must have some particular relevance to the mechanical properties of fibres containing it, and various hypotheses have been put forward to explain the function of tension wood in terms of the structure and properties of the G layer: see for instance Scurfield and Wardrop (1962), Sachsse (1964), Wardrop (1964b, 1965). However, the G layer seems to be rather loosely attached to the older parts of the wall: in sections it is usually seen to be pulled away from the remainder of the wall (as for example in Fig. 114). Although this is probably an artefact

(Robards, 1966) the G layers can fairly readily be entirely removed from the gelatinous fibres in a section of tension wood (Norberg and Meier, 1966). Thus it is difficult to see how any special mechanical property of the G layer can contribute to, or explain, the apparently abnormal shrinkage of tension wood fibres: especially is this so in view of the existence of anomalous tension wood fibres, lacking a G layer, described by Scurfield (1964).

Another form of variability in wood is shown by the marked difference in tensile strength which may exist as between the inner and outer heartwood of many trees. This has been observed in many Australian trees, particularly in eucalypts, and in some tropical hardwoods like African mahogany, obeche, gaboon and seraya. The more central part of the trunk is brittle (Boas, 1947) and in Australia is distinguished as "heart", while the sound, usable heartwood is referred to as "true-wood". This defect is known as brittle-heart; the terms soft-heart, spongy-heart and punky-heart are also used.

Wood with brittle-heart breaks with a short fracture and not with a long splintery one. Such a fracture is suggestive of fungal decay and while brittle-heart may apparently sometimes be due to fungal decay, this is not always so. It seems often to be found in over-mature trees, and it is only the central core containing the oldest wood which is affected; the surrounding wood is normal.

In the log, brittle-heart can often be recognised by the fact that the timber in the centre appears to be spongy and its fibres seem torn and not cleanly cut like those of the rest of the wood. In sawn timber it is less readily recognised, but when the wood is planed numerous very fine lines may be detected, running at right-angles to the grain. Where brittle-heart is well developed, thundershakes (fractures across the grain, Fig. 119 C–E) may be present. If these symptoms are not clearly shown the tip of a knife blade may be inserted into the wood, so as to raise the fibres. In brittle-heart, they will break across short, like those of rotten wood, and will not pull out in long splinters (Fig. 119 A, B). The walls of the fibres of wood which possesses this defect are often broken by transverse fractures and these characteristic cross breaks can readily be detected if a small piece of the wood is macerated and examined under the microscope (Fig. 119 F).

Brashness in wood is defined as "The quality of timber which breaks with a short fracture, i.e. with little or no splintering (short grain)" (British Standards Institution, 1934), so that brittle-heart is to be

Fig. 119.—Brittle heart in Red Meranti (*Shorea* sp.): the knife test applied to normal wood (*A*) and brittle heart (*B*); a knife point was inserted into the wood and prised up; note the short splinters in *B* and the longer ones in *A* (about natural size). C. Thunder shake in Dahoma (*Piptadenia africana*) (about natural size). D and E. Brash fractures in brittle heart in African Mahogany (*Khaya* sp.) (about natural size). F. Compression failures in fibre walls in *Pithecolobium* sp. (× 530).

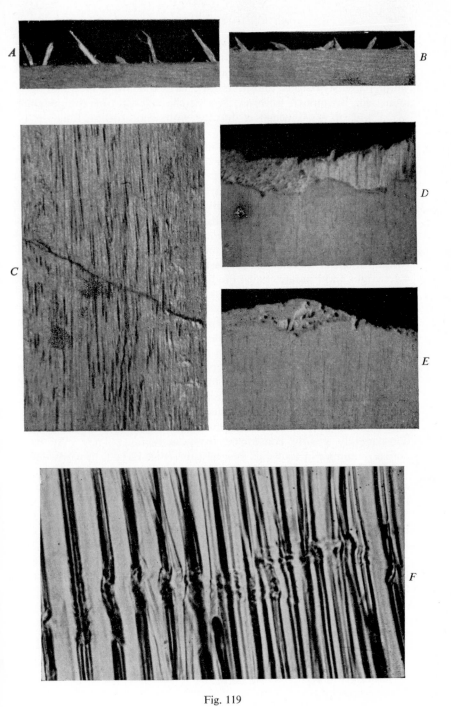

Fig. 119

considered as a form of brashness. Brashness is often associated with low density, which may be due to unusually fast or slow growth or to abnormal structure, the proportion of fibres in the wood being reduced, while parenchymatous and tracheary elements are correspondingly increased. Brashness, however, is also characteristic of compression wood and of wood which is infected with wood-rotting fungi. It is found also in wood which has been subjected to high temperatures and even in that which has been in a moderately elevated temperature for a prolonged period, and here, as in the early stages of decay, there is reason to think that the changes involve a decrease in length in the cellulose chains of the cell wall (Cartwright and Findlay, 1958).

Other living organisms, especially fungi, may bring about changes in wood, affecting its composition, colour or grain. Almost all the adverse effects on wood brought about by fungi are caused by two types of attack; those of the sap-stain fungi (Fig. 120 *B, C*) and the wood-rotting fungi. A number of genera are responsible for sap-stains (see Cartwright and Findlay, 1958; Findlay, 1967) of which the best known in softwoods is *Ceratocystis*, while in light-coloured tropical hardwoods, where sap-stain causes a great deal of trouble, the most abundant causal fungi seem to be *Lasiodiplodia theobranae* and species of *Diplodia*. The sap-stain fungi invade felled timber and utilize the food materials (chiefly starch) present in the sapwood in the cells of the ray and axial parenchyma. In softwoods the coarse hyphae are most commonly found in the rays and resin canals, but they may occur in the tracheids. The hyphae often pass from cell to cell through the pits, but they also penetrate the cell walls by extremely fine bore holes, very much smaller than the normal diameter of the hyphae, which are consequently greatly constricted in these regions. They may pass across a number of tracheids in succession (Fig. 120 *C*). In hardwoods, most of the hyphae of sap-stain fungi are to be found in the ray and axial parenchyma. The hyphae causing blue stain in softwoods are at first colourless, but they soon become dark brown in colour and the appearance of blue "staining" arises in a peculiar way from these dark hyphae showing through the colourless translucent cell walls; the wood is not actually stained by the fungus in the true sense.

When present in abundance, sap-stain fungi are responsible for a certain diminution in the strength properties of the timber but, except for toughness, the loss in strength is so slight that it may normally be

---

Fig. 120.—Fungi in wood. *A*. Advanced stage of dry rot, showing cubical cracking of the wood (a cubical brown rot). *B* and *C*. Blue sap stain in Pine wood. In *B* the surface of the wood shows heartwood at (h), free from fungus, and below this sapwood (s) with the blue stains (c) caused by the fungus (the darkness of the heartwood has been exaggerated by over-exposing this part of the print). *C*. Hyphae of *Ceratocystis* in wood of Pine (*Pinus* ?*sylvestris*); the hyphae are in the ray cells and the axial tracheids; R.L.S. (× 305). *D*. Black zone lines in Beech caused by fungal invasion; causal organism not known, possibly *Ustulina vulgaris*.

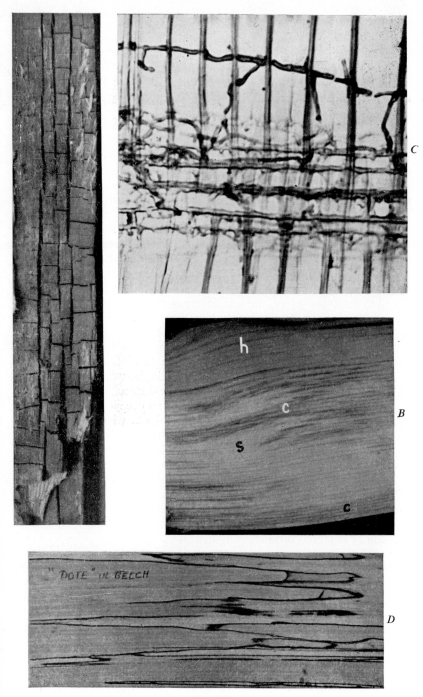

C

B

h

c

s

c

"DOTE" IN BEECH

D

Fig. 120

disregarded. Nevertheless, these fungi may cause unsightly discoloration which is sufficient to affect adversely the value of the infected wood, and indeed to make it unsuitable for some purposes.

Other types of staining, often producing bright colours, occur in both softwoods and hardwoods and are commonly due to the secretion of coloured substances by the fungi concerned.

The wood-rotting fungi, on the other hand, use the actual structural materials of the cell walls as their source of food and in consequence they seriously impair the strength properties of the wood. Their fine hyphae readily penetrate cell walls, leaving bore holes that become larger than the diameter of the hyphae. Some of these fungi, termed brown rots, break down the cellulose and related materials, but as they lack the enzymes necessary to attack lignin they leave a brown residue consisting largely of this substance. The wood shrinks and cracks into brick-shaped pieces which eventually crumble. Others, known as white rots, attack all the constituents of the cell walls and reduce the wood to a white fibrous residue.

The course of an infection of a wood-rotting fungus is usually divisible into two stages, the incipient stage and the characteristic or advanced stage. In the incipient stage the wood appears to be little affected, except that it commonly darkens or, rarely, becomes lighter in colour than normal. This colour change may be uniform or irregular. Darkening may be due to oxidation of the tannins in the wood by enzymes secreted by the fungal invader, while the wood may become paler in colour apparently as the result of the destruction of pigmented materials. The change in colour during incipient decay may be striking: thus *Chlorosplenium aeruginosum* (Oed.) de Not., which invades oak and other hardwoods, turns the timber a vivid green (the "green wood" of inlaid Tunbridge Wells ware) while *Fistulina hepatica* (Huds.) Fr. produces a rich brown coloration in the heartwood of oak and chestnut (brown oak, p. 236). Neither of these two fungi causes serious decay of the wood, though *Chlorosplenium* commonly grows on wood which has already been attacked by another fungus and which may thus be valueless. The colours are, it is thought, caused by the production of coloured substances by the fungi.

Although, to all appearances, the wood remains sound during the incipient stage of decay, its strength properties may be seriously impaired even at this early stage. In the main, however, the incipient stage of an infection may be regarded as the period during which the fungal hyphae are first invading the wood, before they have caused extensive break-down.

In the advanced stages of attack by a wood-rotting fungus, it is very apparent that the wood is weakened and it assumes the rotten appearance characteristically associated with attack by the particular fungus which is causing the breakdown (Fig. 120 *A*). Thus, in pocket-rots the regions of decay appear as isolated pockets, in cubical rots the rotten

wood breaks up into approximately cubical pieces and in spongy rots
the timber becomes spongy in texture. The wood also becomes less
dense and may have a characteristic odour. In the white rots, which are
produced by attack on all the constituents of the cell wall, advanced
decay is marked by a decreasing thickness of the cell walls of the wood
as the fungus breaks them down, whereas in brown rots this thinning
of the wall comes at a much later stage. Here, it is mainly the cellulose
framework which is being broken down, and even when most of the
cellulose has been removed, the lignin may still substantially retain the
original shape of the cell.

Fungal attack may lead to the deposition of dark, gummy or resinous
material in the cells of the wood. Some fungi, usually those of white
rots (though very rarely those of brown rots also), cause the formation
of zone lines or invasion zones. These appear on the surface of the
infected wood as black or dark-brown lines surrounding decayed
areas (Fig. 120 D). These zone lines are formed either by the compacting
of the hyphae of the fungus invader in certain regions, or by the
deposition of gummy material (and the growth of tyloses) which the
living tree is stimulated to produce when attacked by the fungus.

Another type of wood rot occurs generally in the more superficial
layers of timber, causing the wood to become soft, and when dry,
brittle. This type of decay, known as soft-rot, occurs in the wooden
parts of water-cooling towers and other situations in which wood is
liable to be water-logged. It is caused by a number of ascomycetous
micro-fungi, notably species of *Chaetomium*, and by certain Fungi
Imperfecti. Breakdown seems to occur principally in the S_2 layer of
the secondary wall, the S_1 and the S_3 being more resistant. The rot is
produced in the form of lozenge-shaped cavities within the thickness
of the wall, these having their long axes obliquely inclined, parallel to
the direction of the microfibrils. As the rot develops and the cavities
increase in number and size, they coalesce, so that the wall is progressively dissolved away (Bailey and Vestal, 1937; Savory, 1954;
Aaron and Wilson, 1955; Oliver, 1959; Levy, 1965).

Though not a wood rot, a disease of some varieties of apple, known
as "rubbery wood", is one which influences wood structure. It is due
to a virus infection, which induces fundamental disorders in cell wall
organization, as a result of which the wood becomes abnormally highly
extensible. The normal pattern of cellulose deposition in the fibre wall
is disarranged (the microfibrils tending to be more transversely orientated than normal) and lignification is greatly reduced. The rubbery
nature of the wood can be attributed to these structural features
(Nelmes and Preston, 1968).

CHAPTER 10

FIGURE IN WOOD

One of the outstanding characteristics of wood is its infinite variety. Some woods, such as poplar and kauri, are very uniform, both in texture and colour, and there is little or no visible difference between one piece and another. Many timbers, however, like oak and elm among dicotyledons, or Douglas fir and hemlock among conifers, show variations in texture and perhaps also in colour, over relatively small distances, e.g. in different parts of a growth ring. In other woods, like olive and walnut, variety of appearance may be due to colour differences alone. For many woods it is no exaggeration to say that no two pieces are alike.

To all such variation, from whatever cause, the term "figure" is here applied; figure may be defined as any inherent feature which relieves the surface uniformity of a piece of wood. This use of the term differs from the usual one; generally figure is used to describe some pattern which enhances the beauty of a piece of wood. This usage seems to be implicit in the British Standard definition (British Standards Institution No. 565): "The ornamental markings on the surface of timber produced by the relative arrangement of the different elements of the timber or by inherent colouring matter". It is common practice to refer to figure in softwoods as "grain", although the use of the term grain in this sense is not correct; "grain" should be restricted to describing the direction of the tracheids (or other axial elements) in the trunk of a tree. The term can be used, correctly, to describe certain types of figure, but certainly not for the kind most commonly seen in softwoods. Further, the restriction of the term figure to a lack of uniformity, or the presence of a pattern, which is ornamental or beautiful, cannot be defended, since there is no uniformity of opinion as to what is beautiful or ornamental. A pattern in one timber, which by general consent is pleasing, may be produced in exactly the same way as one in another timber which has no aesthetic appeal. Hence, for present purposes, the wider and less subjective definition seems justified.

Figure may be produced in a number of ways, and in this Chapter an attempt will be made to analyse and classify its causes. What causes some types of figure is, however, not fully understood, so that no complete survey of the subject is at present possible.

Lack of uniformity in a piece of wood may be due to colour alone, and figure due to colour variation is not uncommon. Colour, of course, results from the presence of extractives in the walls or lumina of the

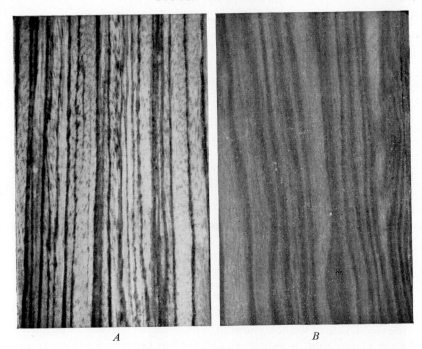

Fig. 121.—Figure due to colour variations. *A*. Zebrano (?*Brachystegia* sp.): the general colour of the wood is a pale golden brown, with streaks varying from dark-brown to almost black. *B*. Macassar Ebony (*Diospyros* ?*macassar*): the ground colour is a rich deep brown with stripes of darker brown to almost black.

elements, although it is, generally, not known what causes this variation. Colour variation in some woods (Fig. 121) is striking, as, for example, the rich greys, grey browns and blacks seen in some walnuts, or the various shades of yellow and brown in olive wood. In snakewood or letterwood (*Piratinera* spp.) the dull reddish-brown wood is marked with axial or radial streaks of black. In American whitewood the heartwood is commonly yellow with a greenish cast, but is subject to much variation, so much so that a single board may show patches of colour ranging through shades of yellow and green, purples, browns and black, producing an effect which is at least striking, if lacking in beauty.

Such local differences in colour are not necessarily characteristic of a genus or even of a species. Thus, the heartwood of the butternut (*Juglans cinerea*) and of the black walnut (*J. nigra*) tend to be uniformly coloured, while that of the European walnut (*J. regia*) may be similarly uniform or may show striking differences in colour even in a small piece. In the past, walnut obtained from the Ancona district of Italy was frequently richly figured with dark streaks, while much walnut coming from France was of a uniform pale purplish grey colour. It thus became customary to refer to all richly-coloured streaky European walnut as Ancona walnut, whatever its origin, while pale, self-coloured wood goes by the name of French walnut.

A piece of wood which contains both heartwood and sapwood could logically be described as figured, although in such pieces, the sapwood is often stained to match the colour of the heartwood when the wood is to be used for decorative purposes. At times, however, the wide, pale-coloured sapwood and dark heartwood of walnut are used in conjunction for ornamental purposes. Sometimes, heartwood is formed irregularly and patches of pale-coloured wood are enclosed within the heartwood, a feature referred to as included sapwood and well shown by some of the ebonies. In *Diospyros marmorata* Park. the included sapwood may form more or less concentric zones alternating with areas of heartwood, or its distribution may be more irregular: the black or dark-brown heartwood contrasts sharply with the greyish white sapwood, producing a striped appearance where the included sapwood is more or less regularly disposed (zebra wood) and simulating black and white marble (marble wood) where the included sapwood is less regularly distributed (Fig. 31).

Some striking colour effects may be produced by fungi parasitic in the wood. One of the best known is brown oak. In the early or incipient stage of infection, wood-rotting fungi often produce a discoloration of wood, although there is little disorganisation of the cell walls at this stage and little decrease in the strength properties of the wood. Brown oak (or chestnut) is wood which shows the incipient stage of infection by the beefsteak fungus (*Fistulina hepatica* (Huds.) Fr.) and it is to this fungus that the enhanced colour of the heartwood is due (Cartwright, 1937). The colour produced is a uniform rich brown—the most highly prized brown oak—but frequently the brown develops in patches (tortoise-shell type). Left under the natural conditions, the rot would develop to the advanced or characteristic stage which, for *Fistulina*, is a cubical brown rot. When the wood is dried, however, the activity of the fungus is arrested and there is no danger that the infection will develop farther. It is true that the richly coloured wood has strength properties somewhat inferior to that of normal oak (Latham and Armstrong, 1934), but since such wood is used for ornamental purposes, like panelling, where strength is of secondary importance, this does not matter. The colour in brown oak is probably due to the formation of some coloured substance by the fungus.

Sometimes oak is attacked by the ascomycetous fungus, *Chlorosplenium aeruginosum* (Oed.) de Not. and, in the incipient stage of the infection, becomes vivid green, a coloration due to a substance which has been called xylidein and for which the fungus is responsible.

Where the wood is uniformly coloured by such fungal invaders, it cannot be claimed that the fungi produced figure in the sense of our definition; indeed, since the definition requires that the figure depends on inherent properties, it is doubtful if the term can be correctly used at all for variation caused by fungi in the wood.

Some fungi, in the early stages of an infection, produce conspicuous thin dark lines (zone lines) in the host wood (Fig. 120 D); such marks are often seen in North American birch and in beech. No use seems to be made of wood so marked for decorative purposes, although the effect is sometimes striking.

Two structural features, growth rings and rays, play an important part in producing figure, and as the figure they produce is closely related to the way in which the log is converted, it will be as well to consider again the grosser features of the trunk and the appearance of boards cut in different planes. We have seen (Chapter 4) that the increase in diameter of the trunk occurs in such a way that the growth increments of wood consist of a sequence of more or less concentric vertical cones, while the rays are vertical sheets of tissue which extend from the pith, or from some point in the wood, into the inner bark; i.e. their direction is radial.

If the trunk is cut across, i.e. transversely, the growth rings will show as a series of concentric circles, and the rays, if they are large enough to be visible, as lines extending radially through the wood. If the trunk is cut obliquely the appearance of the rays will be similar, but the growth rings will then appear as concentric ellipses rather than circles. Oblique or transverse surfaces are, however, rarely needed in commerce, and most logs are sawn longitudinally. If a trunk is halved longitudinally, so that the cut passes through the pith, it will necessarily lie in a longitudinal radial plane, i.e. along a diameter, and the cut surface will show rays to their greatest extent, while the growth rings will appear as a series of parallel lines on each side of the pith (Figs. 28, 122 A). However, a radially cut board will commonly show only one side of the trunk, rather than extending right through from side to side, because a board containing pith might give trouble in drying.

If we consider a log being converted "through and through" (Fig. 123 A), it will be obvious that only one cut can be made through its centre, and the surfaces of the two adjacent boards separated by this cut (assuming the pith to be central in the log) will be strictly radial surfaces; they will be cut along the rays. Further, as the diagram shows, these are the only radial surfaces exposed when the log is converted in this manner, so that in neither of the boards in question can the other faces be strictly radial; indeed, down the middle line of those faces the rays will be cut at right-angles to their length and the surfaces are here tangential. Towards the margins of the boards, of course, their surfaces will be approximately radial.

If we turn now to one of the uppermost boards in the diagram we see that this has surfaces more or less at right-angles to the radial; i.e. they are approximately tangential. In fact, it is only the rays in the

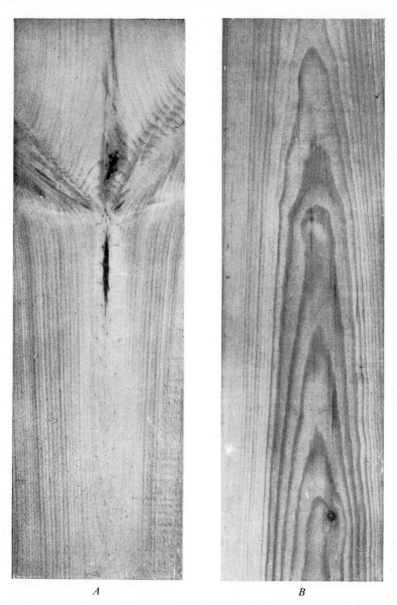

A   B

Fig. 122.—Figure due to growth rings; Scots Pine (*Pinus sylvestris*). *A*. Radial (quarter-sawn) surface; the growth rings show as parallel lines, somewhat distorted in the region of the two spike knots; a small piece of pith (black) is seen in the centre and the small dots and horizontal lines in this region are traces to the short shoots of the sapling tree. *B*. Tangential (plain-sawn) surface showing growth rings of characteristic ∧ shape; near the bottom, just to the right of centre, is a round knot.

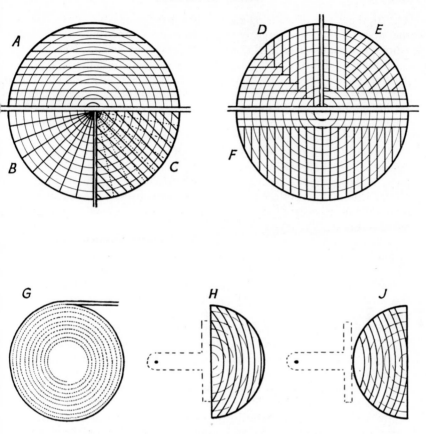

Fig. 123.—Methods by which timber may be converted. *A*, "through and through", giving mostly plain-sawn boards. *B, C, D, E*, methods for obtaining quarter-sawn boards: *B* gives true radial surfaces, but the boards are feather-edged; like *C* this method is no longer used; *D* and *E* are used for small logs. *F*, which gives only a small proportion of boards with surfaces approximating to radial, is probably the most practical method: in *C* the rays are indicated by broken lines. *G*, rotary cutting; the log is peeled against a stationary knife, giving strictly tangential surfaces. *H* and *J*: here also the log moves and the knife does not, but instead of rotating, the log swings in an arc; *H* is the half-round method, *J* the back-cut; compared with the "through and through" method, the cut surfaces in *H* approximate more closely to tangential ones, while in J they more nearly approach the radial.

centre-line which are cut strictly at right-angles to their length and are truly tangential. Nevertheless, elsewhere on these surfaces the rays nearly enough resemble those seen on a strictly tangential cut, so these surfaces may be regarded as tangential for all practical purposes. It follows, however, that it is not possible to cut one board with a wholly truly tangential surface in this manner. On these tangentially cut boards the growth rings appear as a series of concentric ∩'s or ∧'s (Figs. 28

122 *B*), the result of a slicing cut through a series of concentric cones: the rays, if they are large enough, appear as longitudinal streaks. Another question may now arise: why should the growth increments on a tangential face sometimes appear as ∩'s and sometimes as ∧'s? This depends on the exact direction in which the log has been cut, for most trunks have some taper, and the direction of the cut may be more or less parallel either to the slope of the taper, or alternatively, to the longitudinal axis of the trunk. If the direction of the cut approximates to that of the taper the board will show ∧-shaped growth increments, and these ∧'s will tend to be long; in fact they may be so long as to appear on the board as two very slightly converging series of parallel lines. If, however, the direction of the cut follows more closely that of the longitudinal axis of the tree, the lines of the growth increments will tend to more steeply inclined, forming blunter apices, in other words ∩-shaped rather than ∧-shaped.

A board with a radially cut face is termed quarter-sawn, while one which has been cut tangentially, or nearly so, is plain- or slash-sawn.[1]

It is possible to obtain boards in which both faces are strictly radial, but such boards cannot be of even thickness; they must be wedge-shaped in cross-section (i.e. feather-edged) for they can only be cut along radii, i.e. as sectors of the log (Fig. 123 *B*).

While it is impossible to obtain a true tangential surface by sawing a log in the usual way, such a surface can be obtained by peeling, i.e. by rotating the log against a fixed knife so that the wood comes off in a continuous thin sheet (Fig. 123 *G*). Such rotary cutting is extensively used in the preparation of veneers for the manufacture of plywood.

Another method of cutting veneers is to mount a piece of the log firmly and to move it vertically against a fixed vertical knife. Such sliced veneers, cannot, any more than quarter-sawn or plain-sawn surfaces, have strictly radial or tangential faces. A variation of this process is to mount the wood (usually half a log) in such a way that it does not move in a straight line, but in an arc (the radius of which can be varied) against a fixed vertical knife. If the outside of the log faces the knife, and if the arc in which the log swings has a radius approaching that of the log itself, it will be clear that the veneers will represent fairly tangential surfaces (Fig. 123 *H*). If, on the other hand, the centre of the log is nearer to the knife (Fig. 123 *J*) more nearly radial surfaces will be produced. The former method of slicing veneers is known as half-round cutting, the latter as back-cutting.

----

[1] The British Standard definitions of Quarter-sawn and Plain-sawn (British Standards Institution No. 565) are wider than those adopted in this chapter. They are:—

Quarter-sawn. Timber converted so that the growth rings meet the face in any part of an angle of not less than 45° (rift-sawn).

Flat-sawn (= plain-sawn). Timber converted so that the growth rings meet the face over at least half its width at an angle of less than 45° (slash grain, flat grain).

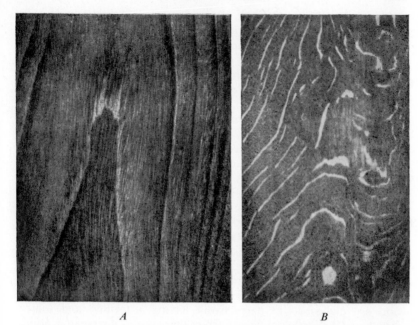

A   *B*

Fig. 124.—*A*. Tangential (plain-sawn) surface of Teak (*Tectona grandis*); the figure is caused by the growth rings, of which one shows as a ∩, the others as lines, i.e. the limbs of ∩'s. The pale zone at the margin of the growth rings, well seen in the apex of the central one, is the initial parenchyma of the growth ring. *B*. Radial (quarter-sawn) surface of Oak (*Quercus* sp.) showing the prominent figure (silver grain) produced by the large rays which are much paler in colour than the rest of the wood.

Knots are another gross feature of the trunk which are sometimes responsible for figure. Branches, which give rise to knots, pass out of the trunk along radii. Hence on a radial face knots will be cut along their length, and so appear as spike knots (Fig. 122 *A*), while on a plain-sawn face they will be cut transversely or (since branches commonly grow obliquely upwards) nearly transversely, and so will appear as round knots (Fig. 122 *B*).

Figure arising from the growth increments is common in softwoods, and occurs wherever there is sufficient difference in texture between early and late wood for the two to be visibly distinct. It is very prominent, for example, in the pitch pines and in Douglas fir, where the change from early to late wood is abrupt and pronounced; in spruces and soft pines, however, where this transition is more gradual, the figure is not nearly so distinct.

This type of figure, which is especially characteristic of temperate timbers with prominent growth rings, is not, however, confined to coniferous woods. Hardwoods of temperate regions may have fairly uniform growth throughout the season, but it is seldom that the beginning or end of the season's growth is not different in some way from that of the rest of the increment; there may be a pore ring at the beginning of the season, or the ring may terminate in a zone of thick-walled fibres or parenchyma. In either case the characteristic "cone-in-cone" structure will appear on tangential faces. Thus in birch it is seen as thin shining lines, due to terminal bands of flattened cells which, because of the thickness of their walls, have offered greater resistance to the tools used in preparing the surface of the wood and, in consequence, have become burnished or polished. In American whitewood there is a similar line at the end of each growth ring, due to the terminal parenchyma, and in American mahogany the presumed growth rings also arise from so-called terminal parenchyma which differs somewhat in colour from the rest of the wood, and so is distinct on plain-sawn surfaces. In oaks and other ring-porous woods, the large vessels of the early wood show up as a series of scratches (vessel lines), arranged in parallel lines on the radial faces and as ∩'s or ∧'s on the tangential surfaces. Teak, which is often ring-porous or, at least, semi-ring-porous, has the same type of figure, which is especially prominent on tangential surfaces, because the vessels of the early wood are embedded in parenchyma having a texture, and sometimes a colour, rather different from that of the intervening fibres (Fig. 124 A).

So far, it has been assumed that the growth rings are perfectly regular, although this is often not so in nature, for some portions of the ring may increase more rapidly than others. This will lead to irregularities in figure due to growth rings. In a simple case we may imagine that in a small portion of the bole the growth increment in one season is greater—or smaller—than elsewhere; the result would be a bulge, or an indentation, in this region, and even if growth in future years were similar to that elsewhere in the bole, the irregularity would remain. In a radial face this bulge will show in the parallel markings, while in a tangential face it would be cut through completely and appear as a number of concentric circles. In some woods such areas are quite small, e.g. the depressions producing bird's-eye figure in maple (cf. pp. 252–54), sometimes they are many cms. across. An excellent example of this type of figure is sometimes seen in pitch pine and in Douglas fir and is termed blister figure (Fig. 125 A). It is also sometimes seen in hardwoods, e.g. not uncommonly in Japanese ash or tamo.

A good illustration of the irregularity of the growth rings is seen in rotary-cut wood (say on the surfaces of a piece of birch plywood). Such surfaces are strictly tangential and it will be apparent that if we peel a set of concentric cones, which in effect is what takes place when a log is rotary-cut, the growth rings should appear on the surface as a series of horizontal, or rather, slightly oblique lines. Inspection of a piece of rotary-cut birch plywood will show that this does not occur;

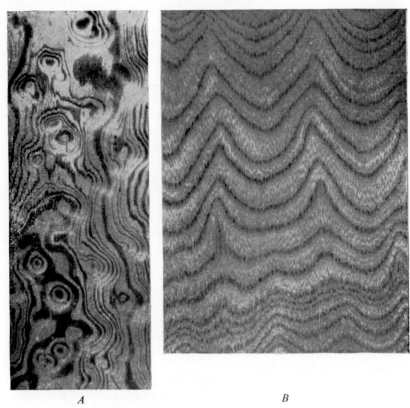

A   B

Fig. 125.—*A*. A Pitch Pine (*Pinus* sp.); a tangential (plain-sawn) surface showing blister figure caused by irregularities in the growth rings. *B*. Sen (*Acanthopanax ricinifolius*); a rotary-cut surface. The dark undulating bands are caused by irregularities in the pore rings although this pattern, produced by rotary cutting, differs from that on a plain-sawn surface (cf. p. 239).

there are irregularities arising, of course, from irregularities in the growth rings (cf. Fig. 125 *B*).

Figure produced by growth rings is nearly always more attractive on tangentially cut surfaces than on radial ones; the quarter-sawn wood is rarely pleasing. In contrast, figure which is produced by rays is generally more beautiful on radially cut surfaces, while plain-sawn faces, as their name implies, have a more uniform appearance. In not a few timbers figure is due to the rays. To produce a distinctive figure the rays, or at least some of them, must in general be large enough to be individually distinct to the unaided eye. The most familiar example of figure of this type is seen in oak, most species of which possess some large rays, up to 5 cms. or more high, as well as numerous small ones which are not visible to the unaided eye. Since the rays take a radial course they will be seen to their greatest extent on quarter-sawn faces, and least on plain-sawn wood. The familiar "silver grain" or "flower" of oak is seen on radial surfaces (Fig. 124 *B*); on tangential surfaces the rays appear as rather dark longitudinal streaks. Clearly, if maximum ray figure is to be obtained, the surface must follow the course of the rays. This, however, is hardly possible, for it is rare for the rays to run strictly radially throughout the whole of their course. Some of the Japanese oaks show a most disappointing figure, in spite of their large rays, and however carefully the wood may have been quartered, because the rays do not run truly radially but tend to be somewhat sinuous. There is a very real practical difficulty in cutting up a log to show the maximum of ray figure for, as has been seen, it is impossible to obtain a board of even thickness with two strictly radial surfaces, and the only method by which two radial surfaces may be obtained is by cutting out wedge-shaped boards. In the past it was a practice, when maximum figure was required in oak, to cut such feather-edged boards and they are still sometimes found in old houses (wainscott oak). The nearest approach to perfection was achieved by cleaving the wood into boards of approximately the size required, the large rays constituting lines of weakness along which splitting most readily occurred. Such cleft surfaces were not, of course, flat and were subsequently smoothed by a plane. Such a method of conversion is costly and economically impracticable at the present time. The methods now used for obtaining quartered oak are a compromise and never yield the maximum possible figure.

Other trees besides oak possess large rays and figure in their timbers is due mainly to these rays (Fig. 126). Among such trees are members of the Casuarinaceae; Proteaceae, e.g. silky oak (*Cardwellia sublimis* F.Muell. and *Grevillea robusta* A.Cunn.) and rewarewa (*Knightia excelsa* R.Br.); Myrsinaceae, e.g. Cape beech (*Rapanea melanophloeos* (L.) Mez.) and Rhizophoraceae (some mangroves). In some of the casuarinas the rays are so large (up to 10 cms. high) and dark in colour that they mar the beauty of quarter-sawn surfaces.

In beech and the maples the rays are smaller than those which have just been considered, but are still large enough to produce an attractive figure on radial surfaces. In the antarctic beeches (*Nothofagus*), however, the rays are much smaller and the radial faces are not considered to be figured. Nevertheless, if they are examined with a lens the characteristic beech figure, in miniature, will be evident.

Apart from the course of the rays and their size, a further condition is necessary before they produce figure; their colour or texture must contrast with the rest of the wood. In hornbeam (*Carpinus betulus* L.), for example, the aggregate rays (which in the present context may be regarded as single large rays) do not produce figure because they are of the same colour as the rest of the wood. They may be seen, if looked for closely, but this is insufficient to give figure.

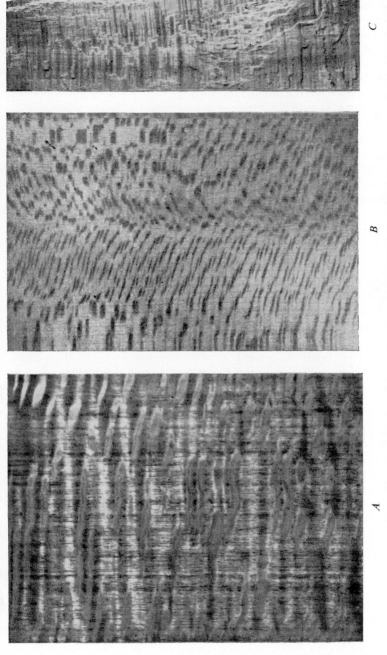

C

B

A

Fig. 126.—Figure caused by rays. *A.* Radial (quarter-sawn) surface of Silky Oak (*?Grevillea robusta*) showing large rays; the fine vertical lines are vessels. *B.* Radial (sliced) surface of Plane or Lacewood (*Platanus* sp.) showing numerous dark-coloured rays. *C.* Cleft radial surface of Beech (*Fagus sylvatica*) showing numerous rather small rays, darker in colour than the rest of the wood.

Even where rays are too small, individually, to produce figure on quarter-sawn surfaces, they may nevertheless affect the appearance of a piece of wood. Thus, in the American mahoganies and especially in Honduras mahogany (*Swietenia macrophylla* King) the rays are storeyed, that is, arranged in regular horizontal layers, and in certain lights this arrangement produces a very characteristic appearance, on tangential faces, known as ripple marks, the wood appearing to have a texture somewhat resembling fabric (Fig. 66). Some of the tropical Tiliaceae, e.g. danta (*Nesogordonia papaverifera* Caupron = *Cistanthera papaverifera* A.Chev.) from West Africa and the Burmese thitka (*Pentace burmanica* Kurz) show the best ripple marks. Not only rays, but also vessel elements, parenchyma and, less frequently, fibres, may have a storeyed arrangement and this regularity of some or all of the cells may often be seen on longitudinal surfaces as a ripple-mark type of figure. Good examples occur in many Sterculiaceae (e.g. *Pterospermum*) and Leguminosae (e.g. *Brachystegia*). Ripple marks are generally inconspicuous and while it is convenient to mention them here, they are scarcely prominent enough to be included within the term figure.

The regular, localised disposition of fibres and parenchyma is also sometimes responsible for figure. Vasicentric, and especially confluent parenchyma, if abundant, may show on longitudinal surfaces as thin dusty streaks. The difference in appearance between the parenchyma and the more shiny fibres is, of course, due to the thicker walls of the latter, which become burnished when the surface is prepared and, if the wood is polished, present a more compact and less absorbent surface to the polish. Figure of this type is well shown by many leguminous woods and by some of the terminalias, e.g. Indian laurel wood (*Terminalia* spp.). It is also seen in iroko (*Chlorophora excelsa* Benth. et H.f.) (Fig. 170 *B*) but here, on plain-sawn surfaces, it shows as dusty zig-zag lines. In the elms similar zig-zag lines (partridge-breast figure) are seen on tangential surfaces, between the loops formed by the pore rings: these are not due to parenchyma but to the numerous small vessels or vascular tracheids of the late wood, which are arranged, as seen in transverse section, in undulating tangential lines (Figs. 142, 143).

If we visualise these groups of vascular elements in the solid wood, it will be evident that since they appear as wavy tangential lines in transverse sections, they are in fact in the form of cones between those of the pore rings of the early wood, but unlike the latter they are in

Fig. 127.—Figure produced by parenchyma; all are tangential (plain-sawn) surfaces. *A*. Panga panga (*Milletia stuhlmannii*); light-coloured bands of parenchyma alternate with dark bands of fibres; the parenchyma is confluent. *B*. Camwood (?*Pterocarpus soyauxii*); the narrow pale areas are the parenchyma, which is confluent. *C*. Utile (*Entandrophragma utile*); the dark lines are parenchyma.

A

B

C

Fig. 12'1

R

cones with corrugated surfaces. In the same way, the somewhat undulating confluent parenchyma of iroko may be regarded broadly as forming corrugated cones (or rather, parts of cones); hence the zig-zag appearance when these cones are sliced tangentially. Figure due to the regular alternation of fibres and parenchyma (Fig. 127) may be rather elusive, only showing at its best when the wood is illuminated at certain angles; it is consequently apt to be disappointing for ornamental purposes.

Although comment has been made on the misuse of the term grain to designate a certain type of figure, grain is nevertheless responsible for some kinds of figure, which may be of great beauty and variety.

In describing the axial elements of wood it has been tacitly assumed that they run strictly axially, but this is not always so. In straight-grained timbers like ash and greenheart (*Ocotea rodiaei* Mez.) the normal course of the fibres is axial, but in common elm, for example, the fibres pursue more devious courses and their twisting and undulation result in a cross-grained wood which is difficult or impossible to split, since a cleavage crack tends to follow the course of these elements.

Spiral grain is a common defect in logs of some species. Where it occurs, the direction of the axial elements is regularly spiral, the spiral being either right- or left-handed. Spiral grain has been reported in more than 200 species; it is common, for instance, in Scots pine and sweet chestnut. There is no satisfactory explanation of its true cause, though there is evidence that in conifers it is related to the predominantly right- or left-handed inclination of pseudo-transverse (i.e. anticlinal) divisions in the fusiform initials of the cambium (Bannan, 1966). It has no claim to be regarded as figure.

In tropical trees a modified form of spiral grain may occur, the axial elements being aligned obliquely to the longitudinal axis of the trunk, but alternately in right- and left-handed directions. Thus the wood is built up of a series of cones in which successive ones have their elements running obliquely in opposite senses. Growth of this type is referred to as double spiral grain, or interlocked grain. How this type of growth comes about is not known. It seems reasonable to suppose that it may arise in the same kind of way as that suggested for spiral grain in conifers, but the factors underlying the alternating changes of obliquity are obscure.

If we examine a plain-sawn surface of a log with interlocked grain no very striking features will be noted, except that on close examination the grain will be seen to be oblique. If this is difficult to see it can be readily demonstrated by the application to the surface of a small drop of ink, which will spread most rapidly along the grain. A radial surface, however, will possess a striking figure consisting of alternating lighter and darker stripes, of widths dependent on the thicknesses of the zones of different obliquity. Such ribbon or stripe figure is very commonly seen in quarter-sawn sapele (*Entandrophragma cylindricum* Sprague)

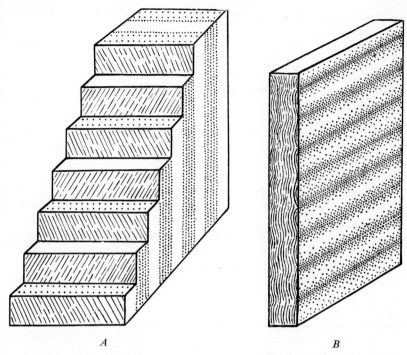

A   *B*

Fig. 128.—*A*. Diagram to illustrate wood with double spiral grain (interlocked grain); the block is viewed tangentially and the radial surface, on the right, shows the characteristic ribbon figure; the block has been cut into a series of steps at the boundaries of successive zones of spirally running fibres, hence the tangential faces of successive steps show the fibres running obliquely to the vertical in opposite directions; on the transverse (end-grain) surface these zones will probably give the appearance of wide growth rings. *B*. Diagram to illustrate wavy grain (fiddle-back figure); the undulating fibres are seen on the narrow face (tangential); the characteristic figure on the broad face (radial).

(Figs. 128 *A*, 130 *A*) and it is of frequent occurrence in many other tropical woods.

If a piece of wood having this type of grain is split radially—not an easy operation—the split will, as usual, tend to follow the direction of the fibres and a more or less corrugated surface will be produced because of the interlocked grain (Fig. 129 *A*, *A'*). The preparation of a smooth radial surface is not easy. If the wood is planed longitudinally in one direction, the fibres of alternate bands, which slope downwards towards the front of the plane, are cut without difficulty: in the adjacent bands, however, the fibres slope in the reverse direction and tend to be plucked out instead of being cut smoothly. Hence, if only roughly finished, the surface will show alternate smooth and rough bands of wood. If now, planing is attempted in the reverse direction, the same thing will happen, except that stripes which formerly finished smoothly will be plucked out, while those which previously proved recalcitrant will now plane smoothly.

It is important to realise that colour differences in different regions of the wood play no part in producing ribbon figure. The apparent colour or shade differences shown by the stripes are optical effects; if a piece of wood with ribbon figure is moved about in relation to the direction of the incident light it will probably be possible to observe a reversal of the apparent colour differences. The ribbon figure effect is due to the different alignment of the fibres in relation to the surface of the wood; they are not cut in the same direction in adjacent bands, and consequently reflect the light differently.

Sometimes, instead of running obliquely, the axial elements undulate, such undulations normally occurring in a tangential plane. Wood with this construction should cleave tangentially and give a reasonably plane surface, but if split radially the surface will be transversely corrugated (Fig. 129 *B, C*). Plain-sawn wood of this type does not show any figure as a result of the unusual course of the longitudinal elements, although it is often possible to detect the sinuous elements on the tangential surface with the aid of a hand-lens (Fig. 130 *D*). On the quarter-sawn surface, however, the wavy fibres produce a transversely barred effect, which likewise is due to varied reflection of the incident light and not to irregular distribution of colour, for here again the fibres are cut in different directions, and hence reflect the light differently. This type of figure, sometimes called wavy grain, is frequently seen in some mahoganies and maples; because it has become almost a convention to use wood so figured for the backs of violins, it is commonly known as fiddle-back figure (Figs. 128 *B*, 130 *B, C*).

Undulating fibres may lie in an oblique direction, or in other words, wood with interlocked grain may have its elements undulating as well. In its simplest form the superposition of fiddle-back and ribbon figure results in a breaking up of the stripes so that a kind of mottle results, which is commonly known as roe figure (Fig. 131 *A, B*). A further complication may arise when, as sometimes happens, the interlocked grain occurs only in localised areas in the trunk. Irregularities in the distribution of wavy grain and interlocked grain, either singly or together, produce a number of beautiful types of figure, some of which are designated by special names by veneer merchants. As there is little uniformity in such nomenclature, there is little point in attempting to give it here. If interlocked grain and wavy grain and their effects on the surface of the wood are clearly understood, it should not be very difficult to get some idea of the cause of the variants which may be met with.

Occasionally wavy grain is seen in plain-sawn surfaces (Fig. 130 *E*), although it would appear to be more rare than that which has just been described. A log in which this occurs, i.e. in which the undulations are in the radial and not in the tangential plane, will, of course, show fiddle-back figure on plain-sawn surfaces and not on quarter-sawn ones.

Fig. 129.—*A*. Cleft radial surface of Aformosia (*Afrormosia ?elata*) with double spiral (interlocked) grain. *A*. End-grain surface of the specimen, showing the irregular cleavage of the radial surface. *B*. Cleft radial surface of a Maple (*Acer* sp.) with wavy grain. *C*. Cleft block of Apple (*Malus pumila*); the figure shows a tangential surface in which the wavy course of the fibres can be seen; the left-hand edge is the edge of the radial surface and the irregularity of this cleft surface, as seen in profile, is striking.

Other well-known and highly ornamental types of figure are associated with irregularities in the orientation of the fibres and other axial elements of the wood. Among these may be mentioned the blister (as applied to decorative hardwoods), quilted and bird's-eye types of figure. In blister figure the surface is marked out into irregular blister-like areas by varying shades of colour. Quilted figure is somewhat similar except that these areas have a sort of honeycomb pattern, rather like that seen in old-fashioned honeycomb quilts (Fig. 131 C), but on a larger scale. Bird's-eye figure shows numerous small, more or less circular areas, superficially resembling pin knots (Fig. 132 C) and at one time often described as such. Blister figure may occur in African mahogany, where wood with a small blister figure goes by the name of pomele mahogany. Another wood which may show blister figure is maple and it is in maple that the quilted and bird's-eye figures occur, the former apparently being confined to Pacific or Oregon maple (*Acer macrophyllum* Pursh) and bird's-eye being generally associated with rock maple (*Acer saccharum* Marsh), although it occurs in other woods as well. Here may also be mentioned dimpled grain, a type of figure which is formed characteristically in lodgepole pine (*Pinus contorta* var. *latifolia* S.Wats.) and occasionally in other softwoods (Phillips, 1948).

Blister, quilted, and bird's-eye figure, as well as dimpled grain, are all caused by irregularities of the growth rings, either in the form of depressions or prominences which, once formed, are perpetuated. Logically, they should have been considered along with the blister figure of softwoods which has been described earlier in the chapter; but this type of figure results from irregular distribution of early and late wood on tangential surfaces and is thus distinct from the type under consideration, which is due entirely to irregularity in the course of the fibres and other longitudinal elements in the area. Hence, on a tangential surface, instead of running longitudinally, these elements run in various directions more or less at right-angles to the surface, with the result that the incident light is reflected differently from different parts of the surface. These irregularities of the growth rings will, of course, show on radial and transverse surfaces as depressions or prominences in the growth rings, but it is only on tangential surfaces that the highly ornamental figure is to be seen. A very striking type of blister figure, due also to undulations in the growth rings, is sometimes seen in ring-porous woods, the effect of the undulations being heightened by the presence of pore rings (Fig. 131 D).

Fig. 130.—Ribbon and fiddle-back figures. *A*. Sapele (*Entandrophragma cylindricum*) showing ribbon or stripe figure; radial surface. *B*. Peroba showing a small fiddle-back figure (radial surface). *C*. ? Sapele showing fiddle-back figure (radial surface). *D*. A small part of a tangential surface of *C*, showing the wavy courses of the vessels (× about 2). *E*. Ash (*Fraxinus* sp.); a tangential surface showing fiddle-back figure; fiddle-back is less common on tangential surfaces than on radial ones.

Fig. 130

How such irregularities arise is not understood. According to Eades (1932) they are sometimes caused by the death of buds on the young stem or trunk, which become buried by the growth of the wood. It is claimed by Hale (1932) that bird's-eye figure in rock maple is caused by a fungus which is parasitic in the cambium. Owing to the presence of this fungus, small areas of the cambium are temporarily inactivated, the activity of the surrounding unaffected cambium leaving the non-active areas in shallow depressions. The infected cambium resumes its activity after a time, but owing to the check in its growth it remains in a depression and the presence of a depression leads to irregular growth of the fibres in this region.

Whether blister or quilted figure may be due to the same cause is not known. Quilted maple appears to occur in leaning trees and below large limbs and it is possible that the fibres owe their tortuous course to stresses which are set up in the living tree. It is not improbable, however, that some other types of figure due to irregular growth of the longitudinal elements will be found to be due to fungi, while it may well be that some colour variations will also be found to owe their origin to fungal invaders.

Record (1934) states that mottle, a type of figure very similar to roe figure, is sometimes caused in American whitewood by injury to the vascular cambium by "sap-sucking" birds. The North American sap-suckers (species of woodpeckers) bore holes in the bark, feed on the inner bark, and in so doing often damage the cambium, with results similar to those already described. The markings so produced are usually in tangential rows, as might easily be produced by a sapsucker which when feeding, makes holes in regular lines.

The dimple grain of lodgepole pine has an entirely different origin, for it is caused by resin blisters, produced in the phloem, which press on the cambium and to some extent retard its activity.

Another type of figure which arises mainly from the irregular course of the axial elements of the wood is that which is formed near the origin of a branch or the base of a fork. In these regions, apparently because of the pressure caused by the expanding trunk and branch (or by the expanding arms of the fork) the vascular cambium and its derivatives become much distorted. Space is more limited on the upper side of such a region than on its lower side, and consequently a wilder figure is likely to occur on that side. Beautiful feather-like markings are often found when the fork of a tree is cut radially, and veneers cut from this region, showing "feather-crotch" figure, are highly prized for decorative

Fig. 131.—*A*. Pepperwood (? *Umbellularia californica*); roe figure, caused by the superposition of ribbon upon fiddle-back figure (radial surface). *B*. Australian Maple (*Flindersia* sp.); roe figure (radial surface). *C*. Pacific Maple (*Acer macrophyllum*); quilted figure, a type of blister figure due to irregularities in the course of the fibres (tangential surface). *D*. Ash (*Fraxinus* sp.); an irregular figure due to irregularities in growth rings, comparable to blister figure in a softwood (tangential surface).

A

B

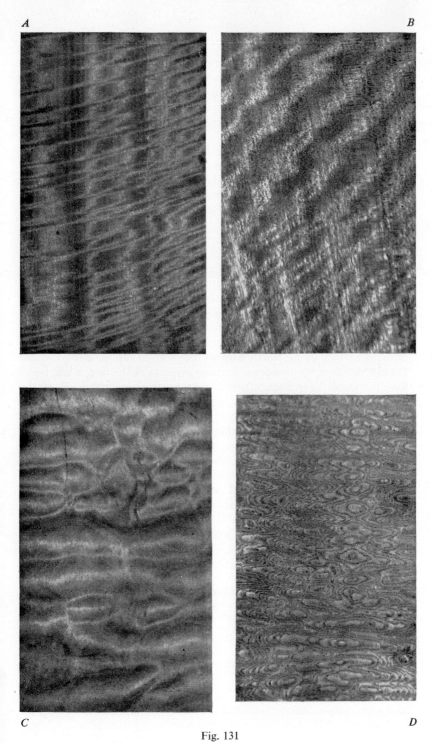

C

D

Fig. 131

work. Some of the mahoganies and walnuts are specially valued for crotch figure. When used for decoration of vertical surfaces feather crotches are nearly always placed upside down, i.e. with the part which came lowest in the tree forming the top of the veneer. The more tangentially placed surfaces of a crotch yield a softer, more wave-like figure which is often termed swirl.

As might be expected, there are usually growth irregularities where the trunk joins the roots of the tree, especially if, as sometimes happens, the roots in this region are flattened laterally and form buttresses, or when, as in walnut, the base of the trunk is swollen. Walnut stumps are highly valued for the beautiful decorative veneers which they give, the beauty of the irregularities of the grain often being enhanced by the irregular distribution of colour. Such logs are commonly halved longitudinally and converted into veneer by the half-round rotary cutting method. No little skill and experience is required to obtain the best figured veneers from such a stump.

The large excrescences which sometimes occur on trees, and which are known as burrs, often yield wood with a highly ornamental figure. They are often caused by injury to the tree and are very common in some trees, like yew and common elm. It is said that they were formerly induced to form in the North African thuya wood (*Tetraclinis articulata* (Vahl) Masters), by deliberate burning of parts of the tree, while burrs in olive wood have been attributed to goats eating the bark of the trees. Any form of wounding or irritation may induce the development of buds from the margins of the wounded area and it is to these buds, or rather to the knots to which they give rise, that burr figure is mainly attributable (Fig. 132). At the same time the presence of numerous knots in the wood will lead to twisting of the fibres in the adjacent wood, so that twisted grain is also, in part, responsible for burr figure. The knots are quite small, and hence if the wood is sectioned tangentially, they show as pin knots, while, if a radial face is exposed, they take the form of small spike knots.

It will be realised that any wood in which the various elements deviate from their normal course will present difficulties in seasoning, since regular transverse and longitudinal shrinkage will not occur, owing

---

Fig. 132.—*A*. Elm (*Ulmus* sp.) burr and *B*. Thuya (*Tetraclinis articulata*) burr; both are tangential surfaces and show numerous small round knots (pin knots); the beauty of the figure depends not only on the knots but also on the irregularities in the grain around the knots. *C*. Block cut from a burr of Plane (*Platanus* sp.); the narrow face to the right is the external surface of the burr (beneath the bark) and shows the remains of numerous epicormic or adventitious buds, while the larger surface is a radial one, in which the numerous small spike knots, caused by the growth of these buds, can be seen. *D*. Pacific Maple (*Acer macrophyllum*); an irregular type of figure; at the top is some irregular quilted or blister figure, below this are a few small knots, clearly from the region of a burr, while the irregular grain on the right suggests that the wood may have come from near the base of a branch or a crotch.

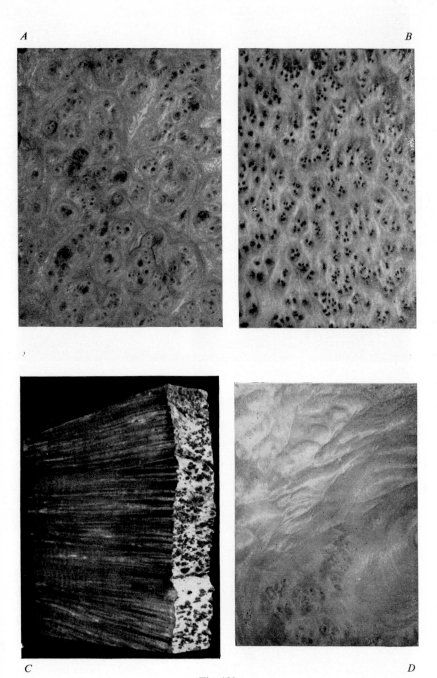

A

B

C

D

Fig. 132

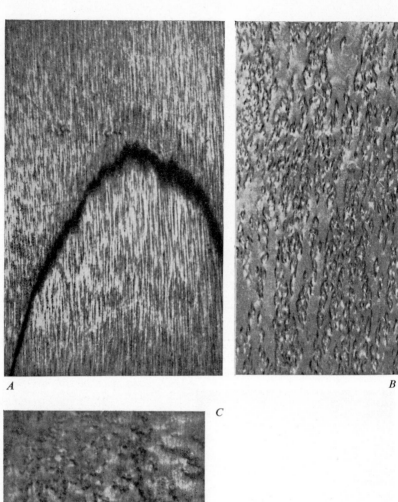

A

B

C

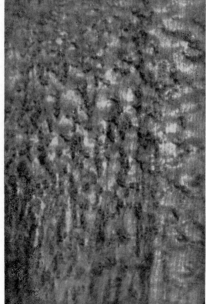

Fig. 133.—*A.* African Walnut (*Lovoa klaineana*); dark gum-vein on tangential surface. *B.* Masur Birch (*Betula* sp.); the numerous small dark lines are pith-flecks. *C.* Bird's-eye maple (*Acer* sp.); the bird's-eye figure simulates burr figure, although it has an entirely different cause (cf. p. 254); tangential surface.

A   B

Fig. 134.—Pith-fleck in Alder (*Alnus glutinosa*). *A*. Transverse section. *B*. Radial
longitudinal section; (both × 27).

to the irregular orientation of the elements of the wood. Thus in a
straightforward case of interlocked grain the normally transverse
shrinkage will be slightly oblique, the obliquity depending on the angle
of orientation of the fibres. But in one zone of fibres this shrinkage will
be oblique in one direction relative to the transverse plane in the trunk,
while in the next zone the obliquity will be in the opposite sense.
Longitudinal shrinkages will be similarly affected. Such variations in
the movement of the fibres in losing or absorbing water will clearly set
up stresses in the wood, which are likely to pull the wood out of shape
or to cause checking. In practice, difficulties of this kind are reduced to
a minimum, since the wood is most often used in the form of thin
veneers rather than as "solid" timber. However, some idea of the
stresses set up in the wood can be gained from examination of a leaf
of veneer cut from, say, a burr of elm or oak. Such a veneer becomes
distorted and far from flat as it dries.

Normally, the presence of gums or resins in ducts or canals, large enough to be visible to the unaided eye, does not improve the appearance of a wood (Fig. 76 B) although, by the definition used in this chapter, figure may be produced by them. Generally, such structures are regarded as defects, since they detract from the beauty of the wood; in hardwoods they are often referred to as gum galls. They are often seen in Tasmanian oak (*Eucalyptus* spp.) and in timbers from trees of the Dipterocarpaceae. Occasionally, however, gum galls contribute materially to the beauty of a timber and may be referred to in connection with figure even when the term is used in its more restricted sense. An excellent example of figure of this type is seen in African walnut, in which the somewhat honey-coloured wood is often marked by thin, dark brown lines of gum (Fig. 133 A). These axial gum ducts run in the same direction as the vessels and consequently if they are fairly abundant, will appear as parallel longitudinal lines on quarter-sawn surfaces and as concentric ∧'s or ∩'s on plain-sawn ones. Occasionally, the ducts are large and numerous and the gum which they contain is almost black. Such gum ducts, occurring, as often happens, in wood which is more deeply coloured than normal, produce a very handsome figure indeed.

It remains to mention one other type of figure which normally mars the appearance of wood, but which nevertheless sometimes makes the surface extremely attractive. This figure is in the form of thin brown lines of varying length which occur on longitudinal surfaces, and which go by the name of pith flecks (Fig. 134 B). Pith flecks (which of course have no connection with the pith of the tree) are caused primarily by the larvae of midge-like dipterous flies belonging to the genus *Agromyza*, and perhaps also to allied genera. The female fly lays her eggs beneath the bark of the tree, and the grubs which hatch out bore longitudinal galleries in the vascular cambium. After the attacks of one species (at least) the galleries become filled with parenchyma cells produced by the ray cells of the phloem; these parenchyma cells have dark-brown contents. The grubs finally escape at the base of the tree and pass into the pupal stage. The parenchyma-filled galleries subsequently become buried in the wood by later cambial activity, and so appear on transverse surfaces as hemispherical or elliptical spots, rarely exceeding 3 mm. across their greatest width; on longitudinal surfaces they occur as the dark-brown streaks already referred to. Pith flecks tend to be more abundant in butt logs because the grubs often bore more extensively in this part of the tree.

Pith flecks are not uncommon in close-textured hardwoods. They are seen, for example, in the birches, alders and soft maples, but are rather rare in hard maple. They are often abundant in the European birches. Rotary-cut birch shipped from Sweden and Finland under the name of Masur birch has a most attractive figure due largely to the very numerous pith flecks which it contains.

CHAPTER 11

THE PROPERTIES AND USES OF WOOD IN RELATION TO ITS STRUCTURE

Different woods vary greatly in their properties; some are soft, others hard; some are heavy, others are light; one wood is flexible, another brittle; or again, some woods are more hard-wearing or resistant to decay than others, while some burn easily, others less readily. There is great diversity in the anatomical structure of different woods and the notion that the properties of timbers should be explicable in terms of their structure is both plausible and attractive. It soon becomes evident, however, that a relationship between the anatomy and the properties of a timber can be demonstrated only in special instances and then only in regard to certain characteristics; in fact microscopical study gives only limited information on the properties of a timber, nor does it assist in the prediction of suitable uses for a newly described wood. For example, although rock maple is very resistant to abrasion and wears away slowly and evenly when used for flooring or escalator treads, it seems to possess no peculiar anatomical features which might explain this valuable quality. Under the microscope it can be seen that the several types of element of which it is composed vary but little in size throughout the growth ring, that they are evenly distributed and that the fibres are fairly thick-walled, and from such characteristics it might be reasonable to infer that rock maple is a wood which should wear evenly and well. Nevertheless, it would not be difficult to select another dozen timbers, including the closely related sycamore, which possess similar microscopic features, although none of them would, in practice, serve as a substitute for rock maple for the purposes mentioned. In the same way, Western hemlock is superior in most of its properties to Eastern hemlock, although structurally these two woods are very similar and such differences as may exist between them do not seem to furnish a satisfactory explanation of the differences in their properties.

Nevertheless, it would seem reasonable that clues to the characteristics of any and every timber must, ultimately, lie in what the wood is made of and how what it is made of is arranged. Since, moreover, the properties of a wood must determine the uses for which it is suited, it is a logical inference that the wood technologist should attempt to investigate the structure of a timber and to make an accurate assessment of its properties and of the uses to which it may best be put. That progress in this direction has been slow does not invalidate this contention. It reflects rather on the present state of our knowledge of wood.

Mere examination of sections of a wood under the microscope cannot yield a full picture of its structure: the study of wood anatomy, or more accurately, wood histology, is so fascinating that it has taken a prominent, perhaps a too prominent place in wood technology. Wood has also a gross structure, a fact not likely to be overlooked; it also has a less obvious ultimate or molecular structure, of which our knowledge is, however, rapidly increasing. In its widest sense, the study of wood structure is concerned at one extreme with gross features, like knots and growth rings—features measured in terms of centimetres or inches—and at the other with molecules, for which the scale of measurement is the Ångstrom unit, i.e. one hundred-millionth of a centimetre, far below the limit of resolution of the highest powers of the light microscope.

It is not too much to say that data on this ultimate structure of wood, with which must be coupled our knowledge of wood chemistry, have been obtained from only relatively few species. It seems likely, however, that the broad generalisations which have been made on these somewhat limited data are justifiable. Although electronmicroscopy has proved a valuable technique for the study of the minutiae of wood structure, as yet our knowledge of these features is very incomplete, particularly at the molecular level, and until much more is known it will not be possible to relate the structure and the properties of wood in a comprehensive manner. In these circumstances it is not surprising that the properties of timbers so often appear to bear little relation to their structure, insofar as this may be seen under the microscope. To attempt to obtain a complete picture by a study of wood anatomy or histology alone is to court disappointment and shows a lack of appreciation of what wood structure embraces.

Although all woods have certain features in common, for instance, the broad pattern of their gross structure, their cellular micro-structure and porosity, their lack of homogeneity and their general similarity of chemical and physical make-up, they differ in diverse ways. Thus, for example, they vary in the types and sizes of the cells present in them,

Fig. 135.—Transverse sections of: *A*, a heavy wood, Greenheart (*Ocotea rodiaei*), *B*, a light wood, Balsa (*Ochroma* sp.) and *C*, another very light wood, Ambach (*Herminiera elaphroxylon*) (all × 170).

In *A* the greater part of the section is occupied by small, thick-walled fibres; the paired vessels on the right are bounded by parenchyma to the left and top, while a weak ray curves round them on the right; neither vessels nor parenchyma are very thick-walled. In *B* there are parts of two vessels on the left and the fibre and parenchyma are very thin-walled. In *C* there is a vessel surrounded by relatively thin-walled fibres, and above and below, thin-walled parenchyma. Note that Greenheart, air-dry, weighs 66–77 lbs. per cu. ft. (S.G. 1·05–1·23), Balsa around 8 lbs. per cu. ft. (S.G. about 0·13) air-dry, while Ambach is even lighter.

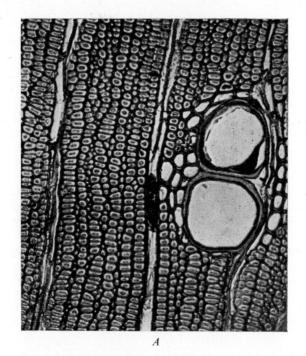

A

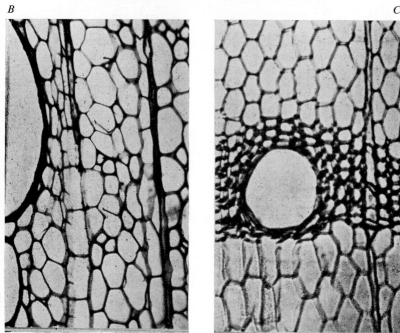

B

C

Fig. 135

S

the arrangement and relative proportions of these cell types, their orientation in relation to the trunk of the tree, the chemical composition and physical structure of their cell walls and middle lamellae, and the presence, distribution and chemical and physical nature of extractives produced by or deposited in them.

The properties and uses of a wood may depend on one or more of these variables. Thus the presence of extractives may alone give a timber certain peculiarities and perhaps determine the uses to which it may best be put. Density might appear to be another property dependent on a single feature, that is on the thickness of the walls of the wood elements, but it is often affected by the presence of extractives, while the suggestion has been made that it may also be affected by cell wall ultrastructure. Very commonly, any readily assessable property of a wood may depend on more than one factor.

The specific gravity of the wall material of wood is approximately 1·53. If all the extraneous materials could be removed from a piece of wood, whatever its natural density,[1] and the wood then compressed until it consisted of solid cell wall material without any spaces, it would weigh about 95·3 lbs. per cubic foot (1·53 kg. per litre). Woods, of course, vary in density; air-dry balsa ranges between 7 and 10 lbs. per cubic foot (specific gravity 0·11 to 0·16), while the wood of one of the pith trees (*Aeschynomene hispida* Willd.) weighs only 2·3 to 4 lbs. per cubic foot, or has a specific gravity of 0·04. At the other extreme are lignum vitae (*Guaiacum* spp.) with an average density of 78 lbs. per cubic foot, or a specific gravity of 1·25, and axemaster of British Honduras [*Krugiodendron ferreum* (Vahl.) Urban], which may weigh as much as 89 lbs. per cubic foot (specific gravity 1·42).

Apart from the wood substance, extractives and water contribute to the weight of wood. The water can be driven off by drying the wood in a steam-heated oven, i.e. at a temperature of 100° C., until it reaches a constant weight (the dry weight or oven-dry weight). The weights of equal volumes of oven-dried woods (ignoring extractives) will be accounted for by the weight of the wood substance present. In a wood of low density, like balsa, the elements are unusually thin-walled and the greater part of the gross volume of the wood is occupied by air; in a dense wood, on the other hand, the walls of the cells are very thick and the lumina are consequently relatively very small; hence the bulk of the wood consists of wood substance, not of air (Fig. 135). The

---

[1] Density is the actual weight of a substance per unit volume, and may be expressed in any convenient units, e.g. in lbs. per cubic foot, as is commonly done for wood. Specific gravity (or relative density) is the ratio of the density of a substance to that of water. Thus taking the density of water as 62·4 lbs. per cubic foot, a wood with a density of 30 lbs. per cubic foot has a specific gravity of 0·48.

Specific gravity of wood is usually calculated as the ratio of the weight of an oven-dry sample to the volume of the sample in the green state. This ratio is often termed the basic density.

following table shows the relative proportions of air and wood substance in woods of different densities.

Density (lbs. per cu. ft.)	Proportions Wood	Air	Relative Density (Specific Gravity)
1	0·011	0·989	0·016
10	0·105	0·895	0·160
20	0·210	0·790	0·320
30	0·316	0·684	0·481
40	0·421	0·579	0·640
50	0·526	0·474	0·801
60	0·631	0·369	0·962
62·4 (Water)	—	—	1·000
70	0·737	0·263	1·121
80	0·842	0·158	1·282
90	0·945	0·055	1·444
95·35	1·000	0·000	1·528

This table is, of course, of theoretical rather than practical interest, in that extractives have been ignored; if abundant, these substances may contribute materially to the density of timber. Thus in Douglas fir, resin is normally not responsible for more than 1 per cent of the dry weight of the wood substance proper, but it may account for as much as a third of the dry weight of the whole timber.

Since the density of wood is an indication of the amount of wood substance contained in unit volume, it might appear that density should be a guide to the general strength of a timber, and it is well-established that this is so. It has been stated, indeed, that where the average density and strength values for a species are known, the density of a given clear specimen may be a better indication of its strength properties than actual strength tests. Some strength properties, like stiffness, vary almost directly with density, while for others the relation is less direct; toughness, for example, varies almost as the square of the density. Dadswell and Nicholls (1959) found that in *Pinus elliottii* var. *elliottii* specific gravity (i.e. relative density) was a good index of average cell wall thickness, this latter being related, in its turn, to the proportion of late wood present in the rings. It was found that specific gravity increased in successive rings from the pith, becoming fairly constant from about the 15th ring outwards, although the specific gravity of the early wood tended to decrease from the pith outwards and that of the late wood to remain more or less constant. An increase in specific gravity was to be explained therefore, by an increase in the proportion of late wood present. We have seen (p. 200) that juvenile wood has less dense late wood than does mature wood, and that this late wood forms a smaller proportion of the growth ring, so that these results are what might be expected.

The rate of growth of a tree may have an important effect on the density and strength properties of a wood. In even-textured woods the rate of growth is generally relatively unimportant in this context, but where the texture is less even the rate of growth may play a large part in determining the strength of a timber. In slowly-grown oak and other ring-porous woods, the successive pore rings of the early wood are close together. The early wood, consisting largely of vessels with large lumina and thin walls, has relatively little wood substance and a relatively low density. A good proportion of the late wood, however, consists of fibres, which are of course the main strengthening cells of a hardwood. Whatever the growth rate, the pore rings vary little in width, so that the closer they are together the lower will be the density of the wood and also its strength. Slowly-grown woods of this type are generally easy to work, for they have little wood substance. On the other hand, fast-grown oak, containing a high proportion of late wood with its dense fibre tissue, has greater density and strength and requires much greater effort to work. Hence, within limits, the faster a ring-porous wood has been grown, the denser it is and the greater its strength. The qualification "within limits" is necessary, since very fast-grown ring-porous woods do not always follow the rule, for their fibres may be only slightly lignified and very thin-walled, so that in consequence much of the bulk of the wood laid down each year may consist of air and little of wood substance. Sometimes the weakness may be due to abnormally high numbers of vessels or an unusually high proportion of parenchyma in the late wood, when of course there is a corresponding reduction in the amount of fibre tissue. Very approximately, for it is difficult to generalise, a ring-porous hardwood possesses maximum strength when its growth rings number between 6 and 10 to the inch (2·5–4 per cm.). This statement of course applies to mature wood, for in juvenile wood the relationship between ring width and strength is likely to be less definite.

In diffuse-porous woods, where the texture is more homogeneous, ring width does not, as a general rule, bear any obvious relation to strength. Nevertheless, the curves drawn by Rochester (1933) indicate that very slowly-grown diffuse-porous woods are slightly less strong than those which have been more rapidly grown. Since these curves show a similarity to the ones relating specific gravity to rate of growth, it is to be inferred that there is an optimum ring width corresponding to which more wood substance is added than in narrower or wider rings. According to Hale (1932) the lighter diffuse-porous woods show density variations which seem to be related to rate of growth, for very fast- or very slowly-grown specimens are rather less dense than those of medium growth rate. He points out that for some purposes the less dense slowly-grown wood is to be preferred, because as it contains less wood substance, and shrinks and swells less with changes in humidity, it is less likely to check when in use.

Broadly, the position in those softwoods where there is a marked difference between the early and late wood, is the reverse of that in ring-porous hardwoods: in general, that is, the production of early wood varies with the width of the growth increment and the formation of late wood remains unaffected. In such timbers the late wood tracheids are thicker walled and smaller than those of the early wood; as a result the late wood is denser and stronger. Consequently, the lower the proportion of early wood there is in a ring, the stronger is the wood. It is sometimes specified that Douglas fir and pitch pine timber which is to be used for structural work shall have an average of at least one-third late wood in the growth rings. In loblolly pine Bethel (1950) found that for compression strength parallel to the grain the optimum percentage of late wood in a ring is about 48.

Where growth is very slow, it would seem that the proportion of late wood to early wood is smaller than usual, with a resultant decrease in strength properties. The evidence here, however, is conflicting, for Lodewick (1933) found that in general the proportion of late wood increases as the ring width becomes less. Hale (1932) explained that in spruce, where the late wood is narrow in normal growth rings, the proportion increases as the ring narrows and that the slower the growth the heavier the wood. According to Rochester, for white spruce the curve indicating the relationship between maximum crushing strength parallel to the grain and ring width rises to a maximum at the slowest growth rate tested (40–42 rings per inch). On the other hand, Hale's curve for Douglas fir indicates a maximum strength at 16 rings per inch and a sharp decrease as the rings narrow; the curve for red pine (*P. resinosa* Ait.) is similar, where the peak lies at 22 rings to the inch. Hale (1932) considered that in dense softwoods, e.g. Douglas fir, where the growth rings contain a high proportion of late wood, the amount of late wood relative to early wood tends to decrease at both extremes of growth rate. It seems clear from a study of the graphs of these two investigators (Fig. 136) that the relationship is not always as simple as has been suggested. It might have been expected that white pine would behave in the same way as spruce, for it also has very narrow zones of late wood. In fact, according to Rochester's curve, white pine has a maximum strength at about 24 rings to the inch; above this, diminution in strength is gradual, but none the less apparent. It looks as though there may be a good deal of variation among conifer species in this respect, indeed perhaps, not only among species, but possibly also among individual trees of the same species. At present, the usual statement that softwoods are strongest when their rings number 6–20 to the inch, must be accepted as no more than giving an approximate indication of where maximum strength is likely to be found.

The density of wood must also be considered from other aspects, as for example, in relation to the effect of water in wood. The amount present is expressed as a percentage of the dry weight; thus 20 per cent

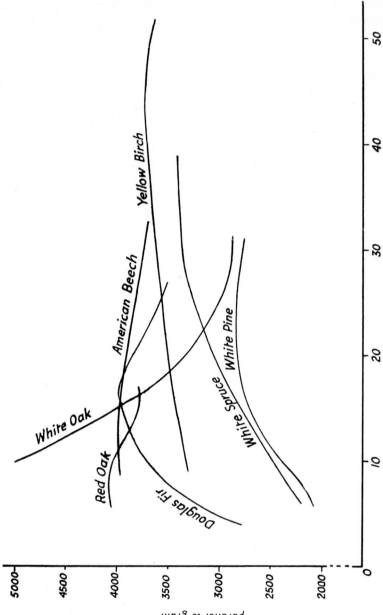

Fig. 136.—Curves illustrating the relationship between a strength property of timber (maximum crushing strength, compression parallel to the grain) and the width of the growth rings.

Curves from Hale (1932) and Rochester (1933)

moisture content means that the amount of water present is 20 per cent or one-fifth of the oven-dry weight. Clearly then, for a given percentage moisture content, the amount of water present will be much greater in a sample of a very dense wood than in one of a less dense wood of the same dimensions. Of course, for moisture contents below fibre saturation point (say about 30 per cent) wood shrinks as it loses water, so that the wood substance comes to occupy a smaller volume and the weight of the wood itself, per unit volume, thus increases as it dries. Above fibre-saturation point there is no change in volume as water is lost or gained. Consequently, in drying, wood loses weight at a greater relative rate above fibre-saturation point than below it.

The proportion of wood substance to air also affects the heating value of dry wood. As fuel, "light" woods give out far less heat than equal volumes of "heavy" woods, because the calorific value lies in the solid matter of the wood and weight for weight the calorific value of most timbers is approximately the same. This statement requires qualification since it ignores the possible presence of inflammable extractives. Oils, waxes and resins are all inflammable and, if present, add to the calorific value. Moreover, the presence of resin, for example, has a disproportionate effect, because the calorific value of resin is about double that of wood. It seems also that extractives must play a part in influencing the way in which a wood burns. Consider some woods of about the same density and without any obviously inflammable extractives like resin: sweet chestnut tends to smoulder rather than blaze, robinia makes a hot fire but gives out a rather objectionable smoke, ash burns well, even when green, while cherry is excellent when fully alight but difficult to ignite in the first instance. Assuming that the wood substance in these woods is essentially the same, we must look to extractives to account for the differences in burning properties.

Extractives may also affect the odour emitted by burning wood. The heartwood of palo santo (*Bulnesia sarmienti* Lorentz) contains an abundance of a gum-resin, and the wood is burnt as incense. Webster (1919) referred to the fragrant scent of burning cedar of Lebanon, but recorded that on one occasion a considerable quantity of bacon was ruined because it had been smoked with cedar wood smoke. Extractives apart, it is generally true that the heavier a wood the more slowly it burns; this might be expected by reason of the greater amount of actual wood present in a given gross volume.

Although the wood substance itself is a tolerably good conductor of heat, the thermal conductivity of dry wood is generally low, on account of the high proportion of air contained in it. Heavy woods are better conductors than light woods, and in consequence feel colder to the touch: light woods, like balsa, have in fact been used as thermal insulators. The insulating properties of wood are valuable also in the fire resistance of wooden beams and doors. Though the surface of a piece of wood may be set on fire, the interior, some 6–7 mm. distant from the charred zone, may have a temperature no higher than 180° C,. and the advance of the high temperature region into the beam or door is relatively slow.

Moisture in wood will of course significantly increase its thermal conductivity, and this may also be modified by the presence of extractives. Thus lignum vitae, though a dense wood, is not cold to the touch, because it is usually coated with the waxy, resinous substance, gum-guaiacum, which is a poor conductor.

As might be expected, the thermal conductivity of wood is dependent on the direction in which it is measured; thus it is 2–3 times faster along the grain than across it. As measured along the grain in coniferous wood there is some evidence [Wangaard, quoted from Forsaith, 1946), and further discussed by Preston (1949a)] that it varies according to the orientation of the micellae in the tracheid walls.

Resilience in wood is also connected with the amount of air which it contains, although other factors also affect this property. Resilience is the ability to withstand temporary deformation, the original shape being resumed when the deforming stress is removed. Under impact, a fairly light wood, like willow, becomes indented, but once the stress is removed, it may regain its original shape—the deformation is temporary. While wood itself is not a very elastic substance, when relatively thin cell walls become distorted, the air in the cells is simultaneously compressed. The compression of the air assists in the recovery; in fact, the wood behaves in some degree like a pneumatic tyre. This resilience makes willow a useful wood for artificial limbs, for its resilience lessens the shock of impact. It also makes it a good wood for cricket bats, although our knowledge of wood structure is not yet sufficient to enable us to explain why the blue willow (*Salix alba* v. *caerulea* Sm.) makes the best bats. The various willows cannot be distinguished by the structure of their timbers and there is indeed little difference between them and the poplars in this respect. Judged on anatomy alone, sound wood of any member of the Salicaceae, provided it came from a tree of suitable growth rate and had the requisite density, should be suitable for the purpose. Very light woods, with extremely thin-walled cells, are not resilient, for their cell walls tend to break under a stress and the deformation is thus permanent. In heavy woods, the thick walls are not sufficiently flexible to suffer temporary deformation under impact, although, of course, the stresses may be sufficient to break some of the wood elements and so cause permanent distortion.

A practical application of the value of resilience in timber is seen in the use of Scots pine for railway sleepers. Some of the heavy eucalyptus woods have been tried in this country for the same purpose, but with less success. Their limited resilience made a less comfortable track and they were found to wear rather badly because, under the pounding of a passing train, the rail chairs tended to break them up, whereas softwood

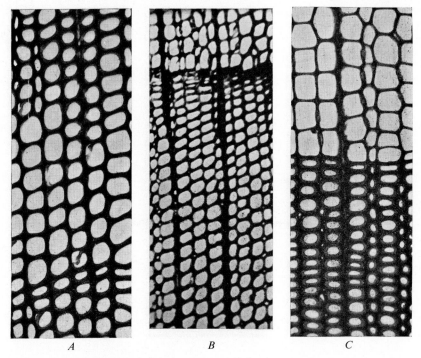

A   B   C

Fig. 137.—Texture of coniferous woods. *A*. Matai (*Podocarpus spicatus*); even-textured; there is very little difference between the early and late wood of a growth ring. *B*. Pencil Cedar (*Juniperus virginiana*); another even-textured wood, the late wood being limited to two or three rows of smaller tracheids. *C*. Douglas Fir (*Pseudotsuga taxifolia*); a wood of uneven texture; usually, the late wood forms a large proportion of the rings and its tracheids are smaller and much thicker-walled than those of the early wood. All T.S. (× 135).

sleepers were sufficiently resilient to withstand repeated compression of this kind and to recover their original form.

The texture of a wood depends on the size of its cells and on the distribution of the different kinds of cells which it contains (Figs. 137, 138). A wood with small cells has a fine texture, a feature which is frequent in, but not confined to, heavy woods, while the elements of a coarse-textured wood are large. An even texture depends on an even distribution of the different types of cell present and also on uniform wall thickness, or sometimes on the latter alone. In softwoods like larch or pitch pine, the early wood consists of large, thin-walled tracheids, and the late wood of much thicker-walled and rather smaller ones; thus the wood has an uneven texture, the soft early wood alternating with the hard, dense late wood. In rotary-cut or plain-sawn Douglas fir the striking figure due to differences between early and late wood may be visible even in panels which have been thoroughly

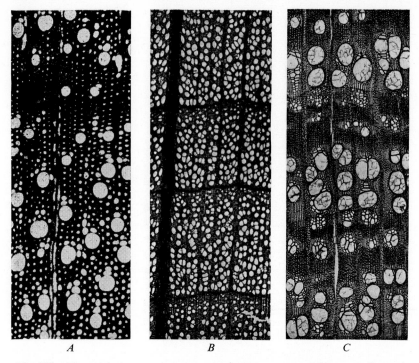

A   B   C

Fig. 138.—Texture in hardwoods. *A.* Cape Box (*Buxus macowani*); texture fine and even; note the small, regularly distributed vessels and the small, thick-walled fibres; there is little difference between early and late wood; T.S. (× 120). *B.* American Beech (*Fagus grandifolia*); texture fine and even, due to the relatively small size of the elements and their regular distribution; there is little difference between early and late wood; T.S. (× 16). *C.* Robinia (*Robinia pseudoacacia*); texture uneven: the vessels in the early wood are much larger than those of the late wood. There are tyloses in most of the vessels. T.S. (× 16).

prepared and have received several coats of paint, the explanation being that since there is more actual wood substance in the late wood zones than in those of the early wood, these are able to take up more water and hence to swell more than the early wood. Paint does not form a coating completely impervious to water and hence does not entirely check the hygroscopicity of the wood, so that swelling or shrinking occur with changes in atmospheric humidity; in common parlance "the grain lifts". In rotary-cut Douglas fir the difference between early and late wood is sometimes emphasised by sand-blasting, sharp sand being blown against the wood with considerable force. The softer early wood is thus worn away more rapidly than the harder late wood and a pleasing "waterworn" appearance is produced. In a similar manner, soft woods like pine, used for grain chutes, may acquire a very irregular surface because constant friction with the moving cereal

Fig. 139.—A piece of Pine, probably Scots Pine (*Pinus sylvestris*), which formed part of a chute in a flour mill. The eroded surface is due to the more rapid wearing away of the softer early wood by the passage of the cereal grains. *Above*, Surface view. *Below*, End view.

grains erodes the softer early wood much more rapidly than the late wood (Fig. 139).

Other softwoods, like pencil cedar (*Juniperus* spp.), kauri (*Agathis* spp.) and yew (*Taxus*), show far less difference between early and late wood and consequently these woods have a more even texture, which is somewhat coarse in kauri, because of the large size of the tracheids, and finer in pencil cedar, where the tracheids are small. Yew is a denser wood than kauri or pencil cedar, for its tracheids are all rather thick-walled and those of the early wood are not much thinner-walled than those of the sparse late wood. Softwoods with such even texture can be put to special uses. Yew, being dense as well as even-textured, is an excellent wood for turnery, for which purpose evenness of texture may be important. Similarly, kauri has been used as a lining for fermenting vats in breweries, since it wears evenly in spite of frequent scouring and the surface remains smooth and does not afford a haven for micro-organisms which might seriously affect the successive brews passing through the vat. Clearly, for such a use it is important that any extract-ives the wood may contain must not adversely affect the flavour of the wort being fermented, and kauri is satisfactory also in this respect. Other woods are used for vats holding corrosive chemicals, the choice of wood depending on the chemical concerned (Farmer, 1967).

Pencil cedar is the best wood for making pencils, a use which makes exacting demands on a wood. To mention some of the qualities necessary—the wood must groove accurately to accommodate the lead; it must cut easily obliquely to the grain; for this is the direction in which a pencil is sharpened; it must cut in this manner with a blunt tool, since most pen-knives merit this description; it must not have an unpleasant taste, since pencils are commonly chewed as well as used for writing; it must finish with a smooth surface, so that it is comfort-able to hold, and it must also take paint or varnish well, since these are frequently applied to pencils.

An even texture also characterises many hardwoods, in which, anatomically, the several types of element are evenly distributed and in which there is no great variation in cell wall thickness throughout the growth increment. Sometimes the cell walls of such woods are thin and the wood is soft. Lime is such a wood, and is valued for carving, for it cuts easily in any direction without chipping. It is also used for curriers' cutting boards; its uniform structure ensures that the knife is not biased, whatever the direction of the cut, while, as it is soft, it does not blunt the knife rapidly. Among harder woods of homogeneous texture is pear, also valued for carving and formerly much used for making blocks for wood-cuts, while the harder maples, like rock maple, have a special value because they wear well and evenly. Maple was used for dairy utensils and furniture because scrubbing does not alter its smooth surface and consequently it holds little dirt. Similarly, because of their even wear, sycamore and hard maple are used for textile and laundry rollers, the smooth surface of the wood being maintained even when it is wet. Dogwood or cornel (*Cornus* spp.) is another hardwood of even texture, much in demand for weavers' shuttles, which receive sufficiently harsh treatment to require a hard, tough even-wearing wood with special properties. In box (*Buxus*) the fibres or fibre tracheids are small and thick-walled and the wood has an almost flinty texture; this is an excellent turnery wood and for wood-engraving blocks it is without equal.

Armstrong (1948, 1949, 1957) has made extensive investigations into the suitability of timbers for flooring, where the most important quality required is resistance of longitudinal surfaces to abrasion. Evenness of texture and density are factors of great importance; hardness is less so, a hard timber being not necessarily suitable. Dimensional stability is an important asset, especially in situations subjected to a wide range of humidity. The presence of extraneous materials, as in teak, may retard abrasion and reduce wear, although hard and gritty substances like mineral deposits and some gums may increase it. In comparing fine, even-textured hardwoods, those with thick-walled fibres are more resistant than those with thinner-walled and larger ones; birch and hard maple are more satisfactory than poplar for this reason. Where the vessels are large, even if the fibres are thick-walled and the wood is therefore hard, the vessels tend to collapse under abrasion and this is followed by rupturing of the tissue between neighbouring vessels, leading to splintering and disintegration. Where the vessels are zoned in regular patterns, such as in oblique lines in Tasmanian oak, they constitute planes of weakness which hasten disintegration. The pore ring in ring-porous timbers clearly constitutes a weak zone and its restriction to the smallest possible space is desirable. An abrupt change from a pore ring to dense late wood with small vessels gives a better wearing floor than if the transition is a gradual one. Quarter-sawn wood, despite its greater stability, may give trouble if it has large rays, which of course, are bands of tissue running in a different direction from the other elements, and of a different texture. In quarter-sawn oak the rays tend to flake off the surface, while quarter-sawn plane needs careful machining to prevent flaking of the large rays in this operation. Softwoods with an even texture like yew and matai, (see Fig. 137 *A*), wear evenly, but where there is a marked difference between early and late wood, the former is less resistant to wear and either becomes compressed or breaks down. In rift-sawn wood (i.e. where the growth rings meet the surface at an angle of not less than 45°), abrasion will thus lead to the development of a somewhat corrugated surface, while in plain-sawn surfaces, where larger areas of the softer wood are exposed to wear, extensive breakdown may take place, and if the wood is laid pith side uppermost the late wood zones may be undercut so that they "shell out". In rift-sawn material the best wear will be obtained in rings which contain the highest proportion of late wood.

For some purposes the length of the fibrous elements is of importance. This applies, for example, to paper making, for the strength of paper depends in large measure on the length of the "fibres" of which it is made. Watson and Dadswell (1961) found a direct linear relation between fibre length and tearing resistance in both softwood and hardwood fibre used for paper making. Softwoods, with their relatively long tracheids, are especially suitable. Hardwood fibres, being shorter (even in the more primitive woods such as poplars), produce a less strong and rather bulky paper. Spruce and silver fir produce pulps which are much used for paper-making, their low resin content and pale colour reducing costs in preparation. Douglas fir and some of the pines, which are much more resinous and which produce a coloured pulp, can nevertheless make very strong paper and their wood is used for the manufacture of dark coloured paper.

It is well-known that when wood splits, it does so along the grain, that is, the plane of cleavage follows the course of the axial elements. For this reason it is important, where wood has to be converted into kindling wood on a large scale, that it shall be sufficiently straight-grained to cleave easily with an axe.

A tree in which the fibres or tracheids pursue an axial or nearly axial course in the bole will, if properly converted, yield straight-grained timber. Where the course of the fibres tends to be variable, a "cross-grained" wood will result. The grain of greenheart is often remarkably straight, so much so that slender pieces, for the joints of fishing rods, can be riven longitudinally into a number of sections and glued and bound together again to make the "split cane" type of rod, which is stronger than one made of solid wood. Similarly, slim osier wands are cleft into several pieces for use in basket making, while the ease with which sweet chestnut cleaves has led to its use for cleft-chestnut fencing.

Toughness depends largely upon the amount of wood substance present, for it is a property not found in very light woods with very thin-walled elements. It probably depends also on the composition of the cell walls and perhaps of the middle lamellae; it may also be affected by the grain of the wood. The toughness of common elm is due, at least in part, to the fact that it is cross-grained and thus cannot readily be split. Its selection for maul heads, butchers' blocks and the felloes of wheels are examples of the use which has been made of its toughness and non-splitting properties. Hornbeam, another hard, tough wood, is also cross-grained and is used for mallet heads and for tool handles. Its very high resistance to shearing stresses makes it valuable for wood screws and wooden cogs and cog teeth. Irregular grain may have disadvantages, however; thus Armstrong (1948) found that in danta, used for quarter-sawn flooring, interlocked grain led to the development of surface cracks along the boundaries of successive zones. Toughness is not, however, confined to cross-grained woods:

hickory and ash are both straight-grained, but at the same time they are very tough.

The rough, dull lustre of common elm is probably due, in part, to the fact that, on longitudinal surfaces, many of the elements are cut obliquely and not strictly longitudinally, so that the varying directions of the fibres makes it impossible to obtain a perfectly smooth finish.

Skilful conversion of timber follows the primary rule of cutting for maximum length of grain. Ideally the longitudinal axis of a board should follow the grain and any deviation from this results in a diminution of strength properties. Reduction in strength is not marked for small deviations from the direction of the grain, but a slope of more than one in ten has a serious effect on the compressive strength of wood, while in tension, diminution in strength becomes appreciable when the slope exceeds one in twenty-five. Great care must be taken to select straight-grained wood for handles of tools which have to withstand impact stresses, for here a small deviation of the haft from the direction of the grain produces a decided reduction in strength. Similarly, any diminution in the strength of ladder rungs and sides due to oblique grain might have serious consequences. Wood for manufacture of the rungs is best cleaved, not sawn, to the rough shape, for then the surfaces will follow the direction of the grain and straight-grained rungs will be obtained.

Sloping or diagonal grain can to a large extent be controlled in conversion, for if a log has taper, the saw cuts should follow the outside of the log and not the centre, in order to obtain maximum length of grain. The natural form of the tree, however, may make it impossible for the sawyer to convert his log into straight-grained boards. A natural defect, all too common in some trees, is spiral grain, that is, where the fibres or tracheids run spirally round the tree, instead of pursuing a strictly longitudinal course. Where this type of grain occurs it is clearly impossible to produce lumber which is straight grained—the wood must, inevitably have "short" grain and suffer from the defects associated with such a structural peculiarity. Spiral grain may often be detected in standing trees by the oblique direction assumed by normally longitudinal fissures in the bark. It is a common defect in large trees of sweet chestnut and is also frequent in Scots pine (Fig. 140).

The effects of wavy grain and interlocked grain on the appearance of wood have already been explained in Chapter 10, where it was seen that these types of figure are caused by the fibres being cut in different directons and consequently reflecting the light differently according to the direction in which they have been cut. Both types of grain are really special types of cross grain. Interlocked grain is, more precisely, double spiral grain, but here the strength properties of the wood are less affected, for the shortness of grain is counteracted by the different directions of the fibres in successive zones of the wood.

The longitudinal shrinkage of straight-grained wood in drying is

Fig. 140.—Spiral grain. *A*, in a telegraph pole, shown by the direction of the surface checking. *B*, Horse Chestnut (*Aesculus ?hippocastanum*) and *C*, Hawthorn (*Crataegus ?oxyacanthoides*), both showing spiral twisting in the bole.

much less than the transverse shrinkage, which is equivalent to saying that the individual fibres and other elements shrink less along their length than across or around it. In woods where the fibres run obliquely, and especially if the obliquity changes periodically either in degree or direction, as in wood with wavy or interlocked grain, it will be apparent that shrinkage is likely to be very irregular and that, in consequence, seasoning of this type of wood will present difficulties which will not be met in straight-grained wood.

In the same way, irregularities in shrinkage will occur in knotty timber. Knots in wood may, for present purposes, be considered fundamentally as regions in a piece of wood where the direction of the grain is decidedly different from elsewhere. Here, considerable irregularities

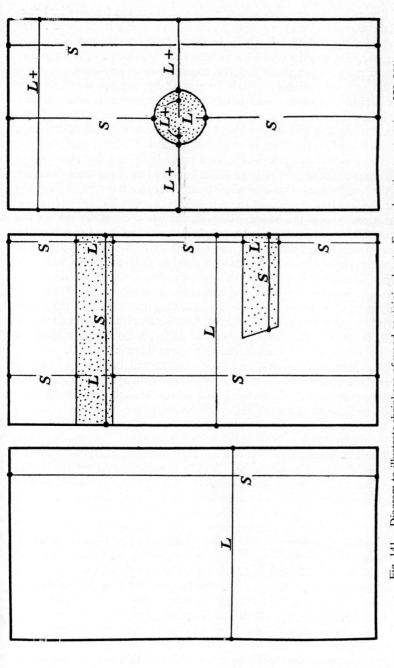

Fig. 141.—Diagram to illustrate shrinkage of wood containing knots. For explanation see text (pp. 278–281).

Left: Radial face (clear); *Centre*: Radial face with two spike knots; *Right*: Tangential face with round knot. L, radial shrinkage; L+, tangential shrinkage; S, longitudinal shrinkage.

T

in drying are to be expected, since in the knots the longitudinal axes of the elements lie in an entirely different direction from those in the rest of the wood The diagrams in Fig. 141 illustrate, in a simplified manner, the way in which knots affect the shrinkage of a board. In a clear radial or tangential face (i.e. a quarter-sawn or plain-sawn piece) with the grain running perfectly longitudinally, the board will shorten very slightly in drying, and it will narrow appreciably, more so in a plain-sawn than in a quarter-sawn piece. There should, however, be no unusual stresses and drying should not produce warping or twisting. If, however, we consider a quarter-sawn board with a medially cut live knot (which will, of course, be a spike knot) running right across the board, the radial shrinkage of the knot will be in the same direction as the longitudinal shrinkage of the board. Because it is regular through-out the width of the board, there should be no unusual stresses in this direction. Across the board, however, the wood on either side of the knot will shrink much more (radial shrinkage) than in the region of the knot (longitudinal shrinkage) and consequently irregular stresses will be set up as the wood dries, which may be relieved by the wood on either side of the knot drying in a permanently stretched condition or, perhaps, by the occurrence of checking. If, however, the knot runs only part of the way across the board, then not only will the radial shrinkage in this region be affected, but the longitudinal shrinkage as well, because in the part which contains the knot overall shrinkage in length will be greater than in the part where there is no knot.

In a plain-sawn board, any knot present will be a round one or nearly so. In parts where there is no knot, shrinkage across the board will be greater than where the board passes through the centre of the knot, because in this latter region shrinkage of the knot will be radial, and almost certainly less than the tangential shrinkage, while in the rest of the width shrinkage will be tangential. As concerns length, shrinkage will be less where the wood is clear than where it passes through the centre of the knot, where the matter is complicated by the radial shrinkage of the knot. An additional complication, of course, is that tangential shrinkage (round the knot) may be more than three times as great as shrinkage across the knot (radial shrinkage).

It will thus be apparent that the presence of knots in a piece of wood introduces complications in drying which are not present in clear, straight-grained timber, and it is important to emphasise that the examples just analysed have been greatly simplified by considering the boards as two-dimensional. Obviously, in either knotty board, allowance should have been made for both kinds of transverse shrink-age, and further, it is unlikely that knots will always be so conveniently placed as those which have been described: they will probably run somewhat obliquely and so will not necessarily be cut strictly radially. It has also been convenient to ignore the fact that the grain round a knot is almost certain to be distorted, and further that the knot consists of denser timber than the rest of the wood: in this connection it may be recalled that dense wood normally shrinks more on drying than less dense wood of the same species. Even in such simplified examples, however, it will be clear that the stresses set up in drying are very different from, and much more complex than those in straight-grained knot-tree timber. The claim that a piece of knotty timber, provided the knots are sound, live ones, is as strong as a clear piece, has no basis of fact. Knotty timber is bound to contain regions of sloping and excessively sloping grain, which, as has been explained earlier in this chapter, must adversely affect its compressive and tensile strengths.

In the visual grading of timber, attention is paid to such gross features as knots, growth rings and the direction of the grain, as well as to defects like shakes and decay, for it has long been realised that such features affect the strength of a piece of timber. For structural timbers, the precise influence of such features upon the strength of the wood, expressed in terms of safe working stress, has been studied, and it is now possible for certain timbers to be graded into strength classes on the basis of a rapid inspection of the size and distribution of knots, the number of growth rings to the inch, the direction of the grain and other gross features (Chaplin, 1945; Desch, 1968). It is also possible to grade timber by non-destructive mechanical testing (Sunley and Curry, 1962; Curry, 1966). These methods are referred to as stress-grading; i.e., the timber is graded according to the stresses it may reasonably be expected to withstand. (See also F.P.R.L., 1968.)

Fibre direction has an important effect on the resonance of timber. Sound travels nearly ten times more rapidly along the grain of wood than it does in air, while its velocity across the grain is about three times faster than in air. In selecting wood for its resonating properties it is of the utmost importance that it possesses a perfectly regular, even structure. Any irregularities of grain will clearly affect the velocity of the sound waves and it is important, for this purpose, that the wood respond to the vibrations everywhere in the same way. Similarly, any defect, like fungal decay, which affects the elasticity of the wood on which its resonating properties depend, will mar its perfection in this respect. It has long been known that spruce, of even and fairly slow growth, has excellent resonating properties, and for this reason it is much used for parts of musical instruments (e.g. for the top-plates of violins) where this particular property is required.

The penetrability of wood, especially to preservatives, has an important bearing on its uses. This is a complex phenomenon, dependent in part on the structure of the wood, and in part on the nature and physical state of the preservative and the manner of its application (Hunt and Garratt, 1967). In studies of the problem in relation to soft-woods particular attention has been paid to the axial tracheids, in which the passage of preservatives from cell to cell is known to occur mainly through the bordered pits. Bailey (1913) showed that the pit membranes are porous, and that finely divided particles in suspension in water (the carbon particles in Indian ink) would pass through them: (see also Fig. 100). In the change from sapwood to heartwood the pits commonly become aspirated, the somewhat extensible pit membrane allowing the torus to be deflected from its median position, by a difference in the pressures on its two sides, so that it more or less blocks the aperture of one of the members of the pit-pair. Once this deflection has occurred it appears to be a permanent one, and it is to the aspiration of the bordered pits that the low permeability of heartwood, as compared with sapwood, has been attributed There may also be differences in this respect between early wood and late wood. Thus Phillips (1933), in a study of the air-dry wood of a number of conifers, showed that in the early wood a very small percentage of pits was unaspirated, whereas in the late wood the percentage was larger and more variable: 25 per cent in Douglas fir, 29 per cent in larch and 31 per cent in spruce. These are timbers which are regarded as being resistant, or very resistant, to penetration by preservatives. In Corsican pine and Scots pine the percentage of unaspirated pits was higher, at 40 per cent and 60 per cent respectively; both these timbers are only moderately resistant to penetration.

Data of this kind accord with the observation that the dry late wood of the growth ring may be more permeable to preservatives than the thinner-walled earlywood. This difference, Bailey (1958) has suggested, may come about because, even if the pits are aspirated, in the narrower late wood tracheids the circular torus does not wholly block the more or less slit-like pit aperture, whereas in the early wood it makes a more effective seal for the circular pit aperture.

In a study of the permeability to air of the wood of Douglas fir, hemlock and Western red cedar, Krahmer and Côté (1963) found that the permeability of the heartwood of these trees was low and much the same, although their sapwoods showed large differences in permeability. In Douglas fir, sapwood was about 34 times as permeable as heartwood, in Western hemlock about 10 times, and in Western red cedar only about 6·5 times. Electron micrographs of the membranes of the bordered pits show that they contained radially arranged microfibrils, which were up to about 1μ apart in Douglas fir, whereas in Western red cedar (where the pits are smaller and the membrane has no torus) these microfibrils were less than $0·1\mu$ apart. The observed differences in permeability of the sapwood were explained in part as resulting from differences in the size of the pores in the pit membranes, and possibly, in Douglas fir, also from the presence of axial resin canals which may have increased the penetrability of the wood. It is probable also that other factors were involved in the permeability properties of the heartwood of the different species; in Douglas fir the permeability of the heartwood, relative to that of the sapwood, may well have been reduced by blockage of the resin canals by tylosoids. In aspirated pits in the heartwood of all three timbers one aperture of each pit pair appeared to be tightly sealed, although in a different manner in each timber. In Douglas fir the torus fitted tightly against the pit aperture: in hemlock the warty layer lining the pit cavity prevented such tight contact, although in this species and in Western red cedar (where it might be expected that because of the absence of a torus the pit aperture would not be effectively closed) there was a heavy lignin-like incrustation on the pit membrane. Solvent extraction of the heartwood of all three timbers gave improved penetration, though in Western red cedar at least the solvents did not appear to affect the incrustation. Probably, extractives, which also contributed to the resistance offered to penetration, were dissolved away

It must be recognised, of course, that the longitudinal permeability is likely to be much greater than the lateral permeability, since, for a given movement of liquid across a given thickness of wood, fewer cell walls would have to be traversed; the difference in permeability may be by a factor of 10^3–10^5. Thus it is of interest that Banks (1968) has devised a technique for the measurement of lateral permeability, using thin tangential slices which could be selected, at will, from early wood or late wood. In Scots pine in the green state he finds that the early wood is more permeable than the late wood, though after air-seasoning the early wood permeability falls and this difference becomes very small; the late wood may then even be the more permeable, as others have found. In the heartwood the permeability is lower than in the sapwood by a factor of 10 or more, and is not much affected by seasoning; broadly, therefore, these data are probably interpretable in terms of the aspiration of pits.

The pits are not, of course, the only pathway for solutions from one lignified wood cell to another, since the cell walls are not impermeable. Rudman (1965), in an electronmicroscope study of the penetration of preservatives into wood of *Eucalyptus* spp., showed the presence in the cell walls of capillaries of up to 450 Å in diameter, though even so the pits were considered to be the major pathway of movement across the wall.

In hardwoods, the vessels, unless blocked by tyloses or extractives, facilitate the movement of preservatives. In most red oaks, where the heartwood vessels are free from tyloses, penetration is good, but where there are tyloses, as in most white oaks and in robinia, the heartwood is very resistant to penetration. For the same reason, red oaks cannot be used for tight cooperage, though white oaks (English oak is of this type) are suitable for this purpose. In diffuse-porous woods, because of the more even distribution of the vessels, preservatives tend to become more evenly dispersed than in ring-porous timbers.

The foregoing account does no more than indicate the nature of the structural factors which may be involved in the varied penetration of preservatives into timber. An interesting instance of another rather different factor is given by *Pinus radiata* and *P. muricata* D. Don, in which the sapwood, while readily penetrated by creosote, is resistant to aqueous preservatives Wardrop and Davies (1957) found that penetration of aqueous preservatives was impeded by the presence of fatty material in a membrane lining the cell wall and pit cavities, this membrane probably representing a residue of the protoplast which formerly occupied the lumen of the cell wall. Such fatty material might be expected to be resistant to wetting by water, but might be dissolved in, or more readily wetted by, an oily preservative like creosote.

The penetration of water into wood is also of interest where logs have to be floated long distances. It has been found that where heart-wood and sapwood are sharply defined, little water enters the heart-wood although the sapwood is readily permeable. Since small logs and those with wide growth rings have proportionately more sapwood, it is these which are likely to absorb enough water to sink.

Of the effects of the composition of the cell wall upon the properties of wood, little is at present known. Clarke (1937a) claimed to show that tropical hardwoods are richer in lignin than those of temperate regions and that this property is related to the relative weakness of these woods, as compared with temperate woods, in shock resistance, although when in compression parallel to the grain they prove stronger. Although Clarke used methods of assessing lignin content which the chemist would now regard at least as of unproven reliability, his work is nevertheless confirmed by that of Norman and Besson (1946). It is well known also that the cell walls become appreciably altered when attacked by wood-rotting fungi, and that the walls, depleted of much of their cellulose or lignin, lose many of their characteristic properties and become considerably weakened. It is also known that the structure and composition of the cell walls of reaction wood differ from those of normal wood (Chap. 9): the abnormal properties of timber derived from reaction wood can be related, in part, to these differences.

There is some reason to believe that the elasticity of wood, as well as other properties already mentioned, is related to the orientation of its cellulose microfibrils. Garland (1939) believed that the stiffness of wood, and to a lesser degree, its tensile and compressive strengths, are related to the micellar orientation. When wood dries, its compressive strength and stiffness are increased, the more so when the microfibrils of the cell are steeply inclined. Moreover, the variability of these properties then seems to be greater. Phillips (1941), however, was unable to discover any relation between micellar angle and crushing strength in normal mature wood of Sitka spruce.

The effect of water on the cell wall is of considerable scientific interest and of great economic importance, for one of the great disadvantages of wood, as a constructional material, is its dimensional instability arising from changes in its moisture content.

In standing or freshly-felled timber the cell cavities contain water to a greater or lesser extent (sapwood and heartwood will of course differ in this respect) and the sub-microscopic spaces in the cell walls are also water-filled. As the wood dries, the "free" water in the cell cavities tends to be lost first, so that these become largely emptied while the walls still hold their "bound" water. This is the so-called "fibre saturation point", which commonly corresponds to a water content of about 28–30 per cent of the dry weight of the wood. However, the distinction between "free" and "bound" water is not an absolute one, and the fibre saturation point is not very sharply defined. In the drying of timber shrinkage begins as the fibre saturation point is approached, though the main part of it occurs as the water content is reduced still further: for example, to 20 per cent or so in air-dried timber, or to 8–12 per cent in kiln-dried wood intended for use in furniture making. The part of the wall which influences this shrinkage most is its thickest layer, the S_2 layer, in which, in mature normal wood, the pitch of the microfibrillar helices is steep. Shrinkage on drying, and of course, swelling accompanying re-wetting, are thus proportionately much greater across the cell than along it, and in a piece of wood the behaviour of the individual cells, as they swell or shrink with changes in moisture content, results in appreciable movement across the grain but in little along the grain; so little, in fact, that for practical purposes longitudinal swelling and shrinking are generally ignored. Where the microfibrils of the S_2 are less steeply inclined, as in juvenile wood and compression wood, longitudinal shrinkage is greater. However, this explanation of the difference between longitudinal and transverse shrinkage does not account for the difference between the radial and tangential transverse shrinkage of timber, a difference which may be considerable. One explanation advanced to account for the smaller radial shrinkage is that the rays exert a restraining effect in this direction. Lindsay and Chalk (1954) and McIntosh (1954, 1957) have shown that the broad rays in some timbers shrink radially to a lesser degree than do the tissues between them. Other explanations have been suggested (cf. Pentoney, 1953) Thus Frey-Wyssling (1943) observed that the radially directed compound middle lamellae (i.e. the middle lamellae and primary walls) may be thicker than the tangentially directed ones. He was of the opinion that this difference may account for the greater tangential shrinkage. Preston (1952) and more recently, Mark (1967), have described differences in the micellar orientation in radial and tangential walls of conifer tracheids, which may also contribute to the difference in shrinkage in the two directions.

It is interesting to consider means whereby wood could be made to lose its affinity for water, in other words, some means by which its hygroscopicity might be reduced, for then its swelling and shrinking could be minimised. Heating to a high temperature may reduce the hygroscopicity of wood, probably by altering its chemical composition, while protective coatings, like paint and varnish, retard the entry and exit of water, although they do not entirely prevent its movement. The introduction of various substances (e.g. salts, sugars, synthetic resins, polyethylene glycol) into the spaces between the micellae has been shown to have a marked effect in reducing hygroscopicity, and consequently, swelling and shrinking. The effect of their presence is that less water can be gained or lost by the cell walls, so that the range of swelling or shrinking is reduced It is also possible to stabilize cell wall structure by the introduction of additional cross-linkages within it, by chemical combination with formaldehyde and other substances (Stamm, 1964; Bryant, 1966; Laidlaw et al., 1967). Chipboard, made from wood chips pressed into boards with a synthetic resin glue, similarly shows less hygroscopicity than natural timber.

Lignin, like water, occupies some of the interfibrillar spaces in the cellulose framework and its removal can be accomplished without total breakdown of the cell wall. The highest proportion of lignin occurs in the outer wall layers and in the middle lamellae; in the latter it reaches its greatest concentration at the corners of the cells, and there is also more between the radial than between the tangential walls (Wardrop, Dadswell and Davies, 1961). Lignin is removed by chemical means in the manufacture of wood pulp for paper, artificial silk, cellophane and other purposes. There is evidence that the region outside the S_2 layer is more porous than the inner parts of the wall, and that it may be more readily penetrated and attacked by chemicals.

When a piece of wood breaks under tension, failure might occur in either of two different ways. The fibres and other elements might not necessarily break up themselves, but might simply pull apart, due to breakdown in the middle lamellae, which here can be regarded as the cementing material between them. Alternatively, the actual walls of the cells might fail and fracture, the middle lamellae holding firm. Forsaith (1946) found that, in thick-walled cells, failure in tension tended to occur within the walls, which might show an irregular fracture due to the pulling apart of the microfibrils (or bundles of microfibrils), principally in the S_2 layer. Cells, or groups of cells, were also found to pull apart at their ends, but they rarely separated along the middle lamellae. Separation occurred between the S_1 and S_2 layers; that is in a region of the wall where there is a discontinuity of microfibrillar inclination. An observation of some interest in this context is that where a failure occurred in the neighbourhood of a bordered pit it did not pass through the pit aperture, but followed the outer rim of the border; that is, it followed the direction in which the microfibrils lie in this region. Similar observations have been made by Kollman and Antonoff (1943), Wardrop (1951) and Mark (1967). Mark discusses the tensile properties of softwood tracheids in considerable depth, in relation to their mode of fracture and their ultrastructure. He finds that either the S_2 and S_3 layers pull out of the enclosing sheath of the S_1, or there may be a spiral breakdown along the direction of the microfibrils of the S_2: the middle lamella is not a plane of weakness. He shows how the ultrastructure of the bordered pit is well adapted to resist tensile stress in wood, and suggests how the difference between brash and normal fracture may be related to the breakdown of different types of chemical bond in the wall, dependent in turn on microfibrillar orientation.

In wood under compression Thunell (1947) found, in Scots pine, birch and oak, that the secondary walls also failed first, low pressures producing transverse cracks, which increased in number with increasing pressure. Under high pressures the middle lamellae also suffered deformation. A more recent study by Dinwoodie (1967) shows how, in spruce, compression failures appear as dislocations in the structure of the tracheid cell walls. Initially they take the form of slip-planes in individual cells (cf. Fig. 115), each involving a double bend or kink in the microfibrils of the wall: the resultant discontinuity in micellar orientation makes the slip-plane readily visible by polarizing microscope. As the compression load is increased, the slip-planes become more numerous, forming, in the aggregate, microscopically visible creases in the wood: these increase in size and eventually produce the macroscopic crumpling associated with obvious mechanical failure. It is interesting to note that the initiation of slip-planes seems to occur most frequently in the parts of tracheids near the margins of rays, related perhaps to the sweep of the tracheid wall around the ray. Dinwoodie finds (1966) also that the act of sectioning wood may itself produce slip-planes unless due precautions are observed.

Reference has already been made to juvenile, mature and senescent wood (p. 203), and that in old trees the wood is far from uniform throughout the trunk: there is a definite pattern in its development which reflects the changing activities of the vascular cambium and changes in cellular differentiation at different periods in the life of the tree. There is a central zone of juvenile wood, the oldest wood of the tree, a zone of mature wood, occupying probably the greater part of the trunk, and in old trees an outer zone of senescent wood, which is of course the youngest wood of the trunk. This pattern may, however, be disturbed, as for instance, when reaction wood is formed. Changes occur, of course, in all three types of wood, for vessels, fibres and tracheids die soon after they are differentiated, and eventually the axial and ray parenchyma also die. In this way two zones in the trunk, the functional outer wood or sapwood, and the completely dead and physiologically inactive inner wood, become differentiated. The latter is often, but not always, clearly distinguished as heartwood.

As has already been indicated (Chap. 9) it is broadly true that the mean length of the fibres or tracheids increases from the pith outwards up to a maximum, and thereafter remains more or less constant. As successive cambial products become longer the microfibrils in their walls (at least those of the S_2 layer) become more steeply inclined, this change being greater in softwood tracheids than in hardwood fibres. This affects the dimensional changes in tracheids and fibres associated with changes in moisture content, since these are related to the orientation of the S_2 microfibrils. When these are steeply inclined the longitudinal change is less than when the microfibrillar inclination is less steep, and conversely for transverse dimensional changes. In Scots pine it has been found that tensile strength also increases as the microfibrils become steeper (Kollmann and Antonoff, 1943). Wardrop (1951) also found in several softwoods an increase in the tensile strength of tangential longitudinal sections of wood taken from successive growth rings, and Kraemer (1951) noted, in red pine, a correlation of certain properties, like stiffness and cross-breaking strength, with microfibrillar orientation He found here a gradual increase in density up to a more or less constant value, with an increase in cellulose content and a diminution in the lignin.

The formation of heartwood is accompanied perhaps by the accumulation of extraneous materials and the growth of tyloses. If the heartwood is durable, the outer heartwood may be more durable than the inner (Findlay, 1957), suggesting a greater accumulation of extraneous materials in the younger heartwood, or the accumulation here especially of substances toxic to wood-rotting fungi. In older hardwood trees, the more central heartwood, which includes the juvenile wood, may develop brittleheart (p. 228), becoming brash and of reduced tensile strength, while its fibres are more readily fractured transversely. There is also evidence that at least in certain hardwood trees, a progressive mild acid hydrolysis may occur *in situ* in the wood (Stewart *et al.*, 1961) so that in the older heartwood the bonding between the fibres appears to be progressively weakened, making them more readily separable in certain pulping treatments. In older trees the most recent wood (senescent wood) may have very narrow growth rings and may also often be brittle and of low density.

Considerable attention has been given to this growth pattern in relation to the utilisation of wood, and to the problem of the production of timber having the qualities most desirable for the use for which it is intended. Since it is now possible to think of producing wood, in some parts of the world, in a much shorter period than in the past, it becomes more practicable to attempt to foresee the purpose for which the crop may be needed and to plan accordingly. Dadswell has given much attention to his problem and his articles (especially those of 1957 and 1958) should be consulted for a fuller account of what is summarised here. He prophesies that it may be possible to grow some kinds of timber in as little as 15–20 years and that, in the future, much timber may be produced from trees under 40 years old. Under normal conditions, the largest increments to the wood are made in the early years of a tree's life, though it must be recognised that some trees as much as 20 years old may have nothing but juvenile wood, and even in a 40-year-old tree, at least half the bole may be of this nature. For carpentry or joinery, the inclusion of such large amounts of juvenile wood, of low density and less strength than mature wood, and also with a greater longitudinal shrinkage on drying, would be undesirable, and for these purposes it would be less advantageous to grow trees in which the maximum bulk of timber has been produced in the minimum of time. For paper pulp, however, it might serve to produce bulk as quickly as possible, although this would not give the maximum amount of long fibre desirable in pulp. It may, however, be possible to overcome this difficulty by the selection of parent trees for the plantation stock which have the desirable qualities. Attention has thus been given to discovering which desirable qualities are likely to be transmitted to the offspring (Dadswell and Nicholls, 1959; Dadswell and Wardrop, 1959; Dadswell et al,, 1959). It is believed that mean tracheid length, wood density and percentage of late wood in the growth ring, though affected by the conditions of growth of the tree, are nevertheless genetically controlled characters (Echols, 1955; Zobel and Rhodes, 1957). It may thus be possible to select and grow strains of trees with these qualities developed to the required degree: see discussion by de Zeeuw (1965).

It remains to consider how the presence of extractives may effect the properties and uses of wood, for they occur in great variety (Kurth, 1946) and sometimes in abundance.

Mineral matter in wood, as we have seen, consists mainly of silica and salts of calcium, the silica being located in the cell walls or in the lumina of the cells, and the calcium deposits in the lumina.

Calcium salts, which may occur in vessels as well as in parenchyma cells, are sometimes abnormally abundant, filling cracks and shakes in the living tree, as may be seen in teak. The large rock-like masses, appropriately known as stone, which are sometimes found in iroko logs (Fig. 70), are good examples of the occurrence of excessive quantities of mineral matter in wood. When plentiful, these white deposits may blunt cutting tools very rapidly and the conversion of logs in which they are very abundant may be uneconomic.

Silica, when abundant in timber, also has a very deleterious effect upon tools, although (Amos 1952) observes that not all timbers with inclusions of silica cause blunting of saws. In Queensland walnut, the silica content of the wood is high and wear on machine saws used for conversion is very heavy. Curiously enough, the same trouble does not seem to arise when the wood is cut into veneers, nor is the wood as hard on hand tools.

It is also believed that the presence of sufficiently large amounts of silica in the cell lumina may make a wood resistant to shipworm, provided that it possesses a compact enough texture (Gonggrijp, 1932; Amos, 1952) Some confirmation of this view was obtained in connection with Australian turpentine (*Syncarpia laurifolia* Ten.), a wood which is remarkably resistant to shipworm and consequently, is in demand for marine constructional work. This property of the timber led to the species being planted in Hawaii, but when timber from these trees was used for marine work it was found to be readily attacked by shipworm. The only difference which could be detected between the Australian and the Hawaiian timber was that the latter either lacked the silica deposits, which are abundant in Australian grown wood, or, at most, contained very little silica (Amos and Dadswell, 1948) The possibility that the silica may affect the alimentary tract of the borer has been suggested as an explanation of the resistant quality of the Australian wood.

The occurrence of gums and resins (here the terms are used loosely) may detract from the value of timber, but equally, these substances may enhance its worth. Large deposits of gum may be found in cavities in the wood of agba (Fig. 72 *A*) and complaints are made that the gum in this wood tends to ooze out so that close-piled boards may become firmly stuck together. Gummy materials may seriously interfere with the working of a wood and no doubt resin is at least partly responsible for the difficulty of sawing Western hemlock.

If the cell cavities are repositories for a good deal of gummy material, the penetration of preservatives will be seriously affected, while the density of the wood may be appreciably increased. Gummy materials may also mar the beauty of the surface, as sometimes happens in the Australian rose mahogany, where an oily material may ooze out on to prepared surfaces. In a like manner, the resin of softwoods may "bleed", and the minute, dirty specks so often seen on Douglas fir are due to this, the soft resin oozing out of the resin canals and picking up dirt.

Resinous material may, however, enhance the value of timber for fuel. That in *Amyris balsamifera* L., the tropical American torchwood, makes the timber burn so well that it is used for torches. Armstrong (1948) found that the presence of gums and resins in vessels and fibres may make the wood more resistant to wear when it is used for flooring, by retarding break-down of the cells. He referred particularly to pyinkado (*Xylia dolabriformis* Benth.) as a wood which, by reason of the size of its vessels, might be expected to be a second-rate flooring timber, although its resistance to wear is in fact, very high, because the dense fibres are plugged with gum.

Gum may sometimes enhance the beauty of the surface of wood, as has been shown for African walnut (p. 260), while in some woods it sparkles and adds to the surface lustre. On the other hand, the presence of gum galls, as in the Tasmanian oaks, spoils the appearance of the wood.

The gum resin in lignum vitae is the well-known gum guaiacum, regarded at one time as a universal panacea and giving the name "wood of life" to the tree. The wood owes its waxy feel to gum guaiacum and it is this material which makes the wood self-lubricating. Its use for pulley blocks and for bushing the propeller shafts of ships (which are so situated that they cannot readily be lubricated) stems from this property. Apparently, with water, gum gaiacum forms a lubricant and thus the wood serves this purpose admirably. Lignum vitae is a very easy wood to saw, even with a blunt saw, again, no doubt because of its waxy deposits. Progress, of course, in so hard a wood, is not rapid.

Tannins are usually obtained from bark rather than wood, but chestnut wood is rich enough in these substances to provide a commercial source of tannin. Quebracho wood, from *Schinopsis lorentzii* Engl. and *S. balsamae* Engl. of South America, may have as much as 20–30 per cent of tannins in its heartwood and is a very important source of these materials. Quebracho wood is extremely durable, for tannins are inhibitory to most wood-destroying fungi. It is well-known that iron nails and screws should not be used in such woods as oak and Western red cedar, which contain tannins, the reason being that the tannins react with the iron in the presence of moisture to make an ink-like substance which produces unsightly black zones round any iron in the wood. Serious corrosion of both the iron and the wood eventually occurs.

Some timbers contain colouring matters which can be used as dyes, although with the advent of synthetic dyes, they are of less importance than formerly. Logwood (*Haematoxylon campechianum* L.) is the source of haematoxylin, which was much used as a black dye for textiles. Old fustic, a yellow colouring matter, comes from the wood of *Chlorophora tinctoria* L., while the wood of the osage orange (*Maclura pomifera* (Raf.) Schneider) yields a dye which is sometimes used in place of fustic. Cutch, the source of a dye which can be made to give various brown shades, is obtained from the wood of *Acacia catechu* Willd , while among the woods yielding a red dye, red sanders wood (*Pterocarpus santalinus* L.f.) is well-known.

Of woods which produce oil, sandal wood (*Santalum album* L.) is probably the best known; the extraction of sandalwood oil from the wood is a lucrative industry in parts of India.

Many other chemically different types of extractives are to be found in wood. Greenheart is thought to owe its immunity from certain types of shipworm to the alkaloids which it contains. These, and other substances present in some timbers, may account for their poisonous nature. It is well known that splinters of some woods may cause unpleasant, festering wounds, and that some timbers, such as East Indian satin wood (*Chloroxylon swietenia*), mansonia (*Mansonia altissima*), guarea (*Guarea cedrata* and *G. thompsonii*) and Makoré (*Mimusops heckelii*), may prove harmful to operatives converting or working them. These unpleasant effects are no doubt due to toxic or irritant substances in the timber, although it is not improbable that at times very fine gritty sawdust may act simply as a mechanical irritant. The quassias or bitterwoods contain an intensely bitter principle, quassine and extracts of the wood of *Quassia amara* L. and *Aeschrion* (*Picraena*) *excelsa* (Sw. Kuntze) have been used for medicinal purposes as well as for insecticidal washes in horticulture.

Other woods, like the true cedars and the cypresses, contain volatile substances. The timbers named are sometimes used for making clothes chests, because the smell which they give off is obnoxious to the clothes moth. In the same way the smell of cigar-box cedar is said to preserve cigars, packed in boxes made of this wood, from insects.

Care must be taken to select suitable wood for the manufacture of containers and wood-wool in which certain foodstuffs are packed. Such woods as poplar and silver fir, which presumably contain no volatile extractives, serve this purpose admirably. On the other hand, pine timbers, with their resinous scent, may taint food packed in them.

This account of extractives refers only to certain aspects of their economic importance, on which further information is given by Hill (1937), Howes (1949), Brown (1947) and Farmer (1967). There is also a very considerable chemical interest and literature in the variety and molecular structure of wood extractives, but this is outside the scope of the present work.

CHAPTER 12

THE IDENTIFICATION OF WOOD

It is often desirable or necessary to establish the identity of a specimen of timber and it seems generally, if tacitly, to be assumed that this is always possible. It is worthwhile, therefore, to consider how far the identification of wood can be accomplished with any degree of exactitude.

The facility shown by some individuals, who are constantly handling wood, for recognising the different kinds with which they are dealing, is sometimes remarkable; no less remarkable are the mistakes which they can make. Here, identification is a matter of experience and is based on the general appearance of the wood. In assessing this, the practised eye takes note, probably subconsciously, of minutiae of surface features which would be missed by the inexperienced but which alone make it possible to differentiate between superficially similar woods.

Identification in this way serves for some purposes, when relatively few woods are being dealt with. But an occasional mistake is a contingency which must always be reckoned with.

In this chapter, however, we are concerned with more scientific methods of identification, based upon thorough systematic examination of the specimen and of its physical and sometimes its chemical properties. Ideally, it may be thought, it should be possible for an experienced wood anatomist, with such data at his disposal, to identify any wood specimen which may come into his hands. In fact this is not possible at the present time and maybe it never will be wholly possible. Plant species are, in the main, recognised and described by reference to external features, and the relatively small differences which exist among the species of a genus do not necessarily have their counterparts in differences of internal structure. Wood seems to have behaved, in the course of evolution, as a rather conservative tissue, showing much less tendency to change than many other parts of the plant, so that distinct but closely related species may have woods which appear identical. Some timbers may be identified with particular species, but it is more usual, especially in large genera, that timbers can only be separated into groups of species, e.g., in the genera *Pinus* and *Quercus*. Differences between genera are of course larger, plants of different genera being more distinct from one another. It is thus more likely that this greater degree of dissimilarity will extend to the wood.

A further difficulty in the scientific description and identification of wood is that of obtaining authentically named specimens. For systematic studies in the identification of trees the botanist collects shoots,

TABLE 2

Sanio's (1872) data for late wood tracheid size in a trunk of a Scots Pine.

Position in tree (Tree 110 years old)	Growth ring	Mean length of tracheids of late wood in millimetres	Mean tangential width of tracheids of late wood in millimetres
Near top Disc 21 years old	1*	0·78	0·016
	14	1·74	0·016
	18	2·21	0·016
	20	2·91	0·016
	21	2·82	0·026
Above thick branches of crown Disc 35 years old	1	0·80	0·016
	15	2·60	0·016
	17	2·74	0·016
	20	2·82	0·016
	35	2·78	0·028
Trunk, 36 feet from ground Disc 72 years old	1	0·95	0·017
	17	2·74	0·017
	19	3·13	0·017
	31	3·69	0·017
	37	3·87	0·017
	40	4·04	0·017
	46	4·21	0·017
	72	4·21	0·032
Close to ground Disc 105 years old	1	—	0·011
	20	1·87	0·011
	29	2·48	0·011
	30	2·60	0·011
	31	2·65	0·011
	60	2·65	0·011
	80	2·69	0·011
	105	2·65	0·028

* i.e. ring nearest pith.

including leaves, flowers and fruits, and possibly also samples of bark, which are dried and preserved as herbarium material. The wood anatomist would thus wish to have, from the same tree, specimens of the secondary xylem, the collection of which, it will be appreciated, would be a much more onerous task, since, as has already been indicated (pp. 199–203), the wood of small twigs is not representative of that of the mature timber; juvenile wood cannot be used for diagnostic purposes. The manner in which the elements of the wood may vary in size in different parts of the trunk is well known; some of Sanio's (1872) data are given in Table 2. Although this work is nearly a hundred years old, and numerous other investigations of the same kind have been published since; see for instance Anderson (1951), Richardson (1964), Schultze-Dewitz (1965) the general picture presented by Sanio still stands.

Besides these normal variations, which are part of the internal growth pattern of the tree, there are also environmental influences on wood structure, some affecting a tree throughout its life and others having a more ephemeral influence, affecting perhaps one or a few growth rings. Consideration must also be given to the inherent variation to which any species is subject. Thus growth rings vary in width, and may contain proportionately more or less late wood. In ring-porous woods like ash and oak, very narrow growth rings are largely occupied by the early wood with its numerous large vessels; as the rings become wider the proportion of late wood, often composed largely of fibres, increases. In abnormally wide rings, however, the fibres differ from those of narrower rings in being much thinner walled. Some softwoods, like Douglas fir and Californian redwood, show a good deal of variation in the proportion of early and late wood in their rings and consequently in the proportion of thick- and thin-walled tracheids. Teak may be nearly ring-porous, semi-ring-porous or diffuse-porous. To give but one other example, the rays of Californian redwood, in what may be described as an average sample, range from about ten to twenty cells high and include a proportion of partially biseriate rays. In their study of the variation in this species Bailey and Faull (1934) figure a tangential section showing uniseriate rays from two to thirty-five cells high, another in which the rays are only one and two cells high, a third containing some rays partially biseriate and in which the tallest is twelve cells high and another in which the rays are predominantly biseriate and of which the tallest certainly exceed forty cells in height. Even an experienced wood anatomist might find it difficult to identify the first two and the last of these sections. Bailey's (1917) paper and those of Bannan should be consulted by those who desire to find further examples of such variations.

It will be clear, then, that the wood of a single species may exhibit a wide range of variation. Ideally, the extent of this variation needs to be fully explored, not only by the study of specimens taken from all parts of the same tree, but also by reference to specimens taken from individual trees throughout the range of the species, and from trees grown under all conditions to which the species is subject. Without this information it is unrealistic to draw up a minutely detailed description of the structure of the wood of a species, in the hope that this will enable others to identify specimens of it. This does not mean that nothing can be done in the way of identification. Nevertheless, it

U

is necessary to know which features of a wood are to be regarded as characteristic of it and reliable for its identification, and which are variable and not to be trusted.

The selection of suitable characters must depend on experience, and it is impossible to lay down hard and fast rules. Characters which are useful for some timbers are valueless for others. The proportion of late wood in the growth ring is of no use for the identification of Douglas fir, but it is a useful character for Western red cedar or for the pencil cedars, while the considerable variation in the proportion of late wood in successive rings is often a useful guide for swamp cypress. Spiral thickening in all the tracheids is a useful feature when the yews are under consideration, for it is invariably present; but it is worthless as a character for the spruces, since it is only very occasionally found in them.

It must be emphasised that identification cannot be safely attempted on the basis of a single character, although very occasionally this may be sufficient; for smell alone serves to identify some woods. The more characters that are used, the better, for it is unlikely that all those selected will vary, in any one specimen, from what is regarded as normal. One or two examples will illustrate this contention. So far as is known, in all the oaks, transverse surfaces show the vessels of the late wood arranged in either radial or slightly oblique lines; apotracheal paren-chyma is present, appearing in narrow tangential bands. Nearly every species has large rays, and all, so far as is known, have small uniseriate rays as well. Some of the oaks, including the commoner commercial species, are ring-porous. The ring-porous nature would nevertheless furnish a very unreliable guide to generic identity if any one of the two hundred odd species of oak might be encountered, for the majority are in fact diffuse-porous. The large rays (and silver grain on the radial surfaces) provide, in general, a reliable guide, although one or two species do not possess large rays.

The small, uniseriate rays, thin bands of apotracheal parenchyma and the radial arrangement of the vessels, are, so far as is known, features which are constant in all species of the genus. It is unlikely that anyone is in a position to make a more positive statement, for no one has examined, thoroughly and critically, wood of every species of oak. Even so, with a little practice, no student will be unable to identify any piece of oak timber with which he is confronted as some kind of oak, but he will only do so by considering the aggregate of characters. Plenty of woods possess one or more of the characters of oak, but none, except oak, possesses all of them.

Turning to the elms, it will be found that all species are ring-porous; the rays are fairly conspicuous; the vessels and tracheids of the late wood are numerous and, as seen on the end grain, are in undulating tangential bands. These features, however, are possessed by some species of the allied genus *Celtis*, which differ in having wider rays, so that here it is necessary to determine, in terms of the number of cells, the width of the wider rays as viewed in tangential section. Not all species of *Celtis*, however, possess woods with these elm-like characters; those that do belong to temperate species like the hackberry (*C. occidentalis* L.). Some tropical species, however, like *C. soyauxii* Engl. have a diffuse-porous structure, with narrow rays and vessels surrounded by abundant confluent parenchyma, while growth rings are absent.

An excellent illustration of the danger of selecting unreliable features, as a result of studying too few specimens, is furnished by the three North American soft pines: yellow pine (*Pinus strobus* L.), sugar pine (*P. lambertiana* Dougl.) and western white pine (*P. monticola* Dougl.). Table 3 gives a number of the supposed differences between the wood of the three species. It was drawn up with the aid of several standard works on wood structure.

It is not suggested that the authors of the works from which these data were drawn would hold that it is possible to distinguish these three pine timbers with certainty, but if the characters which they give for each of these timbers have any value, the implication is that there should be little difficulty in distinguishing the three woods on the aggregate of these characters.

To test the value of this comparative table, three slides were examined, one of each of these three species of pine, from material of which there was no reason to doubt the authenticity. It will be apparent from the table that the three species represented by the slides could not be differentiated. It is possible that they were from abnormal trees, although it would be a remarkable coincidence for all three to have been made from abnormal wood. It is more likely that the original descriptions are at fault, in having been based on insufficient ranges of material. It might of course be contended that it is not reasonable to expect that the relatively minute amount of wood visible in a single slide will show all the characters given in the description of a species. While this must be admitted, the divergences, in these instances, between the structure shown in the slides and the published descriptions are so considerable that there seems ample justification for questioning whether the descriptions make allowance for the range of variation in these species.

To summarise—the selection of reliable characters depends on the examination of a wide series of specimens and calls for experience and judgement. A character may be valuable for some woods but not necessarily for all woods. Identification should rarely be attempted on the basis of one character; such a practice is risky, if not fundamentally unsound.

For identification, reliance is placed so much on visible features, that there is a risk of forgetting that smell, taste and touch are occasionally useful for this purpose, although, admittedly, they play a very small part as compared with sight.

The odour of a wood may be characteristic. The pleasant smell of

TABLE 3

SUPPOSED DISTINCTIVE FEATURES OF WOODS OF THREE SOFT PINES

	Yellow Pine (P. strobus)	Sugar Pine (P. lambertiana)	Western White Pine (P. monticola)	Features in Slides Examined
1. Texture.	Finer (i.e. tracheids smaller than in the other two species).	—	—	No appreciable difference in size of tracheids in the three species.
2. Late wood.	May be wide.	—	Narrow.	All species had narrow late wood zones. Yellow Pine showed largest resin canals. Western White Pine showed smallest resin canals.
3. Axial resin canals.	Smallest diameter of the three species.	Largest diameter of the three species.	—	
4. Axial resin canals.	In late wood.	In outer early wood and in late wood.	In late wood.	Yellow Pine. Canals mainly in late wood but as near beginning of season's growth as in Sugar Pine in one or two rings. Sugar Pine. In outer half of early wood and in late wood. Western White Pine. Tendency to occupy outer part of ring; one at beginning of ring.
5. Axial resin canals.	—	—	Sometimes paired.	Paired canals seen only in Western White Pine.
6. Height of uniseriate rays.	1–8 cells or more.	1–12 cells or more.	1–12 cells or more.	Western White Pine possessed lowest uniseriate rays.
7. Height of fusiform rays.	Up to 12 cells or more.	Up to 20 cells or more.	Up to 20 cells or more.	Yellow Pine. Most fusiform rays long. Sugar Pine. Fusiform rays long. Western White Pine. Short fusiform rays.
8. Bordered pits of axial tracheids.	Rarely in two rows.	In one or two rows.	Rarely in two rows.	Yellow Pine. Two rows of pits frequent. Sugar Pine and Western White Pine. Two rows of pits extremely rare.
9. Pits in ray parenchyma (cross-field).	1–2.	1–2, occasionally up to 4.	1–2, occasionally up to 4.	Yellow Pine. Occasionally three pits per cross-field. Sugar Pine and Western White Pine. Never more than two pits per cross-field.

sandalwood (*Santalum album* L.) is not likely to be forgotten, while the odours of the pencil cedars (*Juniperus* spp.) and of some members of the Meliaceae, in particular the "cigar-box" cedars (*Cedrela* spp.) and guareas (*Guarea* spp.) are equally characteristic. Wood of Port Orford cedar (*Chamaecyparis lawsoniana* (A.Murr.) Parl.) has a pungent, spicy smell, while a variety of spicy odours is found among lauraceous timbers. Raspberry jam wood (*Acacia acuminata* Benth.) does smell of raspberry jam, and sycamore, when hot and wet, of strawberry jam; teak, when worked, has the somewhat pungent odour of burnt leather, while coachwood (*Ceratopetalum apetalum* D.Don) smells of new mown hay. Queensland walnut (*Endiandra palmerstonii* C.T.White) and kabukalli (*Goupia glabra* Aubl.) both possess sour, unpleasant smells; the odour of *Ocotea bullata* E.Meyer is best imagined from its popular name—stinkwood.

Nevertheless, the use of odour as a means of identification has several drawbacks. Odour is generally ephemeral and rapidly passes off as the wood dries out. It may sometimes be restored by friction or by warmth, but is then often not as strong or distinctive as in fresh damp wood. A further difficulty is that there is no way of describing an odour except by reference to one which is known to everybody; terms like "nauseating" or "spicy" lack precision. Moreover, there is always a possibility that a piece of wood may acquire a smell from its surroundings.

Very occasionally, a wood has a characteristic taste. Any wood which contains a good deal of tannin, like oak or chestnut heartwood, will have an astringent taste. The wood of incense cedar (*Libocedrus decurrens* Torr.) has an acrid taste, while that of quassia wood (*Quassia amara* L.) and some other timbers of the same family (Simarubaceae) is very bitter. In general, taste plays little part in the identification of woods, but it is useful, for example, for differentiating between the acrid tasting incense cedar and the structurally similar, but tasteless Western red cedar.

Odour, of course, is due to the presence of volatile extraneous substances in the wood and taste to soluble ones, for the wood substance itself is both odourless and tasteless.

When extraneous substances are extracted from the wood, the liquid extract sometimes furnishes a useful guide for identification. An aqueous extract of the wood of the padauks (*Pterocarpus* spp.) and especially of red sanders wood (*P. santalinus* L.f.) is fluorescent, being blue by reflected light and yellow by transmitted light. A similar extract of horse chestnut is colourless by transmitted light and bluish by reflected light, this being due to a glycoside, aesculin, which the wood contains. An aqueous extract of the heartwood of oak or chestnut will almost certainly turn greenish- or bluish-black when an iron salt is added, because it contains tannin.

Another test, which is much favoured by Australian workers, is the ash test (Dadswell and Burnell, 1932). This involves burning a splinter of the heartwood, of match-stick size, in still air (still air is essential) and noting the appearance of the residue. These residues are classified as:

(a) Charcoal: wood burns slowly and with difficulty, leaving a charred remnant with fine threads of black or grey ash.
(b) Partial ash: there may be a good deal of ash, which tends to drift away, and a charred stump remains.
(c) Complete or full ash: the specimen burns to an ash, which remains on the specimen and more or less retains the shape of the original wood.

Thus karri (*Eucalyptus diversicolor* F. v. M.) burns to a white ash and jarrah (*E. marginata* Sm.), which is, or at least may be, very similar in appearance, burns to a black charcoal. Similarly, of the two silky oaks, a splinter of *Cardwellia sublimis* F. v. M. burns to a charcoal, while in *Grevillea robusta* A. Cunn. combustion is more complete and the residue is a buff-coloured ash. Details of the results of ash tests on numerous Australian timbers will be found in Dadswell and Eckersley (1935). In this work the test has been a routine one on each timber described and while it is not to be inferred that an ash test is always helpful in identification, it is at times undoubtedly valuable for differentiating between closely similar woods.

The ash test indicates differences in the extraneous materials present, for it is these substances which influence the way in which wood burns and also the colour of its ash. When a splinter burns to a charcoal, combustion is incomplete. With the application of greater heat, this charcoal will be consumed and will leave an ash; hence the importance of burning the splinter in still air, for a draught may induce more complete combustion and thus produce a result which is not comparable with those carried out under standard conditions.

Cohen (1933) has described a simple method for distinguishing the wood of hoop pine (*Araucaria cunninghamii* Ait.) from that of bunya pine (*A. bidwillii* Hook.). Concentrated sulphuric acid is added to an aqueous extract of the wood, prepared by a standardised method. An extract made from bunya pine gives an immediate pink coloration which is succeeded by an orange precipitate. A hoop pine extract shows no immediate colour change on addition of the acid, but later a white, gelatinous precipitate is formed. The pink coloration is said to be a more reliable guide than the orange precipitate.

Dadswell (1931) describes a number of similar tests. One of these is claimed to differentiate between three of the light-coloured eucalyptus woods, tallow wood (*E. microcorys* F. v. M.), blackbutt (*E. pilularis* Sm.) and white mahogany (*E. acmenioides* Schau., *E. carnea* R. T. Bak., and *E. umbra* R. T. Bak.). About two grams of the sawdust are heated in 20 ml. of alcohol for two minutes; the extract is allowed to cool to room temperature, filtered free from sawdust and a portion of it added to an equal volume of water. There is a white turbidity if the extract is from tallow wood or white mahogany. If the solution is allowed to stand, the turbidity in the white mahogany extract changes to a fine white precipitate which can be filtered off, whereas that in the tallow wood extract remains and cannot be filtered off with ordinary filter paper. A blackbutt extract remains clear on the addition of alcohol, although later a precipitate may be thrown down.

Cohen (1935), working on some of the coloured eucalypt timbers, found that he was able to separate them into groups on the alkalinity of their ash; on a ferric chloride test applied to aqueous extracts; on the production of a transient colour in aqueous extracts, when 1 per cent ammonia followed by 1 per cent potassium ferricyanide were added; and on a test similar to that used by Dadswell for separating tallow wood, blackbutt and white mahogany. In using the ferric chloride test, which was, of course, for tannins, two types of tannins were differentiated, those giving a blue coloration (gallotannins) and those a green one (phlobotannins).

Among more recent attempts to distinguish different woods by chemical means may be mentioned that of Stearns (1950), who found that a mixture of benzidine and sodium nitrite gave a light to medium reddish-orange colour to red oak and a dark greenish colour to white oak, and the work of Morgan and Orsler (1967), who describe a simple test to separate the wood of *Khaya anthotheca* from those of *K. ivorensis* and *K. grandifoliolia*.

A number of more elaborate analytical procedures have been applied to the identification of closely related woods; see for example the work of Kanehira (1921), Welch (1922, 1935) and more recently the use by Bevan *et al.* (1965) of thin-layer chromatography in studies of the extractives of meliaceous woods, and the work of Swan (1966) on chromatographic methods of distinguishing certain conifers. However, these more elaborate methods are beyond the scope of this chapter. The wood anatomist requires quite simple qualitative tests, or at most, semi-quantitative ones, which may be applied to timbers or their extracts; such means of differentiating between closely similar timbers are likely to be much more widely used in the future.

The presence of extraneous materials often gives wood a character- istic appearance, and this applies in particular to substances which impart a characteristic colour to the wood. Most woods are some shade of brown, ranging from the rich reddish brown of the mahoganies to the pale browns of the willows and alders and the grey browns of some walnuts. Among the red-coloured woods may be noted the rich purple red of Andaman padauk (*Pterocarpus dalbergioides* Roxb.) and the brighter red of some of the African species of this genus. Yellows range from the pale lemon yellows of the boxwoods (*Buxus* spp.) and haldu (*Adina cordifolia* B. et H. ex Brandis) to the orange of opepe (*Sarco-cephalus diderrichii* de Wild.), while the hollies (*Ilex* spp.) are among the relatively few timbers which may be white. It is the unusual colours, of course, which are most useful as diagnostic characters. Thus few woods are black, although this occurs in the heartwood of a few ebonies. Pink is also an unusual colour, but it is seen in the pink ivory (*Rhamnus zeyheri* Sand.) and in species of *Sickingia*, while the heartwood of the blue mahoe (*Hibiscus tiliaceus* L.) may be of a bluish colour. The rich purple of the purplehearts (*Peltogyne* spp.) again is an unusual colour in wood.

A timber may, however, show a considerable range of colour. The pale greenish cream of American whitewood might be called the typical colour of this species, but the wood may be black and even a small piece sometimes shows a startling range of browns, purples and greens. Irregular distribution of colour in the form of streaks and stripes may, on occasion, be distinctive, as for example, in the dark, irregular streaks which occur in the dark reddish-brown snakewood or letterwood (*Piratinera*); the black and white patches of marblewood (*Diospyros marmorata* Park.); or the pale and dark brown stripes of the zebra wood, also a species of *Diospyros*, and of zebrano (*Brachystegia fleuryana* Chev.).

The chief objection to the use of colour as a character for identification, apart from its variability, is that it is often fugitive. The rich colours of the padauks and purplehearts turn to a dull brown on exposure. In the standing tree, alder wood is white, but after felling the colour changes rapidly to reddish or orange brown and equally quickly fades to a pale warm brown.

Again, the lustre of a wood may provide a distinctive feature. In teak it is dull and greasy; in lignum vitae the wood appears to be coated with a fine wax film, due to the gum guaiacum, which may become slightly oxidised locally and appear as small, somewhat bluish patches. The lustre of brown ash (*Fraxinus nigra* Marsh.) is dull, a useful distinguishing feature, since other species of ash are generally somewhat lustrous. Spruce, especially silver spruce (*Picea sitchensis* (Bong.) Carr.) has a faint, almost satiny lustre, while in some of the ebonies the lustre resembles that of bone.

Attention may also be given to texture, whether fine or coarse; and to hardness, which may be judged approximately with the fingernail, a soft wood indenting easily, a hard one scarcely or not at all.

Weight, or more correctly, density, is a useful feature for identification when used in conjunction with other characters, though in some woods it varies very widely. It is usually given for dry wood (12 per cent moisture content is a common standard) but for precise work it should be based on the oven-dry weight. Density is commonly expressed in pounds per cubic foot, the weight of a cubic foot of water being 62·4 lb.

Since the proportion of a block which is submerged, when the wood is placed in water, depends on its density, a very rough guide to the density of a wood may be obtained by placing a regularly shaped piece, e.g. a cube, in water, and observing how much remains above the surface. The following table will serve as a guide:

One-quarter submerged	Density about 16 lbs. per cubic foot
One-half ,,	,, ,, 32 ,, ,, ,,
Three-quarters ,,	,, ,, 47 ,, ,, ,,
Sinks	,, above 63 ,, ,, ,,

In the Lens Key for the Identification of Hardwoods (F.P.R.L., 1960) woods not exceeding 31 lbs. per cu. ft., air-dry, are referred to as light in weight, those between 31 and 62½ lbs. as medium weight, and those above 62½ lbs. as heavy.

The grain of a wood, using the term in its strict sense, may be a useful diagnostic feature. Examples of straight-grained woods are ash and greenheart (*Ocotea rodiaei* Mez); of interlocked grain, producing stripe figure, sapele (*Entandrophragma cylindricum* Sprague) and of wavy grain, giving fiddle-back figure, sycamore. Localised undulations or indentations are seen in the dimples which produce bird's-eye figure in some maples, while the characteristic dimpled grain of the lodgepole pine, caused by resin blisters in the phloem, is a useful diagnostic feature for this timber.

The features so far described are usually referred to as gross features and an unknown wood should always be examined for any distinctive macroscopic and physical characters before recourse is had to the hand-lens and microscope. It is well to emphasise that both lens and microscope are necessary, for some characters may be seen distinctly with a lens, but are much less apparent, if recognisable at all, under the higher powers of the microscope.

If a hitherto unknown wood is being described so as to enable it to be identified by others, care and experience are necessary to select characters which are likely to be of diagnostic value. One form of description seems to be based on the view that if enough detail is included, essential features are not likely to be omitted, and so it is made very full and detailed, with minute descriptions of all the elements, their arrangement, sizes and other peculiarities. As records, such descriptions may perhaps be useful, but only if due allowance has been made for the inevitable variation within an individual tree and among trees throughout the range of the species in question. Without such precautions, descriptions of this sort, are, to say the least, suspect. Quantitative characters may be important on occasion, but experience shows that they can be largely dispensed with; unless they have been made with the necessary precautions they are worthless.

There is another tendency, to be deprecated, which seeks to ensure that all illustrations which accompany diagnoses shall be at the same magnification. Fundamentally there is only one suitable magnification for the purpose of illustration, and that is the one which best shows the particular character or characters which it is desired to emphasise. It may be argued that it is useful to keep to certain standard magnifications, so that different woods may all be represented as seen, for example, with a ×8 hand-lens, or microscopically with a two-thirds inch objective and a ×10 eyepiece. This opinion is, however, difficult to defend; if a wood can be identified on certain gross features it is unnecessary to provide an illustration of its radial section at ×40 diameters. If, on the other hand, accurate diagnosis depends principally on the shape of its pits or other minutiae of structure, it may be a costly waste to publish an illustration at ×8 diameters simply for the sake of uniformity. As the many illustrations in this book show, photomicrographs furnish extremely valuable adjuncts to descriptions of wood structure. They do not by themselves, however, form ideal means of illustration. A photomicrograph is, or should be, an accurate record of the structure visible in one plane of a section, limited in its depth by the depth of focus of the microscope. It thus cannot display the partially three-dimensional picture which the skilled microscopist builds up in his mind's eye by the use of the fine focussing adjustment. There is thus much to be said for the use of good line drawings of wood structure, especially those which portray only the essential features; these may be slightly exaggerated or emphasised. Such drawings are often of great value to a worker attempting to make an identification from a description.

It remains to indicate the types of anatomical features which experience has shown to be reliable and useful for purposes of identification. Much will depend, of course, on the woods which are being examined, for any given character, as has been seen, does not always have the same diagnostic value. No more than a summary will be attempted here: practical applications are outlined in the following chapters.

In softwoods (Phillips, 1948), the grosser features of anatomy may sometimes be useful, such as the amount of late wood and whether the tracheids in this region are thick-walled or not. The rays may furnish several useful features when examined under the microscope. In a tangential section their height, in number of cells, and the shape of the component cells, may be characteristic, as may also be the presence of resin in these cells. Concerning the height of the rays, it is often sufficient to obtain a general impression as to whether the rays are high or low. In the silver firs, for example, rays may range from two to fifty cells in height, but the general impression gained from a tangential longitudinal section is that they are high, just as the Californian redwood appears, generally, to have rather low rays, although occasionally rays exceeding a height of forty cells may be encountered. Should counts be made of the number of cells, it is most important to give the range in height and not only the average height; a single very high or very low ray may have a marked effect on an average figure unless this is based on counts of a very large number of rays.

Another important feature to look for in the rays is the presence or absence of ray tracheids. Attention must also be given to the regularity with which these cells are present, for they occur only sporadically in some softwoods. Wall thickening of these tracheids is important; the peculiar dentate thickenings in some pines are diagnostic. In the ray parenchyma, the type of pitting and its arrangement in the cross-field, as seen in radial longitudinal section, is of great importance, while help may also be obtained from the presence or absence of pitting on walls of these cells other than the radial ones, as well as from characteristic irregularities of wall thickening.

Resin canals may also be present, in some woods invariably, but in some only as an abnormal feature. No difficulty will be found in distinguishing between those of normal occurrence and those which are traumatic (Fig. 49). The shape of rays containing radial resin canals may be distinctive, as may the type of epithelium which lines these canals (Fig. 51); only in the pines are the epithelial cells thin-walled. To some extent, the number of epithelial cells seen in a cross section of the canal may be a useful guide to identity.

The axial tracheids show some variation in different softwood genera and may thus be used as an aid to identification. Attention may be directed to their shape and to such unusual features of their walls as spiral and callitroid thickening. The arrangement of their bordered pits may be uniseriate or multiseriate and, when multiseriate, the pits in adjacent axial rows may be opposite or alternate. These bordered pits may be large, the diameter of their borders approaching the width of the radial wall of the tracheid or they may be considerably smaller. Again, the shape of the pit aperture, or of the torus, may be distinctive.

The absence or presence of parenchyma among the axial elements, and its abundance and distribution, may be characteristic in certain softwoods, and again, irregularities in the wall thickening of these cells may be worth attention.

Apart from its presence in schizogenous canals, resin may occur in the axial parenchyma. Such resin cells may be regularly distributed over the growth ring or confined to special parts of it. Again, resin may be found in ray parenchyma, or in the form of resin plugs in the axial tracheids.

This does not exhaust the list of possible features which may be of value for diagnostic purposes in softwoods, but it does give an indication of the type of feature to be looked for: the use which can be made of them is demonstrated in Chapter 14. A single feature is rarely sufficiently characteristic, although taken in conjunction with other features it may assist in the identification of an unknown wood.

Among hardwoods, much may be accomplished in identification with no more than a ×8 or ×10 hand-lens (F.P.R.L., 1952, 1953). Growth rings do not normally form a useful diagnostic feature, but in woods in which they are unusual in form, such as alder, where they dip between the large rays, or hornbeam, where they are sinuous, they may prove helpful. Storeyed structure and the presence of ripple-marks should also be looked for.

Vessels provide a number of features which are of greatest value for identification. Their general arrangement, grouping, and the presence in them of tyloses and deposits should be noted. It is worth while recording the colour of any deposits or gummy material, as well as observing whether this is hard, or soft with a tendency to bleed.

Size of vessels if often a useful feature. At its simplest, a purely arbitrary standard may be adopted, basing the estimate of size on personal judgment. This may often be sufficient for an experienced person, although it is useless for descriptive work unless it is on some sort of quantitative basis. The scale proposed by Dadswell and Eckersley (1935) has the merit of simplicity and calls for no more than a hand-lens. It is as follows:

Size Class	Actual Size of largest: determined microscopically	Description	Relation to Texture
Minute	Less than 100 μ	Visible only with aid of lens	Very fine
Small	100–200 μ	Just or barely visible to unaided eye	Fine
Medium	200–300 μ	Readily visible to unaided eye	Medium
Large	Over 300 μ	Very distinct to unaided eye	Coarse

Other standards have been suggested (cf. Chattaway, 1932). That used in the Lens Key (F.P.R.L., 1952) is very similar to the scale just given, but with a different terminology, while that proposed by Chalk (1938) has been used in formulating the standard terms of size of vessel diameters adopted by the Council of the International Association of Wood Anatomists (1939). These standard terms are as follows:

Class	Sub-Class	Tangential diameter
Small	Extremely small	up to 25 μ
	Very small	25– 50 μ
	Moderately small	50–100 μ
Medium-sized		100–200 μ
Large	Moderately large	200–300 μ
	Very large	300–400 μ
	Extremely large	over 400 μ

Brazier and Franklin (1961) in their Microscope Key, which deals with about 380 woods, find three size-classes sufficient.

In making determinations of vessel size in a specimen, a sufficient number of measurements must be made to give the range of size. It is useless to measure one or two of the largest vessels. Chattaway (1932) suggests that random measurement of fifty vessels may give a clear idea of the predominant sizes, although a hundred or more vessels may have to be measured if the range is wide.

Where the vessels are evenly distributed, it may be useful to obtain an indication of the number of vessels which occur in a standard area, although this is a feature which is not greatly used. Clarke (1940) suggested that a standard area of 2 sq. mm. is large enough for this purpose, unless the vessels are fewer than about twenty-five, when an area of 8 sq. mm. is recommended. The standard area may be marked out by a die, or by a circle on glass, or even by a hole punched in paper. A circle of 2 sq. mm. has a diameter of about one-sixteenth of an inch and one of 8 sq. mm. of about one-eighth of an inch.

Chattaway (1932) suggested the following classification for vessel distribution:

Up to 2 per sq. mm.	Very few
2–5 per sq. mm.	Few
5–10 per sq. mm.	Moderately few
10–20 ,, ,,	Moderately numerous
20–40 ,, ,,	Numerous
Over 40 ,, ,,	Very numerous

Another scale is given in the Lens Key (F.P.R.L., 1952), but it is suggested that it is rarely necessary to make use of this feature in identifying the commercial timbers covered by the second edition of the Key.

Details of the appearance of the vessels on the longitudinal surfaces should not be omitted. An indication of the length of the vessel lines, whether this is the same on radial and tangential faces, the length of the vessel elements and the distribution of gum and deposits may all help in identification.

The presence and distribution of parenchyma, as seen with a lens, may also be noted, and an estimate given of its quantity, e.g. apotracheal parenchyma in broad (or narrow) bands; the type of paratracheal parenchyma. In this connection attention should also be given to any distinctive appearance of the parenchyma on the longitudinal surfaces.

Rays on the transverse surface should also be examined; they may run straight or tend to curve around the vessels. They may, as in oak, be of two distinct sizes, or, as in alder, some may be aggregate.

Some difficulty may be found, using a hand-lens alone, in distinguishing aggregate rays from ordinary wide rays, but the latter tend to be more regularly distributed than the former. Rays which are noded at the boundaries of the growth rings may provide a useful feature for identification.

The width of the rays may provide a distinctive feature. A rough and ready, but none the less useful, indication of width may be obtained by comparing, on a transverse section, ray width with the diameter of the vessels, e.g.:

Rays less than half as wide as vessels
Rays half as wide to as wide as vessels
Rays wider than vessels.

Clearly this must be assessed from a general inspection and occasional exceptionally wide rays or vessels ignored.

A more precise classification is that adopted by the Council of the International Association of Wood Anatomists (1939) based on Chalk's (1938) proposals: it is as follows:

Class	Sub-Class	Ray Width
	Extremely fine	up to 15 μ
Fine	Very fine	15– 25 μ
	Moderately fine	25– 50 μ
Medium-sized		50–100 μ
	Moderately broad	100–200 μ
Broad	Very broad	200–400 μ
	Extremely broad	over 400 μ

It may also be worth while to record the number of rays in a standard area of transverse surface. Clarke (1940) suggested recording the number which pass through a circle of one-sixteenth or one-eighth of an inch diameter.

Also concerning the rays, attention should be given to the height and width of the rays in terms of cell number or actual measurements, and account taken of whether the rays are uni- or multi-seriate, and of their shape as seen in tangential section. The presence of rays of more than one type is always worth recording, and the composition of the rays, whether homogeneous or heterogeneous, the types of cells of which they consist, the distribution of these cells and the details of pitting in them are all valuable features for identification; careful study of rays is well worth while.

Other grosser features which may be of value for identification are the presence and arrangement of axial ducts (see p. 140 and Fig. 75), while it is worthy of record if the fibres are individually distinct under a hand-lens.

With the microscope a more detailed examination of the various elements may be made. Attention should be given to the thickness of the walls of the vessels, the type of vessel perforation, the arrangement and type of pits, the presence of spiral thickening and the presence of sclerotic tyloses.

The microscope will reveal details of parenchyma distribution which could not be readily seen with the hand-lens. In addition, the shape of the cells may be distinctive, so may their pitting or perhaps the thickness or irregular distribution of thickening in their walls. Details of storeyed arrangement and of fusiform cells and strand parenchyma may be worth recording.

As has already been indicated, it is often the custom to refer to cells of the fibre type, whether libriform fibres or fibre-tracheids, as fibres, or sometimes the two are treated separately. The presence of septate fibres may be a useful diagnostic feature, as may also be the rare presence of spiral thickening in fibrous cells. An indication of wall thickness, and the shape and distribution of pits, may be worth noting, while storeyed arrangement of fibres, if present, will be a valuable feature, as it is not of frequent occurrence. The presence of gelatinous fibres should also be recorded; although they may not be of diagnostic value (but merely an indication of tension wood), nevertheless in some timbers they seem to be very commonly present. It is not usual to pay much attention to tracheids in hardwoods.

The presence of cells which contain extraneous materials is often helpful in the determination of an unknown wood. Note should be made of oil and mucilage cells, tannin cells and latex canals, of cells which contain crystals (isolated cells of this type may be ignored) and the type of crystal present, as well as the presence of chambered parenchyma. Simple micro-chemical tests on extraneous materials are well worth attempting.

It is not suggested that all the features which have been mentioned in this chapter will be required for purposes of diagnosis or identification. The combination of a few of these characters is generally enough, but what combination of characters may be needed depends upon the wood in question.

The subject is one which is best learnt practically. Frequent use by the student of dichotomous keys and perforated-card keys, and after experience with these, the construction of his own simple reliable keys, will give a far better insight into the value and use of various characters for identification than any such summary as that given in this chapter.

CHAPTER 13

THE IDENTIFICATION OF SOME COMMON TIMBERS

I. SOME COMMON HARDWOODS

In this chapter attention will be given to the way in which some of the commoner commercial woods may be identified with certainty. It is not intended to form a treatise on the structure of these woods; only as much of the structure as is required for purposes of identification will be considered. Many features of interest to the wood anatomist will be ignored, partly because of the limitations of space, but primarily because their consideration, however interesting, would tend to impede, rather than to facilitate identification.

In dealing with hardwoods, much may be done in the way of identification with the unaided eye and with a hand-lens. For softwoods, observations with the high powers of the microscope are often necessary. Hence it is convenient to consider the hardwoods first, and those which will come under review in this chapter are:

Oaks (*Quercus* spp.) Ashes (*Fraxinus* spp.)
Elms (*Ulmus* spp.) Chestnuts (*Castanea* spp.)
Hickories (*Carya* spp.) Beeches (*Fagus* spp.)
Birches (*Betula* spp.) Maples and Sycamore (*Acer* spp.)
Poplars (*Populus* spp.) Willows (*Salix* spp.)
Limes and Basswoods (*Tilia* spp.) Alders (*Alnus* spp.)
Walnuts (*Juglans* spp.) Satin Walnut (*Liquidambar*
American Whitewood *styraciflua* L.)
  (*Liriodendron tulipifera* L.) Magnolias (*Magnolia* spp.)
Horse Chestnuts (*Aesculus* spp.) Hollies (*Ilex* spp.)

This list includes a good many commercial woods, but it is, of course, very far from being a comprehensive one. Other woods might equally well have been included, but those in the list will serve to illustrate the methods of identification, and so will be sufficient for present purposes. The number of timbers in commercial use is continually changing, new ones coming on to the market and old ones becoming perhaps less freely available. In this connection reference may usefully be made to the descriptions of timbers regularly published in "Wood".

It will be noticed, in the list above, that only in two instances have the woods been given more than their generic names, for the good reason that it is essential to be able to recognise genera with certainty before learning to deal with species. Species, or at least, groups of species, can sometimes be identified accurately, but initially it is more important to know how to recognise the wood of oaks or ashes than to attempt to distinguish the different sorts of oak and ash. The reason for giving the specific names of American whitewood and satin walnut is that they happen to be the only species of their respective genera which are of any commercial importance.

In general, the presence or absence of a pore ring is not a very useful character for identification, but it furnishes a valuable means of dividing up the timbers on our list. The term ring-porous is used here as meaning the presence of a ring of early wood vessels, as seen on a transverse surface, which are appreciably larger than those elsewhere in the growth ring. This definition thus excludes some of the limes, walnuts and other woods which sometimes possess a pore ring at the beginning of the growth increment, although the vessels of which it is composed are not appreciably larger than those formed later in the season.

Oak,[1] ash, elm and sweet chestnut are the woods on our list which are ring-porous. Hickory is only semi-ring-porous but since the vessels of its early wood are appreciably larger than those which are formed later in the season, this wood may be considered with those just named. As will be shown subsequently, little difficulty will be found in separating these woods by inspection of solid pieces of timber, but for the beginner, the lens characters are more definite and these will be examined first. All that is required is a clean end-grain surface, trimmed with a razor or sharp knife, and a ×8 or ×10 hand-lens.

On an end-grain surface the pore rings are readily seen, close together if the wood is slowly grown, more widely spaced in faster-grown wood. Between successive pore rings the wood is more compact, for here it consists largely of fibres, the smaller vessels occupying a smaller proportion of the total volume than in the early wood. In oak (Figs. 142 *A*, 143) the vessels of the late wood, which in some species are very small, tend to run in radial or slightly oblique lines, embedded in pale-coloured, radially elongate or V- or Y-shaped bands composed of tracheids and apotracheal parenchyma. In elm (Figs. 142 *C*, 143) the vessels and vascular tracheids of the late wood are very numerous, often larger than those of oak and aggregated into broken, undulating tangential lines. Chestnut differs again (Figs. 142 *B*, 143), in having distinctly oval vessels, those of the early wood graduating less abruptly into those of the late wood than in the case of oak. The vessels of the late wood are disposed in somewhat oblique lines, forming a flame-like pattern. In ash (Figs. 142 *D*, 143) the vessels of the late wood are very small, rather few, and arranged either singly or in twos, rarely in threes; they are all surrounded by pale haloes of vasicentric parenchyma. Hickory (Figs. 142 *E*, 143) is rather similar to ash in that its late wood vessels are in ones and twos, but they lack the vasicentric parenchyma; in

---

[1] This refers to deciduous oaks only: the evergreen oaks are considered in Chapter 17.

X

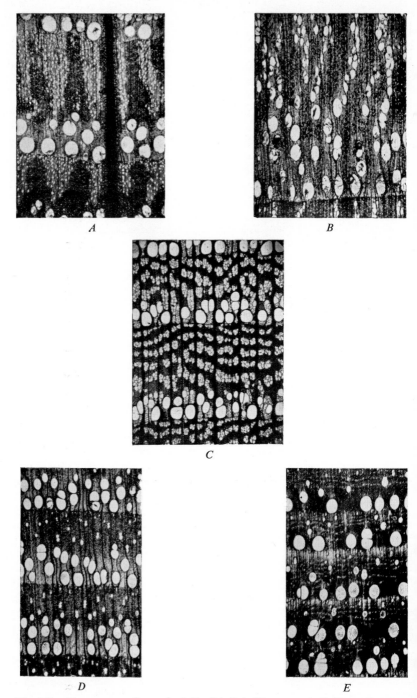

Fig. 142.—Transverse surfaces of: *A*. English Oak (*Quercus* sp.). *B*. Sweet Chestnut (*Castanea sativa*). *C*. Elm (*Ulmus* ?*procera*). *D*. Ash (*Fraxinus excelsior*). *E*. Hickory (*Carya* sp.) (all × 11).

OAK ASH

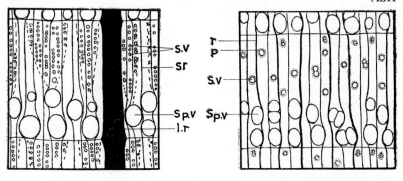

ELM

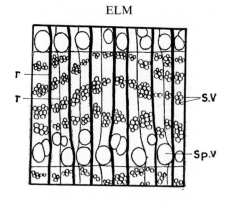

SWEET CHESTNUT HICKORY

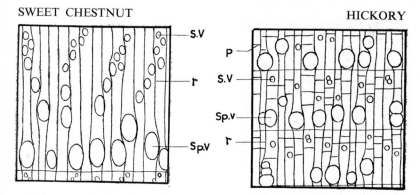

Fig. 143.—Simplified (caricature) drawings of transverse sections to show the features essential for identification of Oak, Ash, Elm, Sweet Chestnut and Hickory (in Oak, the numerous thin lines of apotracheal parenchyma have been omitted, as the other features shown are sufficiently diagnostic for this wood).

l.r., large ray; *p.*, parenchyma; *r.*, ray; *s.r.*, small ray; *S.V.*, vessels of late wood; *Sp.V.*, vessels of early wood.

hickory the parenchyma is in the form of numerous narrow apotracheal bands, like that in oak. Moreover, the vessels of ash are more oval in cross-section than those of hickory. In elm and chestnut the parenchyma is not distinctive enough, under a hand-lens, to concern us here.

The rays must also be examined. In oak they are of two sizes, large ones visible without a hand-lens, and between them smaller, very fine rays which can just be seen with a hand-lens. The rays of elm may just be visible without a lens, especially if the surface is moistened, while those of chestnut, ash and hickory are very narrow, and will certainly not be seen with the unaided eye. Thus the timbers of the five genera may be separated with certainty on the basis of vessel arrangement, ray size and distribution of parenchyma.

The differences visible on the transverse surface have, of course, their counterparts on the longitudinal surfaces. All five genera show the pore rings on the radial and tangential faces, on the former as parallel lines, the vessel lines, which look like small scratches, and on the tangential face as ∧-shaped or ∩-shaped lines of similar scratches. On the radial face of hickory, which may perhaps otherwise be confused with that of ash, these annual lines of vessels are less continuous than in the other four woods, because of its discontinuous pore rings. The large rays of oak will show as broad horizontal sheets or ribbons on the radial face, forming the silver grain, while on the tangential surface they will appear as dark, vertical lines, perhaps as much as 4 cms. in length. In elm the rays will show on the quarter-sawn wood as dark flecks, easily visible to the unaided eye, while on the tangential surface they will probably appear as coarse stippling and will certainly be easily seen with a lens. Ash, hickory and chestnut have very inconspicuous rays and even on the radial surface they are likely to require a lens to reveal them. Oak has a pale-coloured sapwood and a heartwood varying from pale creamy brown to a rich, deep brown colour. Chestnut might readily be confused with oak as far as colour and general appearance are concerned, but the apparent absence of rays, when the wood is viewed with the unaided eye, would be sufficiently diagnostic. Elm timber varies from a pale- to a reddish-brown colour and has a pale-coloured sapwood. Compared with the other woods under consideration it shows two characteristic features, a dull, rather dusty appearance, and numerous thin zig-zag lines on the plain-sawn surfaces, produced by the vessels of the late wood. Ash is white to pale-brown in colour, usually without a distinct heartwood, and is generally little different from hickory in these features. Neither rays, nor parenchyma nor late wood. vessels form distinctive features in these two woods, but, in the solid, ash is less lustrous than hickory and hickory generally has a more silky feel.

Although it is certainly not needed for the purpose of identification, a simple, confirmatory chemical test, based on the fact that oak and chestnut are rich in tannins, may be tried. A few shavings of the heartwood are boiled in water in a test-tube and an iron salt (e.g. ferric chloride) is added. Oak and chestnut give a black colour, resembling ink, while the other three woods give no more than a slight discolouration. This test may be carried out more simply, but less satisfactorily, by painting a little ferric chloride solution on to the timber.

Beech, maple and birch are three common, diffuse-porous timbers, to which attention may next be given. Sycamore is one of the maples and at present no attempt will be made to distinguish this particular maple wood specifically (but cf. p. 402). All three woods are strictly diffuse-porous and the vessels show a slight diminution in size throughout the season, as well as appearing more numerous in the early wood, a feature which is not very marked in birch and maple but conspicuous enough in beech. In all three the growth rings are clearly marked; in beech a useful distinctive feature is that these rings have a somewhat irregular contour, tending at intervals to dip inwards slightly towards the centre of the tree. This commonly occurs at their intersections with the large rays, but may also occur between these. The rays are also distinctive. In beech (Figs. 144 A, 146 A) the rays, like those of oak, are of two groups of size, although there is a less sharp distinction between them: the large rays are noded. Birch (Figs. 144 B, 146 B) also has noded rays, but the rays are very narrow, and their noding is not easy to detect with a lens. The rays of maple (Figs. 144 C, 146 D) are of two sizes, but the large ones are never as wide as those of beech, although they are wider than those of birch.

These differences of ray size give the timbers quite different appearances in the solid. Quarter-sawn beech shows numerous, fairly small, brown flecks or streaks, the large rays, which are equivalent to the silver grain of oak. Maple has a somewhat smoother, more silky texture, although this difference is slight. It shows the same type of figure as beech on its radial surfaces but, of course, on a smaller scale; nevertheless, this figure is visible to the unaided eye. Birch possesses essentially the same ray pattern, but on so small a scale that it only becomes distinct under a lens.

Another useful diagnostic feature of these woods, in the solid, is furnished by the growth rings, which on radial surfaces appear as longitudinal parallel lines, and on tangential faces as $\wedge$'s or $\cap$'s. In beech the growth rings are not very distinct, but in both birch and maple the thin lines of thick-walled parenchyma cells at the ends of the seasons' growth become more polished than the rest of the wood when the timber is worked, because they contain more wood substance. In consequence they show on the surface as shining lines. These lines form a good "spot" feature to distinguish between rotary-cut birch and alder plywood, for they are absent or far less distinct in alder.

The microscope will help with the accurate determination of maple and birch; while it is unnecessary for beech, one or two corresponding features of this wood may nevertheless be mentioned in comparison.

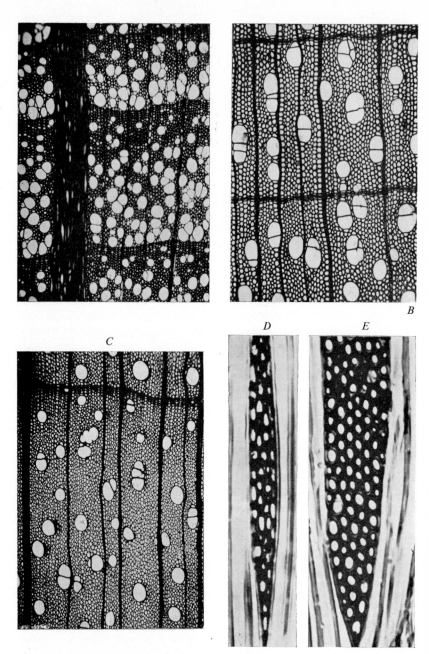

Fig 144.—A. Beech (Fagus sylvatica). B. European Birch (Betula sp.). C. Maple (Acer sp.). All three sections show noded rays; all are T.S. (× 60). D. A ray of Silver Birch (Betula pendula) and E. part of a large ray of Rock Maple (Acer saccharum); in Birch the ray cells have a flattened section, in Maple a rounded one; both are T.L.S. (× 305).

A transverse section, viewed under the low power, will reveal the shape of the vessels and their arrangement. In beech (Fig. 144 *A*) the vessel grouping appears somewhat haphazard; sometimes there are radial groups of two vessels, sometimes tangential ones, and clusters of vessels also occur. Vessel clusters may also be found in birch (Fig. 144 *B*), but here, more often, two or three vessels form short radial chains; a similar arrangement is less commonly seen in the maples, where the vessels are mostly solitary. In maples (Fig. 144 *C*) solitary vessels have a somewhat round section; where they occur in birch they are more oval and somewhat angular.

Tangential longitudinal sections of these three woods show considerable differences in the rays. In beech the rays are of two distinct ranges of size, the larger ones perhaps several millimetres high and as many as 25 cells wide, and the more numerous small ones from 1 to 5 cells wide. Maple (Figs. 145 *B*, 146 *E*) has some relatively broad rays, up to 7 or 8 cells wide, and sometimes up to about a millimetre high (but cf. p. 000). In birch (Figs. 145 *A*, 146 *F*) the rays are small and from 1 to 5 cells wide, but a ray of birch, say 5 cells wide, looks much narrower than one of maple of the same number of cells in width, because of the difference in cell shape. Those of maple, as seen in section, are round, while those of birch are distinctly oval and flattened tangentially, being perhaps no more than half as wide as in maple. (Figs. 144 *D*, *E*, 146 *E*, *F*.)

Among the vessels of these three timbers, only those of maple have spiral thickening (Figs. 145 *D*, 146 *J*). In this wood the vessel perforations are exclusively simple, whereas in birch they are exclusively scalariform (Figs. 145 *C*, 146 *H*). Beech has predominantly simple perforations, although occasionally in some of the smaller vessels they may be scalariform. This, however, is a feature of academic interest; other more obvious characters serve to distinguish beech from any other wood and it is not worth spending time looking for scalariform perforations simply for the purpose of identification.

Other timbers on our list also possess scalariform perforations, either exclusively or in part. Of such, alder, American whitewood and magnolia may be considered together. Alder (Figs. 146 *C*, 147 *A*) is distinctive in possessing aggregate rays[1] and is thus readily differentiated from birch; moreover the rays which are not members of an aggregate are uniseriate (Fig. 146 *G*) and not multiseriate as are a proportion of those in birch. In the solid, the pale reddish-brown colour and lack of lustre of alder are characteristic, and the wood is usually marked with dark-coloured pith-flecks and by the aggregate rays. These are not very prominent on quarter-sawn surfaces, but appear as dark lines, up to a length of many centimetres, on tangential surfaces. The growth rings,

---

[1] According to Kobayashi (1952) some of the Japanese alders do not have aggregate rays.

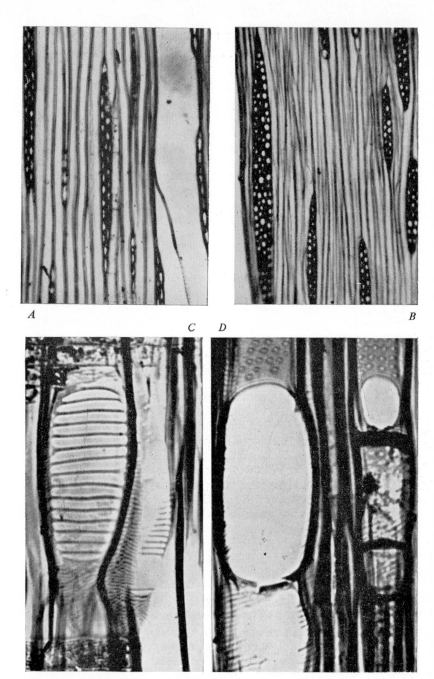

Fig. 145.—*A*. European Birch (*Betula* sp.). *B*. Maple (*Acer* sp.); both are T.L.S. (× 180). *C*. Scalariform perforation of vessel of Silver Birch (*Betula pendula*). *D*. Simple vessel perforations in Rock Maple (*Acer saccharum*). In *D* some spiral thickening is seen below the larger perforation and also in the smaller vessel on the right; the apparent spiral thickening in *C* is, in fact, not spiral thickening, but is caused by rows of very small bordered pits which are out of focus: *C* and *D* are R.L.S. (× 305).

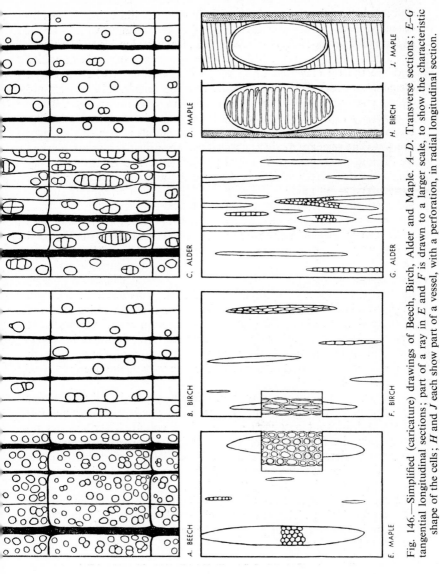

Fig. 146.—Simplified (caricature) drawings of Beech, Birch, Alder and Maple. *A–D*. Transverse sections; *E–G* tangential longitudinal sections; part of a ray in *E* and *F* is drawn to a larger scale, to show the characteristic shape of the cells; *H* and *J* each show part of a vessel, with a perforation, in radial longitudinal section.

as seen on transverse surfaces, are rather characteristic, for they usually dip inwards between the aggregate rays.

Alder has its vessels either clustered, or much more commonly, in radial groups of half a dozen or so. The scalariform perforations (Fig. 147 *D*) have thin and numerous bars.

Magnolia (here only the North American species are considered) and American whitewood, or yellow poplar, have a whitish sapwood and a heartwood varying enormously in colour, although it is usually cream with a slightly greenish tinge. This green tinge, which, to an experienced person, is very characteristic, is a useful guide to identification. In both woods (Fig. 147 *B, C*) the vessels are somewhat angular and are mostly clustered or in radial chains of up to half a dozen elements; occasionally these chains may be longer. The vessels are very numerous and their arrangement is strictly diffuse porous. There is generally little difference in vessel size throughout the growth ring, but at its outer margin there may be a few vessels rather smaller than the rest. The rays are distinctly noded and the growth rings are marked by distinct pale zones of terminal parenchyma. The timbers are very similar in structure, and it is best to use the microscope to distinguish them. The safest guide is the vessel pitting; in magnolia this is scalariform (Fig. 147 *G*), the long, narrow bordered pits extending right across the vessel, while in American whitewood there are several rows of much smaller pits in opposite arrangement (Fig. 147 *F*). In this wood the vessel perforations are exclusively scalariform (Figs. 147 *E*, 150 *N*), but the nature of the perforations is not a useful diagnostic guide to distinguish the two genera, because in *Magnolia acuminata* L. nearly all the perforations are simple, while in *M. grandiflora* L. they are mostly scalariform. In both magnolia and American whitewood the rays, as viewed in tangential longitudinal section, are often somewhat irregular in outline, rather than regularly fusiform, and may be asymmetrical. In no instance is the asymmetry specially obvious, although to an experienced wood anatomist it forms a very distinctive feature of American whitewood.

Poplar, willow, horse chestnut and lime may now be taken together as a group, for they are all soft, fine-textured woods, generally without lustre and without any very characteristic colour. They possess no very distinctive features in the solid and, in fact, are all best identified under the microscope. Lime may be immediately separated from the other three since it is the only one of them possessing multiseriate rays. A transverse section of lime (Figs. 148 *A*, 150 *B*) shows rays of two distinct sizes, the larger ones being distinctly noded at the boundaries of the growth rings. The vessels are clustered: occasionally they are in short radial or tangential groups but a cluster may form a compact group or be partly radially and partly tangentially aligned. Sometimes,

---

Fig. 147.—*A*. Alder (*Alnus glutinosa*). *B*. American Whitewood (*Liriodendron tulipifera*). *C*. Magnolia (*Magnolia grandiflora*). *A–C* are T.S. (× 60). *D*. Alder, showing a scalariform perforation plate in a vessel; R.L.S. (× 305). *E*. American Whitewood, showing a scalariform perforation plate in a vessel; pits, which are situated on the rear wall, and are consequently out of focus, are seen at the top left; R.L.S. (× 305). *F*. American Whitewood, showing an unusual type of perforation plate, partly reticulate, in a vessel; opposite pitting is seen above and below the plate; R.L.S. (× 305). *G*. Magnolia (*Magnolia grandiflora*), showing scalariform pitting in a vessel; R.L.S. (× 305).

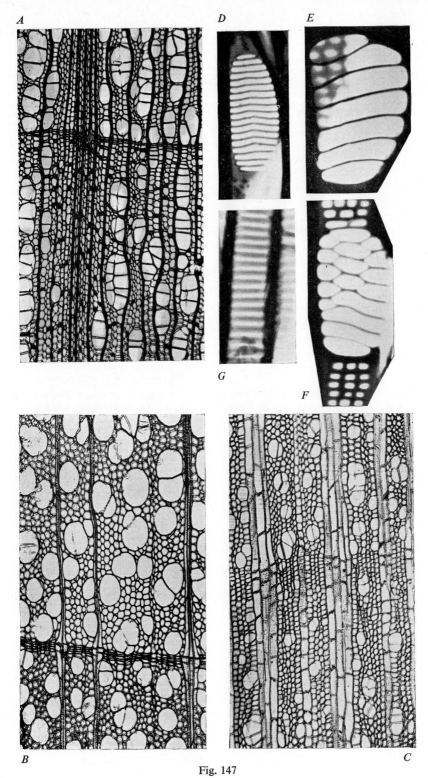

Fig. 147

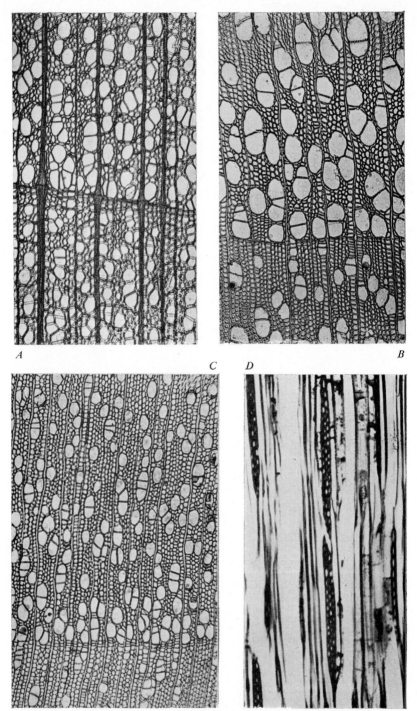

Fig. 148.—*A*. Lime (*Tilia vulgaris*). *B*. Black Italian Poplar (*Populus canadensis* var. *serotina*). *C*. Horse Chestnut (*Aesculus hippocastanum*). *A–C* are T.S. (× 60). *D*. Lime (*Tilia vulgaris*); T.L.S. (× 110).

and especially in the American basswoods (species of *Tilia*), there is a tendency for a pore ring to be formed at the beginning of the season, but the vessels in this region are not appreciably larger than those which follow. Quite characteristic are the very fine lines of aggregate parenchyma, only one cell wide and composed of cells which are very narrow in the radial direction. In tangential longitudinal section the rays are rather irregular and of two distinct sizes, some being uniseriate and others up to six cells wide (Figs. 148 *D*, 150 *G*). The larger rays are often asymmetrical. The vessels bear abundant spiral thickening, and the perforations, which are best examined in the radial longitudinal section, are simple (Figs. 149 *B*, 150 *M*).

As in lime, the vessels of poplar, willow and horse chestnut (Figs. 148 *B*, *C*) are somewhat angular. They are commonly in short, radial chains, and in willow and poplar sometimes show an oblique grouping. All three woods are normally diffuse-porous, although there may be a narrow zone containing a higher proportion of vessels at the beginning of the growth ring. The three timbers cannot be distinguished in the solid with certainty. Sometimes, however, the rays in the horse chestnuts are storeyed; this applies more particularly to the American buckeyes, which belong to the same genus, and to the Japanese horse chestnut. When this occurs, small ripple-marks are visible on the tangential faces. The rays are never storied in the willows and poplars. Horse chestnut may show spirally thickened vessels (Figs. 149 *C*, 150 *L*); this is characteristic of the European species, but is not invariably present in all species of the genus *Aesculus*. Spiral thickening is never present in willows and poplars. Willow possesses heterogeneous rays; in poplar they are homogeneous; in horse chestnut they may be either heterogeneous or homogeneous. A very useful way of separating the three woods is to examine the simple pits in the ray parenchyma, in the regions where the cells are in contact with a vessel. In poplar (Figs. 149 *D*, 150 *J*) these pits are rather large and are in two or three horizontal rows; in willow (Figs. 149 *E*, 150 *K*) the pits are smaller and in three to five horizontal rows, while in horse chestnut there are five to nine rows of pits. Of course, this feature, though it is a good one, must be considered in conjunction with other characters; thus occasionally six rows of pits occur in willow, which taken alone can sometimes mislead, especially if the information obtained from one cell is deemed sufficient. In willow these pits are almost confined to the marginal (upright) cells of the heterogeneous rays. In all three woods the vessel perforations are simple (Figs. 150 *J*, *K*, *L*) and the pits in the vessel walls are relatively large and oval or sometimes rather angular; they tend to be crowded, and the alternate arrangement is very distinct.

Lime has not a distinct heartwood and is variable in colour, sometimes white, sometimes creamy or pale brown. Horse chestnut, likewise, is a sapwood tree with white or yellowish wood, sometimes having a pinkish cast. Poplar wood is generally whitish, but may be pale brown or even have a reddish tinge; it does not often possess a distinct heart-wood. Willow is the only one of these four timbers with a distinct heartwood, which is a pale but rather rich brown, while the sapwood, which may be quite wide, is white.

Walnut, with its heartwood ranging from a purplish slaty grey to a deep brown, often streaked with darker zones, and with its whitish pale-yellow or pale-brown sapwood, is fairly distinctive in the solid. From hand-lens characters, walnut is not an easy wood for the beginner to recognise. One of its distinctive features, the presence of numerous very fine lines of apotracheal parenchyma, is often scarcely visible in the heartwood with a lens, because the parenchyma cells often have the same colour as the surrounding fibres; it is often easier to observe this feature in the sapwood. The vessels are easily visible to the unaided eye, and grade in size throughout the growth ring; in American black walnut there is sometimes a partial pore ring of small vessels. Tyloses are commonly present, giving the vessels a glistening appearance. The rays are narrow. One of the most distinctive features, to be seen with a lens, is the vessel arrangement on the transverse surface (Fig. 172 A). The vessels are disposed singly, or in short radial chains, but the solitary vessels or groups tend to be arranged obliquely to each other, the obliquity being first in one direction in relation to a radius, and then changing, thus; ⊰. Detection of this characteristic arrangement requires practice, as it is not readily obvious to the beginner. Much easier to see in transverse section are the positions of the vessels or vessel groups in relation to the rays; often they do not lie midway between two rays, but are much nearer to one ray, if not touching it. This feature, incidentally, is also very characteristic of woods of the Meliaceae (mahogany family).

In *Liquidambar styraciflua* L., the North American red gum, the heartwood varies in colour from greyish to reddish brown, and is known in Britain as satin walnut: its pinkish white sapwood is known as hazel pine. Despite the name walnut, satin walnut is not in the least like true walnut in any way. It is best examined with the microscope for diagnostic features, since little will be seen with the lens. In a transverse section (Fig. 174 B) the very numerous vessels will probably be noticed first; they are small, usually solitary, or in short radial groups, or clustered, and they are distinctly angular in outline. The vessels are thin-walled, and the rest of the tissue, apart from the narrow

Fig. 149.—*A*. Cricket bat Willow (*Salix alba* var *caerulea*); T.L.S. to show uniseriate rays (× 110). *B*. Lime (*Tilia vulgaris*); R.L.S., showing spiral thickening, pitting and simple perforations of vessels (× 305). *C*. Horse Chestnut (*Aesculus hippocastanum*); R.L.S., showing spiral thickening, pitting (out of focus) and simple perforation in vessel (× 305). *D*. Black Italian Poplar (*Populus canadensis* var. *serotina*); R.L.S., showing pits in ray cells and above, vessels, the one on the right with a simple perforation; pitting can also be seen on the vessels (× 305). *E*. Cricket bat Willow; R.L.S., showing pits in marginal cells of a ray (× 305).

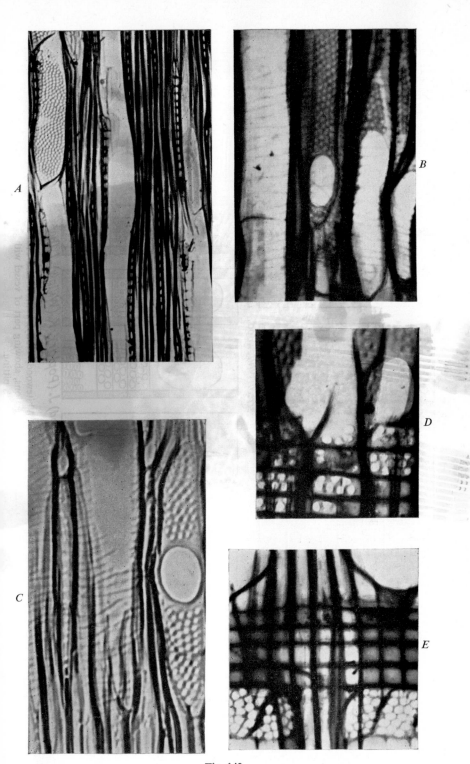

Fig. 149

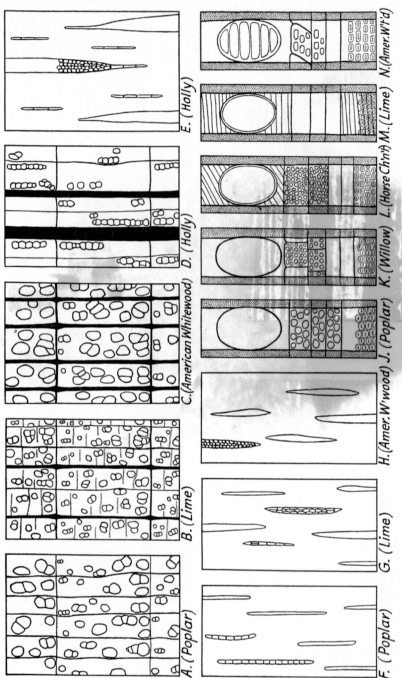

Fig. 150.—Caricature drawings of Poplar, Lime, American Whitewood, Holly, Willow and Horse Chestnut. *A–D* transverse sections; *E–H* tangential longitudinal sections; *J–N* radial longitudinal sections, showing part of vessel with pitting and a perforation, and ray cells with pitting.

A. (Poplar)   B. (Lime)   C. (American Whitewood)   D. (Holly)   E. (Holly)

F. (Poplar)   G. (Lime)   H. (Amer. W'wood) J. (Poplar) K. (Willow)   L. (HorseChn't) M. (Lime)   N. (Amer. W't'd)

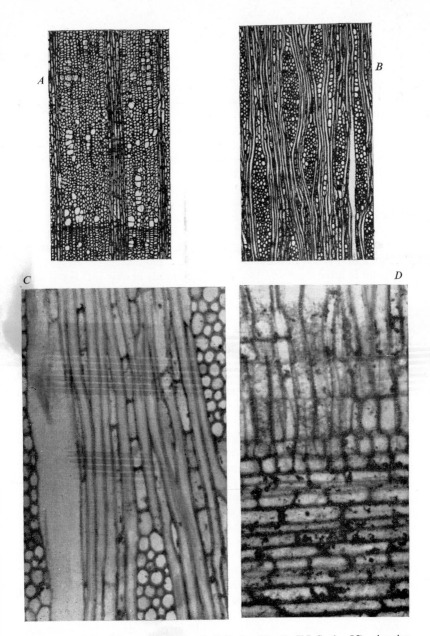

Fig. 151.—Holly (*Ilex aquifolium*). *A*. T.S. (× 50). *B*. T.L.S. (× 85), showing uniseriate and multiseriate rays. *C*. T.L.S. (× 170); part of a large ray lies, slightly obliquely, down the centre line; below is part of the multiseriate region, composed of procumbent cells, with part of the uniseriate "tail" of the ray, composed of marginal or upright cells, extending upwards. *D*. R.L.S. (× 170), part of a ray; in the lower part of the figure are the procumbent cells, and above them the marginal or upright cells.

Y

rays and the not very conspicuous parenchyma, consists of rather thick-walled fibre-like elements. The difference between these thick-walled elements and the thin-walled vessels is striking. These fibre-like cells have distinctly bordered pits, as will be seen in a longitudinal section; they are, in fact, fibre-tracheids. The vessels of red gum have scalariform perforations with numerous fine bars (Fig. 9 C), and they possess spiral thickening, which is, however, confined to the ends of the vessel elements. The rays, seen in tangential longitudinal section, are distinctly heterogeneous, possessing both procumbent and marginal cells. The rays are one to three cells wide; the procumbent cells are almost circular in section, while the marginal cells are elongated. Several rows of marginal cells may occur in a ray, but in a region of this kind the ray is uniseriate. Red gum may sometimes possess axial intercellular canals; these occur sporadically, being traumatic, and if present are arranged in tangential rows. In cross-section they are angular.

Holly is quite distinct from the other woods in this list, being hard and dense, with a very fine and uniform texture; in colour, it is ivory-white, or white with a greenish or greyish tinge. Many of the rays are broad, and visible to the unaided eye on all surfaces, although, because they are of much the same colour as the rest of the wood, the surface must be correctly illuminated if they are to be well seen. Beyond these features, the microscope will be required. Very characteristic are the extremely small vessels, barely visible with a hand-lens, arranged in long radial chains (Figs. 150 D, 151 A). There is little difference between early and late wood, but vessels (no larger than elsewhere) may form something of a pore ring at the beginning of the season. Both vessels and fibres have spiral thickening, which is so abundant that it tends to obscure the scalariform perforations of the vessels, with their numerous bars. The larger rays are heterogeneous and consist of procumbent and marginal cells, the former, in tangential longitudinal section, appearing as small, round or slightly elliptical cells, the latter as tall, thin cells (Figs. 150 E, 151 B, C). In the zone of the procumbent cells the rays may be five cells wide, but in the region of the marginal cells they are uniseriate; where several vertical rows occur the ray appears to be drawn out into a tail. It is not usual to find a tail at both margins of a ray. The small rays are uniseriate, and are composed of cells similar to the marginal cells of the larger rays.

It should now be clear that the identification of some of the common hardwoods of commerce offers no great difficulty. This chapter has, however, been concerned with recognition of genera, not of species. The question will not unnaturally arise: how can species of the different genera be identified? Chapter 17 attempts to answer this question.

CHAPTER 14

THE IDENTIFICATION OF SOME COMMON TIMBERS

II. SOME COMMON SOFTWOODS

In this chapter, as in the last, the aim will be to describe those special features of structure by which certain timbers can be accurately identified. Softwoods, however, are all very similar in fundamental structure, and there are few, if any, gross features of their anatomy which serve as reliable diagnostic guides. It will be apparent, therefore, that attention must be given to detail, and often to minute detail, when attempting to distinguish the different coniferous woods. As a broad general rule, to which there are, of course, exceptions, it is sound policy never to attempt to identify a softwood without the aid of the microscope.

Here attention will be directed to the diagnostic characters of the following coniferous genera:

Pinus (true pines)
Picea (spruces)
Larix (larches)
Pseudotsuga (Douglas fir)
Tsuga (hemlocks)
Cedrus (true cedars)
Abies (silver firs)
Taxus (yews)
Sequoia (redwoods)
Taxodium (swamp cypress)

Chamaecyparis (cypresses, in part
Thuja (arbor vitae, including western red cedar)
Juniperus (pencil cedars, junipers)
Araucaria (hoop-, bunya-, parana-pines)
Agathis (kauris)
Podocarpus (matai, podo, yellow-wood, manio)

The general uniformity of the appearance of softwoods in the solid is only to be expected, since they consist almost wholly of axial tracheids, which are essentially similar in all conifers; moreover, the rays are always inconspicuous. Nevertheless, differences of colour, the presence of heartwood, differences between early and late wood, the distinctness of growth rings, the distribution and appearance of knots (if present), the occurrence of resin, the appearance of the surface, the texture and occasionally the taste and odour of the wood may at times all serve as diagnostic features.

Under the microscope, a transverse section of the wood will, of course, show the axial tracheids in transverse section, as polygonal cells, usually thin-walled at the beginning of the growth ring and thicker-walled, and probably smaller, in the later part. The thicker-walled elements of the late wood may form a zone only two or three cells wide, or they may occupy up to half the growth ring; transition from thin- to thick-walled elements may be gradual or abrupt. In some conifers, the transverse section may show large circular or somewhat polygonal holes, which are the axial resin canals; it may be possible to make out the parenchyma cells which form the epithelium lining these canals, but the walls of the cells may have become crushed or torn. Axial parenchyma, often readily recognised by the fact that it contains dark resin, may be present, but at most it is sparse. The rays show as narrow lines of cells; when the wood contains horizontal resin canals an occasional wider ray may be seen, i.e. a fusiform ray sectioned through the resin canal region, and often dark in colour because of the resin.

In a radial longitudinal section, the axial tracheids will show their characteristic large bordered pits in surface view. These pits are commonly in a single vertical row and their diameter may be nearly as great as the width of the radial wall, although they may be smaller and may sometimes occur in two, or even more, axial rows. Axial resin canals, if present, will appear as longitudinal slits in the section, sometimes empty, or again, filled with dark resin or tylosoids; if the section has passed through the margin of a canal it may show a mass of epithelial cells. The rays, which run across the section at right-angles to the axial tracheids, may be wholly parenchymatous, but they may contain ray tracheids (which have bordered pits), usually along the upper and lower margins of the ray. The pitting of the ray parenchyma cells is frequently useful in identification, the form of the pits and their number and arrangement in the cross-field (cf. pp. 96–97) often being distinctive.

In a tangential longitudinal section, the axial tracheids will have much the same appearance as in the radial section, the greatest difference being that the bordered pits, which are almost entirely on the radial walls, are now seen in section and not in face view. Sometimes, bordered pits are to be seen on the tangential walls of the axial tracheids, but these pits are relatively small and generally not numerous; they occur mostly in the late wood tracheids. Axial parenchyma, if present, will be seen as long, narrow rectangular cells, sometimes filled with dark resin; these cells will have the same appearance as in the radial section. In the tangential section the rays will appear as axial chains of cells 2 to 40 or more cells in height and sometimes even represented by single cells; these rays are normally uniseriate, but in some softwoods a few may be two cells wide in parts. Where radial (horizontal) resin canals are present in the rays, the shape of these rays is altered, for they bulge in the part which contains the canal; such rays are referred to as fusiform rays.

Since the foregoing description is a generalised one, applicable, in the main, to all softwoods, it will be clear why microscopic examination is necessary for identification, for this will depend on small features such as the presence or absence of ray tracheids, the height of the rays, the type of pitting in axial tracheids and ray parenchyma and so on. Nevertheless, as will be seen, grosser features are sometimes useful, provided they are not relied upon solely.

Of the conifers on our list, only four genera possess normal resin canals. These all have ray tracheids, a feature which is, however, shared by two other genera and one species of a third. These two characteristics thus provide a useful starting point for separating the genera on anatomical features.

Axial and radial resin canals are invariably present in *Pinus*, *Picea*, *Larix* and *Pseudotsuga*, so that if a transverse section of an unknown softwood shows axial resin canals, identification is already narrowed down to these four genera. It is true that resin ducts may also be present in Eastern Asiatic *Keteleeria*, but this wood is unlikely to be encountered in commerce, and in any case its lack of ray tracheids, possessed by all the four genera already mentioned, should prove a sufficiently distinctive feature. Axial traumatic resin ducts may be met with in some other genera, e.g. *Abies*, *Sequoia*, but since such canals occur in tangential series, no difficulty will be found in distinguishing them from normal resin canals. It should be added that in the spruces resin canals may be less abundant than in woods of the other three genera; hence, if they are not immediately visible in a section, a search should be made to discover whether or not they do occur.

Examination of transverse sections of woods from these four genera will show differences of contrast between early and late wood of the growth rings. In Douglas fir (Fig. 152 *A*) and larch (Fig. 152 *B*) the change from early to late wood is sudden, the late wood is generally extensive and its tracheids are thick-walled. The same is true of the pitch pines (Fig. 152 *E*), but in Scots pine (*P. sylvestris* L.) (Fig. 152 *D*) the change is more gradual and the late wood is often less dense than that of larch. In the soft pines, like yellow pine (*P. strobus* L.) (Fig. 152 *F*) and sugar pine (*P. lambertiana* Dougl.), and in the spruces (Fig. 152 *C*), the change from early to late wood is gradual, but the late wood is usually neither very extensive nor very dense.

The contrast between early and late wood is, of course, apparent also on longitudinal surfaces. On quarter-sawn faces, the growth increments show as longitudinal layers, consisting alternately of the more open and softer early wood and the denser late wood, while on plain-sawn faces these layers show as a series of ∧'s or ∩'s. In larch, Douglas fir and the pitch pines there is a strong contrast between successive layers, while in Scots pine the contrast is also well marked. The difference is less striking in the soft pines and the spruces.

In the soft pines, axial resin canals are visible in the longitudinal surfaces as prominent brown streaks, while similar, but smaller, streaks are fairly conspicuous in Scots pine.

In spruces, likewise, resin canals can be seen, but they are less

Fig. 152

obvious because they are colourless and look rather like scratches made with a pin. It is unlikely that the smaller resin canals of Douglas fir and larch will be seen without careful search, but in Douglas fir their presence may be indicated by small grimy-looking patches, caused by the rather fluid resin oozing from the canals on to the surface and picking up dirt.

In transverse section the microscope reveals the differences in the resin canals of some of these woods. In the soft pines the canals tend to be large, while in Douglas fir they are commonly in tangential pairs. Moreover, in the pines, the epithelial cells are not likely to be conspicuous because, owing to their thin walls, they will probably have collapsed, or have been torn when the section was cut. In the other genera they will probably be easily visible, since they have thicker walls and are, consequently, less likely to collapse or to be torn.

Spiral thickening is normally present in the axial tracheids of Douglas fir (Fig. 39 A); while it varies considerably in amount, it is particularly well-developed in those of the early wood. It also occurs as a regular feature in the early wood tracheids of the Himalayan spruce (*Picea smithiana* (Wallich) Boissier) a timber of some commercial importance in India. Spiral thickening is also found, very occasionally, in the late wood tracheids of some other spruces, and in *Larix*, but its occurrence in these woods is sufficiently uncommon to be safely ignored.

A detailed study of the ray tracheids in radial longitudinal sections furnishes valuable data for diagnoses. In the pines it is not possible to make specific identifications of their woods, but the genus can be divided into seven sections on the basis of wood characters (Phillips, 1948). Differences in the ray tracheids, coupled with differences in the ray parenchyma, make it possible to identify a wood as belonging to any one of these sections. For present purposes it must suffice to refer to three of these sections, the soft pines of the yellow pine type, e.g. yellow pine (*P. strobus* L.), sugar pine (*P. lambertiana* Dougl.) and western white pine (*P. monticola* Dougl.), the pitch pines, e.g. longleaf pine (*P. palustris* Mill.), slash pine (*P. caribaea* Morelet) and loblolly pine (*P. taeda* L.) and the pines of the red deal type, e.g. Scots pine (*P. sylvestris* L.), red pine (*P. resinosa* Ait.), and Austrian and Corsican pines (*P. nigra* Arnold). It happens that the members of each of these groups possess a more or less common shoot character, the soft pines having five needles on their dwarf shoots, the pitch pines generally three and the pines of the red deal type normally two; the groups may, therefore, be conveniently referred to as the five-, three- and two-needle

Fig. 152.—Transverse sections of softwoods to show differences in growth rings; all show axial resin canals. *A*. Douglas Fir (*Pseudotsuga taxifolia*). *B*. A Larch (*Larix lyallii*). *C*. Sitka Spruce (*Picea sitchensis*). *D*. Scots Pine (*Pinus sylvestris*). *E*. Longleaf Pine (*Pinus palustris*), a Pitch Pine. *F*. Weymouth (Yellow) Pine (*Pinus strobus*). (All × 16.)

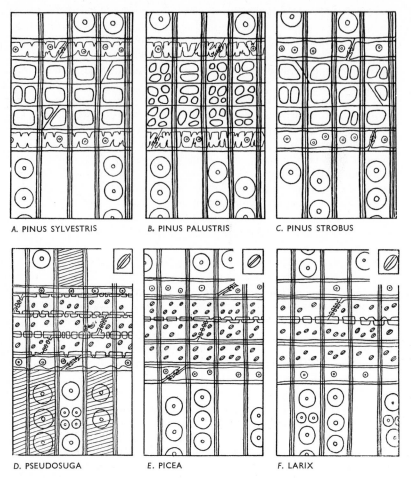

A. PINUS SYLVESTRIS   B. PINUS PALUSTRIS   C. PINUS STROBUS

D. PSEUDOSUGA   E. PICEA   F. LARIX

Fig. 153.—Diagrammatic radial longitudinal sections (high power) of various soft-woods, showing parts of axial tracheids and part of a ray. *A*. Scots Pine (*Pinus sylvestris*). *B*. Longleaf Pine (*Pinus palustris*), a Pitch Pine. *C*. Yellow Pine (*Pinus strobus*). *D*. Douglas Fir (*Pseudotsuga taxifolia*). *E*. A Spruce (*Picea* sp.). *F*. A Larch (*Larix* sp.).

The small diagrams inset in the top right-hand corners of the lower row show the type of pit in the ray parenchyma, more highly magnified.

pines respectively. It must be emphasised that this classification is not a rigorous one; for example, the number of leaves on the short shoots of the pitch pines may be variable, while jack pine (*P. banksiana* Lamb.) is a two-needle pine of which the wood, seen in the solid, resembles red deal, though histologically its structure falls into line with that of pitch pines.

In the ray tracheids the walls vary considerably; they are rarely of equal thickness throughout the cell. Where the thickened areas are relatively large, the walls seen in section have a slightly undulating appearance; such ray tracheids are termed smooth-walled. Sometimes the thickening is more localised, forming peg-like or tooth-like projections into the lumen of the cell; ray tracheids with this type of thickening are said to be dentate.

In the pitch pines (Fig. 153 B) and the pines of the red deal type (Fig. 153 A) the ray tracheids are dentate, the teeth being very strongly developed in the pitch pines, where they sometimes extend almost across the cell lumen. In spruce there are sometimes minute dentations on the ray tracheid walls, as there are—much more rarely—in larch, but frequently the ray tracheids in these two genera appear smooth (Fig. 153 E, F). In Douglas fir (Fig. 153 D) and the soft pines (Fig. 153 C) the ray tracheids are smooth, but those of the former may have spiral thickening.

In pines of the red deal type, and also in the soft pines, the ray parenchyma cells have large, window-like simple pits on their radial walls: commonly one to each cross-field in the former (Fig. 153 A), and more often two in the latter (Fig. 153 C). The pitch pines have pinoid pits in their ray parenchyma cells, numbering 3–6 to the cross-field (Fig. 153 B). In the other three genera, the pits of these cells are always small, of the piceoid type, and varied in their arrangement. In the spruces they tend to occupy the corners of the cross-field (Fig. 153 E), and in Douglas fir and larch (Fig. 153 D and F) to be in an irregular horizontal line, but these are features on which it is unwise to place too much reliance.

In tangential longitudinal sections, the shapes of the fusiform rays and of their resin canals may serve as useful diagnostic features. In the pines, spruces and larches (Fig. 154) these rays often have uniseriate tails above and below the resin canal region, which bulges out more or less abruptly. Sometimes, however, the rays are more smoothly fusiform, a feature which is commonly, but not invariably, shown by Douglas fir (Fig. 154 A). In the pines the resin canal often tends to occupy the whole of the width of the ray (Fig. 154 C), for its thin-walled epithelial cells are commonly crushed. In the other three genera the thicker-walled epithelial cells retain their original form. The radial resin canals in the pines are often of more or less circular section, those of the spruces tend to be oval, while in Douglas fir the canals are small and often polygonal. This polygonal cross-sectional shape is caused by the thick-walled epithelial cells bulging somewhat into the canal. The same thing happens in larch (Fig. 154 B) and spruce, but because of the larger size of the canals, compared with those of Douglas fir, the angular appearance is usually less obvious. The number of epithelial cells surrounding a section of a radial resin canal also helps identification; in Douglas fir there are usually six or fewer, spruce has usually 7–9, and larch 9–12 of these cells. Larch wood, which is difficult to

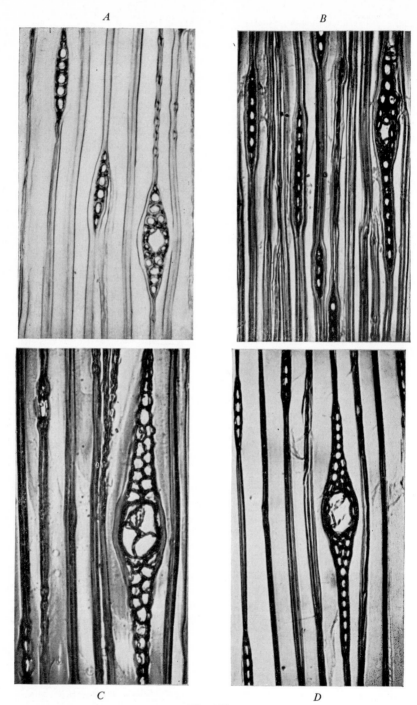

A *B*

C *D*

Fig. 154

distinguish microscopically from spruce, frequently has the radial resin canals excentrically placed in the fusiform rays, so that the upper, or lower, part of the ray may appear to be drawn out into a long tail. Phillips (1948) has examined this feature quantitatively and finds that in 25 fusiform rays taken at random in a section, the average ratio of the numbers of cells in the shorter and longer tails is 2 : 3 in larch and 1·5 : 2 in spruce. This quantitative treatment thus bears out the general impression, gained from inspection of sections, that larch shows "tailed" rays more frequently than spruce.

The fusiform rays of Douglas fir are rather broad and dumpy, so that the marginal ray tracheids seen in tangential sections appear broadly triangular; radial sections may pass through the edges of such tracheids, when of course their full height wll not be seen. Such "low" ray tracheids are not infrequently found in *Pseudotsuga* (Fig. 153 *D*) but rarely in the other three genera. It should, however, be emphasised that these ray tracheids are, in fact, not much lower than those of pine, spruce and larch, although their apparent shallowness serves as a useful diagnostic feature.

The uniseriate rays afford additional help in separating the timbers of these four genera. In *Pseudotsuga* (Fig. 154 *A*) they are usually low, with an average height of 8 cells: in the pines they rarely exceed a height of 12 cells, while in spruces and larches they may be 20 or more cells high.

It may be thought that undue emphasis has been given to microscopic detail in relation to the identification of these four genera, and that diagnoses might be made on the basis of one or two of the characters referred to. This is often true, but it must be remembered that the characters vary and that it is therefore often desirable to study as many characters as possible before making a determination. The timbers of larch and spruce, for example, are notoriously difficult to distinguish in small samples. They are, however, readily distinguished in the log because spruce is a sapwood tree whereas larch has distinct heartwood.

Two other genera, *Tsuga* and *Cedrus*, and one species of a third, *Chamaecyparis nootkatensis* (Lamb.) Spach, the Alaska cedar or yellow cedar also possess ray tracheids (Figs. 155 *A, B* 162 *D*). However they lack resin canals except that traumatic canals may be found occasionally in *Cedrus*. This statement must not be understood to imply that ray tracheids may not be found elsewhere. They occur, for example in *Abies* and *Sequoia*, but in these genera as in others, their

Fig. 154.—Fusiform rays of softwoods in tangential longitudinal section. *A*. Douglas Fir (*Pseudotsuga taxifolia*), with two characteristic uniseriate rays to the left. *B*. European Larch (*Larix decidua*), showing an excentrically placed resin canal. *C*. Weymouth (Yellow) Pine (*Pinus strobus*). *D*. European Spruce (*Picea abies*). (All × 170.)

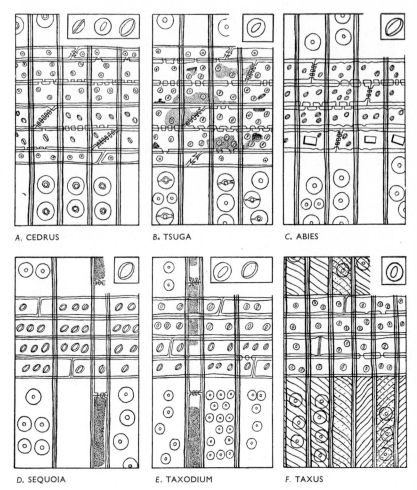

Fig. 155.—Diagrammatic radial longitudinal sections (high power) of various softwoods, showing parts of axial tracheids, axial parenchyma and part of a ray. *A*. Cedar (*Cedrus*). *B*. Hemlock (*Tsuga*). *C*. Silver Fir (*Abies*). *D*. Redwood (*Sequoia*). *E*. Swamp Cypress (*Taxodium*). *F*. Yew (*Taxus*). Resin is shown by stippling. The small diagrams inset in the top right-hand corners show the types of pit in the ray parenchyma, more highly magnified.

occurrence is so sporadic that they cannot be regarded as normal features of the wood. They are thus of no value in identification.

In *Cedrus* (the true cedars) the fresh heartwood has a pleasant pungent odour and the growth rings are distinct. *Cedrus* also has a unique microscopic feature (visible in radial longitudinal sections), in that the tori of the pits in the axial tracheids have scalloped margins. Since the torus is larger than the pit aperture, each pit shows the usual

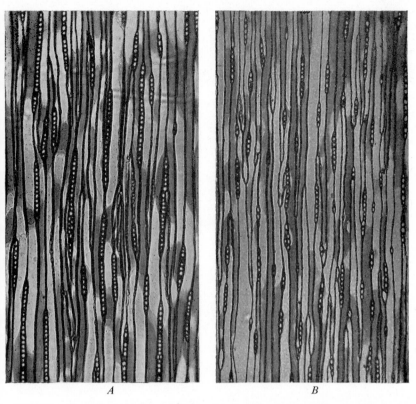

A   B

Fig. 156.—Rays of: *A*. Cedar of Lebanon (*Cedrus libani*) and *B*. Western Hemlock (*Tsuga heterophylla*) in T.L.S. (× 60). In *A* there is a partially biseriate ray to the left of centre, a little below the middle of the figure.

inner and outer rings, the pit aperture and pit border respectively, with a third one, the torus, having a scalloped or crenulate edge, in between them (Fig. 39 *A*).

In *Tsuga* (the hemlocks) the wood resembles that of *Cedrus* in having distinct growth rings. It may however have a sour smell, and differs microscopically also in that the pit membranes commonly show more or less horizontal radial bands extending across them from the torus to the border. *Tsuga* differs from *Chamaecyparis nootkatensis* in having more prominent growth rings with proportionately more late wood. Furthermore the pitting of the axial tracheids is partly biseriate and when this occurs the pits are opposite. Axial parenchyma is sparse or absent in all three genera, but if it is present, the end walls of the cells are characteristically nodular in *Cedrus* and *Tsuga* but not in *Chamaecyparis nootkatensis*.

The woods of these three genera also differ in the height of their

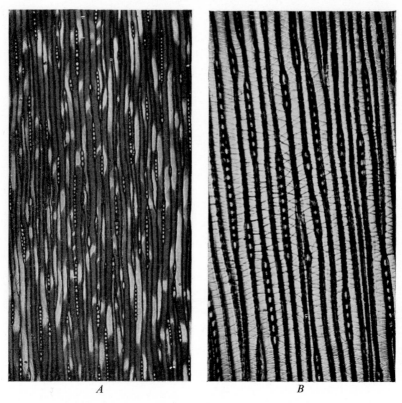

A *B*

Fig. 157.—Tangential longitudinal sections of: *A*. Yellow Cedar (*Chamaecyparis nootkatensis*) (× 60) and *B*. Yew (*Taxus baccata*) (× 170).

rays. Thus in *Cedrus* the rays may exceed a height of 40 cells and some are in part biseriate (Fig. 156 *A*). In *Tsuga* and *Chamaecyparis* the rays are lower, rarely exceeding 16 cells in the former (Fig. 156 *B*) while in *C. nootkatensis* most of the rays are less than 12 cells high (Fig. 157 *A*).

The woods of other species of *Chamaecyparis*, which lack ray tracheids, are best considered together with some from the related genera *Juniperus* and *Thuja*.

In *Juniperus*, which includes the pencil cedars, the woods of the commercially important species have almost white sapwood and dull red or reddish-brown heartwood, and are immediately distinguished by their distinctive odour, familiar as the smell of a freshly sharpened pencil (good pencils are made from these woods). In the growth ring there is very little late wood; hence the wood looks very even in texture (Fig. 158 *C*). The rays are low. rarely exceeding a height of six cells, and in the heartwood usually contain abundant, dark, resinous material

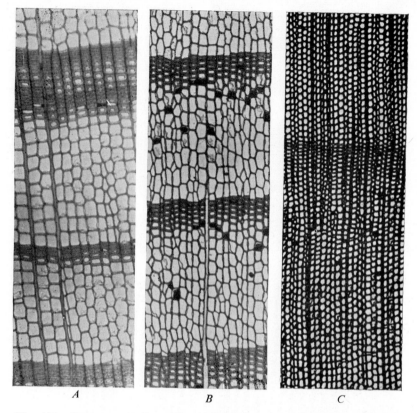

Fig. 158.—Transverse sections of: *A*. Swamp Cypress (*Taxodium distichum*).
B. Californian Redwood (*Sequoia sempervirens*). *C*. Pencil Cedar (*Juniperus virginiana*). (All × 51.)

(Fig. 159 *C*). In the ray parenchyma, the cross-field pitting is generally cupressoid, although it may sometimes be taxodioid, and there are 1–4 pits in a cross-field (Fig. 162 *A*). Very commonly the axial tracheids, as viewed in transverse section, do not fit closely, but have small intercellular spaces between them (Fig. 36), a very unusual feature in the normal wood of conifers (but cf. compression wood, Chapter 9).

Differentiation of the woods of *Thuja* and *Chamaecyparis* (except *C. nootkatensis* already described) is difficult. The chief generic distinctions lie in the generally abundant axial parenchyma of *Chamaecyparis* and the normal sparseness of such cells in *Thuja*, and in the pitting of the ray parenchyma, which is exclusively cupressoid in *Chamaecyparis*, and generally taxodioid, but sometimes cupressoid, in *Thuja*. For present purposes it will be better to consider the differences shown by commercially important woods of the two genera— *Thuja plicata* D.Don (western red cedar), *T. occidentalis* L. (white

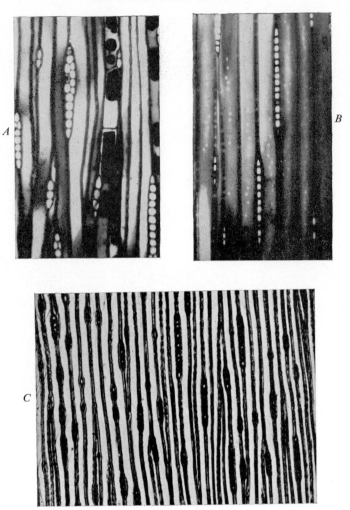

Fig. 159.—Tangential longitudinal sections of: *A*. Californian Redwood (*Sequoia sempervirens*); note biseriate rays and resin cells. *B*. Swamp Cypress (*Taxodium distichum*). *C*. Pencil Cedar (*Juniperus virginiana*), with the rays containing much resinous material. (All × 90.)

cedar or arbor vitae), *Chamaecyparis lawsoniana* (A.Murr.) Parl. (Port Orford cedar) and *C. thyoides* (L.) B.S.P. (southern white cedar).

The heartwood of western red cedar is pinkish- or reddish-brown, sometimes a dull brown; its sapwood is nearly white. It possesses a somewhat cedar-like odour and is slightly bitter to the taste. White cedar also has a whitish sapwood, while its heartwood is pale brown; it has the same taste and smell as western red cedar. Port Orford cedar

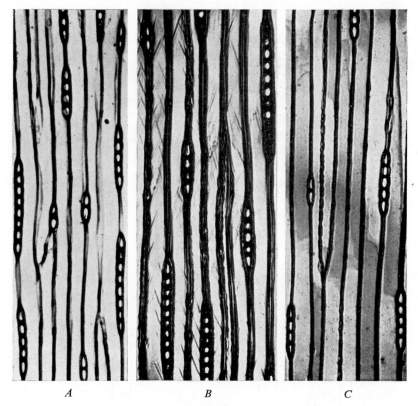

                A   B   C

Fig. 160.—Rays of: *A*. Western Red Cedar (*Thuja plicata*); *B*. Port Orford Cedar
(*Chamaecyparis lawsoniana*); *C*. Southern White Cedar (*Chamaecyparis thyoides*).
(All T.L.S. × 170.)

has a yellowish to brownish heartwood, often not sharply differentiated
from the sapwood, a pungent scent somewhat like ginger and a spicy,
unpleasant taste. A reddish- or pinkish-brown characterises the wood
of southern white cedar, which possesses a slightly bitter taste, a cedar-
like smell and usually a somewhat oily appearance.

It is said that, microscopically, Port Orford cedar has low rays (a
height of 1–6 cells is usual), and may thus be distinguished from the
wood of southern white cedar where the rays are taller (usually from
1–12 cells high); but this is not a reliable difference, as reference to
Figs. 160 *B* and *C* will show. If axial parenchyma happens to be
plentiful in white cedar, the wood is not easy to distinguish from
southern white cedar. The best distinguishing features are the difference
in the colour of the heartwood, for white cedar lacks a pinkish tinge
in its heartwood, and its wood does not have an oily appearance. In
western red cedar the parenchyma is variable and often sparse: the

z

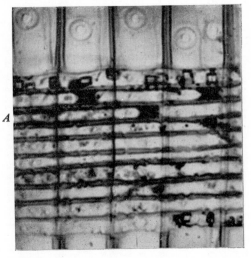

A

B 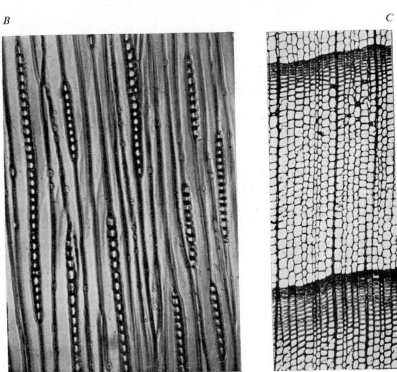 C

Fig. 161.—*A*. Grand Fir (*Abies grandis*), R.L.S. showing part of a ray, with resinous material in some of the cells and crystals in the uppermost and lowermost ones; the pitting on the horizontal walls of the ray cells is well shown (× 305). *B*. European Silver Fir (*Abies alba*), T.L.S.; there is a partially biseriate ray at the top, almost in the centre line (× 170). *C*. Western Red Cedar (*Thuja plicata*), T.S. (× 51).

rays are usually from 1–12 cells high (Fig. 160 *A*) and thus differ from those of white cedar, where the usual height is 1–8 cells. A further useful diagnostic feature is found in the bordered pits of the axial tracheids, which, in the early wood, are often paired near the ends of the tracheids.

The yews (*Taxus*) produce a very distinctive timber, hard, heavy and close-textured, with a pale sapwood and rich brown heartwood, the junction between the two being marked by a thin greyish zone. The tracheids of the late wood are thick-walled and even the early wood is fairly dense: all the tracheids possess abundant spiral thickening (Fig. 157 *B*). The cross-field pits (Fig. 155 *F*) of the ray cells number 1–4 and are either of the cupressoid or taxodioid type. The rays rarely exceed 25 cells in height and a few are partly biseriate (Fig. 157 *B*).

The pale-coloured timbers of *Abies* (the silver firs) resemble those of *Picea* (the spruces) in showing distinct growth rings and a gradual change from early to late wood, but in *Abies* the wood is slightly heavier and of a coarser texture. For a softwood, the rays are fairly conspicuous on quarter-sawn surfaces. The absence of resin canals usually distinguishes the wood from that of *Picea*, though traumatic axial ducts may occur. Ray tracheids are also normally absent, but may occasionally be present, when the wood resembles spruce in radial longitudinal section. Crystals of calcium oxalate occur not uncommonly in the ray parenchyma (Fig. 161 *A*) and are sometimes confined to the upper and lower rows of cells of the rays. There are normally 2–3 pits of the taxodioid type in the cross-field, while the end (tangential) walls of the ray cells are strongly pitted (Fig. 155 *C*). Like *Cedrus*, *Abies* possesses high rays, sometimes 30 or more cells high, and these rays are not uncommonly in part biseriate (Fig. 161 *B*).

The next two softwood genera to be considered—*Sequoia* and *Taxodium*—are fairly distinctive woods in the solid, while under the microscope their identification presents no difficulty. The only species of *Sequoia* of commercial interest is *S. sempervirens* Endl., the Californian redwood, for the other species of the genus, *S. wellingtonia* Seem., the Californian big tree or Wellingtonia, is too rare to be of economic value: nor is its timber of such good quality as that of the redwood. Redwood produces a light-weight, rather coarse-textured timber of which the heartwood is a pale reddish- to a deep reddish-brown colour and the narrow sapwood is whitish or yellowish white. In transverse sections it will be seen that there is a marked difference between early and late wood, for the tracheids of the early wood are large and thin-walled while those of the late wood are thick-walled and radially flattened: the change from early to late wood is abrupt and the late wood normally occupies quite a small proportion of the growth ring (Fig. 158 *B*) although sometimes it may be more extensive. Parenchyma is fairly abundant among the axial tracheids and its cells are conspicuous by reason of their dark resinous contents. In radial longitudinal sections there are a number of distinctive features: the bordered pits of the axial tracheids are often of small size and frequently lie two abreast; the axial parenchyma cells, with their abundant resin, are conspicuous by reason of their dark contents; the pits of the ray cells are taxodioid and are usually 2–3 to the cross-field (Fig. 155 D). The large size of the ray cells is noteworthy and is well seen in a tangential longitudinal section. The rays vary much in height but in general give the impression of being rather low; they are frequently, in part, biseriate (Fig. 159 A). Small bordered pits are abundant on the tangential walls of the late wood tracheids.

The sapwood of *Taxodium* (swamp cypress) is yellowish white, while its heartwood varies from light- to dark-brown, reddish-brown or nearly black, and the names red, yellow and black cypress, which are sometimes used for the timber, normally refer to its colour. When freshly sawn the wood has an unpleasant, rancid smell, often less pronounced in light-coloured specimens. It has a greasy feel and generally a peculiar grubby appearance which is very characteristic. The late wood is sharply differentiated from the early wood, the large thin-walled tracheids of the latter contrasting strongly with the thick-walled and often radially flattened ones of the late wood (Fig. 158 A). The great variation in the relative amount of late wood in successive rings is also usually characteristic, while the growth rings themselves may be somewhat sinuous. Axial parenchyma cells are frequent, and conspicuous by reason of their dark-coloured resin: they may even be visible with a hand-lens on the longitudinal faces. The rays are rather coarse and consequently somewhat more conspicuous on the radial surface than those of most softwoods. In a radial section the bordered pits of the axial tracheids are distinctive, for in some tracheids they occur in 3 or even 4 vertical rows; such pits are opposite (Fig. 155 E) in arrangement. The pits of the ray parenchyma are commonly in a single row, 3–4 in a cross-field, and are either taxodioid or cupressoid. In a tangential longitudinal section, the rays appear fairly high and sometimes partly biseriate, although, unlike *Sequoia*, rays which show this last feature are not common (Fig. 159 B). The axial tracheids of the late wood frequently have numerous small bordered pits on their tangential faces.

Of the remaining genera on our list, *Araucaria* and *Agathis* may be distinguished from other coniferous timbers by the pitting on the walls of the axial tracheids: where this is multiseriate, the pits are commonly in 2–4 vertical rows and the pitting is alternate (Fig. 38 E, F, In other conifers multiseriate pitting, if present, is opposite (but cf. *Cedrus* p. 88). The woods of *Araucaria* and *Agathis* are, however, very similar and there is no certain way of distinguishing between them. Both are characterised by their regular growth, for even when growth rings are apparent, there is generally little difference between early and late wood (Fig. 163 A). The rather large diameter of the axial tracheids

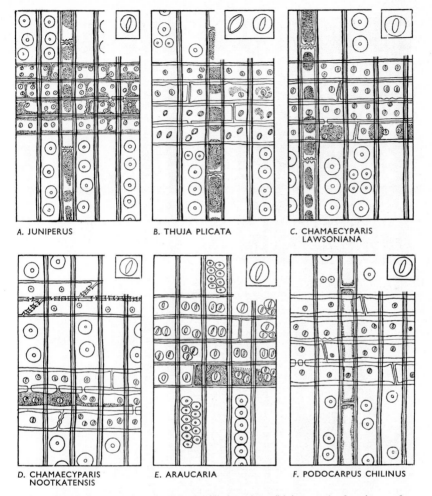

A. JUNIPERUS   B. THUJA PLICATA   C. CHAMAECYPARIS
                                                   LAWSONIANA

D. CHAMAECYPARIS   E. ARAUCARIA   F. PODOCARPUS CHILINUS
   NOOTKATENSIS

Fig. 162.—Diagrammatic radial longitudinal sections (high power) of various soft-woods showing parts of axial tracheids, axial parenchyma and part of a ray. *A.* Pencil Cedar (*Juniperus*). *B.* Western Red Cedar (*Thuja plicata*). *C.* Port Orford Cedar (*Chamaecyparis lawsoniana*). *D.* Yellow Cedar (*Chamaecyparis nootkatensis*). *E. Araucaria. F.* Manio (*Podocarpus chilinus*). Resin is shown by stippling.

The small diagrams inset in the top right-hand corners show the types of pit in the ray parenchyma, more highly magnified.

is sometimes striking. The ray parenchyma cells have thin horizontal walls, so that in tangential sections the rays often appear broken because these walls frequently tear when the wood is sectioned (Fig. 163 *C*). The pitting in the ray cells is characteristically cupressoid (Fig 162 *E*). Neither specialised resin cells nor resin canals occur in these woods, but resin is usually abundant in the ray cells (Fig. 163 *B*)

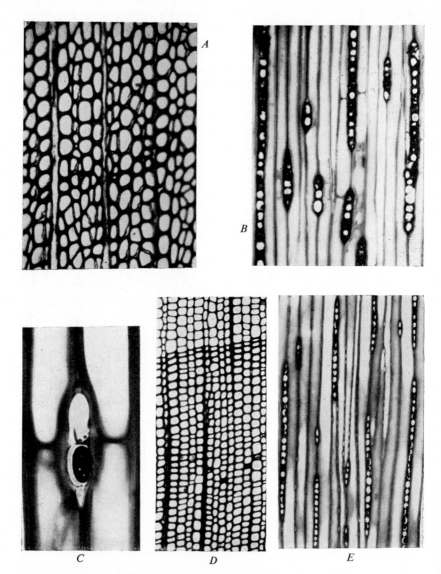

Fig. 163.—*A*. Parana Pine (*Araucaria angustifolia*); T.S. (× 95). *B*. New Zealand Kauri (*Agathis australis*); resin plugs are seen in the tracheid almost in the centre line and in the one on the right of this; T.L.S. (× 95). *C*. Queensland Kauri (*Agathis palmerstonii*); a small ray, only two cells high, the lower cell containing resin; the thin horizontal wall between the two ray cells is partly broken; there is a resin plug in each of the two axial tracheids flanking the ray; T.L.S. (× 330). *D*. Manio (*Podocarpus chilinus*); T.S. (× 95). *E*. Miro (*Podocarpus ferrugineus*); T.L.S. (× 95).

and in axial tracheids, usually near the rays where it takes the form of resin plugs (Fig. 163 *B, C*).

In *Agathis* the heartwood is brownish and in *Araucaria* pale or whitish. In *Agathis* there may be as many as four longitudinal rows of bordered pits in the axial tracheids, although more often, as in *Araucaria*, there are only two or three rows.

Timbers of the genus *Podocarpus* are likely to prove difficult to a beginner, for no single character will serve for their identification. Generally, there is little difference between early and late wood and the growth rings are not distinct (Fig. 163 *D*). Neither resin canals nor ray tracheids are present and in most species the transverse walls of the ray cells are thin and unpitted, while on the longitudinal walls of these cells the simple pits are small. Axial parenchyma is present and usually abundant, but in one or two species it is sparse. In the wood of the New Zealand species *Podocarpus spicatus* R.Br. (matai), the longitudinal walls of the ray parenchyma have large simple pits, a character which is found in one or two other softwoods, apart from some of the pines. This type of pitting, however, associated with the characters already mentioned and with an orange-brown heartwood, is sufficient to identify the wood. Again, in *P. chilinus* Don, one of the American species producing manio, the horizontal walls of the ray parenchyma are thick (Fig. 162 *F*) and pitted, while in the New Zealand kahikatea (*P. dacrydioides* A.Rich) these walls are also pitted but thin.

CHAPTER 15

KEYS FOR THE IDENTIFICATION OF WOOD

The use of keys for the identification of unknown woods is a useful and much used practice. Students, however, often confess to being unable to use such devices, so that a brief account of several types of key, and the ways in which they are used, will not be out of place.

Let us suppose that we have an unknown timber to identify. Its country of origin is known, as also is the fact that the timbers of that particular area have been examined and described in detail. The specimen to be identified might therefore be compared in all its features with these descriptions, one by one, until one was found with which it tallied; thus its identification might eventually be achieved.

This method would, however, obviously be laborious and time consuming, and some more rapid procedure is clearly needed. For the wood anatomist, experience might supply the necessary short cuts: without being able to recognise the wood precisely, he would probably know approximately where to look among the descriptions, and also where a search would probably be a waste of time. A well-constructed key provides similar guidance, by directing the search more quickly to the region of its objective.

The most widely used type of key is that known as the dichotomous key. In making such a key to a group of timbers, for example, the woods of a country, or of a family, or those which are used for some special purpose, the first step would be to attempt to divide them into two groups on the basis of a pair of easily recognised and contrasted characters. Each group would then be sub-divided, again and again into two groups, until the last sub-divisions each separated two woods. The first criterion might be between ring-porous and diffuse-porous woods, and if the unknown specimen were ring-porous, in using the key this alternative would, clearly, be selected. The next division might be based on ray size, for which again two sharply contrasted characters would be needed; for example, "rays easily visible to the unaided eye" and "rays visible only with a lens". Again, the user of the key would select the alternative which fitted the unknown specimen, and so on, until the last alternative led to a single timber with which the unknown should correspond. Working through the key is thus a process of choosing repeatedly between two branches of a fork, or dichotomy; hence the name, dichotomous key.

The value of a dichotomous key depends on several things. Foremost, it rests on the skill of its author in selecting criteria which give two clear unequivocal alternatives at each step, thus enabling the user to decide, without hesitation or error, which branch of the dichotomy to select. A pair of alternatives such as "rays narrow" and "rays broad" is not satisfactory, because it gives no indication of what the author's idea of a narrow or a broad ray may be. While extremely narrow or very broad rays would not cause trouble, those of intermediate size certainly would. If, however, the alternatives were given as: "all rays very narrow, not discernable to the unaided eye" and "at least some rays visible to the unaided eye" no difficulty would be likely to arise in deciding to which group the unknown specimen should be assigned.

The use of a single pair of contrasting characters at each step in the key, as indicated in the foregoing paragraph, may not, however, always be reliable, since a wood specimen may be abnormal in respect of the character used. For this reason a key may usefully make reference to two characters at each step, so reducing the likelihood of abnormality leading to error. Whether this additional complication is worth-while is a matter for the experience and judgement of the compiler of the key, since clearly the key should be kept as simple as possible, and the use of different characters reduced to a minimum consistent with reliability. Where only one pair of characters is available the user of the key must take the greatest care in deciding which path to follow at each dichotomy: one false step will inevitably lead to the wrong conclusion. The effective use of keys calls for experience, but they are not difficult to use if they have been well-constructed. The beginner will find it best to work slowly; speed combined with accuracy comes with practice.

The method may be illustrated by the construction of a key for six purely imaginary timbers, *A*, *B*, *C*, *D*, *E* and *F*. The descriptions of these timbers are supposed to be as follows:

A. Wood white: sapwood tree. Very soft and light in weight. Splinter burns to a complete white ash. Ring-porous. Vessel perforations scalariform, with 30–40 bars. All vessels with spiral thickening. Rays uniseriate: regularly storeyed.

B. Sapwood white; heartwood pink. Very hard and heavy. Splinter burns to a complete white ash. Diffuse-porous. Vessel perforations scalariform, with 25–35 bars. Vessels without spiral thickening. Rays 1–8 cells wide. Ray cells with gummy contents.

C. Sapwood grey; heartwood rich warm brown. Splinter burns to a charcoal. Ring-porous. Vessel perforations simple. All vessels with spiral thickening. Rays uniseriate and also 5–6 cells wide.

D. Wood pale yellow; sapwood tree. Very hard and heavy. Splinter burns to complete buff-coloured ash. Diffuse-porous. Vessel perforations scalariform, with 2–5 bars. Vessels may have spiral thickening. Rays 4–5 cells wide. Rays with sheath cells.

E. Wood white; sapwood tree. Splinter burns to charcoal. Ring-porous. Vessel perforations simple. Vessels without spiral thickening. Rays 2–3 cells wide; regularly storeyed: rays with prominent marginal cells.

F. Sapwood grey; heartwood pale brown. Splinter burns to charcoal. Diffuse-porous. Vessel perforations simple. Vessels without spiral thickening. Rays uniseriate.

To make the first dichotomy for a key to these six woods a structural difference is required which will divide them clearly into two classes. It would not be helpful to divide them into sapwood and heartwood trees, since the user of the key might only have a piece of sapwood. The burning splinter test is not the best one to select, since this must be carried out on the heartwood. The presence of spiral thickening in the vessels might at first sight be useful, but *D* presents difficulties. If it is certain that any section will show vessels with and without spiral thickening, the character might be used, but if spiral thickening occurs only sporadically in *D*, this character is valueless for the key.

The rays however, will not differ in the heartwood and sapwood, nor most probably, in different specimens of a species, and might therefore be used. Thus the first division for the key might be: *Group* 1: rays exclusively uniseriate (*A* and *F*) and *Group* 2: some rays at least, multiseriate (*B, C, D, E*). *Group* 1 is then readily divided on the vessel perforations (*A* scalariform, *F* simple). *Group* 2 might be subdivided into: *Group 2A* with simple perforations in the vessels (*C* and *E*) and *Group 2B* with scalariform perforations (*B* and *D*). *Group 2A* is then readily divided on the rays and *Group 2B* on the vessel perforations.

On these divisions a key could be constructed on the following lines:

1. Rays exclusively uniseriate   2
   At least some rays multiseriate   3
2. Vessel perforations exclusively scalariform   .   .   .   .   *A*
   Vessel perforations exclusively simple   .   .   .   .   .   *F*
3. Vessel perforations exclusively scalariform: spiral thickening
      entirely absent or present only in some vessels   .   .   .   4
   Vessel perforations exclusively simple: spiral thickening present in
      all vessels   5
4. Perforation plates in vessels with 25–35 bars. Rays 1–8 cells wide   *B*
   Perforation plates in vessels with 2–5 bars. Rays 4–5 cells wide   .   *D*
5. Wood white. Rays 2–3 cells wide, storeyed   .   .   .   .   *E*
   Wood grey (sapwood) or brown (heartwood). Rays uniseriate and
      also 5–6 cells wide   .   .   .   .   *C*

To use this key to identify an unknown timber (assuming it to be one included in the key) the character of the rays would first be examined. If there were some multiseriate rays, the second alternative in 1 would be selected, so leading to 3 and by-passing woods *A* and *F* entirely. Here, supposing the vessels to have simple perforations and spiral thickening, the second alternative would lead to 5, when it would be necessary to decide on the colour of the wood and the width of the rays. Supposing the wood to be white, with storeyed rays 2–3 cells wide the key would lead to wood *E*.

It would then remain to check the characters of the unknown wood against those given in the description of the wood *E*. The colour of the wood has already been used in the key, so have the width of the rays and their arrangement. The ash test would not necessarily be conclusive unless it were known whether the wood specimen came from near the outside of the tree or not, but if it did agree with that in the description it would provide additional confirmation. Two further characters could be checked from the description: the vessel arrangement, which is ring-porous, and the presence of marginal cells in the rays.

The key need not have been constructed in the way suggested; other pairs of alternatives might have been selected and the same result achieved. It may be objected that, in spite of what has been written about the disadvantage of using colour in a key, this feature has in fact been used in this example. This is true, but it was used only at a point in the key where it could not possibly have given rise to confusion, unless the unknown specimen had been dyed or stained. As a precaution, however, ray width was associated with colour at this dichotomy. Another objection might be raised to the alternatives in 5, in that the first refers to the rays as being storeyed, while the second makes no mention of their arrangement. This, however, is permissible, for in general rays are not storeyed and the feature is only noted when it occurs; hence the fact that it is not mentioned in the second alternative implies that the rays are not storeyed.

The key just outlined is, of course, an extremely simple one and it was convenient, in describing the six fictitious timbers, to give them characters by which they might readily be separated. A group of real timbers, especially if it is large, is less accommodating, and sometimes in the use of a key it may not be possible to decide with certainty between two alternatives. This may be due to faulty construction of the key, or it may be inherent in the method, which is, admittedly, a short cut. The use of more than one pair of characters at each step in the key may then be a great help and a safeguard against error.

It may also be asked whether a key need be based on microscopic features, or if features visible to the unaided eye or with a hand-lens might be used. Useful keys to hardwoods have been constructed on their gross features alone, and are of practical value in that they can be used when no microscope is available, but in hardwood keys it may be necessary, or at least, very desirable, to refer to microscopic characters on occasion. Gross features might also be used extensively in a softwood key, although to use them to full advantage it would be necessary to refer to quite large specimens for the key to be satisfactory in use. In general, much greater use would be made of microscopic characters in the construction of a softwood key than in making a key for hardwoods.

Keys for the identification of common hardwoods and of common softwoods will be found at the end of this chapter and in Chapter 17; they should afford practice in the use of this method of identifying unknown woods.

A serious objection to the dichotomous key is that the features it uses must be referred to in a definite order, and a point may be reached in the key where the character of the unknown specimen is such that it is not possible to decide between the two alternatives offered; if this is so it is impossible to proceed with the identification. This obstacle may be partly overcome by skill in constructing the key. Thus it may be possible to anticipate the difficulty by putting a wood which is likely to give trouble at an early step in the key in both alternative groups at that point, and separating it at some later dichotomy; however, this is not very practicable in a long key. A second failing of dichotmous keys is their inflexibility; once constructed they cannot be extended to include new timbers without being completely revised.

Some systems of identification are not open to these objections. One such is that proposed by Swain (1927, 1928). The method has not been generally adopted, and need receive no more than brief mention here. It appears, perhaps, to be rather too elaborate, but as this comment is not based on practical experience of the method, it ought not to be regarded as serious criticism.

Swain's description of any timber is summarised in the form of a number which consists of an integer and five decimals, for hardwoods, and an integer and two decimals for softwoods. Thus European ash (*Fraxinus excelsior* L.) is designated 8·78720, box (*Buxus semper-virens* L.) is 19·49501 and yellow pine (*Pinus strobus* L.) is 4·56.

Each numeral denotes some character of the timber. The integer gives the approximate density of the wood, and for hardwoods, an indication of the size of the vessels. The first decimal numeral indicates whether the wood is pale or distinctly coloured, as well as the number of rays in a standard area of transverse surface. For hardwoods, the second decimal figure indicates the number of vessels, in relation to their size, in a standard area of transverse surface, while for softwoods it designates such features as odour, taste and fissility. The third place of decimals is used to indicate vessel arrangement, i.e. ring-porous or diffuse-porous and the arrangement of pore multiples; the fourth concerns parenchyma, as it appears in transverse section, and also the regularity of the rays. Properties such as smell, taste and colour are registered by the fifth decimal figure.

On Swain's system, the formula for European ash (8·78720) means:

8   Wood moderately light (37·5–50 lbs. per cubic foot, air-dry). Vessels easily visible to the unaided eye.

0·7   51–75 rays in a circle of 5 mm. diameter on a transverse surface: wood light coloured.

0·08   221 or more vessels in a circle of 5 mm. diameter on a transverse surface.

0·007   Ring-porous. Pore multiples rare; generally, at most two contiguous vessels.

0·0002   Rays regular; parenchyma apotracheal.[1]

0·00000   Wood fissile.

and for yellow pine (4·56):

4   Wood very light (below 37·5 lbs. per cubic foot, air-dry). Resin ducts present. Non-porous.

0·5   36–50 rays in a circle of 5 mm. in diameter on a transverse surface. Wood light coloured.

0·06   Wood without odour or taste. Ash more or less tawny. Wood fissile.

Allowance is made for variation in any timber by giving another numeral, or even two, o indicate the maximum variation in that wood. Thus after careful study of an unfamiliar wood it should be possible to write down its formula and compare this with those of known woods.

Pfeiffer and Varossieau (1946) also make use of a decimal system to summarise the characteristic features of hardwoods. The system is considerably more elaborate than that of Swain, the features being designated by letters and numerals arranged in columns. Reference must be made to the original paper for details of the system, and also for a critical summary of other systems which have been proposed.

Two other systems make use of perforated cards. In that of Bianchi (1931), a red card is divided into rectangles in each of which is placed the name of a genus or species of timber. A number of white cards of similar size and divided up in the same manner, are also required. A white card is allocated to each feature used for identification, the rectangle allocated to any timber (which corresponds to that on the red card), being cut out if that timber possesses the feature to which the card is allotted. When it is desired to identify an unknown timber, a feature shown by this timber recorded on one of the white cards, is selected and this card is laid over the red card so that the rectangles of the two correspond. Thus only the names of those timbers possessing the feature in question remain visible on the red card. A second feature is now chosen and its white card superimposed on the first one, thus

---

[1] This would appear to be an error. It possibly refers to parenchyma at the end of the growth ring.

eliminating some more timber names from the red card. The process is repeated until finally, if the unknown wood is represented on the red card, this name alone remains uncovered and the identification is complete.

Clarke (1938b, 1939) utilised a punched card system, adapting it for the identification of hardwoods (see also F.P.R.L., 1952, 1953, 1961) while Phillips (1948) made use of the same system for softwoods.

The cards used measure 8 in. × 5 in. : they have one corner removed and are perforated round the edges. One card is used for each wood to be included in the key. Each marginal hole is allocated some feature of diagnostic value, and if that feature is present in a particular wood, its hole, on the appropriate card, is notched out to the edge. The pack of cards is then ready for use. The wood to be identified is examined and any distinctive feature which it may possess, and which is recorded on the cards, is chosen. A long needle or wire is pushed through the appropriate hole in the pack and the pack is shaken. All the cards having this hole notched out fall from the pack, and these are then assembled into a smaller pack, the truncated corner making it possible to orientate all the cards correctly. Other features are used in a similar way until a single card falls out; this should bear the name of the timber it is desired to identify.

Clarke recommends that the appropriate hole be notched even if the timber is "border-line" for the feature in question, while where the timber is variable the hole should not be notched, but the un-notched margin of the hole should be marked with an ink line. In a few instances it may be found that more than one card is necessary for one timber, to cover all possible contingencies. These precautions may not be necessary for identification alone, for it is for the user to select clear well-marked characters; they are, however, useful when it is desired to use the cards to obtain descriptions of timbers. This can readily be accomplished, since the characters of a wood are of course recorded in some detail on its card.

Of special interest in its practical application was the adoption of this system for military purposes in the Pacific during the last war (Dadswell, Eckersley, Griffin and Ingle 1947). Characters requiring the use of a microscope were not used, but the keys were so adapted that they served to determine the uses, strength and durability of timbers, as well as for their identification. The cards appear to have been used successfully even by untrained personnel.

For the two dichotomous keys which follow, the timbers already described in Chapters 13 and 14 are used. It must be emphasised that these do not represent the only ways in which these timbers might have been "keyed". The student who wishes to obtain practice in constructing dichotomous keys might learn much about these devices by attempting to construct alternative keys for some or all of these woods, selecting from the characters which have been given in the relevant chapters.

KEY TO SOME COMMON COMMERCIAL HARDWOODS

1. Ring-porous or semi-ring-porous, with vessels
   of pore ring considerably larger than those of
   late wood   2
   Diffuse-porous, or, if ring-porous, vessels of pore
   ring not much larger than those of late wood .   6

2. Parenchyma apotracheal   3
   Parenchyma not apotracheal   4

3. Large rays easily visible to unaided eye and
   2·5 cms. or more high .   .   .   .   .   *Quercus*
   Rays not visible without lens .   .   .   .   *Carya*

4. Vessels of late wood in undulating tangential lines   *Ulmus*
   Vessels of late wood not in undulating tangential
   lines   5

5. Vessels of late wood few, single or paired, within
   parenchyma sheath .   .   .   .   .   *Fraxinus*
   Vessels of late wood fairly numerous, in oblique
   (more or less tangential) lines   .   .   .   *Castanea*

6. Some rays, at least, distinctly visible to unaided eye   7
   Rays not distinctly visible to unaided eye .   .   11

7. Pits of vessels scalariform   .   .   .   .   *Magnolia*
   Pits of vessels not scalariform   8

8. Vessels in long radial chains .   .   .   .   *Ilex*
   Vessels not in long radial chains   .   .   .   9

9. Vessel perforations exclusively scalariform   .   *Alnus*
   Vessel perforations not, or seldom scalariform .   10

10. Vessels with abundant spiral thickening   .   .   *Acer*
    Vessels without spiral thickening   .   .   .   *Fagus*

11. Rays uniseriate   12
    Some rays, at least, multiseriate   .   .   .   14

12. Vessels with abundant spiral thickening   .   .   *Aesculus*
    Vessels without spiral thickening   .   .   .   13

13. Rays homogeneous; pits of ray cells in 2–3 hori-
    zontal rows   .   .   .   .   .   .   *Populus*
    Rays heterogeneous; pits of ray cells in 3–5 hori-
    zontal rows.   .   .   .   .   .   .   *Salix*

14. Vessel perforations simple   15
    Vessel perforations scalariform   .   .   .   16

15. Vessels clustered; with spiral thickening   .   .   *Tilia*
    Vessels not clustered; without spiral thickening .   *Juglans*

16. Scalariform perforations with 10 or fewer bars .   *Liriodendron*
    Scalariform perforations with 15 or more bars   .   17

17. Rays   heterogeneous: distinct   fibre-tracheids
    abundant .   .   .   .   *Liquidambar*
    Rays homogeneous: distinct fibre-tracheids not
    present   .   .   .   .   *Betula*

KEY TO SOME COMMERCIAL SOFTWOODS

1. Ray tracheids always present 2
   Ray tracheids normally absent 10
2. Resin canals always present 3
   Resin canals normally absent 8
3. Resin canals with thin-walled epithelial cells . 4
   Resin canals with thick-walled epithelial cells . 6
4. Ray tracheids dentate 5
   Ray tracheids smooth . . . . . *Pinus* (Soft Pine Group)
5. Cross-field pits 1, rarely 2; large, window-like . *Pinus* (Scots Pine or Red Deal Group)
   Cross-field pits 3–6, pinoid . . . . *Pinus* (Pitch Pine Group)
6. Spiral thickening normally abundant. . . *Pseudotsuga*
   Spiral thickening not normally present . . 7
7. Fusiform rays often with excentric resin canal: sudden change from early to late wood . . *Larix*
   Fusiform rays sometimes with excentric resin canal; gradual change from early to late wood *Picea*
8. Rays high (sometimes exceeding 40 cells); margin of torus of bordered pit scalloped . . . *Cedrus*
   Rays low (rarely exceeding 16 cells); margin of torus of bordered pit not scalloped . . 9
9. Ray parenchyma often resinous; late wood conspicuous; pit membranes of axial tracheids with radial horizontal bars . . . . *Tsuga*
   Ray parenchyma not resinous; late wood inconspicuous . . . . . . *Chamaecyparis nootkatensis*
10. Axial tracheids with abundant spiral thickening . *Taxus*
    Axial tracheids without spiral thickening . 11
11. Multiseriate pitting frequent on axial tracheids . 12
    Multiseriate pitting infrequent or absent on axial tracheids 15
12. Multiseriate pitting on axial tracheids alternate . *Agathis* and *Araucaria*
    Multiseriate pitting on axial tracheids opposite . 13
13. Rays conspicuously large-celled, commonly in part biseriate . . . . . . *Sequoia*
    Rays not conspicuously large-celled, not frequently biseriate 14
14. Rays usually not over 12 cells high; pits on axial tracheids at most in 2 rows . . . . *Thuja plicata*
    Rays usually not over 16 cells high; pits on axial tracheids in 2, 3 or even 4 rows . . . *Taxodium*
15. Some rays tall, exceeding 15 cells in height . 16
    All rays short, rarely exceeding 12 cells in height 17

16. End walls of ray cells nodular; horizontal walls of
    ray cells strongly pitted   .   .   .   .   *Abies*
    End walls of ray cells not nodular; horizontal
    walls of ray cells thin, not pitted[1] .   .   .   *Podocarpus*
17. Wood with pungent smell and unpleasant spicy
    taste .   .   .   .   *Chamaecyparis*
                                                  lawsoniana
    Scent not pungent, taste not unpleasant   .   .   18
18. Intercellular spaces between tracheids frequent;
    ray cells commonly filled with dark resin   .   *Juniperus*
    Intercellular spaces between tracheids uncommon
    or absent; ray cells not commonly filled with
    dark resin   19
19. Transition from early wood to late wood abrupt   *Thuja plicata*
    Transition from early wood to late wood gradual   20
20. Heartwood pale-brown; parenchyma sparse   .   *Thuja occidentalis*
    Heartwood reddish-brown or pinkish; paren-
    chyma abundant .   .   .   .   .   .   *Chamaecyparis*
                                                    thyoides

[1] In certain species of *Podocarpus* the horizontal walls of the ray cells are pitted

2A

CHAPTER 16

THE IDENTIFICATION OF SOME COMMON TIMBERS

III. TEAK, MAHOGANY AND WALNUT

In the preceding chapters on identification some common commercial woods were selected to illustrate the application of the study of wood anatomy to identification. No attempt was made to limit this selection to timbers which were closely related botanically, or to those which might be confused in commerce. Consideration was, however, given to some such woods, for examples, ash and hickory; silver fir and spruce. In this chapter the emphasis will be shifted to problems of identification within groups of woods which are commonly associated in use, or in the possession of similar trade names.[1] Attention will be given to teak and the teaks so-called, to some of the mahoganies, real and false, and to the commoner woods known commercially as walnut.

There are several reasons for a new timber receiving the name of some well-known one, qualified of course by an appropriate (or sometimes inappropriate) prefix. The name may be that of the tree producing the wood, and applied to that tree because of some real or fancied resemblance to a more familiar tree. Again, the timber itself may be so named from a real or supposed resemblance to some well-known wood, either from want of a better name or in the hope that it will be more favourably received, for users not unnaturally adopt a cautious attitude towards new woods. The name may even be a deliberate attempt to mislead and to market an inferior wood under the guise of one of known merit. Consequently, it would not be correct to regard all such woods as substitutes for better-known ones, nor, on the other hand, to assume that they are necessarily inferior in all circumstances to the woods whose names they bear. Thus iroko (African teak) is as durable as teak and in some ways as good a wood, but it does not possess all the qualities of teak, and thus for some purposes, such as the decking of marine craft, it is inferior to teak.

In this chapter the somewhat different approach to identification will be apparent. Our concern here is not so much to identify the woods as such, but to distinguish the different timbers of an artificial group. It will be assumed that the woods fall into one or other of these groups and the differences between the several woods in a group will be examined.

---

[1] It is not intended to suggest that these names are the commonest ones in use. For every wood mentioned the proposed standard name (B.S. 881 and 589: 1955) is shown in heavy type, although it does not necessarily follow that this name is the one which is generally accepted in the timber trade or by users of the wood.

TEAK

It is not surprising that a wood with the outstanding merits of teak should have substitutes, nor that some of these should be by no means second-rate timbers. Nevertheless, whatever their worth, no other woods possess exactly the same properties as teak.

Teak is produced by *Tectona grandis* L.f., a member of the family Verbenaceae and is found in India, Burma, Thailand and parts of the East Indies. It is always possible that samples of African origin may be encountered, although teak is not a native of Africa and only grows there where it has been planted in experimental plantations. Thus commercial supplies are most unlikely to derive from Africa. A second species of *Tectona* grows in Burma; this is *T. hamiltoniana* Wall., the timber of which goes by the trade name of dahat. Not much is known about dahat, which is much harder and heavier than teak and very unlikely to be used as a teak substitute.

Of timbers to which the name teak is sometimes applied, the more important are:

African or *Nigerian teak*, better called **iroko**, odum or mvule, the wood of *Chlorophora excelsa* Benth. et Hook. f. and *C. regia* A.Chev., trees widely distributed in tropical Africa and members of the Moraceae.

Eng teak, for which the names **eng** or in are to be preferred. This is the product of *Dipterocarpus tuberculatus* Roxb. and of at least one other species of the same genus. The wood comes from Burma and Thailand, and the trees belong to the Dipterocarpaceae.

Borneo teak is a name which has been applied to several distinct timbers. It has been used for the wood of species of *Dryobalanops*, also known as **kapur**, kapor, Borneo camphorwood (and sometimes, not very appropriately, as Mahoborn teak), as well as for timber known as **selangan batu** derived from species of *Hopea* and *Shorea*. All three genera belong to the family Dipterocarpaceae. **Merbau**, the wood of *Intsia bijuga* O.Ktze. and *I. palembanica* Miq., members of the Leguminosae, is also sometimes called Borneo teak.

Rhodesian teak comes from *Baikiaea plurijuga* Harms., also a member of the Leguminosae and sometimes known as Zambesi redwood: it is found in tropical Africa.

This is not an exhaustive list of woods to which the name teak, with some qualifying prefix, has been applied, but it includes the commoner "teaks" over which confusion is likely to arise. Within the limits of the list there is little likelihood of mistaking teak for any of the other woods, for none bears a close resemblance to it, except, sometimes, in colour, and all may be distinguished from it with the unaided eye, or at most with the help of a hand-lens.

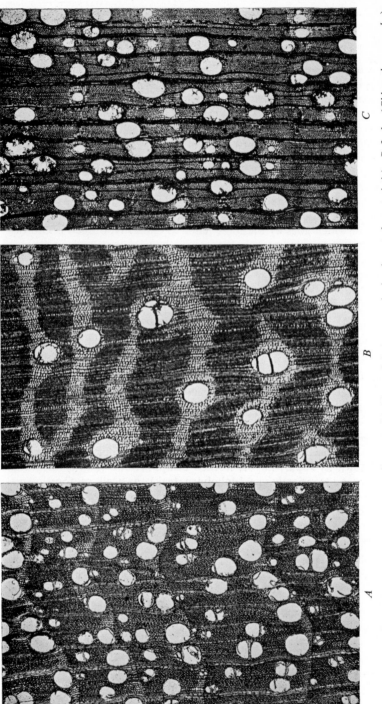

Fig. 164.—Transverse sections of: A. Teak (*Tectona grandis*) (the undulating growth ring is not characteristic); B. Iroko (*Chlorophora excelsa*); C. Eng (*Dipterocarpus tuberculatus*). In Eng the axial canals are solitary or in short tangential rows and are surrounded by a fairly broad zone of parenchyma. (All × 27.)

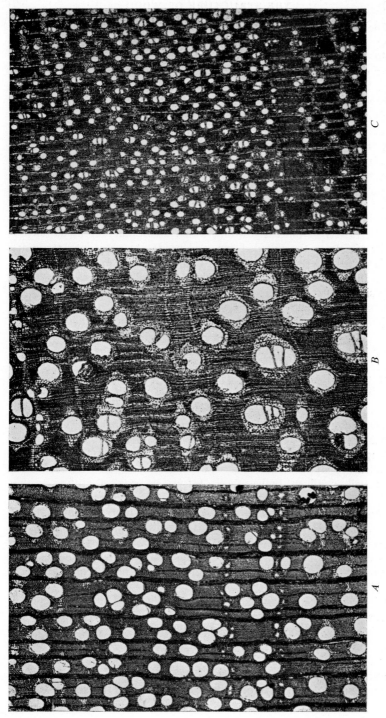

Fig. 165.—Transverse sections of: *A*. Kapur (*Dryobalanops oblongifolia*); *B*. Merbau (*Intsia bakeri*); *C*. Rhodesian Teak (*Baikiaea plurijuga*). In Kapur the axial canals are commonly in long tangential lines; two such lines pass right across the figure. (All × 27.)

The heartwood of teak is generally of a golden-brown colour, sometimes marked with dark streaks; it darkens with age. The sapwood is white or pale yellowish-brown. The wood is rather coarse-textured and has a dull and commonly oily appearance, although it is not invariably oily. When fresh it possesses a characteristic, slightly pungent odour, reminiscent of burnt leather. Viewed under a ×8 or ×10 lens, the transverse surface of teak normally shows well-marked growth rings which are distinct, in fact, to the unaided eye (Figs. 164 A, 166 A). They are conspicuous because of a zone of parenchyma at the beginning of each ring (initial parenchyma) which is paler in colour than the later wood. Usually there is, as well, a conspicuous pore ring embedded in the parenchyma, though it is not always well-developed, and the wood might then be more accurately termed semi-ring-porous; some samples may be virtually diffuse-porous.

The vessels of the early wood, which are solitary or in pairs, are easily visible to the unaided eye, and grade gradually into medium-sized vessels and thence into smaller ones in the outer part of the growth ring. In the heartwood, tyloses are frequent in the vessels. White deposits of apatite (an impure form of calcium phosphate) may occur in some vessels, while others may contain deposits of a gummy nature which are yellowish- to reddish-brown in colour and which either fill the vessel cavity or merely form a lining to it. The rays, which are paler in colour than the rest of the tissue, may just be seen with the unaided eye.

In iroko, the colour of the wood varies from pale golden-brown to dark-brown. The wood possesses little lustre but it is never oily and has no characteristic smell. It is strictly diffuse-porous and the boundaries of the growth rings are not usually well defined (Figs. 164 B, 166 B). Its vessels are generally solitary but they may be in radially arranged pairs or even in larger multiples. They are visible to the unaided eye and are embedded in broad zones of parenchyma, which are usually confluent between adjacent vessels or vessel groups. In the early wood of the seasonal increment, the parenchyma may not be confluent, while in the outermost wood of the ring, the parenchyma bands may be straighter, more continuous and somewhat finer than those in the middle of the ring. The vessels may have tyloses or they may be filled with white mineral deposits consisting largely of calcium carbonate. On the transverse face the rays are barely visible to the unaided eye.

Dipterocarpaceous woods which pass under the name of teak may be recognised by certain general features which characterise the woods of this family. Of these, the most conspicuous, in transverse section, is what may be termed the untidy arrangement of the numerous vessels (Figs. 164 C, 165 A), for they are irregularly distributed, so that there are areas where the vessels are crowded and adjacent ones where they are more sparse. Furthermore, the vessels seen on a transverse surface

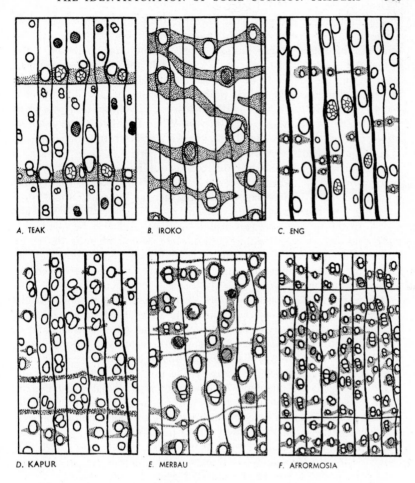

A. TEAK   B. IROKO   C. ENG

D. KAPUR   E. MERBAU   F. AFRORMOSIA

Fig. 166.—Simplified (caricature) drawings of transverse sections of teak and so-
called teaks: *A.* Teak; *B.* Iroko; *C.* Eng; *D.* Kapur; *E.* Merbau; *F.* Afrormosia.
Parenchyma is stippled; gummy material in vessels is hatched; "white deposits"
in vessels are cross-hatched; tyloses are also indicated in some of the vessels.

always have the appearance of deep holes; this feature is accounted for
by the straight courses which the vessels normally pursue, as may be
seen by the long vessel lines on the longitudinal surfaces. Another
characteristic feature is the presence of axial intercellular canals,
often filled with gum or mineral deposits and occurring in tangential
rows. Such canals are rarely absent from a specimen and they may be
very abundant.

Accurate determination of dipterocarpaceous timbers is not an easy matter. Eng and selangan batu have the intercellular canals in short tangential rows, embedded in parenchyma (Figs. 164 C, 166 C,) whereas in kapur these canals form continuous tangential rows (Figs. 165 A, 166 D). Moreover, in kapur, but not in eng and selangan batu, ripple marks are to be seen on tangential faces, for the rays are storeyed. Eng is a lustreless timber, generally of a reddish-brown colour; selangan batu is also without lustre and yellowish-brown when fresh cut, darkening to a greyish-brown. When freshly cut, the wood of kapur is readily identified by the fact that it smells strongly of camphor; it is dull and reddish-brown in colour.

Merbau wood has a slightly oily feel, is dull and of a brown to dark reddish-brown hue. On the transverse surface (Figs. 165 B, 166 E) thin concentric lines of parenchyma will be seen at intervals; these, presumably, are the limits of the growth rings. The vessels, which are visible to the unaided eye, are usually solitary and may be filled with dark contents or with sulphur-yellow ones. A conspicuous sheath of aliform parenchyma occurs around each vessel, and vessels may be linked by confluent parenchyma. The rays are fine and barely visible to the unaided eye.

Rhodesian teak possesses more lustre than the woods already described, and has a closer texture. On an average, it is decidedly heavier than the timbers so far considered, although merbau may be as heavy. In colour, the heartwood is brown to red-brown, and may show lighter and darker colours in alternating bands, as well as irregular dark streaks. Its vessels, as seen in transverse section (Fig. 165 C), are small, barely visible to the unaided eye, numerous and regularly distributed. They are sometimes solitary, but often in radial groups of up to about eight vessels, this last a unique feature among the woods under present consideration. A dark-coloured gum frequently fills the vessels. Parenchyma is abundant, both around the vessels and extending tangentially into irregular wavy lines, but this tissue is not very distinct with a lens, much less to the unaided eye. The rays are not visible without a hand-lens, but their storeyed arrangement produces fine ripples marks on the tangential surface.

The structural characters which have been described here as differentiating between teak and the so-called teaks influence the appearance of the timber surfaces sufficiently to enable these woods to be identified in the solid with the unaided eye. The initial parenchyma of teak appears on the plain-sawn wood (Fig. 124 A) as a series of ∧'s or ∩'s and because it is paler in colour than the rest of the wood, it is conspicuous. The large vessels of the pore ring show up as scratches (vessel lines) within these parenchyma hoops. Parenchyma is also conspicuous in merbau and iroko. In the former it appears on the tangential surface as sheaths round the vessel lines. This also applies to iroko (Fig. 170 B) but here the sheaths are connected because the parenchyma is confluent. and since it is somewhat wavy as seen in transverse section, it appears on the tangential face as a series of more or less zig-zag lines. The dipterocarpaceous timbers will be readily distinguished from the rest by their uniform appearance on the longitudinal surfaces; probably the only conspicuous feature will be the very long vessel lines, due to the straight courses which the vessels pursue. On the tangential surface of kapur, ripple marks will be seen, a feature shared only with Rhodesian teak, which, however, lacks the long vessel lines and in which these lines are inconspicuous to the unaided eye, because of their small size.

Although it has not been called a teak, the timber known as **afrormosia** or kokrodua (*Afrormosia elata* Harms.), which comes from parts of tropical West Africa, has proved to be a valuable alternative to teak, particularly on account of its stability. This wood has a fairly fine texture and a yellowish-brown colour, with fairly well-marked growth rings, abundant paratracheal and confluent parenchyma and storeyed rays (Figs. 170 *A*, 166 *F*). The only one of the woods just considered, with which it might possibly be confused, is iroko. It differs from iroko in a number of characters, of which the most useful are its storeyed rays, finer texture and more numerous and much smaller vessels.

The following key should serve to distinguish the teaks, but it suffers from the limitations of all keys, in that, at each step, emphasis is placed upon a single character, or at most two, instead of upon several:

1. Parenchyma conspicuous to unaided eye on
   tangential face   2
   Parenchyma inconspicuous or not visible to unaided eye on tangential face   5
2. Parenchyma initial . . . . . .   *Tectona grandis*
                                          (Teak)

   Parenchyma not initial   3
3. Parenchyma mostly aliform . . . .   *Intsia* spp.
                                          (Merbau)

   Parenchyma mostly confluent   4
4. Ripple marks present . . . . .   *Afrormosia elata*
                                          (Afrormosia)

   Ripple marks absent . . . . .   *Chlorophora* spp.
                                          (Iroko)

5. Vessel lines conspicuous to unaided eye on longitudinal surfaces   6
   Vessel lines scarcely visible to unaided eye on
   longitudinal surfaces . . . . .   *Baikiaea plurijuga*
                                          (Rhodesian teak)

6. Ripple marks present . . . . .   *Dryobalanops* spp.
                                          (Kapur)

   Ripple marks absent . . . . .   *Dipterocarpus* spp.
                                          (Eng), *Hopea* spp.,
                                          Shorea spp.
                                          (Selangan Batu)

MAHOGANIES

Mahogany has been popular for so long as a cabinet wood that it inevitably has a host of substitutes; many woods, completely unrelated to mahogany, bear its name. Any wood which approximates to it, even remotely, in colour and texture, seems to qualify for the magic name mahogany. The mahoganies of commerce are thus a huge and motley collection of timbers; here only a selection of the more important ones can be considered.

American mahogany is produced by trees of the genus *Swietenia*, which is exclusively American. There are two principal commercial species:

S. mahagoni Jacq., which gives Cuban, Spanish or West Indian mahogany, and

S. macrophylla King, which furnishes the bulk of Central American mahogany, Honduras mahogany or baywood.

Venezuelan mahogany is produced by *S. candollei* Pitt while other species may produce mahogany coming from Brazil, Peru and Mexico.

African mahogany derives from trees of *Khaya*, a genus confined to tropical Africa. Most of that from the west coast is produced from *K. ivorensis* A. Chev., a species of the West African coastal forest belt. *K. grandifoliolia* C.DC. occurs in areas of lower rainfall and hence farther from the West African coast, ranging eastwards to Uganda. *K. anthotheca* C.DC., which is also distributed between the Ivory Coast and Uganda, likewise occurs in areas of lower rainfall than those favoured by *K. ivorensis*. *K. nyasica* Stapf, known as umbaua, as well as under the general name African mahogany, derives from Central and East Africa, while *K. senegalensis* A.Juss., of West and Central Africa, is dry-zone mahogany. Mahoganies shipped from the West African coast are often known commercially by their port of shipment: thus Axim, Grand Bassam, Lagos and Takoradi mahogany are all, in the main, the timber of *K. ivorensis* and hence are not botanically distinct. An expert can often guess at the port of shipment with a reasonable degree of accuracy. He will detect differences in the texture of the wood and in its soundness, depending on the conditions under which supplies to a particular port normally grow; in the way the logs have been prepared in the forest for shipment and even in the condition of the outside of the logs. Shipment in most ports is by floating the logs to the ship standing off-shore, and bruising of the logs may occur to a greater extent on a rocky shore than on a sandy one.

Timber of African mahogany is variable in quality, due in part to its origin from different species of *Khaya*, but particularly to variation in the conditions under which the trees have grown (Rendle, 1956).

Both *Khaya* and *Swietenia* are members of the family Meliaceae, a large family confined to the warmer parts of the earth, and usually known as the mahogany family. Other genera of the Meliaceae which produce woods of the mahogany type are referred to below.

Entandrophragma is an African genus of about ten species. **Sapele** (formerly known as sapele mahogany) derives from *E. cylindricum* Sprague, which ranges from tropical West Africa to Uganda. Heavy sapele, or **omu**, for which there is not much demand in Europe, is produced by *E. candollei* Harms. Occasional logs come out with West African parcels of **gedu nohor**, or tiama, which is derived in the main from *E. angolense* C.DC., a tree of tropical East and West Africa. Gedu nohor, in its turn, may be mixed with parcels of sapele logs. *E. utile* Sprague gives the timber known as **utile**, assié or sipo, and is found in West Africa and Uganda.

Guarea is an African and American genus. The timbers of the African species are marketed as **guarea**, or sometimes distinguished as white guarea (*G. cedrata* Pellegr.) and black guarea (*G. thompsonii* Sprague et Hutch.). The Central American *G. excelsa* H.B.K. known as cramantee and sometimes also as guarea, produces a wood which has received favourable notice.

Dysoxylum is a predominantly Indo-Malayan genus, of which *D. fraseranum* Benth., of eastern Australia, produces rose mahogany, Australian mahogany or rosewood. There are many other meliaceous woods, such as African walnut (*Lovoa*), the "cigar box" cedars (*Cedrela* spp.) and avodiré (*Turraeanthus*), which are not reckoned commercially among the mahoganies.

Of the more important woods of other families, for which the name mahogany is used, are:

Aucoumea klaineana Pierre (family Burseraceae) from West Africa, which produces **gaboon**, gaboon mahogany or okoumé.

Shorea, Parashorea and *Pentacme* (family Dipterocarpaceae) from which come Philippine mahogany, the **lauans** of the Philippines; the **serayas** of North Borneo and the **merantis** of Malaya, Sarawak and Indonesia.

Pentace burmanica Kurz. (family Tiliaceae) of Burma, producing Burma mahogany or *thitka*.

Mimusops (*Dumoria*) *heckelii* Hutch. et Dalz. (family Sapotaceae), the cherry mahogany or **makoré** of West Africa.

As with the teaks, hand-lens characters are sufficient to separate these timbers. Viewed on an end-grain surface the American mahoganies (Figs. 167 *A*, *B*, 171 *A*) are characterised by the presence of fairly prominent rays (which are just visible to the unaided eye, especially if the wood is wet); by the more or less even distribution of the vessels over the season's growth; and by the presence of concentric rings of parenchyma, called terminal parenchyma, because it is supposed to mark the end of the season's growth. The vessels, seen in transverse sections, show a feature which is conspicuous, but by no means unique, in the Meliaceae, in that they seldom lie midway between two rays, but are usually nearer to one than the other. Some of these vessels contain a dark red gum; others, white mineral deposits. There is a little paren-

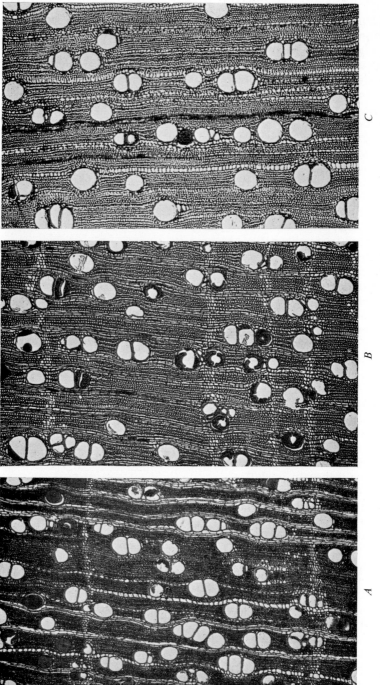

Fig. 167.—Transverse sections of: *A.* Cuban Mahogany (*Swietenia mahagoni*); *B.* Central American Mahogany (*Swietenia macrophylla*); *C.* African Mahogany (*Khaya ivorensis*). (All × 27.)

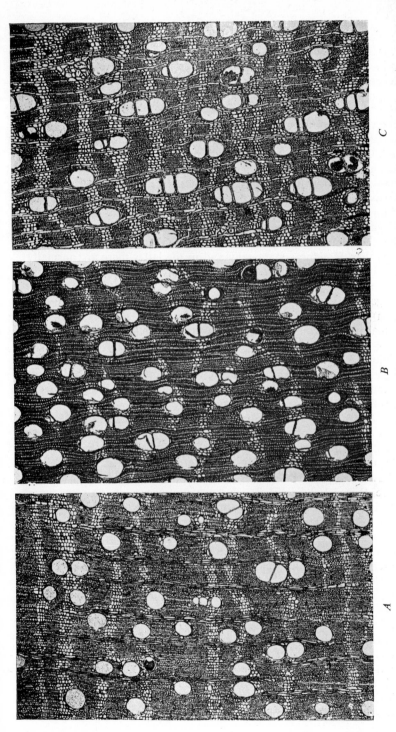

Fig. 168.—Transverse sections of: *A*. Sapele (*Entandrophragma cylindricum*); *B*. Guarea (*Guarea cedrata*); *C*. Australian Mahogany (*Dysoxylum fraseranum*). (All × 27.)

chyma around the vessels, but this is not prominent. The parenchyma, rays included, is always a buff colour. The rays are storeyed, 3–4 cells wide, and are characterised by having distinct marginal cells. The fibres are septate. Both marginal ray cells and septate fibres are characteristic of the Meliaceae, though neither occurs in all members of the family. The timbers of the species of *Swietenia* cannot be distinguished with certainty, but generally that of Honduras mahogany is less dense than that of Cuban mahogany, weighing about 34 lbs. per cubic foot (air-dry) as compared with the 40–50 lbs. per cubic foot of the finer-textured Cuban mahogany. The colour of Honduras mahogany varies from yellowish-brown to light reddish-brown, or a rich dark red, while that of Cuban mahogany is a rich reddish-brown. The colour of Cuban mahogany, however, depends on its age; when freshly cut it is yellowish-white, then darkening to a reddish-brown. Cuban mahogany has more vessels than Honduras mahogany and in the latter there are normally fewer vessels with white deposits and more with red gum than in Cuban mahogany, while ripple marks are more prominent in Honduras mahogany, for its rays are more regularly storeyed than are those of Cuban mahogany. In both timbers plain-sawn surfaces show the terminal parenchyma as ∧- or ∩-shaped lines, but this feature is not always prominent unless the surface is illuminated from the right direction. Venezuelan mahogany is described as being similar to Cuban mahogany, although Brazier and Franklin (1961) could not distinguish commercial specimens of Brazilian, Peruvian and Bolivian origin from Central American *S. macrophylla*.

In *Khaya ivorensis*, which produces the bulk of African mahogany, the wood is pink when freshly sawn, varying, after exposure, from pinkish-brown to deep reddish-brown. The vessels, which may contain dark gum deposits, are usually rather larger than those of *Swietenia*, but have the same arrangement, while the wood is of a rather coarser texture (Figs. 167 *C*, 171 *B*). Parenchyma occurs in narrow zones around the vessels. Terminal parenchyma may also occur, but it is not as well-developed as in *Swietenia* and its occurrence is sporadic. Moreover, a terminal band may be incomplete, for it does not always run all the way round the log. Consequently, if there is no terminal parenchyma in a small specimen, it does not follow that there was none in the log; this can only be ascertained by examination of a large area of transverse surface. All the parenchyma is usually pinkish-brown and not of the decidedly buff colour which characterises that of the American mahoganies. In *Khaya* the rays are not regularly storeyed and hence ripple marks are not seen on plain-sawn surfaces. Nor, of course, are the hoops of terminal parenchyma as regular or as prominent as in the American mahoganies.

It is not always possible to distinguish timbers of the different species of African mahogany, but the following details give an indication of the sort of differences which may exist. In *K. ivorensis*, *K. anthotheca*

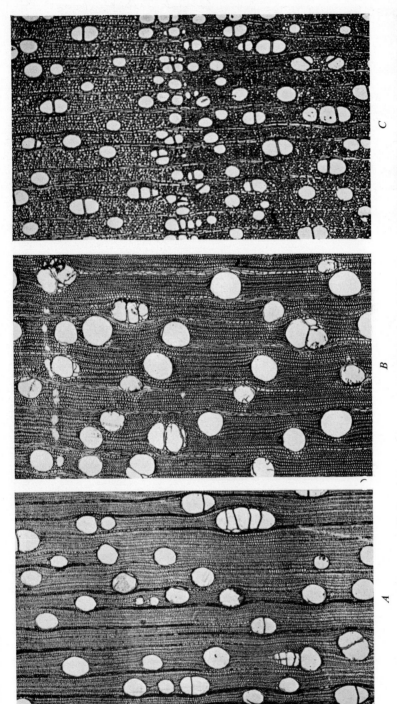

Fig. 169.—Transverse sections of: *A.* Gaboon (*Aucoumea klaineana*); *B.* Red Meranti (*Shorea macroptera*); *C.* Thitka (*Pentace burmanica*). In red meranti a tangential line of axial canals is seen near the top of the illustration. (All × 27.)

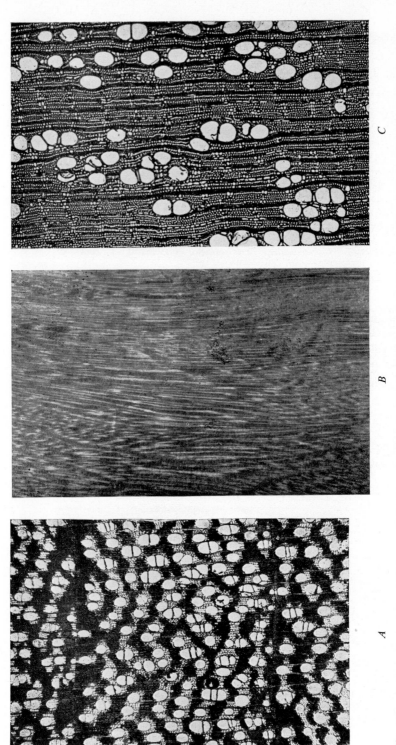

Fig. 170.—*A*. Transverse section of Afrormosia (*Afrormosia elata*) (× 27). *B*. Plain-sawn face of Iroko (*Chlorophora excelsa*) showing zig-zag lines of parenchyma (about natural size). *C*. Transverse section of Makoré (*Mimusops heckelii*) (× 27).

and *K. nyasica*, the timbers have a reddish-brown colour and terminal parenchyma is nearly absent; at most, only occasional, poorly developed bands occur. *K. nyasica*, however, may be somewhat denser than the other two timbers and then it shows some irregularly spaced terminal parenchyma. The wood of *K. senegalensis* is darker in colour than that of the three preceding species, having a deep reddish- to purplish-brown hue and sometimes a rather oily appearance; it is also rather heavier. In this species there are well-developed bands of terminal parenchyma. In *K. grandifoliola* the timber is more or less intermediate in weight (about 45 lbs. per cubic foot) between that of *K. senegalensis* (about 50 lbs. per cubic foot) and *K. ivorensis* (about 35 lbs. per cubic foot). It shows terminal parenchyma, although this is usually less well developed than that in *K. senegalensis*. There are also certain chemical differences: see Morgan and Orsler (1967). For a more detailed account of the differences between the timbers of the Uganda species, *K. nyasica*, *K. anthotheca* and *K. senegalensis*, reference should be made to Eggeling and Harris (1939) and Brazier and Franklin (1961).

Sapele, the most important timber deriving from the genus *Entandrophragma*, weighs about 40 lbs. per cubic foot when seasoned, and is generally a darker brown colour than most African mahoganies. It also has a rather finer texture, for both vessels and rays are small, being barely visible to the unaided eye. Parenchyma is generally abundant (Figs. 168 *A*, 171 *C*), although it is seldom conspicuous, since it is rather dark and does not contrast much with the rest of the wood tissue Terminal parenchyma is present as narrow bands, although it is often incompletely developed. In addition, there are numerous bands of parenchyma, which may include vessels in their midst, and on longitudinal surfaces these bands may show up as dark, purplish lines. Fine ripple marks are usually present on tangential faces, although the rays are not invariably storeyed.

One rather characteristic feature of sapele is the regularity with which it exhibits interlocked grain, giving rise to stripe or ribbon figure on quarter-sawn surfaces. Interlocked grain, wavy grain (which gives fiddle-back mahogany) as well as other irregularities which produce a number of attractive types of figure, are of common occurrence both in *Swietenia* (especially *S. mahagoni*) and in *Khaya*, although ribbon figure does not seem to occur in nearly as high a proportion of the logs of these trees as it does in those of *Entandrophragma cylindricum*.

Sapele possesses a characteristic, cedar-like scent when fresh and it is to this that the old name, scented mahogany, was due. This odour tends to disappear after a time.

Heavy sapele, as its name implies, is a rather heavier wood than sapele, weighing 45–48 lbs. a cubic foot. It has rather larger vessels than those of sapele and very abundant parenchyma. Its rays are just large enough to be visible to the unaided eye, but they are not very conspicuous because of the dark colour of the wood. These rays are

2B

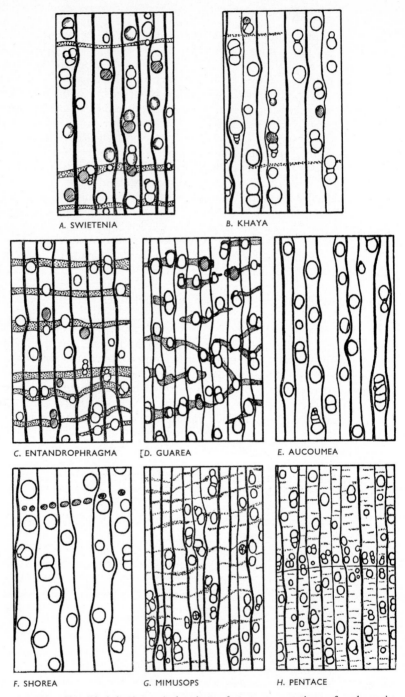

A. SWIETENIA

B. KHAYA

C. ENTANDROPHRAGMA

[D. GUAREA

E. AUCOUMEA

F. SHOREA

G. MIMUSOPS

H. PENTACE

Fig. 171.—Simplified (caricature) drawings of transverse sections of mahoganies and so-called mahoganies. *A*. American Mahogany; *B*. African Mahogany; *C*. Sapele; *D*. Guarea; *E*. Gaboon; *F*. Meranti; *G*. Makoré; *H*. Thitka.
Parenchyma is stippled or shown by dotted lines; gummy material in vessels is hatched.

not usually storeyed, hence ripple marks are absent or, at best, irregular. The wood of heavy sapele has no smell. Gedu nohor, likewise, lacks scent or, at most, is only slightly scented. In this timber, however, there are no long tangential bands of parenchyma, except those which terminate the growth ring, and most of the parenchyma takes the form of occasional short, tangential bands connecting adjacent vessels. In gedu nohor ripple marks are absent, or only occasional, while the rays on the end grain surfaces are just visible to the unaided eye. The wood of *E. utile* resembles sapele, but it has rather larger vessels and is less highly figured. Ripple marks may be present. This timber, again, does not possess a distinctive odour. Eggeling and Harris (1939) give a detailed account of the differences between woods of several species of the genus which occur in Uganda; see also Brazier and Franklin (1961).

The name scented mahogany is also sometimes applied to the African guareas. The commoner white guarea (*G. cedrata*) has a pinkish-brown wood, which darkens less on exposure than other mahoganies, and a fresh cedar-like scent, which is fugitive. In *Guarea cedrata* the vessels are just visible to the unaided eye (Figs. 168 *B*, 171 *D*), solitary, or in radial groups of 2–3 or more, and they sometimes contain dark-coloured gum. The rays are very fine. There is no distinct terminal parenchyma but there are numerous wavy, discontinuous, tangential bands of parenchyma, often joining vessels but sometimes avoiding them. The somewhat heavier, paler[1] and less scented black guarea shows more distinct growth rings and its parenchyma is more conspicuous and in continuous tangential lines. The American *G. excelsa* is rather lighter in weight than *G. cedrata* and has a somewhat coarser texture.

The characters which have been described may suggest that, colour apart, there is little difference between the woods of sapele and guarea as seen with a hand-lens, but the absence of ripple marks in guarea, its smaller rays, the more regularly spaced parenchyma and the more frequent presence of multiple vessels are sufficient to differentiate these timbers.

The wood of Australian rose mahogany closely resembles that of *Guarea* (Fig. 168 *C*). It also, is fragrant, hence the prefix "rose." In general, its vessels are more commonly filled with gummy material, which remains rather fluid and tends to ooze out on surfaces of the wood as dark-coloured, oily-looking patches. Splinters of this wood burn to a white ash, whereas in *G. cedrata* the ash is of a grey colour. The wood is also rather heavier than the guareas, weighing about 45 lbs. a cubic foot, air-dry, as compared with about 40 lbs. in black guarea and 37 lbs. in white guarea.

It may well be asked how far the term mahogany may be legitimately

---

[1] The prefixes white and black refer to the colour of the bark of the tree, not to that of the wood.

used for these woods. If it is agreed to limit it to the woods of the Meliaceae, it is still difficult to decide to which genera to apply the name. Few would now agree with the statement of Record and Mell (1924): "The woods of the different species of *Swietenia* alone are entitled to the name Mahogany, regardless of the quality and characteristics of other woods masquerading under this name." African mahogany has been known for well over 100 years, perhaps a good deal longer, and has some claim to the name. The American Mahogany Association (Lamb, 1948) admits *Swietenia* and *Khaya ivorensis* (and probably other species of *Khaya* as well) into the select circle, while the British Standard (1955) likewise proposes, as standard names, only American mahogany for *Swietenia* and African mahogany for *Khaya*. There is much to be said for a fairly rigid restriction in the use of the name, provided that we are not unduly influenced by the dictates of the more mercenary aspects of commerce, for it is better that a wood of merit should have a distinctive name.

Of the non-meliaceous woods known as mahogany, gaboon or okoumé has a pinkish-brown colour, a light weight (about 27 lbs. per cubic foot, air-dry) and a coarse texture, which features are, in themselves, characteristic. Its vessels, seen in transverse section (Figs. 169 *A*, 171 *E*), are oval and not infrequently in radial chains of two, three or more, and normally without contents. Its rays are fine and tend to bend round the vessels. Growth rings are rarely distinct and parenchyma is inconspicuous. The rays are not storeyed.

The general appearance of dipterocarpaceous timbers has already been noted (p. 364) and these features serve to distinguish a dipterocarpaceous "mahogany" from a meliaceous one (Figs. 169 *B*, 171 *F*). A further characteristic may be the presence of tyloses in the vessels, for these are not common in the meliaceous mahoganies. To attempt a more detailed description would be profitless, for Philippine mahogany is produced by several species of *Shorea* as well as to some extent by *Parashorea* and *Pentacme*. Roughly, the lighter weight woods of these genera come out as Philippine mahogany, lauan, seraya or meranti, depending on their country of origin; the darker ones are distinguished from the light-coloured ones by the prefix red, the light-coloured ones having the prefix white, or for meranti, yellow. Fuller details of the confused nomenclature must be sought by reference to Rendle (1938), British Standards Institution (1955) and Brazier (1956): see also Desch (1941). It should be added that, in addition to their axial intercellular canals, members of the Philippine mahogany group may also possess radial canals in their rays.

Burma mahogany (thitka) is a fine-textured wood of about the same density as Cuban mahogany and of a pleasant red-brown hue. The growth rings are not very distinct and the vessels, which are often in radial chains of 2–3 or sometimes more, are evenly distributed and usually empty (Figs. 169 *C*, 171 *H*). The rays are very fine and not visible to the unaided eye. Parenchyma is present in the form of very fine apotracheal bands, normally only one cell wide, between adjacent rays. This parenchyma may only be discovered with the aid of a microscope. Thitka commonly possesses a narrow ribbon figure and shows fine ripple marks on its tangential faces as distinctly as any wood.

Cherry mahogany or makoré also possesses fine, apotracheal parenchyma, but here it is quite distinct under a hand-lens and even sometimes, to the unaided eye. Its vessels are in short radial chains of 3–4 elements and they are usually devoid of contents (Figs. 170 C, 171 G). The wood is of fine texture, about as heavy as Cuban mahogany and varies from pinkish- to purplish- or reddish-brown in colour. Ripple marks are occasionally present, but are not characteristic of the wood.

KEY TO THE COMMERCIAL MAHOGANIES

1. Ripple marks present 2
   Ripple marks absent 6
2. Terminal parenchyma absent 3
   Terminal parenchyma present and conspicuous . 4
3. Apotracheal parenchyma difficult to see with hand-lens: radial groups of, usually, 2–3 vessels . *Pentace burmanica* (Thitka)

   Apotracheal parenchyma easily seen with hand-lens: radial groups of, usually, 3–4 or more vessels . . . . *Mimusops heckelii* (Makoré)

4. Parenchyma and rays buff-coloured: ripple marks constant . . . . *Swietenia* (American Mahoganies)

   Parenchyma and rays not buff-coloured . . 5
5. Ripple marks constant or nearly constant: cedar-like smell . . . . *Entandrophragma cylindricum* (Sapele)

   Ripple marks irregular: not scented . . . *Entandrophragma candollei* (Heavy Sapele)
   Entandrophragma utile (Utile)

6. Axial intercellular canals frequent . . . *Shorea, Parashorea, Pentacme* (Meranti, Seraya, Lauan)

   Axial intercellular canals absent . . . 7
7. Parenchyma (excluding terminal parenchyma) forming numerous, prominent tangential bands wider than rays 8
   Parenchyma (excluding terminal parenchyma) not forming prominent tangential bands; tangential lines, if present, not wider than rays . 11

8. Vessels predominantly in radial groups   .   . *Dysoxylum frasera-*
                                                 num (Australian
                                                 Mahogany)
   Vessels not predominantly in radial groups   .   9
9. Prominent terminal parenchyma present   .   . *Entandrophragma*
                                                 utile (Utile)
   Prominent terminal parenchyma not present   .   10
10. Parenchyma bands irregularly spaced: rays
    distinct to unaided eye   .   .   .   .   . *Entandrophragma*
                                                 candollei (Heavy
                                                 Sapele)

    Parenchyma bands more or less regularly spaced:
    rays scarcely visible to unaided eye   .   . *Guarea* (Guarea)
11. Numerous fine lines of apotracheal parenchyma
    forming network with rays   .   .   .   . *Mimusops heckelii*
                                                 (Makoré)
    Parenchyma and rays not forming network   .   12
12. Rays distinct to unaided eye   .   .   .   . *Khaya* (African
                                                 Mahoganies)[1]
    Rays barely visible to unaided eye   .   .   .   13
13. Terminal parenchyma present: dark red gum
    common in vessels   .   .   .   .   . *Entandrophragma*
                                                 angolense (Gedu
                                                 Nohor)
    Terminal parenchyma absent: gum in vessels
    infrequent .   .   .   . *Aucoumea klaineana*
                                                 (Gaboon)

[1] May, exceptionally, possess axial intercellular canals.

WALNUTS

Walnut, like mahogany, enjoys immense popularity as a cabinet
wood, and like mahogany, has a host of substitutes which can be distinguished without difficulty from the genuine wood.

The true walnut woods are produced by trees of the genus *Juglans*
(family Juglandaceae). This genus is widely distributed, and species
occur wild from south-eastern Europe to eastern Asia, in North
America and in parts of South America. *J. regia* L. is the principal
Old World species; its home extends from south-eastern Europe to the
Himalayas and China, and it is extensively planted in Europe and
Japan. It is usually called **European walnut**. *J. regia* L., the **American
walnut**, or American black walnut, occurs wild in the eastern parts of
North America. Several other species in tropical and South America
appear to produce excellent timber of the black walnut type, although
they are apparently of little commercial importance, except locally.
The origin of claro, or Californian walnut, which yields well-figured
burrs, crotches and stumps, is uncertain; it is said to be produced by

two closely related trees, *J. hindsii* (Jeps.) Rehder and *J. californica*
S.Wats., or alternatively by black walnut trees introduced into
California. **Japanese walnut** is *J. sieboldiana* Maxim. Another North
American species, *J. cinerea* L., sometimes passes as white walnut, but
its more usual name is butternut; its timber is paler, lighter and weaker
than black walnut; little reaches Britain.

Among the so-called walnuts are:

Queensland walnut, also known as Australian walnut, walnut bean,
and oriental wood. This comes from *Endiandra palmerstonii* C.T.White
et Francis, a tree of the family Lauraceae, found in northern Queensland.

African walnut, Nigerian walnut or Benin walnut, from the West
African *Lovoa klaineana* Pierre ex Sprague (now *L. trichilioides*
Harms.) a meliaceous tree. Another member of the genus, *L. brownii*
Sprague, occurs in tropical East Africa, but is too scarce to be exported.

Mansonia or African black walnut, produced by *Mansonia altissima*
A. Chev. (family Triplochitonaceae), another tree of tropical West
Africa.

Imbuya, or embuia, Brazilian walnut, from *Phoebe porosa* Mez, a
member of the Lauraceae from tropical America.

New Guinea walnut, Pacific walnut or Papuan walnut, from New
Guinea and nearby islands, produced by species of *Dracontomelum*
(family Anacardiaceae).

Satin walnut, the heartwood of *Liquidambar styraciflua* L., known
as **American red gum** in North America, whence it derives. The sapwood
is known in Britain as hazel pine. The tree belongs to the family
Hamamelidaceae.

Kokko, or East Indian walnut, the wood of the leguminous *Albizzia
lebbeck* Benth., from India, Burma and the Andaman Islands.

Swamp walnut, the name sometimes applied to the brown heartwood
of the North American **black willow**, *Salix nigra* Marsh.

Mayombe walnut, a name sometimes given to the dark-coloured
wood of **afara**, or **limba**, *Terminalia superba* Engl. et Diels (family
Combretaceae).

The heartwood of European walnut (*J. regia*), whose sapwood is pale
coloured, varies much in colour and in figure. French walnut is usually
greyer than English walnut; Circassian walnut usually well-figured;
the best quality Italian walnut is dark, well-figured and streaky and is
known as Ancona walnut. Such names, originally at least, referred to
the country of origin, but now have little real meaning. It is, in fact,
customary to term any dark-coloured, streaky walnut, Ancona walnut,
no matter from what part of Europe it derives.

The characteristic features of walnut, as seen with a hand-lens, have
already been given (p. 324). Under the microscope the vessel perforations will be found to be simple. The rays, viewed tangentially, are
narrow—they may be up to 5 cells wide, but those 1–3 cells wide are
commoner—and rather irregular; thus a ray 3 cells wide in part, may

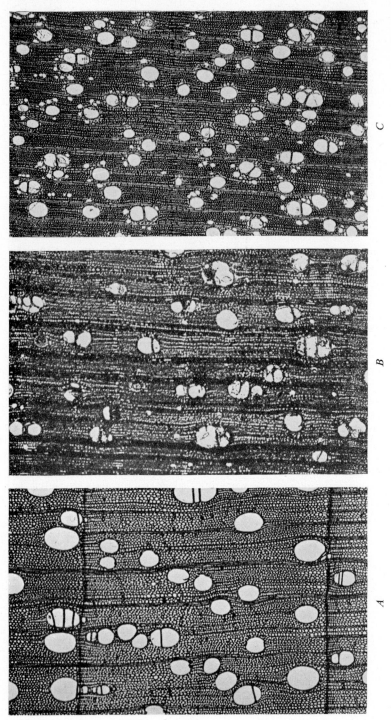

Fig. 172.—Transverse sections of: *A*. European Walnut (*Juglans regia*); *B*. Queensland Walnut (*Endiandra palmerstonii*); *C*. Imbuya (*Phoebe porosa*). In Imbuya there are numerous oil cells (larger than the other cells in the section but much smaller than the vessels) around or near the vessels. (All × 27.)

tail into a line of single cells. The parenchyma is conspicuous under the microscope and its cells often contain crystals (Figs. 14, 172 *A*, 176 *A*).

No certain way is known by which European walnut and American black walnut may be distinguished, but black walnut is typically darker and more uniform in colour and nearly always has a purplish tinge. Though it often happens that the early wood vessels of American black walnut are more numerous than those of European walnut, so that the wood may be semi-ring-porous, both species may show this character. There is not, however, the striking difference in size between the vessels of the early and late wood, as seen for example in ash: see also Brazier and Franklin (1961).

Queensland walnut (*Endiandra palmerstonii*) is readily distinguished from other commercial walnuts, when freshly sawn, by its unpleasant, sour smell. It is very variable in colour, dark-brown, reddish-brown and black, the different colours often appearing as longitudinal streaks. Its texture is rather closer than that of walnut and the wood is rather heavier. The growth rings are indistinct or absent (Figs. 172 *B*, 176 *B*) and the vessels are more or less evenly distributed and either solitary, or sometimes in radial chains of 2–4 elements. At irregular intervals there are conspicuous tangential bands of parenchyma. The vessels commonly contain a dark-brown gummy material, as well as abundant tyloses which are characterised by their thick walls (Fig. 175 *B*), not a common anatomical feature in wood: vasicentric parenchyma is present. The rays are barely visible to the unaided eye. They are from 1–4, and most commonly, 2–3 cells wide.

Brazilian walnut (*Phoebe porosa*) which is found on the high land in southern Brazil, belongs to the same famly as *Endiandra*. Its heartwood is yellowish- to chocolate-brown and often well figured, and when freshly cut the wood has a spicy, resinous scent and taste. In contrast with Queensland walnut, the growth rings are distinct. Here the vessels are solitary or in short radial rows of 2–4 or more, and do not have thick-walled tyloses (Figs. 172 *C*, 176 *C*). The rays, like those of Queensland walnut, are narrow, and usually 1–3 cells wide. Another feature apart from growth rings, which serves to differentiate this wood from Queensland walnut, is the presence of septate fibres (Fig. 175 *C*) while all sections of the timber will show prominent oil cells (Fig. 172 *C*).

African walnut (*Lovoa*) is a meliaceous wood and more nearly resembles mahogany than walnut in structure. Its rich yellowish- to dark-brown colour and almost sparkling lustre are characteristic, as is, nearly always, the presence of at least a few black streaks. In *Lovoa* the growth rings are indistinct (Figs. 173 *A*,176 *E*). The vessels are fairly large, regularly distributed, solitary or often in multiples of 2–5 or more, which may be arranged radially or obliquely, or sometimes, more irregularly in clusters. The vessels often contain a very dark, almost black gum. Parenchyma sometimes occurs as bands and there is a little paratracheal parenchyma, although rarely sufficient to be seen

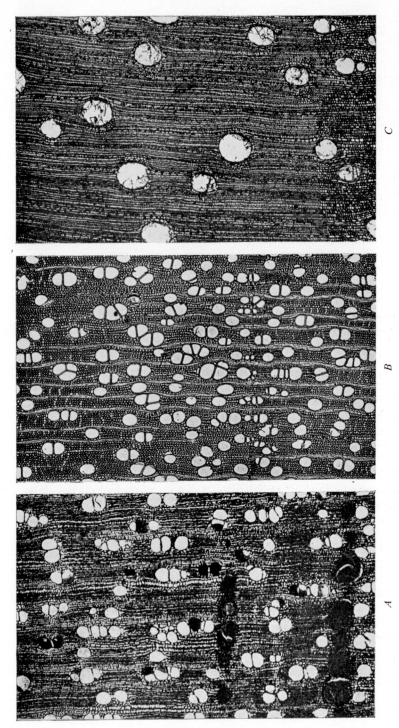

Fig. 173.—Transverse sections of: *A*. African Walnut (*Lovoa klaineana*); *B*. Mansonia (*Mansonia altissima*); *C*. New Guinea Walnut (*Dracontomelum* sp.). (All × 27.)

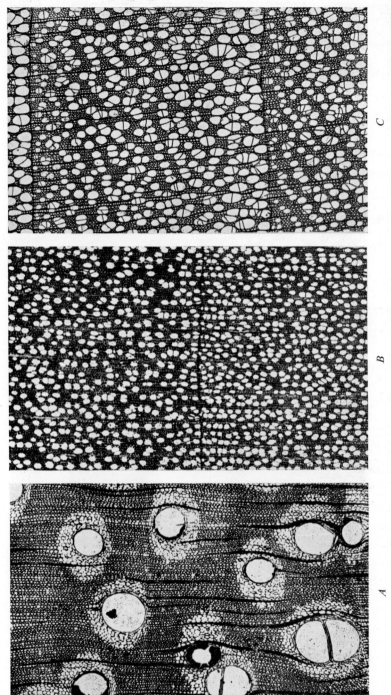

A   *B*   *C*

Fig. 174.—Transverse sections of: *A*. Kokko (*Albizzia lebbeck*); *B*. American Red Gum (*Liquidambar styraciflua*); *C*. Black Willow (*Salix nigra*). (All × 27.)

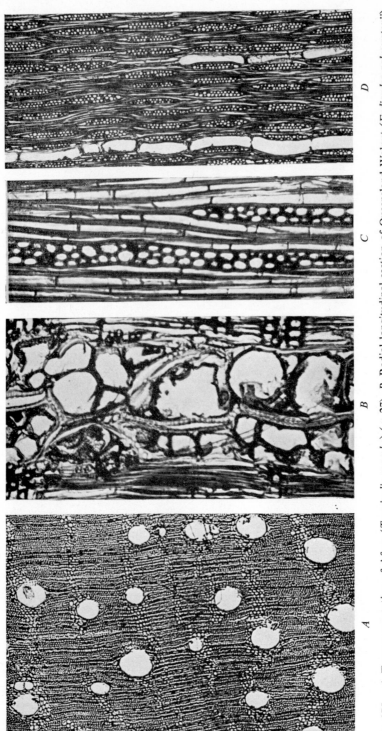

Fig. 175.—*A*. Transverse section of Afara (*Terminalia superba*) (× 27). *B*. Radial longitudinal section of Queensland Walnut (*Endiandra palmerstonii*) showing thick-walled tyloses in vessels (× 110). *C*. Tangential longitudinal section of Imbuya (*Phoebe porosa*) showing septate fibres (× 170). *D*. Tangential longitudinal section of Mansonia (*Mansonia altissima*) showing storeyed rays (× 51).

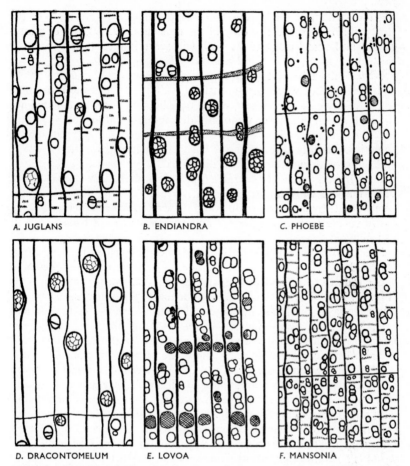

A. JUGLANS   B. ENDIANDRA   C. PHOEBE

D. DRACONTOMELUM   E. LOVOA   F. MANSONIA

Fig. 176.—Simplified (caricature) drawings of transverse sections of Walnuts and
so-called Walnuts. *A*. Walnut; *B*. Queensland Walnut; *C*. Imbuya; *D*. New Guinea
Walnut; *E*. African Walnut; *F*. Mansonia.
Parenchyma is stippled or shown by dotted lines, gummy material in vessels is
hatched; the gum in the gum galls of African Walnut is cross-hatched; oil cells are
shown as black dots.

with a hand-lens. The dark streaks, already referred to, are gum galls,
formed by a localised breakdown and splitting of tissue, the cavities
becoming filled with dark gum. They may occur in tangentially
arranged groups (Fig 133 *A*), and when abundant, and as is usual then,
associated with dark-coloured wood, produce a very handsome
figure.

African black walnut (*Mansonia*) has a colour rather similar to that
of American black walnut, but is a closer-textured wood, with smaller
vessels, which are clustered (Figs. 173 *B*, 176 *F*). This last feature,

together with the very pronounced ripple marks resulting from the storeyed arrangement, not only of the rays (Fig. 175 D), but of parenchyma and vessel elements as well, will serve immediately to identify this timber among the walnuts.

New Guinea walnut (*Dracontomelum*) resembles the more lightly coloured type of wood of Queensland walnut. It lacks the sour smell when freshly cut. The vessels, which may be seen with the unaided eye (Figs. 173 C, 176 D), are uniformly distributed, solitary or in groups of 2 or 3: they usually have tyloses. The parenchyma is paratracheal, sometimes slightly aliform, and is fairly conspicuous. The rays are fine, and the growth rings are at best ill-defined.

East Indian walnut (*Albizzia lebbeck*) is a dull, dark-brown wood, often marked with darker bands. It is readily distinguished from the true walnuts by its coarse texture and its very large vessels (Fig. 174 A), easily visible to the unaided eye and surrounded by a broad zone of parenchyma.

Satin walnut and willow have already been described in some detail (pp. 323–28). In satin walnut the fine, angular vessels often occur in short radial chains and are separated by thick-walled fibre-tracheids (Fig. 174 B). The vessels have scalariform perforations, while the irregular rays (as viewed in tangential section) are 1–3 cells wide and often tailed. Willow also has fine vessels, although they are rather fewer and larger than those of satin walnut, and often in short, radial chains; their perforations are simple. In willow the rays are only one cell wide.

Mayombe walnut, the West African *Terminalia superba*, is more often known as white afara, limba or fraké. This wood is generally pale-coloured but logs may have an irregular, dark-coloured heartwood with markings varying from greyish-brown to almost black. Such dark-coloured wood, which is rather reminiscent of walnut, is the type known as noyer du Mayombe or noyer-limbo on the Continent. The wood is sometimes known as Congo walnut in the United States.

This wood has well-defined rather undulating growth rings. Its vessels can be distinguished with the unaided eye, and are commonly solitary, and oval in section; they have simple perforations. Parenchyma is fairly plentiful. It occurs round the vessels, although it does not always completely ensheathe them, and it may be confluent between adjacent vessels (Fig. 175 A). This parenchyma may be visible to the unaided eye. The rays are one cell wide.

KEY TO THE COMMERCIAL WALNUTS

1. Growth rings distinct 2
   Growth rings inconspicuous or lacking . . 8
2. Parenchyma in numerous, thin concentric lines,
   not as wide as widest rays 3
   Parenchyma not in numerous thin concentric lines 4

3. Rays storeyed, ripple marks prominent . . *Mansonia altissima*
(African Black
Walnut)

 Rays not storeyed, ripple marks absent . . *Juglans* (Walnuts)
4. Rays exclusively uniseriate   5
 Rays not exclusively uniseriate . . .   6
5. Parenchyma paratracheal and confluent . . *Terminalia superba*
(Mayombe Walnut)

 Parenchyma not paratracheal and confluent, very
 sparse . . . .   *Salix nigra*
(Swamp Walnut)
6. Vessel perforations scalariform . . . *Liquidambar*
styraciflua
(Satin Walnut)

 Vessel perforations simple   7
7. Parenchyma abundant . . . . . *Albizzia lebbeck*
(East Indian
Walnut)

 Parenchyma scanty . . . . . *Phoebe porosa*
(Brazilian Walnut)
8. Vasicentric parenchyma very prominent, as thick
 sheaths round vessels . . . . . *Albizzia lebbeck*
(East Indian
Walnut)

 Vasicentric parenchyma, if present, not forming
 very prominent, thick sheaths round vessels .   9
9. Tyloses not frequent in vessels, dark gum galls
 common . . . . *Lovoa klaineana*
(African Walnut)

 Tyloses frequent in vessels, gum galls absent .   10
10. Tyloses thick-walled; irregularly spaced tangential
 lines of parenchyma present . . . . *Endiandra*
palmerstonii
(Queensland
Walnut)

 Tyloses thin-walled; without irregularly spaced
 tangential lines of parenchyma . . . *Dracontomelum* spp.
(New Guinea
Walnut)

CHAPTER 17

SPECIFIC DIFFERENCES IN TIMBERS

In the chapters so far devoted to identification, attention has been paid to generic rather than to specific characters, although it has been seen that well-marked differences in wood structure may exist within a genus, as for example among species of *Chamaecyparis*. In the present chapter emphasis will be placed on specific differences among woods of the same genus, and we shall examine how far it is possible to separate and identify the woods of such closely related trees.

To attempt to carry identification so far might appear to be a matter of academic rather than practical interest, but it not infrequently happens that timbers from different species of a genus differ appreciably in their properties and in the uses to which they may be put. For example, rock elm, wych elm and common elm yield timbers having quite different properties, and among the willows only one species is suitable for use in first-class cricket bats. Consequently, the mere generic naming of a timber, as elm or willow, is not necessarily sufficient, and identification down to species level may sometimes be very desirable.

It will be found that in larger genera the timbers may often be divided into groups on the basis of their structure and other characteristics, but in few, if any, instances is it possible to point to a large genus in which the woods may be accurately identified as species. Why this is so is explained after the range of wood structure in certain genera has been described. The genera selected are *Quercus* (oaks), *Ulmus* (elms), *Fraxinus* (ashes) and *Acer* (maples).

OAKS

Botanists are not all in agreement about the limits of the genus *Quercus*, but there are certainly more than two hundred species. Most of these are found in the northern hemisphere, where in temperate regions they may be important members of the forest floras; in warmer countries they tend to occupy the mountain areas. In America they extend southward to Colombia. They are well represented in the Mediterranean region, in the Himalayas and in Malaya. Most oaks are trees but a few are shrubs.

On the basis of their wood structure the oaks fall into three sections, the white oaks, the red oaks and the evergreen (live) oaks. Those of the first two groups are deciduous species. It is well known that one character is common to all the oaks, the possession of very large rays, as

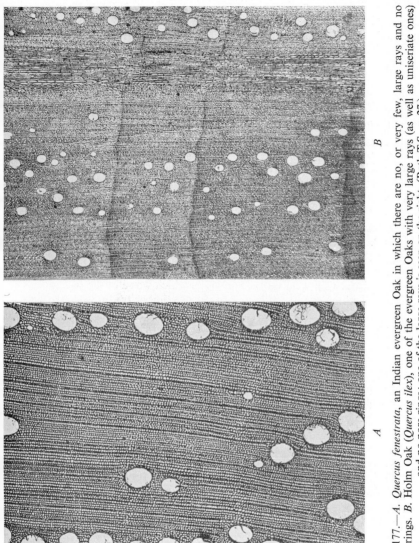

Fig. 177.—A. *Quercus fenestrata*, an Indian evergreen Oak in which there are no, or very few, large rays and no pore rings. B. Holm Oak (*Quercus ilex*), one of the evergreen Oaks with very large rays (as well as uniseriate ones) and no pore rings; one of the large rays is seen on the right. (Both T.S. × 27.)

2c

well as uniseriate ones. According to Gamble, a few of the Indian oaks (*Q. pachyphylla* Kunz, *Q. lappacea* Roxb. and *Q. fenestrata* Roxb.) (Fig. 177 *A*) have no large rays. Possibly such oaks, all of them evergreen, should form another section, but at present it is better to regard oak timber as belonging to one or other of the three sections already mentioned.

The deciduous oaks are generally ring-porous. English oak (Fig. 178 *A*) may serve as an example. Here the wood is strictly ring-porous and the large vessels of the early wood, in the heartwood, are usually filled with tyloses. The change from early to late wood is abrupt, and in transverse section the late wood shows small and numerous vessels arranged in radial lines, or in somewhat fan-shaped groups, which are surrounded by pale-coloured tissue consisting of parenchyma and tracheids. Numerous fine lines of apotracheal parenchyma stretch between the rays. The large rays are conspicuous, while there are numerous, small, uniseriate rays between them which are only discernible with a hand-lens. English, or European oak, consists of two species, *Q. robur* L. (= *Q. pedunculata* Ehr.), the pedunculate or common oak, and *Q. petraea* Liebl. (= *Q. sessiliflora* Salisb.), the durmast oak. It happens that wood known to be derived from trees of the latter species is sometimes mild and very evenly grown, as in the famous Spessart oak from Germany, but no way is known by which wood of the two species can be distinguished with certainty. In the timber trade, various types of European oak are known, the distinguishing names being based on the districts or countries from which the wood originates, e.g. Austrian, Polish, Volhynian, Danzig, Slavonian oak. These oaks may differ to some extent in texture, rate of growth, size of logs and other features which might be expected to vary with the conditions under which the trees grow. Thus Slavonian oak is mild and seasons well, while Volhynian oak is the name used for the better quality Polish oak. These various oaks, however, cannot be distinguished with certainty, for they are all derived from one or other of the two species of oak, *Q. robur* and *Q. petraea*, which are together known as European oak.

The wood of a true white oak (*Q. alba* L.) (Fig. 178 *B*), of North America, has a structure and colour similar to European oak and the same is true of several other North American species, like *Q. montana* Willd., the chestnut oak. The timbers of all species from North America which produce wood of this type are collectively known as American white oak. The timbers of the several species cannot be distinguished from one another, although there are some differences between them. Thus in the southern species there is a gradual and not an abrupt change in the size of the vessels from early to late wood, while in *Q. montana* the vessels of the heartwood do not contain many tyloses.

Numerous species of oak come from eastern Asia and the wood of more than one species has been imported into Britain as Japanese oak.

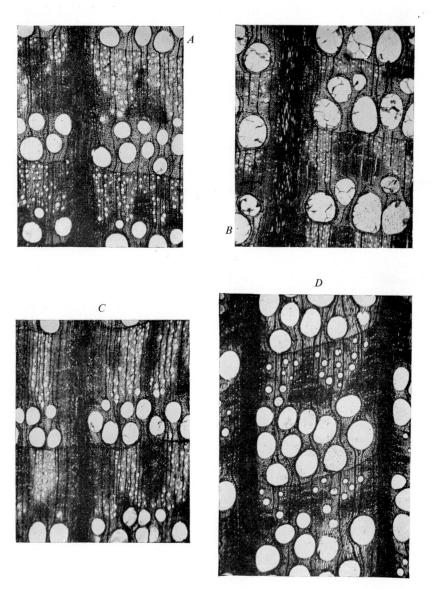

Fig. 178.—Transverse sections of various Oaks. *A*. English Oak (*Quercus petraea*);
B. White Oak (*Q. alba*); *C*. Japanese Oak (*Q. mongolica* v. *grosseserrata*); *D*. Red
Oak (*Q. borealis*).

The bulk of the timber which bears this name is derived from *Q. mongolica* Turcz. var. *grosseserrata* (Bl.) Rehd. et Wils (Fig. 178 *C*), which is structurally a white oak.

There is another group of North American deciduous oaks, typified by *Q. borealis* Michx.f., the red oak, and its variety *maxima* Sarg., the northern red oak, and by *Q. shumardii* Buckl., the shumard oak, in which the wood is generally of a pale reddish-brown colour, as compared to the pale yellowish- or greyish-browns of the white oaks. The vessels of these woods (Fig. 178 *D*), which collectively constitute the red oaks of commerce, are rather more oval in section than those of the white oaks and are usually without tyloses. There is a somewhat gradual change in size between the early wood vessels and those of the late wood, as compared with the very abrupt change in most white oaks, and the vessels of the late wood are fewer and larger (possibly the best distinguishing features). Moreover, the large rays rarely exceed a height of 1–1½ inches (2·5–4 cms.), whereas in the white oaks they may be higher. The timbers of these red oaks are not individually distinct, as far as is known at present.

Quercus cerris L., the Turkey oak of southern Europe and western Asia, produces a hard, heavy wood, closely resembling that of red oak in colour and in structure, except that it is less distinctly ring-porous and possesses smaller early wood vessels. In the heartwood, these may contain tyloses. Like the red oaks, which are less durable than the white oaks, Turkey oak does not produce a durable timber.

The structure of the wood of the evergreen oaks is well seen in *Q. ilex* L. (Fig. 177 *B*), the holm oak, another species native of southern Europe. The wood is hard and heavy. There is no pore ring and seen in transverse section the vessels occur in radially elongated groups, which may extend through more than one season's growth; growth rings are not very distinct. The large rays of the holm oak are very conspicuous, and viewed under the microscope in a tangential longitudinal section are seen to be broken up, very irregularly, into smaller rays by intervening fibres—they are, in fact, aggregate rays. In the red and white oaks, the small rays are uniseriate or, very occasionally, in part biseriate; in holm oak uniseriate rays preponderate, but bi- and triseriate rays are not infrequent. Similar in structure to the holm oak and exhibiting what may be regarded as the typical features of the evergreen oaks, are the North American live oak (*Q. virginiana* Mill.) and the holly oak (*Q. morii* Hay) of Formosa.

ELMS

The elms are distributed mainly over north temperate regions and species occur in Europe and Asia as well as in North America. There are about eighteen species, as well as a number of hybrids, like the Dutch elm.

Of the British and European species, those best known for their timber are:

U. procera Salisb. (European, English, common, or red elm).
U. glabra Huds, (wych, mountain, or Scotch elm).
U. hollandica Mills var. *major* (Sm.) Rehd. (Dutch elm).
The chief American species are:
U. thomasii Sarg. (rock or cork elm).
U. americana L. (white or American elm).
U. fulva Michx. (slippery or red elm).

U. japonica (Rehd.) Sarg. (and possibly other species as well), is the Japanese elm.

U. wallichiana Planch. is an elm of the Himalayas and other parts of India and is a well-known local timber.

The principal features of elm timber are the pore rings of large vessels, the smaller and numerous vessels of the late wood, which, seen in transverse section are arranged in undulating tangential bands, and the fairly broad rays, visible on the transverse surface to the unaided eye, at least if the wood is wet. Elm usually shows a very characteristic figure on its plain-sawn surfaces, for the late wood vessels appear here as rather dusty looking zig-zag lines, producing a type of figure sometimes called partridge-breast figure.

Of the three European species already mentioned, common elm and Dutch elm have rays which, viewed in tangential section, are broadly boat-shaped—they may be as many as eight cells or so wide (Fig. 179 *F*); wych elm has narrower rays, up to about five cells wide (Fig. 179 *G*). In common elm (Fig. 179 *A, D*) there is an abrupt change from the large vessels of the pore ring to the closely-packed, tangentially arranged vessels of the late wood, while in both wych elm (Fig. 179 *B, E*) and Dutch elm the change is more gradual and there is a zone of fairly large vessels between the pore ring and the undulating bands of vessels of the late wood. In this transition zone the vessels are neither so numerous nor so compactly arranged as are those of the late wood. Wych elm possesses a rather finer texture than common elm, for it has somewhat smaller vessels, and moreover, it is relatively straight grained, for its fibres run more or less axially; those of common elm pursue much more irregular courses, with the result that this wood is tougher and more cross-grained. English elm is called red elm because of its dull, rather dark-brown heartwood; the wood of Dutch elm is usually rather paler. Wych elm timber is usually pale, hence the name white elm, and often has a greenish tinge or distinct green streaks. While a wood anatomist might identify a piece of elm timber as one of these three, he would more probably show greater caution and refrain from making a specific diagnosis, for the good reason that there are other English elms like *U. hollandica* Mill. var. *vegeta* (Loud.) Rehd. (the Huntingdon elm), and *U. carpinifolia* Gleditsch (the smooth-leaved

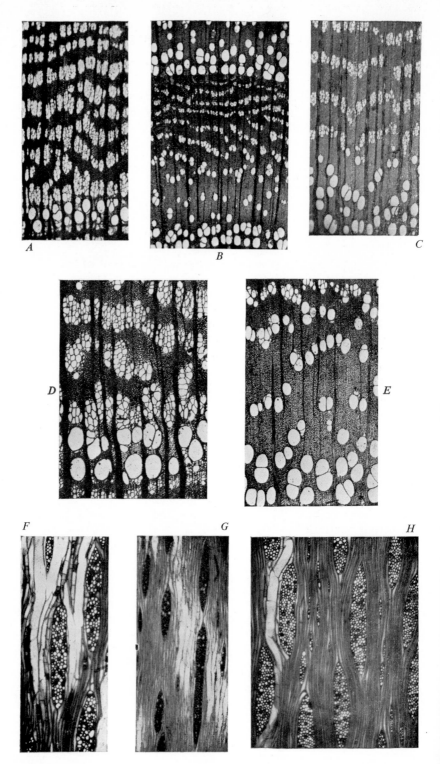

Fig. 179

elm), of which the wood structure has not been studied in any detail. In the trade, it is the three species already mentioned which are distinguished, but the other species sometimes find their way into parcels of these woods.

Of the three principal species of American elm, the red or slippery elm (Fig. 180 *B, E*) has a pore ring normally several vessels wide and an abrupt change between the early and late wood. Both rock elm (Fig. 180 *F*) and white (American) elm (Fig. 180 *A, D*) usually have only a single row of vessels in the pore ring. In white elm these vessels are more or less uniform in size and are easily visible to the unaided eye. Those of rock elm are smaller, and even the largest are barely visible without a hand-lens; nor, in rock elm, is the pore ring—if such it may be called—formed entirely of large vessels, for smaller pores are interspersed among the larger ones and the pore ring has an irregular appearance. In white elm the spring vessels in the heartwood contain few tyloses, whereas tyloses are abundant in rock elm, furthermore white elm shows a rather abrupt transition from early to late wood while in rock elm the change may be more gradual. Rock elm, as might be expected, is heavy and rather fine-textured; it is also straight-grained and easy to split. White elm is coarse-textured and, like European elm, often cross-grained. Slippery elm is also coarse-textured but unlike the two preceding species, has rather narrow rays.

Another genus of the Ulmaceae, *Celtis*, has two North American species—*C. occidentalis* L., the hackberry and *C. laevigata* Willd., the sugarberry. The wood of both species is commonly marketed with elm, for it is used for the same purposes as white and slippery elm. The timbers of these two species of *Celtis* (Fig. 180 *C*) are indistinguishable from one another and they closely resemble that of slippery elm, with a conspicuous pore ring several vessels wide and the late wood vessels in undulating tangential lines. The rays, however, are more conspicuous on end-grain surfaces than those of *Ulmus fulva*, for they are rather wider: moreover, they are generally heterogeneous, whereas elm rays are homogeneous. Again, in these species of *Celtis* the heartwood is greyish to yellowish-grey and is scarcely different from the sapwood, whereas slippery elm has a brown, often dark heartwood, frequently of a reddish shade and distinctly marked off from the sapwood.

ASHES

There are between sixty and seventy species of ash, with a wide distribution in the northern hemisphere. The commercial names used

---

Fig. 179.—Sections of European Elms: *A*. English Elm (*Ulmus procera*) T.S. (× 11). *B*. Wych Elm (*U. glabra*) T.S. (× 11). *C*. Huntingdon Elm (*U. hollandica* v. *vegeta*) T.S. (× 11). *D*. as *A*, but × 21. *E*. as *B*, but × 21. *F*. English Elm T.L.S. (× 50). *G*. Wych Elm T.L.S. (× 50). *H*. Huntingdon Elm T.L.S. (× 50).

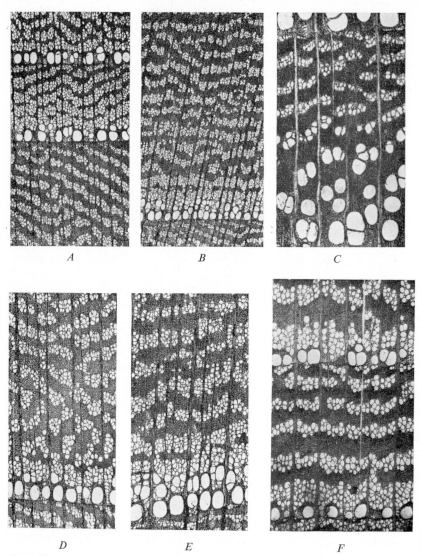

Fig. 180.—Sections of North American Elms and Hackberry. *A*. White Elm (*Ulmus americana*) T.S. (× 11). *B*. Red Elm (*Ulmus fulva*) T.S. (× 11). *C*. Hackberry (*Celtis occidentalis*) T S (× 21) *D*. White Elm T.S. (× 21). *E*. Red Elm T.S. (× 21). *F*. Rock Elm (*U. thomasii*) T.S. (× 21).

for the ashes are very confusing. *Fraxinus excelsior* L., the common or European ash, has a wide distribution in Europe and extends eastwards to the Western Himalayas. The timber is usually known by its country of origin; English ash, French ash, Hungarian ash, Polish ash and so on, are all derived from this one species. However much these trees may differ in rate of growth, texture and other qualities, their timbers cannot be distinguished with certainty. The heartwood of this species is whitish to pale-brown and is not sharply differentiated from the sapwood, but in old trees it may become irregularly dark-brown or black. If such timber is marked with dark, irregular streaks it is called olive ash, but again this is not distinct structurally from any other wood of *F. excelsior*.

Fraxinus mandschurica Rupr., which grows in Japan and Manchuria, is known as Japanese or Manchurian ash, or tamo, and is the only Asiatic species of this genus of commercial importance in Britain, although other ashes occur in China and Japan and in the warmer parts of eastern Asia.

North America possesses about eighteen species of this genus. About 98 per cent of the commercial ash timber from that continent is produced by three species:

F. americana L. (white ash).
F. nigra Marsh. (black ash).
F. pennsylvanica Marsh. var. *lanceolata* Sarg. (green ash).

Most of the remaining two per cent comes from:

F. oregana Nutt. (Oregon ash).
F. pennsylvanica Marsh. (red ash).

Among the American ashes there is much confusion over trade names, for little attention is paid to species and a parcel of American or Canadian ash may include several species. Much is sold as white ash, regardless of species, although the wood of black ash, with distinctive mechanical properties, a rather brown heartwood and a less lustrous surface, is usually distinguished as brown ash. Another North American species is *F. tomentosa* Michx.f. (= *F. profunda* (Bush) Britt.), the pumpkin ash, but the trade term, pumpkin ash, is used indiscriminately, not only for timber from old trees of this species but also for timber of green ash, which has been grown in permanently wet soils and which is light, soft and brittle.

As concerns the general structure of ash, the wood is ring-porous in the commercially important, but not in all, the species of the genus. The large vessels of the early wood are rather oval in section and the vessels gradually diminish in size to the small vessels of the outermost part of the growth ring. The small vessels of the late wood are not numerous and are either single or in groups of two or three, surrounded by a sheath of vasicentric parenchyma. The rays are narrow and not visible without the aid of a hand-lens.

No means are as yet established by which it is possible to distinguish the timbers of the different species of ash on an anatomical basis. The only clear-cut distinction lies between black or brown ash (*F. nigra*) and what we may call the white ashes, this latter group including the

North American white, green, red and Oregon ashes as well as European and Japanese ash. In black ash the wood, viewed in transverse section (Fig. 182 *A*, *B*), normally shows narrower rings than that of the white ash type (Fig. 181 *A*, *E*), but the pore rings of the early wood are more conspicuous, for they occupy a relatively larger part of each growth ring. In white ashes generally, the parenchyma around the vessels tends to spread out tangentially into wings and often to connect up with that of neighbouring vessels, i.e. it may be confluent, especially toward the end of the growth ring (Fig. 181 *C*, *F*), but this does not occur in black ash (Fig. 182 *C*). The darker, less lustrous wood of black ash has already been noted, while the sapwood of this tree is narrow and contrasts thus with the wide sapwood of the white ashes.

MAPLES

The maples constitute a genus of over a hundred species spread over Europe, Asia, North Africa and North America and include a number of important timber-producing trees.

Among the European species are:

A. campestre L. (field maple), the only species native to Britain.

A. pseudoplatanus L. (sycamore), a species long established in Britain, regenerating naturally and spreading in many woodlands.

A. platanoides L. (Norway maple).

Of the several North American species, the most important timber trees are:

A. saccharum Marsh. (rock or sugar maple).

A. saccharinum L. (silver maple).

A. rubrum L. (red maple).

A. macrophyllum Pursh. (Oregon, big-leaf, or Pacific maple).

The chief species producing Japanese maple timber appear to be:

A. palmatum Thunb.

A. mono Maxim.

The wood of the maples is fairly fine- and even-textured. It is diffuse-porous, the vessels showing little difference in size throughout the growth ring. Seen with a hand-lens the vessels appear strikingly circular in section and are solitary or in short radial chains; they have spiral thickening and simple perforations. The rays are fairly conspicuous

---

Fig. 181.—Sections of Ashes. *A*. European Ash (*Fraxinus excelsior*) T.S. (× 1 1) *B*. as *A* but × 32. *C*. European Ash; T.S. of boundary of growth ring, showing vessels and associated parenchyma (× 185). *D*. European Ash T.L.S. (× 90). *E*. White Ash (*F. americana*) T.S. (× 11). *F*. White Ash; T.S. of boundary of growth ring, showing vessels and associated parenchyma (× 185). *G*. White Ash T.L.S. (× 90).

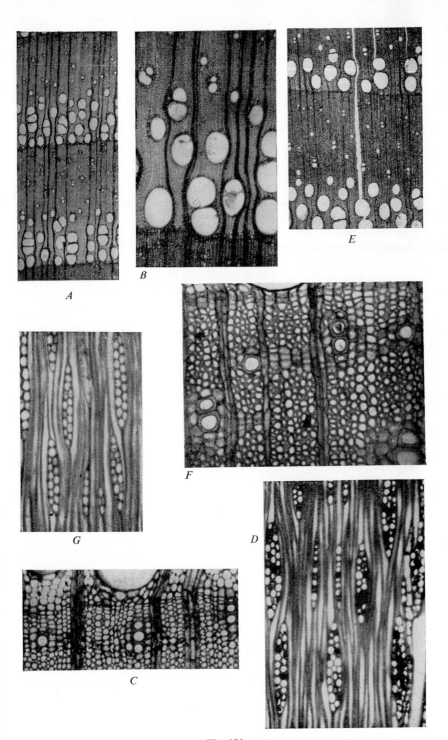

Fig. 181

402 THE STRUCTURE OF WOOD

and in transverse sections they appear straight. In tangential longitudinal section the ray cells appear rounded; the rays are from one to seven or eight cells wide.

The timbers of the American maples fall into three main groups, the hard maples, of which *A. saccharum* is the principal species the soft maples, produced by *A. saccharinum* and *A. rubrum*, and Pacific maple derived from *A. macrophyllum*. Hard maple is a stronger and denser wood than the others. Its heartwood is light reddish-brown; that of soft maple is pale-brown and Pacific maple is a deep pinkish-brown. The sapwood of soft maple is white, while in hard and Pacific maples it is white with a reddish tinge. Colour in maple wood, however, must not be taken too seriously, for it varies considerably. In hard maple, the ray figure on quarter-sawn faces is more prominent than that of Pacific and soft maples, for the rays are larger and up to seven or eight cells wide, while in Pacific maple and soft maple the rays are not more than five cells wide (Fig. 183 *C, D, E*). All these woods have small rays as well as large ones and the two sizes are fairly distinct in hard maple, whereas in soft maple large and small rays tend to intergrade. Pacific maple has few uniseriate rays. Viewed on the end grain, the rays are most prominent in soft maple, for here they are usually darker than the rest of the wood; on the other hand, the growth rings are most prominent in hard maple.

A further feature which is an aid to identification arises from the activities of the grubs of *Agromyza*, which cause pith flecks (cf. p. 260). Pith flecks are common in soft maple but are rare in hard and Pacific maples.

The wood of sycamore is white or yellowish-white, lustrous and usually without distinction between heartwood and sapwood. Its large rays are fairly broad and, seen in transverse section (Fig. 184 *A*), exceed the diameter of the vessels; they are paler than the rest of the wood and consequently show up rather clearly on the end grain. In the harder and denser hard maple the rays contrast less with the rest of the wood and are less conspicuous. Like hard maple, sycamore wood rarely shows pith flecks.

The timbers of field maple and Norway maple are very similar to that of sycamore, although their rays are smaller and more numerous and also less variable in size (Fig. 184 *A–D*). Field maple timber is rather darker and heavier than that of sycamore and is more likely to show pith flecks.

Reference has already been made to bird's-eye maple, of which the

---

Fig. 182.—Sections of Ashes. *A*. Black Ash (*Fraxinus nigra*) T.S. (× 11). *B*. as *A*, but × 32. *C*. Black Ash; T.S. of boundary of growth ring, showing vessels and associated parenchyma (× 85). *D*. Black Ash T.L.S. (× 90). *E*. Red Ash (*F. pennsylvanica*) T.L.S. (× 90). *F*. Japanese Ash (*F. mandshurica*) T.S. (× 11). *G*. Japanese Ash T.L.S. (× 90).

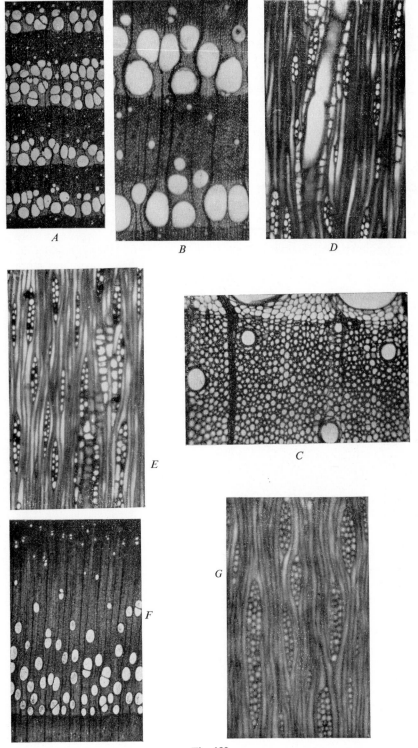

Fig. 182

chief source is hard maple, and to quilted maple, which occurs in Pacific maple (cf. pp. 252–54). The pale-grey timber known as harewood is sycamore which has been artificially coloured by chemical means.

There appears to be much confusion between plane and sycamore, which is perhaps not surprising considering the confusion in their popular names (cf. p. 1). The botanical relationship of plane to sycamore is remote, for the planes belong to the family Platanaceae, a family having no close affinity with the Aceraceae, to which the sycamore belongs. The only resemblance between sycamore and plane is in the shape of the leaf, a character which is not generally a reliable index of affinity among plants. Plane wood (known also as lacewood) does not resemble the wood of sycamore. Its large rays alone are characteristic, and on the longitudinal faces they produce a figure which is rather like that of beech (Fig. 126 B) except that it is larger and more pronounced. Again, in transverse section (Fig. 184 E) the very numerous vessels (sometimes clustered) and the prominent rays are more reminiscent of beech, except that in plane the large rays are more numerous.

These descriptions of differences in wood structure among species or groups of species of a genus exemplify what may be accomplished generally in the way of specific determination of wood. The results, it must be confessed, are disappointing. That it is possible to divide the oaks, on the basis of their wood structure, into no more than three, or at most, four groups, or the ashes (over 60 species) into only two groups, makes it appear that any attempt to proceed much beyond generic diagnoses is a waste of time. In a large measure this state of affairs is to be attributed to lack of knowledge, and it is reasonable to hope that as data on wood structure accumulate it will be possible to do much more in making specific diagnoses. Undoubtedly, in the timbers of the genera which have been selected here as examples, there are more differences between species than have been described in this chapter: colour, lustre and other physical properties may serve as useful guides, and may indeed, on occasion, prove even more useful than anatomical features. It is possible also that much may be done by the use of simple chemical tests on the timbers or their extracts.

There is, however, a fundamental difficulty in this matter. In the illustrations of the ashes, various points of difference may be observed of which no note has been taken in this chapter. Reference might have been made to the relatively coarse rays of common ash (Fig. 181 D) and the finer ones of red ash (Fig. 182 E); to the more oval outline of the early-wood vessels in some species, to differences in the grouping of the vessels of the late wood and in the thickness of their walls— but—to what purpose? Each illustration was taken from a very small piece of a single tree of a particular species, at most with a surface area of a square centimetre and a thickness of less than 20 μ, and the illustration itself represents only part (in some instances a very small part)

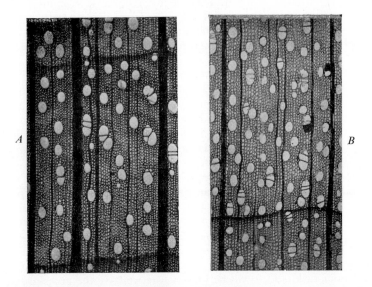

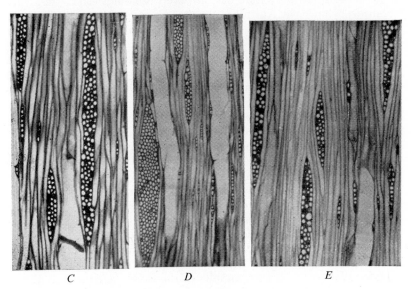

Fig. 183.—Sections of Maples. *A*. Rock Maple (*Acer saccharum*) T.S. (× 39).
B. Silver Maple (*A. saccharinum*) T.S. (× 39). *C*. Pacific Maple (*A. macrophyllum*)
T.L.S. (× 80). *D*. Rock Maple T.L.S. (× 80). *E*. Silver Maple T.L.S. (× 80).

of this small piece of wood. There is no prospect of learning anything of the variation in structure of a species from a single slide, and it is probably no exaggeration to claim that it would be impossible to get a comprehensive and accurate picture of the range of variation in more than one or two species of ash from all the specimens available in this country. It is even unlikely, in fact, that the authentic specimens available could provide sufficient data to enable us to judge the conditions under which the trees which produced them grew. Are, for example, the early wood vessels of some species characteristically more oval in section than those of others, or is this a feature which varies in different samples of the same species and consequently is of no diagnostic worth? Or again, are thick-walled late wood vessels really characteristic of white ash, as might appear from the illustration, or are they due to the special environmental conditions under which the wood of one particular tree was formed? We do not know, and at present must confine ourselves to intelligent guesses. We need a detailed study of the structure of the wood of individual species, from samples taken from trees in all parts of the range of the species in question and under all the environmental conditions in which the trees grow. This, of course would be an enormous task, and it will be long before we have the necessary data.

Some work of this nature has, however, been undertaken, in a very realistic manner, in Australia, on the genus *Eucalyptus*, a genus of some three hundred species (Dadswell and Burnell, 1932; Dadswell, Burnell and Eckersley, 1934).

The genus *Eucalyptus* was a convenient one on which to work, for it is almost confined to Australia, so that the accumulation of wood samples proved less difficult than it would have done had the genus been spread over three or four continents. Even so, the work of collecting samples was laborious and time consuming. Samples were taken from several different parts of the trees and from the corresponding parts of each tree. Collection was not confined to one tree in a locality, and selection was made from localities as widely separated as possible. Full details were recorded of the environment of each tree sampled—aspect, elevation, soil, type of forest and so on. The samples were 20–40 inches (50–60 cms.) long, 4½ inches (11·5 cms.) wide and 2½ inches (6·5 cms.) thick and were thus large enough to be representative. In addition, in order to make accurate identification of the specimens, herbarium material, in the form of fruits, leaves, bark, buds and flowers was, as far as possible, obtained from each tree. In most species studied, at least ten samples of the wood, taken from different trees, in various localities, were examined.

Full particulars of the features used for separating these timbers must be sought in the original papers, but a few details may be given here to indicate the type of character used. The primary division was into coloured woods (i.e. dark-red, red, dark-brown, chocolate and pink timbers) and light- or non-coloured ones (i.e. light-brown, brown,

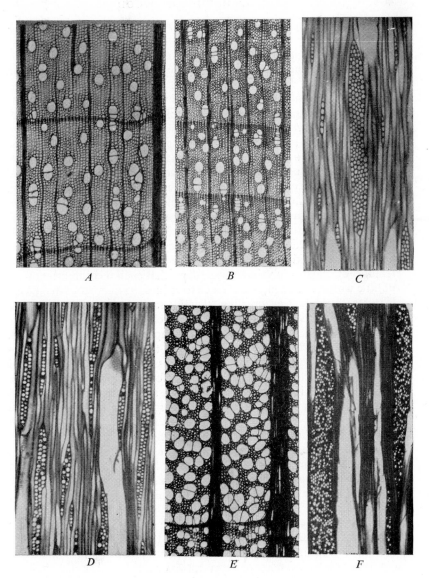

Fig. 184.—Sections of Maples and Plane. *A.* Sycamore (*Acer pseudoplatanus*) T.S.
(× 39). *B.* Field Maple (*A. campestre*) T.S. (× 39). *C.* Sycamore T.L.S. (× 80);
D. Field Maple T.L.S. (× 80). *E.* American Plane (*Platanus occidentalis*) T.S. (× 39).
F. American Plane T.L.S. (× 39).

yellow, white or pale-coloured woods). As the authors point out, this feature does not always form a sharp line of distinction, for some species may fall into either group and due allowance must be made for this contingency. The same difficulty would probably have arisen whatever criteria were used and this is a disadvantage which is inevitable. Thirty-seven dark-coloured species were examined and forty-one light-coloured ones. In the key to the coloured species, use is made of density and the woods of the several density groups are then separated on the result of the burning splinter test, depending on whether the splinter burns to a complete ash, or partial ash, or merely to a charcoal with little ash. Further divisions are made on the average number of vessels seen in a circle of five millimetres diameter on the end grain, on the average number of rays per square millimetre of tangential section, on the presence or absence or abundance of triseriate rays, on parenchyma and so on. Such physical properties as hardness and fissility were called into service where they were of use. Little attention however, was paid to measurements, for in the preliminary survey for features of diagnostic value it was found that such measurements were of little worth. An attempt was made to reduce the number of diagnostic features to as few as possible, thereby saving much laborious and unnecessary work and making the key much easier to use.

The following extract from the first paper (Dadswell and Burnell, 1932), should act as a sufficient warning to those who base descriptions on a single specimen: "Descriptions of structural features and of wood characters based on three or four samples are apt to be misleading and it is strongly urged that all future work should be carried out with as many samples as possible for each species. The variation within a species made it difficult to draw up a key which would definitely separate all the species investigated. . . ." That this variation may be considerable is borne out by the work of Jansonnius (1950) who, from a study of the wood of nearly a thousand Javan species, found that in large genera variations within a single species are often wider than variations between different species of smaller genera.

Even in the keys carefully prepared by Dadswell and his co-workers it will be found that sometimes no certain way is given of separating some species. This deficiency may be due to either of two things. On the one hand it is possible that the authors missed certain minute but constant points of difference between two or more very similar timbers, and that, in the future, differences (anatomical or perhaps chemical) will be found which will enable such apparently similar woods to be distinguished. On the other hand, it is also possible, and perhaps more probable, that the timbers of two or three species of a large genus *are* more or less identical and cannot therefore be separated with certainty. It is quite likely, as has already been suggested (pp. 293) that the characters of the secondary wood may not be as useful for purposes of classification as certain other parts of the plant. The timbers of distinct but closely related tree species may not necessarily differ. Nevertheless, when our knowledge of wood structure is more advanced, it may be that we shall sometimes be able to use it as a basis for specific distinctions between trees—sometimes, but not invariably. How far we are from attaining that goal should now be apparent; so too should the amount of collecting and investigation called for if work of this nature on a large genus is to be put on a sound scientific basis.

TECHNIQUES FOR THE STUDY OF WOOD ANATOMY

Examination of a wood specimen for details of its structure and for the purpose of identification should be systematic. It should begin with such gross features as are readily observed with the unaided senses and proceed to those which are rendered visible with a simple hand-lens and thence to such as require a microscope for their elucidation.

EXAMINATION OF GROSS FEATURES

While the visual sense is of greatest use, smell, taste and touch may sometimes play a part in studying wood. A specimen may have a characteristic odour when fresh, and even old samples may prove to be scented if they are rubbed briskly, or warmed. Chewing a fragment of the wood may reveal a distinctive taste, e.g. acrid, astringent, bitter, while if the specimen feels greasy or waxy or otherwise unusual, this feature is worth recording. It is, however, scarcely worth while to note such features unless they are definite and out of the ordinary. To record, for example, that a light wood feels warm or a heavy one cold, is clearly of little value, since it is characteristic of timber that the heavier it is, the colder it feels. On the other hand, it would be worth recording the fact that a heavy wood felt warm, as this would be an unusual feature and probably indicative of the presence of copious quantities of some extraneous material which was a poor conductor of heat.

The colour and texture of the specimen will, of course, be noted, as well as the appearance of the surface, e.g. rough, smooth, dull, lustrous or greasy, while it may be of value to observe the direction of the grain and, in a straight-grained wood, whether it gives long or short splinters. A note should be made of storeyed structure, if present.

A rough estimate of the hardness of the specimen may be obtained by pressure with the finger-nail, using the following arbitrary scale:

Wood easily indented by finger-nail   SOFT
Wood not readily indented by nail   FAIRLY HARD
Wood scarcely indented by nail   HARD

If the sample is of reasonable size, it should be weighed and its volume calculated, when the density may readily be estimated. From this the weight per cubic foot can easily be ascertained (a cubic foot of water weighs 62·4 lbs.). If the sample has been in the laboratory for some time, it will be sufficiently accurate, for a determination of this kind, to assume that it has a moisture content of about 15 per cent.

A splinter of the specimen, of about the dimensions of a matchstick, should be burnt to determine whether the wood burns to a charcoal or to a complete ash and, if the latter, the colour of the ash should be observed. Any special features of burning, e.g. a bright flame, a smoky flame, burns quietly, crackles when burning, burns readily, burns with difficulty, a distinct odour of burning, should be noted. In carrying out this ash test it is essential that the splinter be burnt in perfectly still air, for even a slight draught may be sufficient to invalidate the result. Moreover, heartwood should always be used for the test.

A few shavings from the specimen should be boiled in a little water and a note made of any peculiarities of the extract, e.g. a distinctive colour or fluorescence, while the presence of tannins in the extract is indicated by a bluish- or greenish-black coloration when ferric chloride is added to it. Here, again, heartwood should always be used.

EXAMINATION WITH A HAND-LENS

For the lens examination of timber, a × 8 or a × 10 lens is the most useful. At times, a lens of higher power (× 20) is valuable, but its services will not be in very great demand: it must be regarded as supplementary to, and certainly not as a substitute for, the one of lower power.

When in use, the lens should be held close to the eye, both eyes being kept open, and the specimen brought into focus. To hold the specimen stationary and to focus with the lens is a far less satisfactory procedure, as the field of view is likely to be severely restricted.

Preparation of a specimen for lens examination consists of cleaning the transverse surface with a sharp, heavy razor. Safety razor blades may be used in place of the open type razor, but most students will find them too weak for the task, even if their sharpness is beyond reproach. It is also a good plan to examine a cleft radial surface, on which scalariform perforations, if present, will show to advantage.

Much information on the structure of a timber may be obtained by the intelligent use of a lens. The distribution and shape of the vessels in hardwoods are often readily ascertained, so also is the presence of tyloses and deposits, the length of vessel elements and the type of vessel perforation. Information can also be obtained concerning the distribution of axial parenchyma, the shape, arrangement and distribution of the rays and the presence of ducts and canals.

EXAMINATION WITH A MICROSCOPE

A. The Microscope.—For detailed examination of wood structure a microscope is necessary. This need not be an elaborate instrument, but it should have a $\frac{2}{3}$ inch (16 mm.) and a $\frac{1}{6}$ inch (4 mm.) objective. A $1\frac{1}{2}$ inch (40 mm.) objective is sometimes useful and very occasionally a $\frac{1}{12}$ inch (2 mm.) oil-immersion objective may be required for the observation of certain minutiae of structure. However, neither of the latter lenses need be regarded as a necessary item of equipment. Some regard a mechanical stage, by means of which the mounted sections can be moved systematically across the field of view, as a desirable accessory, but most experienced microscopists are likely to look upon the mechanical stage as a troublesome piece of equipment for routine work, and one to be avoided except when needed for special purposes. The effective use of a microscope is very dependent on an understanding, in general terms, of the optical principles involved. Barer (1959) and White (1966) give clear accounts, and reference may be made also to those works cited on p. 423 in connection with photomicrography.

B. Preparation of Wood for Microscope Examination.—For the detailed examination of wood under the microscope, very thin sections are needed. They must be free of air and mounted in some suitable medium. For rapid, temporary mounting, water, or better, dilute glycerine, will serve, but if it is desired to preserve the sections permanently, they should be mounted in glycerine jelly or Canada balsam (Franklin, 1938; Jane, 1932–3).

Several methods are available:

a. A rapid technique for temporary sections.—This method will be found very useful when identification of wood is the aim. Cut very small and very thin shavings from the transverse, radial and tangential faces of the specimen with a sharp razor[1]—shavings a few millimetres long and wide will be sufficient. Put the shavings in a test-tube with a little alcohol and heat to boiling: this will drive the air out of the cells. Add water to the alcohol—at least twice as much water as alcohol—tip the liquid into a watch-glass and mount the sections on a slide in water. Should the sections be very transparent they can be coloured with aniline sulphate (or hydrochloride). This is purely a temporary method, although special sections, which may be required for future reference, can be preserved by mounting direct into glycerine jelly, or after staining, dehydration and clearing, in Canada balsam.

b. The microtome.—Generally, for permanent mounts in Canada balsam, or rather less permanent ones in glycerine jelly, larger and more accurately cut sections are to be preferred. Such sections are best cut on a sledge type (sliding) microtome. Failing this, however, quite good longitudinal sections can be cut with a perfectly sharpened plane, set with a fine mouth; though transverse sections are less easy to obtain by this method, fairly good ones may be cut with a low-angle block plane.

Fairly satisfactory sections may also be cut in a hand microtome, especially if this is firmly supported and clamped to the bench, and the razor moved across the cutting table with an oblique cut. Here also, transverse sections usually prove the more troublesome.

The sledge microtome is essentially a device by means of which a block of wood can be firmly held and accurately presented to a moving knife which, as it passes across the block, removes a section of a predetermined thickness. For general work, sections 20 μ (0·02 mm.) thick are the most suitable, although for special purposes it may be necessary to cut much thinner ones.

In a type of sledge microtome very suitable for cutting wood sections (Fig. 185), the block of wood, of which the transverse face should not exceed 1 cm. in width, and the longitudinal faces should not exceed 2 cm., is held in a Naples clamp, a device which enables it to be accurately orientated with respect to the knife. The knife is a heavy one, wedge-shaped in section, and is firmly clamped to the sledge, which slides back and forth along a groove on three bearing surfaces, so carrying the knife across the uppermost face of the block. In some models the Naples clamp and block must be raised for each section by turning a graduated head; this operates a screw mechanism which raises the clamp. In others, the sledge, on being

---

[1] A razor with a blade of wedge-shaped section is preferable. Hollow ground razors may not be strong enough for harder woods. Safety-razor blades, especially those of the single-edged, stiff back variety, will serve for softer woods.

Fig. 185.—A heavy sledge microtome, suitable for cutting wood sections. In essentials, the wood block (b) from which sections are to be cut, is held in a clamp (c) which moves up the dove-tail slide (g). The thickness of the sections depends on the distance up the slide which the clamp moves between each cut; this is determined automatically or by turning the head (h); the knife (k) is carried by the sledge (s) which moves in a V-groove, on the top of the instrument.

returned to its starting point after a section has been cut, automatically turns the screw and so raises the block through a previously determined increment in readiness for the next section.

   c. *Preparation of Blocks.*—Before sections can be cut, the block of wood requires some preliminary preparation, although it is possible to section soft to moderately hard woods without previous treatment, by means of Kisser's steam method (see p. 414). In general, however, initial treatment, after blocks of suitable size have been cut, consists of repeatedly boiling them in water until they sink. The blocks become water-logged more rapidly if the hot water is replaced by cold as soon as it boils. Such water-logging, besides driving out the air, helps to soften the wood. Many timbers are then ready for sectioning and they should preferably be sectioned immediately, while warm. If this cannot be done at once, the blocks should be stored in a mixture of equal parts of glycerol and alcohol. For prolonged storage the proportion of glycerol to alcohol should not exceed 1 to 4.

   Hard woods may require additional softening, for which purpose several methods have been used. Of such, the more useful are:

   1. *Hydrofluoric Acid.*—This is the best known and probably the most generally satisfactory method for really hard timbers (Harlow, 1944). The acid is highly corrosive and, since it attacks glass, is stored in gutta percha or polythene bottles. For softening wood blocks, polythene beakers, lead cups or boxes may serve as containers, or even glass dishes

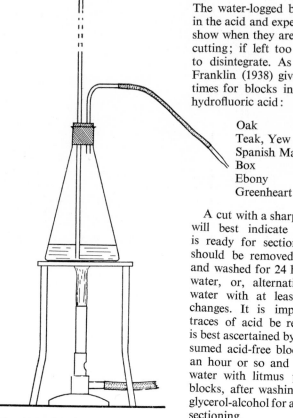

which have been thoroughly cleaned and then coated with paraffin wax. The water-logged blocks are placed in the acid and experience alone will show when they are soft enough for cutting; if left too long they begin to disintegrate. As a rough guide, Franklin (1938) gives the following times for blocks in 50–60 per cent hydrofluoric acid:

Oak	2 days
Teak, Yew	4 ,,
Spanish Mahogany	5 ,,
Box	6 ,,
Ebony	9 ,,
Greenheart	12 ,,

A cut with a sharp knife or scalpel will best indicate when a block is ready for sectioning. Specimens should be removed from the acid and washed for 24 hours in running water, or, alternatively, boiled in water with at least half a dozen changes. It is important that all traces of acid be removed and this is best ascertained by leaving the presumed acid-free blocks in water for an hour or so and then testing the water with litmus paper. Softened blocks, after washing, are stored in glycerol-alcohol for a few days before sectioning.

It should be emphasised that hydrofluoric acid is an unpleasant liquid to handle and inexperienced users would be well advised to wear rubber gloves when using it. Removal of specimens from the acid is best

Fig. 186.—Kisser's steam apparatus. Water is boiled in the flask and steam passes through the right-hand tube, the nozzle of which is placed near the block which is being cut. The vertical tube on the left is a safety valve.

accomplished with a pair of home-made wooden forceps, which should also be used for putting the blocks in the acid, thus avoiding splashes.

2. *Kisser's Steam Method.*—This method may be used on dry wood, but it is better on specimens which have been water-logged. The apparatus is shown in Fig. 186. A few chips of unglazed porcelain in the flask reduce "bumping" when the water boils. The steam jet is directed on to the specimen.

The two chief objections to Kisser's method are that it results in the accumulation of a good deal of water on the microtome and knife, which thus need careful cleaning and oiling after use and, secondly, that the steam which impinges on the specimen may be too cold to be very effective as a softening agent. This second difficulty may be met by using a copper or monel metal coil instead of a glass delivery tube, the coil being heated by a second bunsen flame.[1]

It is sometimes claimed that the steam has a deleterious effect on the edge of the knife, but the opinion of those competent to judge is that no temperature below 400° C. is likely to affect the temper of the knife, and certainly a temperature approaching 400° C. will not be reached with this apparatus.

3. *Acetic Acid—Hydrogen Peroxide.*—This method is due to Franklin (1946). Blocks are softened in a mixture of equal parts of glacial acetic and hydrogen peroxide (20 volume). The flask which contains this mixture is fitted with a reflux condenser and the blocks are allowed to simmer for about an hour, very hard woods requiring rather longer and softer ones a shorter period. The wood will become macerated if kept too long in the mixture. On removal, the blocks are washed in several changes of running water before cutting.

A method of softening wood by means of cellulose acetate was described by Williamson (1921), who claimed to have succeeded in softening hard timbers in from three days to a few weeks by means of a solution of cellulose acetate in acetone. This method cannot, however, be recommended from personal experience.

d. Using a Sledge Microtome.—The use of a sledge microtome is best learnt by demonstration and experience. Here, no more than a few notes relevant to the cutting of wood specimens will be given.

The block, when ready for cutting, should be trimmed so that its sides represent transverse, and radial and tangential longitudinal faces. It should be firmly mounted in the clamp with the face from which sections are to be cut uppermost. It is sometimes recommended that for the cutting of transverse sections the rays should be parallel to the direction of movement of the knife, but it often seems preferable for the knife to move obliquely across the specimen, i.e. neither radially nor tangentially. For longitudinal sections similarly, an oblique cut is better than a longitudinal one.

The knife must be firmly clamped to the sledge. As a rule it should meet the block at an angle of about 10° to the direction of travel and at about 10° from the horizontal plane, but these angles are only approximate, and must be varied somewhat to suit the specimen.

If the microtome is an automatic one the sledge must be pushed back to its fullest extent after each cut, otherwise the subsequent section will be thinner than intended.

In cutting sections, both the block and the knife should be flooded with 70 per cent alcohol. Flooding, as concerns the knife, means that it should

---

[1] It seems to be a general experience that the steam method is not sufficient to soften very hard woods, but Mr F. R. Richardson, of the Jodrell Laboratory, Kew, informed Professor Jane that he has found no difficulty in sectioning the hardest timbers with the aid of this method. He uses a glass delivery tube, but obtains a sufficient pressure of steam by using a very long glass tube as a safety valve. In his opinion, adjustment of steam pressure to suit the wood is important and is brought about by varying the force of the steam jet and the distance of the nozzle of the delivery tube from the specimen.

carry as much liquid as possible on its upper surface; then the sections, which are fragile, do not drag against the knife but are buoyed up by the liquid. When using the steam-softening method, alcohol tends to cool the wood and it is better to rely on the water which condenses on the knife, or to use (in place of alcohol) warm water to which a little glycerol has been added.

As the section is being cut it should be held down on the knife with a soft camel-hair brush; this will normally prevent it curling. With hard woods, curling is sometimes troublesome. It may be prevented to some extent by replacing the alcohol with a mixture of equal parts of alcohol and glycerol, and after keeping the section flat with the brush, allowing it to remain on the knife for a minute or so before removal. If curling is still troublesome the only satisfactory way of dealing with the sections is to slide them from the knife to a slide, and to carry out staining and subsequent operations on the slide, using the minimum of liquid at each stage.

It sometimes happens, with a rather hard specimen, that alternate cuts fail to produce sections, while those which are obtained are of double the required thickness. This is indicative of a dull knife, or sometimes of a specimen which is really too hard to be cut without further softening. Except when very thin sections are required the difficulty can sometimes be obviated by raising the block twice for each section (each time to half the required thickness) instead of moving it up in one operation. There seems to be no adequate explanation as to why this trick should sometimes work.

Sections are removed from the knife with a brush, or better, with the ball of the second finger, moistened with 70 per cent alcohol.

e. Care of the Microtome and Knife.—It is very important that the microtome should run smoothly. It should be cleaned after use and all bearing surfaces, screws and so on, thoroughly oiled with light machine oil. To prevent grit and dust getting on to the microtome, it should be covered when not in use. It is a good plan periodically to wipe all bearing surfaces free of oil with a xylene-soaked rag and then to re-oil them.

Sections cannot be cut with a blunt knife, and for hard woods, or gritty ones, frequent sharpening is necessary. Moreover, while a slightly dull knife is very soon sharpened, a thoroughly blunt one, which in any case has not cut good sections for a good deal of the time it has been in use, takes a long while to recondition.

A slightly dull knife may only require stropping, or at most, a few strokes on a water-stone, but where more extensive treatment is required it should be honed on a fine oil-stone. A fine Belgian stone, like a razor hone, is suitable, using a light machine oil as a lubricant. After honing, the edge of the knife should be examined under the low power of the microscope to make sure that it is not nicked; if it is, honing should continue until such blemishes are removed. The knife is then honed on a finer stone, which should be a water-stone lubricated with soapy water. It is then stropped on a "solid" strop, i.e. one which is mounted on a block of wood.

In honing and stropping, the knife is fitted with a back or bevel (Fig. 187), which is merely a metal tube that slips over the back of the knife and is held there firmly by two screws. The knife suitable for cutting wood sections has a wedge-shaped section, and it is necessary to form a steeper

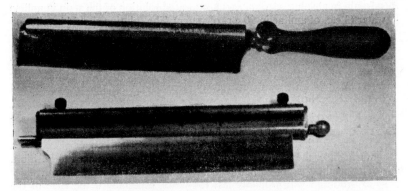

Fig. 187.—Heavy wedge-shaped microtome knives suitable for cutting wood sections. The upper one has been fitted with the usual type of "back" which is slipped on the back of the knife when the knife is to be sharpened; it has a removable handle. The lower knife has a back fitted with rollers; its handle has been removed.

bevel for the cutting edge, hence the use of the back, which raises the back of the knife off the stone. The objection to the type of back mentioned is that its sides are gradually worn away on the hone and consequently the angle of the cutting bevel is continually changing. A back in which the bearing surfaces are silver-steel rollers has been designed to overcome this defect (Jane, 1935).

When honing, the knife is pushed edge foremost along the stone with an oblique motion, so that the whole edge is covered at each stroke. It is then turned over on its back and the process repeated. The movements in stropping are similar except that the knife is moved back foremost. For honing and stropping a detachable handle is fitted at the heel end of the knife and it is important to ensure that even pressure is applied throughout each stroke; this is best accomplished by pressing the left-hand thumb on the toe of the knife.

Stones and strops should be kept covered when not in use. Stones should be wiped free of lubricant after use and, before they are covered a few drops of clean oil or water (as the case may be) should be put on their surface. Occasionally, the oil-stone should be cleaned with xylene or paraffin.

After prolonged use, stones tend to wear hollow. They may be relevelled by rubbing on a sheet of fine emery paper fixed to a board and lubricated with oil (for an oil-stone) or water (for a water-stone).

f. Staining and Mounting Sections.—The process of mounting sections is similar to that used in general botanical technique and need not be described in detail. Sections of pale-coloured woods, at least, will need to be stained before they are mounted, otherwise they will be too transparent for microscopic examination. The student will probably stain the sections of all the timbers which he cuts. Safranin is normally used and appears to be without equal, although there are numerous other stains available, on the use of which a book on botanical technique (Johansen, 1940; Rawlins, 1933) should be consulted.

Safranin is made up by mixing equal parts of a saturated solution of safranin in absolute alcohol and a saturated solution of the stain in aniline water (3 c.c. of aniline in 90 c.c. of water). The solution should be allowed to ripen for a few months before it is used.

To obtain a good, bright, red colour, sections should be left in the stain for some hours, in fact they may safely be transferred to safranin after cutting, and left there for days, until it is convenient to mount them. The safranin should not be thrown away after use, but filtered and returned to the stock bottle.

1. *Glycerine Jelly Mounts.*—After safranin staining, the sections are rinsed in 50 per cent alcohol and transferred to weak glycerine (about 10 per cent aqueous). A drop of melted glycerine jelly is placed on a warm slide, the section added, and a warm coverslip placed in position. This method is not so permanent as that using balsam, although slides so produced will probably last for years, especially if the edge of the coverslip is ringed with gold size.

An alternative method, which is preferred by some workers, is to mount unstained sections in glycerine jelly to which a little safranin has been added; the section gradually takes up the stain.

2. *Canada balsam Mounts.*—For balsam mounts, the sections are removed from the stain, washed twice in alcohol, dehydrated in absolute alcohol, cleared in xylene or cedar-wood oil, and mounted in the usual way.

It is customary to mount transverse, radial and tangential longitudinal sections on one slide, the transverse section with its rays at right-angles to the long axis of the slide and the longitudinal sections with the axial elements in a similar direction.

The most convenient size of coverslip is 1½ in. × ⅞ in. and for most work a No. 1 or 2 thickness will be suitable. If it is intended to use a one-twelfth inch (2 mm.) objective on the slide at any time, a No. 0 or No. 1 coverslip must be used. It is preferable, for ease of manipulation, to mount the coverslip in the centre of the slide and not towards one end, as is so often done.

In mounting three sections under one cover, difficulty may be experienced in keeping them in position. This is fairly easily avoided if the sections are placed on the slide in the minimum quantity of balsam and a streak of balsam is placed along the centre of the coverslip before it is lowered on to the sections. When the coverslip is in position it is a good plan to allow the slide to dry with a small lead weight on the coverslip, as flatter sections are thus obtained. For visual work, this is not very important, but it is strongly recommended that this procedure be adopted if sections are likely to be photographed subsequently. Drying of the slide may be hastened if the slide is put on a hot-plate: the top of a radiator, or a biscuit tin in which a 60-watt lamp is mounted will also serve. If dried by heat, the slide may be cleaned up in a few days, but if heat has not been used it is best left for at least a fortnight before cleaning. Most of the excess balsam can be scraped off with an old scalpel and the remainder cleaned off with a rag moistened with xylene. In a well-mounted slide, little cleaning should be required, for only just enough balsam to fill the space below the coverslip should have been used in the first instance.

g. Examination of Separate Elements.—It is sometimes necessary to examine isolated elements of a piece of wood, as for example, for measurement of the length of elongated elements like fibres. For this purpose the middle lamellae are broken down, so that the cells fall apart. There are several methods by which this process of maceration may be accomplished.

1. *Schultze's Method.*—This is the most rapid method. Small slivers of wood are put into a test-tube to which is added a little concentrated nitric acid and a few crystals of potassium chlorate. The tube is warmed gently, preferably in a fume-cupboard. It requires experience to decide when the macerating process has proceeded far enough. Insufficiently macerated wood cannot be teased out, while if the process goes too far, the splinters disintegrate completely. The stage at which the maceration should be stopped will depend upon the wood and on the size of the fragments. For pieces about 12 mm. long and 1–2 mm. thick, the process should cease as soon as the splinters assume a white, ragged appearance. The maceration is stopped by filling the tube with cold water.

2. *Jeffrey's Method.*—Thin slivers of wood, from which the air has been expelled by boiling in water, are macerated in a mixture of equal parts of 10 per cent nitric acid and 10 per cent chromic acid. The solution may be gently warmed (e.g. by placing in an embedding oven). The process is much less violent and more satisfactory than Schultze's method. It may take some hours or days.

3. *Franklin's Method.*—This has already been described (cf. p. 415) for softening. For maceration, the process is merely carried farther, the length of time required depending on the timber. This is the best method.

If maceration is continued too far the cells themselves may disintegrate. Thus if it is desired to preserve the macerated material it must be washed thoroughly. This may be achieved by repeatedly allowing it to settle in a large volume of water, and pouring off and replacing the supernatant. The final change may then be into dilute formalin.

The macerated material may be made into a temporary or a permanent mount, as follows:

a. Temporary Mount.—Wash the material in several changes of water, place a fragment on a slide in a drop of dilute glycerine, tease apart thoroughly with needles and mount a coverglass.

It is often possible to separate the elements sufficiently by mounting a coverglass on it and gently tapping this with a needle.

β. Permanent Mounts:

1. *Glycerine Jelly.*—Place a drop of well-melted glycerine jelly coloured with safranin, on a well-warmed slide. Add a splinter of the macerated wood and tease out quickly with warm needles. Mount a warm coverslip. If air bubbles should be present in the mount they may be driven off by judicious warming.

2. *Canada balsam.*—Two useful methods may be mentioned:

(i) *Jane's Method.*—Smear a clean slide with a very thin film of Mayer's albumen. Add a drop of water and tease out a macerated splinter in it. Warm the slide, on an oven or over an electric lamp, until nearly dry, then flood with alcohol. Stain, dehydrate, clear, and mount in balsam. A fairly generous amount of the macerated wood should be used as a good deal washes off in the subsequent treatment; enough, however, is retained to give all that is required.

(ii) *Franklin's Method.*—Wash the macerated material in water followed by three changes of alcohol. Soak in clove oil[1] for a few minutes. Transfer to 1 per cent light-green in a mixture of one part of clove oil and three parts of alcohol and allow to stain for ten minutes: warming facilitates staining. Rinse in clove oil, followed by xylene. Place the maceration on a slide in a little thin Canada balsam, tease out, then add coverslip.

h. Tension Wood Fibres.—Although double-staining of sections of normal wood is unnecessary, it is valuable for some special purposes, as in the study of tension wood. Safranin and light-green may be used, or better, the method of Robards and Purvis (1964), which is very effective. Stain sections in 1 per cent aqueous lignin pink (5 mins.), wash in 95 per cent alcohol, differentiate briefly in water and dehydrate with 95 per cent alcohol followed by absolute alcohol. Then stain in 1 per cent chlorazol black E in methyl cellosolve (5 mins.), dehydrate in absolute alcohol, clear in xylene and mount in Canada balsam.

i. Fungal Hyphae in Wood.—If the wood is reasonably sound, it may be sectioned in the usual way and subsequently stained to differentiate the fungal hyphae from the woody tissue. This may be accomplished by several methods. A good one, due to Cartwright (1929), stains the wood red and the hyphae blue. The following procedure should be adopted:

Stain sections for one minute or less in 1 per cent aqueous safranin. Wash in distilled water. Flood sections on a slide with picro-aniline blue (five parts saturated aqueous aniline blue, two parts of saturated aqueous picric acid) and warm the slide over a flame until the liquid is just about to simmer. Wash out the blue in distilled water. Wash in two changes of 70 per cent alcohol. Transfer to absolute alcohol, clear in clove oil, then transfer to xylene and mount in balsam.

j. Storage of Slides.—Permanent slides may be stored in the usual types of cardboard or wooden slide box. There is also a very convenient system which uses aluminium holders which carry four slides. These holders are the size of standard index cards (5 in. × 3 in.) and may be filed, like cards, in a card-index cabinet.

k. Describing the Microscopic Characters of a Specimen.—No general advice can be given on how much detailed information should be recorded from a specimen. It is a simple matter to draw up elaborate schedules or forms on which full details of all the elements can be recorded. Much, however, must depend on the purpose for which the information is required. Thus, if an attempt is being made to find characters on which a number of woods from different species of a genus can be distinguished, it is clearly a waste of time to record the shape of vessel pits, or the dimensions of fibres and tracheids, if these are similar in all the species. Similarly, detailed dimensions of different elements serve little useful purpose unless they are

---

[1] Clove oil should clear from industrial alcohol, but if it fails to do so and turns milky, place the specimen in absolute alcohol for a minute or so and then proceed to the clove oil.

taken from several specimens from the same species of tree, as well as from several parts of the trunk of each specimen. The advantage of filling up schedules or recording all the data on a definite plan is that the specimen is examined systematically and no details are missed.

As a guide to the type of schedule which may be used, the student is referred to those of Clarke (1938b) for hardwoods and Phillips (1948) for softwoods, while schemes for both hardwoods and softwoods will be found in Brown, Panshin and Forsaith (1949), and Panshin, de Zeeuw and Brown (1964). These will serve to indicate what is useful, and from them the student can make up his own scheme, bearing in mind, it is hoped, that rigid uniformity is likely to lead to mere description for its own sake.

ILLUSTRATIONS

If a description of a wood is to be illustrated, choice will lie between drawings and photomicrographs. The former are not difficult to make, but there is usually a tendency on the part of a beginner to put in too much detail, and that in too great a hurry. A few cells carefully delineated are worth more than a hundred drawn with little regard to accuracy. In any drawing or sketch it is important to aim at simplicity, and in general to include only such features as are useful for diagnosis or for whatever purpose the sketch is intended. It may be useful, sometimes, to exaggerate slightly, or at least, to emphasise, salient features. For example, a sketch of a transverse section of ash, or especially of chestnut, as seen under a hand-lens, would stress the oval outline of the vessels of the early-wood, while one of lime, as seen in tangential longitudinal section under a low power of the microscope, would bring out the asymmetry of the rays. Careful study should be made of the simplified sketches which appear in this book; they are, essentially, caricatures, emphasising certain details at the expense of others. They have been made, in many instances, from the photomicrographs which accompany them.

Where accurate drawings have to be made of details visible with the microscope, an outline sketch is obtained with the aid of some drawing device. Probably that most widely used is the Abbé camera lucida, a piece of apparatus consisting essentially of a half-silvered prism and a mirror, which fits over the eye-piece of the microscope (Fig. 188). It is so arranged that, on looking down the microscope, the observer sees not only an image of the specimen, but also his pencil, so that the image can be traced on a suitably placed piece of paper. Another device is the drawing prism, which also fits over the eye-piece of the microscope and which projects a real image of the specimen on to paper, so that its outlines can be traced with a pencil. Whichever is used, such detail as is required must be filled in subsequently.

It is worth while to add a word about the shading of drawings. The only justification for shading is to emphasise some feature or to show it more clearly. Shading should always be used with restraint. It is too frequently used to cover up slovenly work, an artifice which never succeeds.

Simple photomicrography is not difficult, provided the photographer understands the principles of correct illumination of microscopical specimens. A satisfactory method is to use a 35 mm. single-lens reflex camera, fitted by means of a suitable adaptor to the eye-piece tube of the microscope (Fig. 189). The major manufacturers of cameras of this type can supply adaptors for

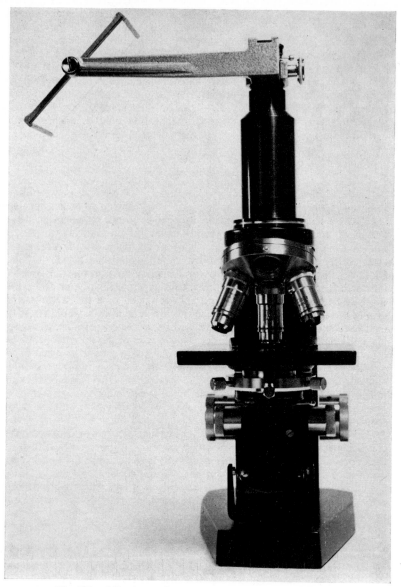

Fig. 188.—Microscope fitted with camera lucida, for drawing.

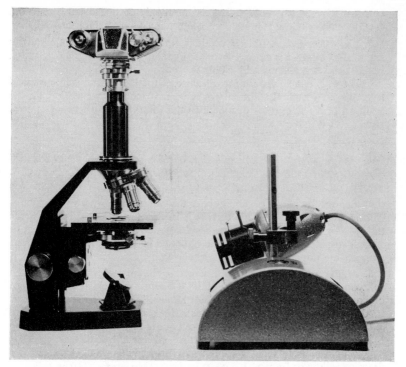

Fig. 189.—Reflex camera (using 35 mm. film) fitted, by means of an adaptor, to the eyepiece tube of a microscope.

photomicrography. If the lighting conditions are standardised, correct exposure can be judged sufficiently accurately after some experimenting. There are, of course, many more elaborate forms of photomicrographic apparatus, for which the microscope manufacturers' catalogues should be consulted, but these are only worth while if a great deal of work is to be done. Reference may be made to the following books for further information and guidance on photomicrography: Barnard and Welch (1936), Allen (1958), Lawson (1960), Shillaber (1963), Barron (1965).

MICROCHEMICAL TESTS

It is sometimes worth while to apply standard microchemical tests to wood, especially to extraneous materials. Such tests leave much to be desired, but they are, nevertheless, sometimes useful and a few of the simple, better known ones are listed below:

(*a*) *Cellulose:*

1. *Iodine and Sulphuric Acid.*—Soak sections in a dilute (straw-coloured) solution of iodine in potassium iodide. After about a minute drain off the iodine and add sulphuric acid (about 70 per cent by volume). Cellulose is

2E

coloured blue, but lignified cell walls commonly do not give this reaction, even though cellulose is present; the lignin masks the cellulose.

2. *Chlor-zinc-iodine.*—Place sections in chlor-zinc-iodine (Schultze's solution). Cellulose is coloured violet; lignified tissue turns yellow; starch grains swell and assume a blue colour.

This test is not as certain for cellulose as the iodine and sulphuric acid test, although a good solution works well. If trouble is experienced, the addition of a few crystals of iodine to the solution will often put matters right.

(*b*) *Lignin:*

1. *Aniline sulphate* (or *aniline hydrochloride*).—Soak sections in acidified aqueous aniline sulphate. Lignified tissues turn bright yellow.

2. *Phloroglucinol.*—Soak sections in 1 per cent phloroglucinol in 95 per cent alcohol for about one minute, drain and replace with strong hydrochloric acid. Lignified tissues turn red. In this test the acid may precede the phloroglucinol, with the same result.

Unfortunately, the bright colours obtained in lignified tissues with these reagents are not permanent.

3. *Mäule reaction.*—This test, which differentiates hardwoods from softwoods, is included because of its academic interest. It is based on differences in the composition of their lignins, but is unlikely to be of use to the wood anatomist (Gibbs, 1958). Soak material in 0·5–1 per cent aqueous potassium permanganate for ten minutes. Wash in water, followed by dilute hydrochloric acid, and transfer to dilute ammonia.

Angiospermous wood turns red: gymnospermous wood turns a nondescript yellow or brown.

(*c*) *Cork:*

1. Stains with fat stains (q.v.).

2. *Potassium hydroxide.*—Immerse sections on a slide in strong potassium hydroxide solution: cork is coloured yellow. On heating, the yellow colour deepens and yellow drops of phellonic acid, visible under the microscope, are formed.

(*d*) *Starch:*

1. *Iodine in potassium iodide.*—Starch stains blue. The colour disappears if the section is warmed, but reappears on cooling.

Unless the reagent is used very weak the starch grains are stained a deep blue-black.

2. *Polarized light.*—If starch is examined in a polarizing microscope with the polaroids in the crossed position, the grains show a black, maltesetype cross, indicative of their essentially radial internal organization.

(*e*) *Oils and Fats:*

Oils dissolve certain stains (fat stains). Of these, the best known are sudan III (fett ponceau) and sudan IV (scharlach R), both of which stain oils red. They should be made up for use in equal parts of alcohol and glycerine.

As oils may themselves sometimes be deep yellow or brownish in colour, greater visibility of staining is sometimes obtained with sudan blue, which colours oils blue.

(*f*) *Gums:*
True gums are soluble in warm water, but not in alcohol.

(*g*) *Resins:*
Resins are soluble in alcohol, but not in water. Resins are stained by fat stains (q.v.).

(*h*) *Tannins:*
Tannins react with iron salts to form an ink. Five per cent ferric chloride solution gives a deep greenish-black or bluish-black colour, the colour depending on the type of tannin.

(*i*) *Mineral Matter:*

1. *Calcium carbonate.*—Dissolves in acetic acid. Dissolves in dilute hydrochloric acid with effervescence.

2. *Calcium oxalate.*—Insoluble in acetic acid. Dissolves in dilute hydrochloric acid without effervescence.

3. *Silica.*—Insoluble in hydrochloric, nitric or sulphuric acids. Soluble in hydrofluoric acid.

BIBLIOGRAPHY

AARON, J. R. and WILSON, K. (1955). Soft-rotting fungi in timber. *Wood* **20**, 186–9.

ALLEN, R. M. (1958). Photomicrography. New York.

ALVIM, P. DE T. (1964). Tree growth periodicity in tropical climates. *In* Zimmermann (1964), pp. 479–95.

AMBRONN, H. and FREY, A. (1926). Das Polarisationsmikroscop. Leipzig.

AMOS, G. L. (1952). Silica in timber. *C.S.I.R.O. (Australia), Bull.* **267**, 1–55.

AMOS, G. L. and DADSWELL, H. E. (1948). Siliceous inclusions in wood in relation to marine borer resistance. *J. Coun. sci. industr. Res. Aust.* **21**, 190–6.

ANDERSON, E. A. (1951). Tracheid length variation in conifers as related to distance from the pith. *J. For.* **49**, 38–42.

ANON. (1952). Manual of the Polarising Microscope. Cooke, Troughton & Simms, York.

ARMSTRONG, F. H. (1948). Flooring hardwoods: their wear and anatomical structure. *For. Prod. Res. Lab. Bull.* **21**.

— (1949). Flooring softwoods: their wear and anatomical structure. *For. Prod. Res. Lab. Bull.* **23**.

— (1957). Timbers for flooring. *For. Prod. Res. Lab. Bull.* **40**.

ASTBURY, W. T. (1933). Fundamentals of fibre structure. London.

AUDUS, L. J. (1964). Geotropism and the modified sine rule: an interpretation based on the amyloplast statolith theory. *Physiol. Plant.* **17**, 737–45.

BAILEY, I. W. (1913). The preservative treatment of wood. II. The structure of the pit membranes in the tracheids of conifers, and their relation to the penetration of gases, liquids and finely divided solids in green and seasoned wood. *Forestry Quarterly* **11**, 12–20.

— (1917). The role of the microscope in the identification and classification of the "timbers of commerce". *J. For.* **15**, 1–13.

— (1920). The cambium and its derivative tissues. III. A reconnaissance of cytological phenomena in the cambium. *Amer. J. Bot.* **7**, 417–34.

— (1923). The cambium and its derivative tissues. IV. The increase in the girth of the cambium. *Amer. J. Bot.* **10**, 499–509.

— (1932). Preliminary notes on cribriform and vestured pits. *Trop. Woods* **31**, 46–8.

— (1933). The cambium and its derivative tissues. VIII. Structure, distribution and diagnostic significance of vestured pits in dicotyledons. *J. Arnold Arbor.* **14**, 259–73.

— (1954). Contributions to Plant Anatomy. Waltham, Mass.

— (1958). The structure of tracheids in relation to the movement of liquids, suspensions and undissolved gases. *In* Thimann, pp. 71–82.

BAILEY, I. W. and BERKELEY, E. E. (1942). The significance of X-rays in studying the orientation of cellulose in the secondary wall of tracheids. *Amer. J. Bot.* **29**, 231–41.

BAILEY, I. W. and FAULL, A. F. (1934). The cambium and its derivative tissues. IX. Structural variability in the redwood, *Sequoia sempervirens*, and its significance in the identification of fossil woods. *J. Arnold Arbor.* **15**, 233–54.

BAILEY, I. W. and HOWARD, R. A. (1941). Imperforate tracheal elements and xylem parenchyma. *J. Arnold Arbor.* **22**, 432–42.

BAILEY, I. W. and KERR, T. (1935). The visible structure of the secondary wall and its significance in physical and chemical investigations of tracheary cells and fibres. *J. Arnold Arbor.* **16**, 273–300.

BAILEY, I. W. and NAST, C. G. (1944). The comparative morphology of the Winteraceae. III. Wood. *J. Arnold Arbor.* **25**, 97–103.

— (1945). The comparative morphology of the Winteraceae. VII. Summary and conclusions. *J. Arnold Arbor.* **26**, 37–47.

BAILEY, I. W. and VESTAL, N. R. (1937). The significance of certain wood-destroying fungi in the study of the enzymatic hydrolysis of cellulose. *J. Arnold Arbor.* **18**, 196–205.

BALCH, R. E. (1952). Studies of the Balsam Woolly Aphid, *Adelges piceae* (Ratz) and its effects on Balsam Fir, *Abies balsamea* (L.) Mill. *Pub. Dept. Agric. Can.* **867**.

BANKS, W. B. (1968). A technique for measuring the lateral permeability of wood. *J. Inst. Wood Sci.* **20**, 35–41.

BANNAN, M. W. (1941–2). Wood structure of *Thuja occidentalis*. *Bot. Gaz.* **103**, 295–309.

— (1942). Wood structure of the native Ontario species of *Juniperus*. *Amer. J. Bot.* **29**, 245–52.

— (1944). Wood structure of *Libocedrus decurrens*. *Amer. J. Bot.* **31**, 346–51.

— (1950). The frequency of anticlinal divisions in fusiform cambial cells of *Chamaecyparis*. *Amer. J. Bot.* **37**, 511–9.

— (1952). The microscopic wood structure of North American species of *Chamaecyparis*. *Can. J. Bot.* **30**, 170–87.

— (1956). Some aspects of the elongation of fusiform cambial cells in *Thuja occidentalis*. *Can. J. Bot.* **34**, 175–96.

— (1960a). Cambial behaviour with reference to cell length and ring width in *Thuja occidentalis* L. *Can. J. Bot.* **38**, 177–83.

— (1960b). Ontogenetic trends in conifer cambium with respect to frequency of anticlinal divisions and cell length. *Can. J. Bot.* **38**, 795–802.

— (1962a). The vascular cambium and tree ring development. *In* Kozlowski, pp. 3–21.

— (1962b). Cambial behaviour with reference to cell length and ring width in *Pinus strobus*. *Can. J. Bot.* **40**, 1057–62.

— (1963a). Cambial behaviour with reference to cell length and ring width in *Picea*. *Can. J. Bot.* **41**, 811–22.

— (1963b). Tracheid size and rate of anticlinal divisions in the cambium of *Cupressus*. *Can. J. Bot.* **41**, 1187–98.

— (1964). Tracheid size and anticlinal divisions in the cambium of *Pseudotsuga*. *Can. J. Bot.* **42**, 603–31.

— (1965). The rate of elongation of fusiform initials in the cambium of Pinaceae. *Can. J. Bot.* **43**, 429–35.

BANNAN, M. W. (1966). Spiral grain and anticlinal divisions in the cambium of conifers. *Can. J. Bot.* **44**, 1515–38.

BARBER, G. A., ELBEIN, A. D. and HASSID, W. Z. (1964). The synthesis of cellulose by enzyme systems from higher plants. *J. Biol. Chem.* **239**, 4056–61.

BARER, R. (1959). Lecture notes on the use of the microscope. Oxford.

BARNARD, J. E. and WELCH, F. V. (1936). Practical photomicrography. London.

BARON, A. L. E. (1965). Using the microscope. London.

BAYLIS, P. E. T. (1960). Lignin. *Science Progress* **48**, 409–34.

BEEKMAN, W. B. (1964). Elsevier's wood dictionary. Vol. I. Commercial and botanical nomenclature of world timbers. Amsterdam, London and New York.

BERLYN, G. P. (1961). Factors affecting the incidence of reaction tissue in *Populus deltoides* Bartr. *Iowa State Journal of Science* **35**, 367–424.

BETHEL, J. S. (1950). The influence of wood structure on the strength of Loblolly Pine wood (*Pinus taeda* L.). *Tech. Rep. Sch. For. N.C. St. Coll. 3.*

BEVAN, C. W. L., EKONG, D. E. U. and TAYLOR, D. A. H. (1965). Extractives from West African species of the Meliaceae. *Nature, Lond.* **206**, 1323–5.

BIANCHI, A. T. J. (1931). Een nieuwe determinatiemethode. *Tectona* **24**, 884–93.

BISSET, I. J. W. and DADSWELL, H. E. (1949). The variation of fibre length within one tree of *Eucalyptus regnans* F.v.M. *Aust. For.* **13**, 86–96.

— (1950). The variation in cell length within one growth ring of certain angiosperms and gymnosperms. *Aust. For.* **14**, 17–29.

BISSET, I. J. W., DADSWELL, H. E. and AMOS, G. L. (1950). Changes in fibre length within one growth ring of certain angiosperms. *Nature, Lond.* **165**, 348–9.

BISSET, I. J. W., DADSWELL, H. E. and WARDROP, A. B. (1951). Factors influencing tracheid length in conifer stems. *Aust. For.* **15**, 17–30.

BOAS, I. H. (1947). The commercial timbers of Australia: their properties and uses. Melbourne.

BOLKER, H. I. (1963). A lignin carbohydrate bond as revealed by infra-red spectroscopy. *Nature, Lond.* **197**, 489–90.

BOSSHARD, H. (1951). Variabilität der Elemente des Eschenholzes in Funktion von der Kambiumtätigkeit. *Schweiz. Z. Forstw.* **102**, 648–65.

— (1952). Elektronenmikroskopische Untersuchungen im Holz von *Fraxinus excelsior*. *Ber. schweiz. bot. Ges.* **62**, 482.

— (1956). Der Feinbau des Holzes als Grundlage technologischer Fragen. *Schweiz. Z. Forstw.* **107** (1), 81–95.

BOYD, J. D. (1950). Tree growth stresses. II. The development of shakes and other visual features in timber. *Aust. J. Applied Science* **1**, 296–312.

BRAUNS, F. E. and BRAUNS, D. A. (1960). The Chemistry of Lignin. New York.

BRAZIER, J. D. (1956). Meranti, Seraya and allied timbers. *For. Prod. Res. Lab. Bull.* **36**.

BRAZIER, J. D. and FRANKLIN, G. L. (1961). *See* For. Prod. Res. Lab. Microscope Key.

BRITISH STANDARDS INSTITUTION (1934). Terms and definitions applicable to softwoods. *B.S.* **565**. London.

— (1946). Nomenclature of commercial timbers. *B.S.* **881** and **589**. London.

— (1955). Nomenclature of commercial timbers including sources of supply. *B.S.* **881** and **589**. London.

BROWN, H. P., PANSHIN, A. J. and FORSAITH, C. C. Vol. I (1949); Vol. II (1952); Textbook of Wood Technology. New York.

BROWN, N. C. (1947). Timber products and industries. New York.

BROWNING, B. L. (1963). (*Editor*) The chemistry of wood. New York.

BRYANT, B. S. (1966). The chemical Modification of Wood. *For. Prod. Journ.* **16**, *No. 2*, 20–7.

BUCHER, H. (1957a). Die Tertiarwand von Holzfasern und ihre Erscheinungsformen bei Coniferen. *Holzforsch.* **11**, 1–16.

— (1957b). Die Struktur der Tertiarwand von Holzfasern. *Holzforsch.* **11**, 97–102.

BUCHHOLZ, J. T. (1939). The generic segregation of the Sequoias. *Amer. J. Bot.* **26**, 535–8.

BUNN, C. W. (1945). Chemical Crystallography. Oxford.

BURNS, G. P. (1920). Excentric growth and the formation of red wood in the main stem of conifers. *Vermont Agric. Expt. Stn. Bull.* **219**, 1–16.

CARTWRIGHT, K. ST. G. (1929). A satisfactory method of staining fungal mycelium in wood sections. *Ann. Bot.* **43**, 412–3.

— (1937). A reinvestigation into the cause of "Brown Oak", *Fistulina hepatica* (Huds.) Fr. *Trans. Brit. mycol. Soc.* **21**, 68–83.

CARTWRIGHT, K. ST. G. and FINLAY, W. P. K. (1958). Decay of timber and its prevention. H.M.S.O., London.

CHALK, L. (1930). Tracheid length, with special reference to Sitka spruce (*Picea sitchensis* Carr.). *Forestry* **4**, 7–14.

— (1937). The phylogenetic value of certain anatomical features of dicotyledonous woods. *Ann. Bot. Lond. N.S.* **1**, 408–28.

— (1938). Standardisation of terms for vessel diameter and ray width. *Trop. Woods* **55**, 16–23.

CHALK, L. and CHATTAWAY, M. M. (1937). Identification of woods with included phloem. *Trop. Woods* **50**, 1–31.

CHALK, L., MARSTRAND, E. B. and WALSH, J. P. DE C. (1955). Fibre length in storeyed hardwoods. *Acta Bot. Neerland.* **4**, 339–47.

CHAPLIN, C. J. (1945). Stress grading of timber. *Timber Development Assoc.* London.

CHATTAWAY, M. M. (1932). Proposed standards for numerical values used in describing wood. *Trop. Woods* **29**, 20–8.

— (1933). Tile cells in the rays of the Malvales. *New Phytol.* **32**, 261–73.

— (1949). The development of tyloses and secretion of gum in the heartwood formation. *Aust. J. Sci. Res. B.* **2**, 227–40.

CHOW, K. Y. (1946). A comparative study of the structure and chemical composition of tension wood and normal wood in beech (*Fagus sylvatica* L.). *Forestry* **20**, 62–77.

CHOWDHURY, K. A. (1934). The so-called terminal parenchyma cells in the wood of *Terminalia tomentosa*. *Nature, Lond.* **133**, 215.
— (1936). Terminal and initial parenchyma cells in the wood of *Terminalia tomentosa* W. & A. *New Phytol.* **35**, 351–8.

CLARKE, S. H. (1935). Recent work on the relation between anatomical structure and mechanical strength in English Ash (*Fraxinus excelsior* L.). *Forestry* **9**, 132–8.
— (1937a). A comparison of certain properties of temperate and tropical timbers. *Trop. Woods* **52**, 1–11.
— (1937b). The distribution, structure and properties of tension wood in Beech (*Fagus sylvatica* L.). *Forestry* **11**, 85–91.
— (1938a). Fine structure of the plant cell wall. *Nature, Lond.* **142**, 899.
— (1938b). A multiple entry perforated-card key with special reference to the identification of hardwoods. *New Phytol.* **37**, 369–74.
— (1939). Catalogue of features for use in the construction of a key to the identification of hardwood timbers. *For. Prod. Proj. 9, Progress Rep.* **4** Pt. 2.
— (1940). A lens key to hardwood timbers. *For Prod. Res. Proj. 9, Progress Rep.* **4**, Pt. 3.

COHEN, W. E. (1933). A simple chemical test for separating the woods of Hoop Pine (*Araucaria cunninghamii*) and Bunya Pine (*Araucaria bidwilli*) *J. Coun. sci. indust. Res. Aust.* **6**, 126–7.
— (1935). The identification of wood by chemical means. Pt. II. Alkalinity of ash and some simple tests for the identification of the coloured woods of the genus *Eucalyptus*. *Pamphl. Coun. sci. indust. Res. Aust.* **53**.

COLVIN, J. R. (1964). The biosynthesis of cellulose. *In* Zimmermann (1964).

CÔTÉ, W. A.(Jr.) (1965). (*Editor*) Cellular Ultrastructure of woody plants. Syracuse, N.Y.

CÔTÉ, W. A. (Jr.) and DAY, A. C. (1965). Anatomy and Ultrastructure of Reaction Wood. *In* Côté (1965), pp. 391–418.

CRONSHAW, J. (1965). Cytoplasmic fine structure and cell wall development in differentiating xylem. *In* Côté (1965), pp. 99–124.

CRONSHAW, J. and MOREY, P. R. (1965). Induction of tension wood by 2-3-5-tri-iodobenzoic acid. *Nature, Lond.* **205**, 861–18.

CURRY, W. T. (1966). Stress grading machines. *Timb. Tr. J.* **259**, 71–7.

DADSWELL, H. E. (1931). The identification of wood by chemical means. Pt. I. *Pamphl. Coun. sci. indust. Res. Aust.* **20**.
— (1957). Tree growth characteristics and their influence on wood structure and properties. Seventh British Commonwealth Forestry Conference.
— (1958). Wood structure variations occurring during tree growth and their influence on properties. *J. Inst. Wood Sci.* **1**, 11–33.

DADSWELL, H. E. and BURNELL, M. (1932). Method for the identification of the coloured woods of the genus *Eucalyptus*. *Bull Coun. sci. indust.Res Aust.* **67**.

DADSWELL, H. E., BURNELL, M. and ECKERSLEY, A. M. (1934). Methods for the identification of the light coloured woods of the genus *Eucalyptus*. *Bull. Coun. sci. indust. Res. Aust.* **78**.

DADSWELL, H. E. and ECKERSLEY, A. M. (1935). The identification of the principal commercial Australian timbers other than *Eucalyptus*. *Bull. Coun. sci. indust. Res. Aust.* **90**.

DADSWELL, H. E., ECKERSLEY, A. M., GRIFFIN, F. V. and INGLE, H. D. (1947). The extension of the card sorting method to war-time problems in timber identification. *J. Coun. sci. indust. Res. Aust.* **20**, 321–37.

DADSWELL, H. E., FIELDING, J. M., NICHOLLS, J. W. P. and BROWN, A. G. (1961). Tree to tree variations and gross heretability of wood characteristics of *Pinus radiata. Tappi* **44**, 174–9.

DADSWELL, H. E. and NICHOLLS, J. W. P. (1959). Assessment of wood qualities for tree breeding. I. In *Pinus elliottii* var. *elliottii* from Queensland. *C.S.I.R.O. Australia Div. of For. Prod. Tech. paper No.* **4**.

DADSWELL, H. E. and WARDROP, A. B. (1946). Cell wall formation in wood fibres. *Nature, Lond.* **158**, 174-5.

— (1949). What is Reaction Wood? *Aust. For.* **13**, 22–33.

— (1955). The structure and properties of tension wood. *Holzforsch.* **9** (4), 97–104.

— (1959). Growing trees with wood properties desirable for paper manufacture. *Appita* **12**, 129–36.

DADSWELL, H. E., WATSON, A. J. and NICHOLLS, J. W. P. (1959). What are the wood properties required by the paper industry in the trees of the future. *Tappi* **42**, 521–6.

DALLIMORE, W. and JACKSON, A. B. (1948). A Handbook of coniferae. (3rd edition.) London.

— (1966). (*Revised* Harrison, S. G.) (4th edition).

DE BARY, A. (1884). Comparative anatomy of the vegetative organs of the Phanerogams and Ferns. Oxford.

DESCH, H. E. (1932). Anatomical variation in the wood of some dicotyledonous trees. *New Phytol.* **31**, 73–118.

— (1941). Dipterocarp timbers of the Malay peninsula. *Malayan Forest Records No.* **14**.

— (1968). Timber: its structure and properties. (4th edition.) London.

DINWOODIE, J. M. (1963). Variation in tracheid length of *Picea sitchensis* Carr. *D.S.I.R. For. Prod. Res. Special Report* **10**.

— (1966). Induction of cell wall dislocations (slip-planes) during the preparation of microscope sections of wood. *Nature, Lond.* **212**, 525–7.

— (1967). Recording the initiation of failure in timber. *Nature, Lond.* **216**, 827–8.

DOBBS, C. G. (1951). A study of growth rings in trees. *Forestry* **24**, 22–35

DOUGLASS, A. E. (1919). Climatic cycles and tree growth: a study of the annual rings of trees in relation to climate and solar activity. I. *Publ. Carneg. Instn.* **289**.

— (1928). Climatic cycles and tree growth: a study of the annual rings of trees in relation to climate and solar activity. II. *Publ. Carneg. Instn.* **289**.

— (1936). Climatic cycles and tree growth: a study of cycles. III. *Publ. Carneg. Instn.* **289**.

EADES, H. W. (1932). British Columbia softwoods: their decays and natural defects. *Bull. For. Serv. Can.* **80.**

ECHOLS, R. M. (1955). Linear relation of fibrillar angle to tracheid length and genetic control of tracheid length in slash pine. *Trop. Woods* **102,** 11–22.

— (1958). Variation in tracheid length and wood density in geographic races of Scots Pine. *Yale Sch. For. Bull.* **64.**

EGGELING, W. J. and HARRIS, C. M. (1939). Fifteen Uganda timbers. Forest trees and timbers of the British Empire. IV. Oxford.

ELLIOTT, G. K. (1960). The distribution of tracheid length in a single stem of Sitka spruce. *J. Inst. Wood Sci.* **5,** 38–47.

EMERTON, H. W. (1957). Fundamentals of the beating process. Kenley.

ENGLER, A. and PRANTL, K. (1897–1915). Die natürlichen Pflanzenfamilien. 1st ed. Leipzig. (A number of volumes of the second edition have already been published.)

ESAU, K. (1964). Structure and development of the bark in dicotyledons. *In* Zimmermann (1964), pp. 37–50.

— (1965). Plant anatomy. 2nd edition. New York.

ESAU, K. and HEWITT, W. B. (1940). Structure of end walls in differentiating vessels. *Hilgardia* **13,** 229–44.

EWART, A. J. and MASON-JONES, A. J. (1906). The formation of red wood in conifers. *Ann. Bot. Lond.* **20,** 201–3.

FAHN, A. and ARNON, N. (1963). The living wood fibres of *Tamarix aphylla* and the changes occurring in them in the transition from sapwood to heartwood. *New Phyt.* **62,** 99–104.

FARMER, R. H. (1967). Chemistry in the utilization of wood. London.

FEGEL, A. C. (1941). Comparative anatomy and varying physical properties of trunk, branch and root wood in certain north eastern trees. *Bull. N.Y. St. Coll. For. Tech. Pub.* **55.**

FINDLAY, W. P. K. (1957). Durability of African mahogany—*Khaya ivorensis. Empire Forestry Review* **36,** 91–3.

— (1967). Timber pests and diseases. London.

FOREST PRODUCTS RESEARCH LABORATORIES (1952). Identification of hardwoods; a lens key. *For. Prod. Res. Bull.* **25.**

— (1953). An atlas of end-grain photomicrographs for the identification of hardwoods. *For. Prod. Res. Bull.* **26.**

— (1956). Reaction Wood (Tension Wood and Compression Wood). Lft. **51.**

— (1960). Identification of hardwoods; a lens key. *For. Prod. Res. Bull.* **25,** (2nd ed.).

— (1961). Identification of hardwoods; a microscope key. *For. Prod. Res. Bull.* **46,**

— (1968). Grade stresses for structural timbers. *Bull.* **47.**

FORSAITH, C. C. (1926). The technology of New York State timbers. *Tech. Pub. N.Y. St. Coll. For.* **18.**

— (1946). The physical properties of wood. *In* Wise (1946), 54–81.

FOUARGE, J. and SACRÉ, E. (1943). Analyse physique, mechanique et anatomique de bois de pin sylvestre. *Bull. Inst. agron. Gembloux* **12,** 14–43.

FRANKLIN, G. L. (1938). The preparation of woody tissues for microscopic examination. *For. Prod. Res. Lab.* [cf. also: The preparation of wood for microscopic examination. *For. Prod. Res. Lab. Lft.* **40** (1951)].

— (1946). A rapid method of softening wood for microtome sectioning. *Trop. Woods* **88**, 35–6.

FRASER, D. A. (1952). Initiation of cambial activity in some forest trees in Ontario. *Ecology* **33**, 259–73.

FREI, E., PRESTON, R. D. and RIPLEY, G. W. (1957). The fine structure of the walls of conifer tracheids. VI. Electron-microscope investigations of sections. *J. Exp. Bot.* **8**, 139–46.

FREUDENBERG, K. (1964). The formation of lignin in the tissue and *in vitro*. *In* Zimmermann (1964), pp. 203–18.

FREY-WYSSLING, A. (1943). Weitere Untersuchungen über die Schwindungs-anisotrophie des Holzes. *Holz. a. Roh-u. Werkst.* **6**, 197–8.

— (1948). Submicroscopic morphology of protoplasm and its derivatives. Elsevier, New York.

— (1964). Cytology of ageing ray cells. *In* Zimmermann (1964), p. 457.

FREY-WYSSLING, A. and BOSSHARD, H. H. (1959). The cytology of ray cells in sapwood and heartwood. *Holzforsch.* **13**, 129–37.

FREY-WYSSLING, A., MUHLETHALER, K. and WYCKOFF, R. (1948). Mikro-fibrillenbau der pflanzlichen Zellwände. *Experientia* **4** (12), 475.

FROST, F. H. (1930). Bordered pits in parenchyma. *Bull. Torrey bot. Cl.* **56**, 259–63.

GARLAND, H. (1939). A microscopic study of wood in relation to its strength properties. *Ann. Mo. bot. Gdn.* **26**, 1–94.

GERRY, E. (1915). Fibre measurement studies; length variations, where they occur and their relation to the strength and uses of wood. *Science* **41**, 179.

— (1916). Fibre measurement: a comparison of tracheid dimensions in Longleaf Pine and Douglas Fir. *Science* **43**, 360–1.

GIBBS, R. D. (1958). The Mäule reaction, lignins and the relationships between woody plants. *In* Thimann (1958), pp. 269–312.

GIDDINGS, J. L. (1962). Development of tree-ring dating as an archaeological aid. *In* Kozlowski (1962), pp. 119–32.

GLOCK, W. S. (1941). Growth rings and climate. *Bot. Rev.* **7**, 649.

GLOCK, W. S., STUDHALTER, R. A. and AGERTER, S. R. (1960). Classification and multiplicity of growth layers in the branches of trees at the extreme lower forest border. *Smithson. misc. Coll.* **140** (1), Public. 4421.

GONGGRIJP, J. W. (1932). Gegevens betreffende een onderzoek naar Neder-landsch-Indische houtsoorten, welke tegen den paalworm bestand zijn. *Meded. boschbouw. Proefst.* **25**, 1–100. English Summary in *Trop. Woods* **33**, 51–2.

GREEN, M. L. (1931). Rules of Botanical Nomenclature. *Emp. For. J.* **10** 54–72.

GROOM, P. (1926). Excretory systems in the secondary xylem of Meliaceae. *Ann. Bot. Lond.* **40**, 631–49.

HALE, J. D. (1932). The identification of woods commonly used in Canada. *Bull. For. Serv. Can.* **81**.

HARADA, H. (1965). Ultrastructure and organization of Gymnosperm Cell Walls. *In* Côté, (1965), pp. 215–33.

HARLOW, H. W. (1944). The chemical softening of wood for microtome sectioning. *Bull. N.Y. St. Coll. For. Tech. Publ.* **63**.

HARTMANN, F. (1932). Untersuchungen über Ursachen und Gesetzmässigkeit exzentrischen Dickenwachstums bei Nadel- und Laubbaüme. *Forstwiss. Centralbl.* **54**, 497–517, 547–66, 581–90, 622–34.

— (1942). Das statische Wuchsgesetz bei Nadel- und Laubbaüme. Neue Erkenntnis über Ursache, Gesetzmässigkeit und Sinn des Reaktionsholzes. Vienna.

— (1943). Die Frage der Gleichgewichtsreaktion von Stamm und Wurzel heimischer Waldbaüme. *Biol. Gen.* **17**, 367–418.

HARTSHORNE, N. H. and STUART, M. J. (1960). Crystals and the Polarizing Microscope. London.

HEJNOWICZ, A. and HEJNOWICZ, Z. (1958). Variations of length in vessel members and fibres in the trunk of *Populus tremula. Acta Soc. Bot. Polon.* **27**.,131–59.

— (1959). Variations of length of vessel members and fibres in the trunk of *Robinia pseudoacacia. Acta Soc. Bot. Polon.* **28**, 453–60.

HERMANS, P. H. (1949). Physics and chemistry of cellulose fibres. New York.

HESS, R. W. (1950). Classification of wood parenchyma in dicotyledons. *Trop. Woods* **96**, 1–20.

HILL, A. F. (1937). Economic Botany. New York.

HODGE, A. J. and WARDROP, A. B. (1950). An electron microscopic investigation of the cell wall organisation of conifer tracheids and conifer cambium. *Aust. J. sci. Res. B* **3**. 265–9.

HOWES, F. N. (1949). Vegetable gums and resins. Waltham, Mass.

HUNT, G. M. and GARRATT, G. A. (1967). Wood Preservation. 3rd ed. New York and London.

HUTCHINSON, J. (1959). The families of flowering plants. I. Dicotyledons. Oxford.

INTERNATIONAL ASSOCIATION OF WOOD ANATOMISTS (1932). Glossary of terms used in describing woods. *Trop. Woods* **36**, 1–13.

— (1939). Standard terms of size for vessel diameter and ray width. *Trop. Woods* **59**, 51–2.

— (1957). International glossary of terms used in wood anatomy. *Trop. Woods* **107**, 1–36.

— (1964). (Committee on Nomenclature.) Multilingual glossary of terms used in wood anatomy.

JACCARD, P. (1938). Exzentrisches Dickenwachstum und anatomisch-histologische Differenzierung des Holzes. *Ber. schweiz. bot. Ges.* **48**, 491–502.

— (1940). Tropisme et bois de reaction provoques par la force centrifuge chez des feuilles. *Ber. schweiz. bot. Ges.* **50**, 279–84.

JACOBS, M. R. (1945). The growth stresses of woody stems. *Common. For. Bur. Aust. Bull.* **28**.

JANE, F. W. (1932–3). The microscopic examination of woody material. *Watson's micr. Rec.* **27**, 3–6; **29**, 8–9; **30**, 8–11.

— (1934). Terminal and initial parenchyma in wood. *Nature, Lond.* **133**, 534.

— (1935). A "back" for use when honing microtome knives. *Ann. Bot. Lond.* **49**, 399–400.

— (1949). The living tree. *Essex Nat.* **28**, 104–18.

— (1951). The natural history of a piece of wood. *Sch. Nat. Stud.* **46**, 34–8.

JANSONNIUS, H. H. (1950). The variability of the wood anatomy in large and small genera. *Blumea* **6**, 462–4.

JOHANSEN, D. A. (1940). Plant microtechnique. New York.

JUTTE, S. M. (1956). Tension wood of Wane (*Ocotea rubra* Mez.). *Holzforsch.* **10**, 33–5.

JUTTE, S. M. and ISINGS, J. (1955). The determination of tension wood in Ash with the aid of the phase-contrast microscope. *Experientia* **11**, 386.

KAEISER, M. (1955). Frequency and distribution of gelatinous fibres in eastern cottonwood. *Amer. J. Bot.* **42**, 331–4.

KANEHIRA, R. (1921). Identification of Formosan woods. *Bull. Formosa Bur. prod. Ind.*

KAY, D. H. (Editor). (1965). Techniques for Electron Microscopy. 2nd edit. Oxford.

KENNEDY, R. W. and FARRAR, J. L. (1965). Induction of tension wood with the anti-auxin 2-3-5-tri-iodobenzoic acid. *Nature, Lond.* **208**, 406–7.

KENNEDY, R. W. and WILSON, J. W. (1954). Studies in smooth and cork barked *Abies lasiocarpa* (Hook.) Nutt. I. Fibre length comparisons. *Pulp Pap.* (*Mag.*) *Can.* **55**, 130–2.

KERR, T. and BAILEY, I. W. (1934). The cambium and its derivative tissues. X. Structure, optical properties and chemical composition of the so-called middle lamella. *J. Arnold Arbor.* **15**, 327–49.

KOBAYASHI, Y. (1952). Identification of Japanese Alder woods. I. The properties of wood rays. *Bull. For. Exp. Sta. Meguro* **52**, 181–97. [For English summary cf. *Forestry Abstracts* **14**, (1953).]

KOEHLER, A. (1924). The properties and uses of wood. New York.

KOLLMANN, F. and ANTONOFF, M. (1943). Beitrag zur Erforschung des submikroscopischen Feinbaus von Holz. *Holz. a. Roh-u. Werkst.* **6**, 41–5.

KÓRÁN, Z. and CÔTÉ, W. A., Jr. (1965). The ultra-structure of tyloses. *In* Côte (1965), pp. 319–33.

KOZLOWSKI, T. T. (Editor). (1962). Tree Growth. New York.

KRAEMER, S. H. (1951). Agric. Expt. Stn., Purdue University *Bull.* **560**.

KRAHMER, R. L. and CÔTÉ, W. A. (Jr.) (1963). Changes in coniferous wood cells associated with heartwood formation. *Tappi* **46**, 42–9.

KRATZL, K. (1965). Lignin, its biochemistry and structure. *In* Côté (1965), pp. 157–80.

KRIBS, D. A. (1935). Salient lines of structural specialisation in the wood rays of dicotyledons. *Bot. Gaz.* **96**, 547–57.

— (1937). Salient lines of structural specialisation in the wood parenchyma of dicotyledons. *Bull. Torrey bot. Cl.* **64**, 177–86.

— (1950). Commercial foreign woods on the American market. Pennsylvania.

KURTH, E. F. (1946). The extraneous components of wood. *In* Wise (1946), pp. 385–445.

LAIDLAW, R. A., PINION, L. C. and SMITH, G. A. (1967). Dimensional stability of wood. II. Grafting of vinyl polymers to wood components. *Holzforsch.* **21**, 97–102.

LAMB, G. N. (1948). The Mahogany Book 7th Ed. Mahogany Assoc. Inc. Chicago.

LARSEN, P. R. (1957). Effect of environment on the percentage of summerwood and specific gravity of Slash pine. *Yale Sch. For. Bull.* **63**, 1–80.

LATHAM, J. and ARMSTRONG, F. H. (1934). The mechanical strength properties of "Brown Oak". *Forestry* **8**, 131–5.

LAWSON, D. F. (1960). The technique of photomicrography. London.

LEVY, J. (1965). The soft-rot fungi: their mode of action and significance in the degradation of wood. *Adv. Bot. Res.* **2**, 323–57.

LIESE, W. (1957). Zur Struktur der Tertiarwand bei den Laubholzern. (The structure of the tertiary wall in hardwoods). *Naturwiss.* **44**, 240–1.

— (1965a). The warty layer. *In* Côté (1965), pp. 251–69.

— (1965b). The fine structure of bordered pits in softwoods. *In* Côté (1965), pp. 271–90.

LIESE, W. and CÔTÉ, W. A. (1962). Electron microscopy of wood. Results of the first ten years of research. Fifth World Forestry Proceedings, Seattle, Washington (1960), Vol. II, 1288–98.

LIESE, W. and DADSWELL, H. E. (1959). Über den Einfluss der Himmelerichtung auf die Länge von Holzfasern und Tracheiden. *Holz. a Roh-u. Werkst.* **17**, 421–7.

LIESE, W. and HARTMANN-FAHNENBROCK, M. (1953). Elektronenmikroskopische Untersuchungen über die Hoftüpfel der Nadelhölzer. *Biochim, Biophys. Acta.* **11**, 190–8.

LIESE, W. and LEDBETTER, M. C. (1963). Occurrence of a warty layer in vascular cells of plants. *Nature, Lond.* **197** (4863), 201–2.

LINDSAY, F. W. and CHALK, L. (1954). The influence of rays on the shrinkage of wood. *Forestry* **27**, 16–24.

LINNAEUS, C. (1753). Species Plantarum. Holm. [Facsimile of First Edition: *Ray Society, London:* Vol. **140** (1957) and Vol. **142** (1959).]

LODEWICK, J. E. (1933). Some summerwood percentage relationships in the southern pines. *J. agric. Res.* **46**, 543–54.

LONSDALE, K. (1948). Crystals and X-rays. London.

MACDOUGAL, D. T. and SMITH, G. M. (1927). Long-lived cells of the Redwood. *Science (N.S.)* **66**, 456–7.

MACMILLAN, C. (1904). Note on some British Columbian dwarf trees. *Bot. Gaz.* **38**, 379–81.

MACMILLAN, W. B. (1925). A study in the comparative lengths of tracheids of red spruce grown under free and suppressed conditions. *J. For.* **23**, 34–42.

MAHESHWARI, P. and VASIL, V. (1961). *Gnetum.* Botanical Monograph No. 1. Council of Scientific and Industrial Research, New Delhi.

MCELHANNEY, T. A. *et al.* (1935). Canadian woods, their properties and uses. Ottawa.

MCINTOSH, D. C. (1954). Some aspects of the influence of rays on the shrinkage of wood. *J. For. Prod. Res. Soc.* **4**, 39–42.

— (1957). Transverse shrinkage of red oak and beech. *For. Prod. J.* **7** 114–20.

MARK, R. E. (1967). Cell wall mechanics of tracheids. Newhaven, Conn., U.S.A.

MEIER, H. (1961). The distribution of polysaccharides in wood fibres. *J. Polymer Sci.* **5**, 11–8.

MEIER, H. and WILLKIE, K. C. B. (1959). The distribution of polysaccharides in the cell-wall of tracheids of Pine (*Pinus sylvestris* L.). *Holzforsch.* **13**, 177–82.

METCALFE, C. R. and CHALK, L. (1950). Anatomy of the Dicotyledons. Oxford.

MEREWETHER, J. W. T. (1957). A lignin-carbohydrate complex in wood. *Holzforsch.* **11**, 65–80.

— (1960). The linkage of lignin in the plant. *In* Brauns and Brauns (1960), pp. 630–58.

MEYER, K. H. (1950). Natural and synthetic high polymers. New York.

MISRA, P. (1939). Observations on spiral grain in the wood of *Pinus longifolia* Roxb. *Forestry* **13**, 118–33.

MORGAN, J. W. W. and ORSLER, R. J. (1967). A simple test to distinguish *Khaya anthotheca* from *K. ivorensis* and *K. grandifoliolia*. *J. Inst. Wood Sci.* **18**, 61–4.

MYER, J. E. (1930). The structure and strength of four North American woods as influenced by range, habitat and position in the tree. *Bull. N.Y. St. Coll. For. Tech. Pub.* **3**.

NEČESANÝ, V. (1958). Effect of β-indolacetic acid on the formation of reaction wood. *Phyton* **11**, 117–27.

— (1960). Bewertung "normalen" Holzes vom Standpunkt der Struktur. *Faserforschung und Textiltechnik* **12**, 169–78.

— (1966). Die vitalitätsveranderung der Parenchymzellen als physiologische Grundlage der Kernholzbildung. *Holzforsch. u. Holzverwert.* **18**, 61–64.

NELMES, B. J. and PRESTON, R. D. (1968). Cellulose microfibril orientation in rubbery wood. *J. Exp. Bot.* **19**, 519–25.

NORBERG, P. H. and MEIER, H. (1966). Physical and chemical properties of the gelatinous layer in tension wood fibres of aspen (*Populus tremula* L.). *Holzforsch.* **20**, 174–8.

NORMAN, D. and BESSON, A. (1946). Caractéristiques des bois tropicaux. *Rev. Bois appl.* **1**, 3–10.

OLLIVER, C. W. (1951). The intelligent use of the microscope. London.

OLIVER, A. C. (1959). Soft rot: a summary of existing knowledge. *T.D.A. Inform. Bull.* B/1B/2.

ONAKA, F. (1949). Studies on compression and tension wood. *Wood Res. Kyoto* **1**.

OTT, E. (1943). Cellulose and cellulose derivatives. New York.

PANSHIN, A. J., DE ZEEUW, C. and BROWN, H. P. (1964). Textbook of Wood Technology, Vol. I: Structure, identification, uses and properties of commercial woods of the United States. New York.

PATEL, R. N. (1962). On the occurrence of gelatinous fibres with special reference to root wood. M.Sc. Thesis, Univ. of London.

PAUL, B. H. (1924). Influence of growth conditions upon the properties of wood. *J. For. Washington* 22, 707–23.

PEARL, I. A. (1967). The Chemistry of Lignin. New York.

PENTONEY, R. E. (1953). Mechanisms affecting tangential vs. radial shrinkage. *J. For. Prod. Res. Soc.* 3, 27–32.

PFEIFFER, H. (1926). Das abnorme Dickenwachstum. *In* Linsbauer, K., *Handbuch der Pflanzenanatomie* 9, Berlin, pp. 1–268.

PFEIFFER, J. P. H. and VAROSSIEAU, W. W. (1946). Classification of the structural elements of the secondary wood of dicotyledons, using decimal indices for classification and identification of wood species. *Blumea* 5, 437–89.

PHILLIPS, E. W. J. (1933). Movement of the pit membrane in coniferous woods, with special reference to preservative treatment. *Forestry* 7 109–20.

— (1937). The occurrence of compression wood in African Pencil Cedar. *Emp. For. J.* 16, 54–7.

— (1940). A comparison of forest and plantation-grown African Pencil Cedar (*Juniperus procera* Hochst.) with special reference to the occurrence of compression wood. *Emp. For. J.* 19, 282–8.

— (1941). The inclination of fibrils in the cell wall and its relation to the compression of timber. *Emp. For. J.* 20, 74–8.

— (1948). Identification of softwoods by their microscopic structure. *For. Prod. Res. Bull.* 22, 1–56.

PILLOW, M. Y. (1931). Compression wood records hurricane. *J. Forestry* 29, 575–8.

PILLOW, M. Y. and LUXFORD, R. F. (1937). The structure, occurrence and properties of compression wood. *Tech. Bull.* 546, *U.S. Dept. Agric.*

PRESTON, R. D. (1947). The fine structure of the walls of the conifer tracheid. II. *Proc. Roy. Soc.* (*London*) Ser. B 134, 202–18.

— (1948). The fine structure of the walls of the conifer tracheid. III. *Biochim. et Biophys. Acta* 2, 370–83.

— (1949a). The organisation of the cell wall in relation to the structure of fibres. *In* Preston, J. M., *Fibre Science*, 218–47. Manchester.

— (1949b). Spiral structure and spiral growth: the development of spiral grain in conifers. *Forestry* 23, 48–55.

— (1952). The molecular architecture of plant cell walls. London.

— (1959). Wall organisation in plant cells. *Int. Rev. Cytol.* 8, 33–58.

— (1965). Interdisciplinary approaches to wood structure. *In* Côté, (1965), pp. 1–31.

PRESTON, R. D., NICOLAI, E., REED, R. and MILLARD, A. (1948). An electron microscopic study of the wall of *Valonia ventricosa. Nature, Lond.* 162, 665.

PRESTON, R. D. and RANGANATHAN, V. (1947). The fine structure of the fibres of normal and tension wood in Beech (*Fagus sylvatica* L.) as revealed by X-rays. *Forestry* 21, 92–8.

PRESTON, R. D. and RIPLEY, G. W. (1954). An electron microscopic investigation of the walls of conifer cambium. *J. Exp. Bot.* 5, 410–3.

PRESTON, R. D. and WARDROP, A. B. (1949). The fine structure of the walls of the conifer tracheid. IV. *Biochim. et Biophys. Acta* **3**, 549–59.

PRIESTLEY, J. H. (1945). Observations on spiral grain in timber. *Amer. J. Bot.* **32**, 277–84.

PRITCHARD, R. P. and BAILEY, I. W. (1916). The significance of certain variations in the anatomical structure of wood. *For. Quart.* **14**, 662–71.

RAO, SUNDARASIVA B. (1959). Variation in the structure of the secondary xylem in individual dicotyledonous trees. Ph.D. Thesis, Univ. of London.

RAWLINS, T. E. (1933). Phytopathological and botanical research methods. New York.

RAY, JOHN (1724). Synopsis methodica stirpium Britannicarum. London.

RAYNE, A. F. (1945). The investigation of failures in wood by microscopical examination. *Royal Aircraft Establishment, Farnborough Report No.* **Ch. 421**. Oct. 1945.

RECORD, S. J. (1934). Identification of the timbers of temperate North America. New York and London.

RECORD, S. J. and MELL, C. D. (1924). Timbers of tropical America. New Haven.

REHDER, A. (1940). Manual of cultivated trees and shrubs (2nd ed.). New York.

RENDLE, B. J. (1938). Commercial mahoganies and allied timbers. *For. Prod. Res. Bull.* **18**.

— (1956). Variation in the quality of African mahogany. *Wood*, 349–54.

— (1960). Juvenile and adult wood. *J. Inst. Wood. Sci.* **5**, 58–61.

RENDLE, B. J. and PHILLIPS, E. W. J. (1958). The effect of rate of growth (ring width) on the density of softwoods. *Forestry* **31**, 113–20.

RICHARDSON, S. D. (1964). The external environment and tracheid size in conifers. *In* Zimmermann (1964), pp. 367–88.

ROBARDS, A. W. (1965a). Tension wood and excentric growth in crack willow (*Salix fragilis* L.). *Ann. Bot. N.S.* **29**, 419–31.

— (1965b). Electron microscopic observations on the bordered pits of *Cedrus libani* Loud. *J. Inst. Wood Sci.* **15**, 25–35.

— (1966). The application of the modified sine rule to tension wood production in the stem of crack willow (*Salix fragilis* L.). *Ann. Bot. N.S.* **30**, 513–23.

— (1967). The xylem fibres of *Salix fragilis* L. *J. Roy. Micr. Soc.* **87**, 329–52.

ROBARDS, A. W. and PURVIS, M. (1964). Chlorazol black E as a stain for tension wood. *Stain Technol.* **39**, 309–15.

ROBINSON, W. (1920). The microscopical features of mechanical strains in timber, and the bearing of these on the structure of the cell walls in plants. *Phil. Trans. Roy. Soc.* **210B**, 49–82.

ROCHESTER, G. H. (1933). The mechanical properties of Canadian woods. *Bull. For. Serv. Can.* **82**.

ROELOFSEN, P. A. (1959). Handbuch der Pflanzenanatomie Bd. III, Teil 4. The plant cell wall. Berlin-Nikolassee.

ROGERS, H. J. and PERKINS, H. R. (1968). Cell Walls and Membranes. London.

RUDMAN, P. (1965). Fine structure of wood. *Nature, Lond.* **208**, 55–6.

2F

440   THE STRUCTURE OF WOOD

SACHSSE, H. (1964). Uber submikroscopische Bau der Faser Zellwand beim Zugholz der Poppel. *Holz. a. Roh-u. Werks.* **22**, 174–82.

SANIO, K. (1872). Ueber die Grösse der Holzzellen bei der gemeinen Kiefer (*Pinus sylvestris*). *Jb. wiss. Bot.* **8**, 401–20.

SAVORY, J. G. (1954). Breakdown of timber by ascomycetes and fungi imperfecti. *Ann. Appl. Biol.* **41**, 336–47.

SCHENCK, H. (1892). Beiträge zur Biologie und Anatomie der Lianen. *In* Schimper, A. F. W., *Bot. Mitt. Trop.* **4**.

SCHMID, R. (1965). The fine structure of pits in hardwoods. *In* Côté, (1965), pp. 291–304.

SCHMID, R. and MACHADO, R. D. (1964). Zur Entstehung und Feinstruktur skulpturierter Hoftüpfel bei Leguminosen. *Planta* **60**, 612–26.

SCHNIEWIND, A. P. (1966). Irregularities of finished surfaces caused by unequal ray shrinkage. *For. Prod. J.* **16**, 66.

SCHULTZE-DEWITZ, G. (1965). Variation und Haufigkeit der Faserlange der Kiefer. *Holz. a. Roh-u. Werks.* **23**, 81–6.

SCHWANKL, A. (1956). Bark. (Trans. Edlin, H. L.) London.

SCURFIELD, G. (1964). The nature of reaction wood. IX. Anomalous cases of reaction anatomy. *Aust. J. Bot.* **12**, 173–84.

SCURFIELD, G. and WARDROP, A. B. (1962). The nature of reaction wood. VI. The reaction anatomy of seedlings of woody perennials. *Aust. J. Bot.* **16**, 93–105.

SEIFRIZ, W. (1936). Protoplasm. New York.

SETTERFIELD, G. and BAYLEY, S. T. (1961). Structure and physiology of cell walls. *Ann. Rev. Pl. Phys.* **12**, 35–62.

SHILLABER, C. P. (1963). Photomicrography. New York.

SIEGEL, S. M. (1962). The plant cell wall. Oxford, London, New York and Paris.

SINNOTT, E. W. (1952). Reaction wood and the regulation of tree form. *Amer. J. Bot.* **39**, 67–78.

— (1960). Plant Morphogenesis. New York.

SOLEREDER, H. (1908). Systematic anatomy of the dicotyledons, p. 1100. Oxford.

SOMERVILLE, W. (1927). How a tree grows. Oxford.

SOUTH AFRICAN BUREAU OF STANDARDS (1947). Nomenclature of South African home-grown timbers. Pretoria.

SPURR, S. H. and HYVÄRINEN, M. J. (1954a). Compression wood in conifers as a morphogenetic phenomenon. *Bot. Rev.* **20**, 551–60.

— (1954b). Wood fibre length as related to position in tree and growth. *Bot. Rev.* **20**, 561–75.

STAMM, A. J. (1964). Wood and Cellulose Science. New York.

STANDARDS ASSOCIATION OF AUSTRALIA (1940). Australian standard nomenclature of Australian timbers. *Tech. Standard No.* **0.2-1940**. Sydney.

STEARNS, T. L. (1950). Distinguishing Red Oak from White Oak by chemical colour reaction. *Sth. Lumberm.* **184**, 50.

STEWART, C. M., KOTTEK, J. F., DADSWELL, H. E. and WATSON, A. J. (1961). The Process of Fibre Separation. III. Hydrolytic degradation within living trees and its effects on the mechanical pulping and other properties of wood. *Tappi* **44**, 798–813.

SUNLEY, J. G. and CURRY, W. T. (1962). A machine to stress-grade timber. *Timb. Tr. J.* **241**, 73–5.

SVENSSON, A. A. (1956). The surface fine structure of conifer cell walls. *Arkiv. Kemi.* **10**, 239–50.

SWAIN, E. H. F. (1927). A universal index to wood. *For. Bull. Qd.* **7**.

— (1928). The timbers and forest products of Queensland. Brisbane.

SWAN, E. P. (1966). Chemical methods of differentiating the wood of several western conifers. *For. Prod. Journ.* **16**, *No.* 1, 51–4.

THIMANN, K. V. (Editor) (1958). The physiology of forest trees. New York.

THORNBER, J. P. and NORTHCOTE, D. H. (1961a). Changes in the chemical composition of a cambial cell during its differentiation into xylem and phloem tissue in trees. 1. Main components. *Biochem. J.* **81**, 449–55.

— (1961b). Changes in the chemical composition of a cambial cell during its differentiation into xylem and phloem tissue in trees. 2. Carbohydrate constituents of each main component. *Biochem. J.* **81**, 455–64.

— (1962). Changes in the chemical composition of a cambial cell during its differentiation into xylem and phloem tissue in trees. 3. Xylem, glucomannan and α-cellulose fractions. *Biochem. J.* **82**, 340–6.

TIMELL, T. E. (1964). Wood hemicelluloses. Pt. I. *Adv. Carbohydrate Chem.* **19**, 247–302.

— (1965). Wood hemicelluloses. Pt. II. *Adv. Carbohydrate Chem.* **20**, 409–83.

— (1965). Wood and bark polysaccharides. *In* Côté, (1965), pp. 127–56.

THUNELL, B. (1947). Undersökning av cellbyggnadens reaktion für tryck-päkänniger päfuru-, björk, och ekvirke. *Medd. svenska Traforskn-Inst* (*Träktekn. Avd.*) **13** (English summary).

TOMLINSON, P. B. (1961). Anatomy of the Monocotyledons. II. Palmae, p. 151. Oxford.

— (1964). Stem structure in arborescent monocotyledons. *In* Zimmermann (1964), pp. 65–86.

WANGAARD, F. F. (N.D.). Transverse heat conductivity of wood. Thesis N.Y. St. Coll. For. [quoted from Wise (1946)].

WARDROP, A. B. (1948). The influence of pressure on the cell wall organisation of conifer tracheids. *Proc. Leeds phil. lit. Soc.* 128–35.

— (1951). Cell wall organisation and the properties of the xylem. I. Cell wall organisation and variation of breaking load in tension of the xylem in conifer stems. *Aust. J. sci. Res. B.* **4**, 391–414.

— (1954). The mechanism of surface growth involved in the differentiation of fibres and tracheids. *Aust. J. Bot.* **2**, 165–75.

— (1956). The nature of reaction wood. V. The distribution and formation of tension wood in some species of *Eucalyptus. Aust. J. Bot.* **4**, 152–66.

— (1957a). The organisation and properties of the outer layer of the secondary wall in conifer tracheids. *Holzforsch.* **11**, 102–10.

— (1957b). The phase of lignification in the differentiation of wood fibres. *Tappi* **40** (**4**), 225–43.

— (1960–1). The structure and formation of reaction wood in Angiosperms. *News Bull. International Assn. of Wood Anatomists* **2-8**.

— (1964a). The structure and formation of the cell wall in xylem. *In* Zimmermann (1964), pp. 87–134.

WARDROP, A. B. (1964b). The reaction anatomy of arborescent angiosperms. *In* Zimmermann (1964), pp. 405–56.
— (1965). The formation and function of reaction wood. *In* Côté, (1965), pp. 371–90.
WARDROP, A. B. and DADSWELL, H. E. (1947). The occurrence, structure and properties of certain cell wall deformations. *Coun. sci. industr. Res. Aust. Bull.* **221**.
— (1950). The Nature of Reaction Wood. II. The cell wall organisation of compression wood tracheids. *Aust. J. sci. Res. B.* **3**, 1–13.
— (1952). The cell wall structure of xylem parenchyma. *Aust. J. sci. Res. B.* **5**, 223–36.
— (1955). The Nature of Reaction Wood. IV. Variations in cell wall organisation of tension wood fibres. *Aust. J. Bot.* **3**, 177–89.
— (1957). Variations in the cell wall organisation of tracheids and fibres. *Holzforsch.* **11**, 33–41.
WARDROP, A. B., DADSWELL, H. E. and DAVIES, G. W. (1961). Aspects of wood structure influencing the preparation of semi-chemical pulps. *Appita* **14**, 185–202.
WARDROP, A. B. and DAVIES, G. W. (1958). Some anatomical factors relating to the penetration of water into xylem of Gymnosperms. *Aust. J. Bot.* **6**, 96–102.
— (1964). The Nature of Reaction Wood. VIII. The structure and differentiation of compression wood. *Aust. J. Bot.* **12**, 24–38.
WARDROP, A. B. and HARADA, H. (1965). The formation and structure of the cell wall in fibres and tracheids. *J. Exp. Bot.* **16**, 356–71.
WARDROP, A. B., LIESE, W. and DAVIES, G. W. (1959). The nature of the wart structure in conifer tracheids. *Holzforsch.* **13**, 115–20.
WARDROP, A. B. and PRESTON, R. D. (1947). Organisation of the cell walls of tracheids and wood fibres. *Nature, Lond.* **160**, 911.
— (1951). The submicroscopic organisation of the cell wall in conifer tracheids and wood fibres. *J. Exp. Bot.* **2**, 20–30.
WAREING, P. F. (1959). Problems of juvenility of flowering in trees. *J. Linn. Soc. London, Botany* LVI (No. 366), 282–9.
WATSON, A. J. and DADSWELL, H. E. (1961). Influence of fibre morphology on paper properties. I. Fibre length. *Appita* **14**, 168–78.
WEBSTER, A. D. (1919). Firewoods, their production and fuel values. London.
WELCH, M. B. (1922). A method of identification of some hardwoods. *J. roy. Soc. N.S.W.* **56**, 241–8.
— (1935). Effect of chemical solutions on some woods. *J. roy. Soc. N.S.W.* **69**, 159–66.
WERSHING, H. F. and BAILEY, I.W. (1942). Seedlings as experimental material in the study of "redwood" in conifers. *J. For.* **40**, 411–4.
WESTING, A. H. (1965). Formation and function of compression wood in gymnosperms. *Bot. Rev.* **31**, 381–480.
— (1968). Formation and function of compression wood in gymnosperms. II. *Bot. Rev.* **34**, 51–78.

WHITE, D. J. B. (1962). Tension wood in *Sassafras. J. Inst. Wood Sci.* **10**, 74–80.

— (1965). The anatomy of reaction tissues in plants. *Viewpoints in Biology* **4**, 54–82. Ed. Carthy, J. D. and Duddington, C. L., London.

WHITE, D. J. B. and ROBARDS, A. W. (1965). Gelatinous fibres in ash (*Fraxinus excelsior* L.). *Nature* **205**, 818.

— (1966). Some effects of Radial Growth Rate upon the Rays of Certain Ring-Porous Hardwoods. *J. Inst. Wood Sci.* **17**, 45–52.

WHITE, G. W. (1966). Introduction to Microscopy. London.

WILLIAMSON, H. S. (1921). A new method of preparing sections of hard vegetable structures. *Ann. Bot. Lond.* **35**, 139.

WILLIS, J. C. (1931). A dictionary of the flowering plants and ferns (6th Ed.). Cambridge.

— (1966). (7th Ed., revised Airy Shaw, H. K.)

WISE, L. E. (1946). Wood Chemistry. New York.

"WOOD". Publ. monthly. London.

WYCKOFF, R. W. G. (1949). Electron microscopy technique. New York.

de ZEEUW, C. (1965). Variability in wood. *In* Côtè, (1965), pp. 457–71.

ZIMMERMANN, M. H. (Editor) (1964). The formation of wood in forest trees. New York.

ZOBEL, B. J. and RHODES, R. R. (1957). Specific gravity indices for use in breeding Loblolly pine. *Tappi* **41** (*4*), 167–70.

ZOBEL, B. J., WEBB, C. and HENSEN, F. (1959). Core or juvenile wood of loblolly and slack pine trees. *Tappi* **42**, 345–56.

INDEX

Principal references are in heavy type: references to illustrations are in italics

2H

2G